INSTRUCTIONAL SUPERVISION

A Behavior System

Robert J. Alfonso
KENT STATE UNIVERSITY

Gerald R. Firth
UNIVERSITY OF GEORGIA

Richard F. Neville
UNIVERSITY OF MARYLAND, BALTIMORE COUNTY

INSTRUCTIONAL SUPERVISION

A Behavior System

ALLYN AND BACON, INC.
BOSTON • LONDON • SYDNEY • TORONTO

LIBRARY OF CONGRESS CATALOGING IN PUBLICATION DATA
Alfonso, Robert J   1928–
    Instructional supervision.

    Includes bibliographical references and index.
    1. School supervision—United States. I. Firth,
Gerald R., joint author. II. Neville, Richard F.,
1931–   joint author. III. Title.
LB2805.A448   371.2'00973   74–30022

ISBN 0–205–04775–0
Third printing…August, 1977

To all those
who have shared the fascination of new possibilities, the frustration of unexpected barriers, the fortune of subsequent progress, and the fellowship of open colleagues this book is sincerely dedicated.

Contents

Contents

Preface

The material compiled for this book represents an adventure in educational thought.

It is not a chronicle, although the record of events relevant to its development are included. It is not a report, although the findings of research fundamental to its evolution are described as deemed appropriate. It is the expression of a viewpoint that both substantiates and indicts existing supervisory practices in American schools.

The unique contribution of this book to the educational field is its statement of a concept of instructional supervisory behavior that is defined in theory, described from research, delineated as components, and demonstrated through skills. The purpose of this approach is to help people alter their present beliefs regarding supervision, elevate supervision to professional prestige, and increase its priority of service within the school organization.

A team of individuals worked on this project; the book, therefore, is a collaborative effort. The various sections of the book offer a rationale, provide a research base, present critical components, express technical skills, explore organizational considerations, identify accountability aspects, and suggest future directions.

The approach to instructional supervision presented herein differs substantially from other such analyses in two ways: first, the phenomenon of instructional supervisory behavior was identified from empirical data exclusively, rather than from descriptions of current practice; and secondly, an operational definition of instructional supervision evolved, rather than an extension of pre-established dimensions.

The authors have taken particular care to avoid a compendium of varied chapters lacking general direction or total impact. The preparation of the manuscript has been entirely a team operation. Even when one individual assumed primary responsibility for initial drafting of a particular section, the results were reviewed by both of the other members. Eventually all three participated in the processes of critique and revision. This has produced joint editorship of the material into a common format. The entire publication represents efforts to analyze and interpret the results.

Part I—*A Rationale for Instructional Supervisory Behavior*—establishes the frame of reference for the entire book. It stems from the recognition in Chapter 1 of "Supervision: An Organizational Imperative." Chapter 2 deals with "The History of Supervision in Education." Chapter 3 breaks with tradition by conceptualizing "The Nature of Instructional Supervisory Behavior" as an identifiable system among others within the educational context.

The four chapters that comprise Part II provide *A Research Base for ISB* by summarizing knowledge in selected fields. Chapter 4 is devoted to "Leadership Theory," Chapter 5 to "Communication Theory," Chapter 6 to "Organization Theory," and Chapter 7 to "Change Theory." Each of these chapters contains basic propositions drawn from research findings and their implications for instructional supervisory behavior.

Part III, *The Critical Components of ISB*, was derived from combining and interpreting the meaning of the propositions involved. Chapter 8 deals with the "Definitions of Critical Components" that constitute ISB operationally in the intervention, interpersonal, and milieu dimensions. Chapter 9 is devoted to an explication of "Component Relationships" based upon a dynamic matrix.

Part IV deals with *The Technical Skills of ISB*. It is through the intervention dimension of ISB that technical skills are applied. They exist in a functional relationship to the interpersonal or human components and the milieu or managerial components.

Part V describes the influence of various *Organizational Considerations* on Instructional Supervisory Behavior. Chapter 11 examines "The Impact of School Environment," including that of the administrative behavior system in terms of the organizational structure, the teacher behavior system through its personnel characteristics, and portions of the student behavior system and other systems within the educational context in terms of the learning setting. Chapter 12 explores "The Structure of Supervisory Services," including behavior exhibited by the supervisor as an individual agent, as a member of an instructional service team, or as an operative within a total delivery system. Chapter 13 considers "The Preparation and Selection of Supervisory Personnel," including essential competencies, selection processes, and professional programs that focus upon technical skills and their application in various organizational situations.

The three chapters of Part VI deal with *Accountability in Supervision*. Chapter 14 examines "Indices of Effective ISB" by suggesting appropriate principles and guidelines both for the supervisor and for the organization in evaluating supervisory effectiveness. Assessment of the possession and demonstration of "Technical Competence" by the individual engaged in instructional supervisory behavior is discussed in Chapter 15. Determination of "Organizational Viability," as provided and evidenced through conditions that support effective supervision, is considered in Chapter 16.

In the single chapter of Part VII, the potential of *Future Directions for ISB* is explored. This chapter anticipates additional ones that remain to be developed at a later time after more experience.

The authors readily acknowledge the complexity of the task that they have set before themselves. However, they also believe that this book offers insights, proposals, and guidelines to action that have immediate and pragmatic meaning while offering a base for further theoretical advancement.

Robert J. Alfonso
Gerald R. Firth
Richard F. Neville

PART I

A Rationale for Instructional Supervisory Behavior

Supervision in education is taken as an article of faith. The emergence of schools and formal educational activities quite naturally gave rise to systems of management and supervision. Obviously such conditions were not unique to educational development. Over the range of institutional human activity such as government, business, religion, and health care, supervisory programs were needed, designed, and set in motion. For complex reasons the study of supervision in education has tended to remain apart from, if not denying its relationship with, similar phenomena in other fields of activity. It is as if instructional supervision exists sans both counterpart and tradition.

The principle is advanced here that supervision in schools shares many commonalities with supervision in industry; it represents a different manifestation of an imperative feature of all organizations. Moreover, the specialized form in which instructional supervision exists currently is related more to its evolution than to its basic character. Once these assertions are accepted as tenable, it is possible to examine instructional supervision as a distinct behavior system.

The three chapters of Part I establish a different frame of reference for consideration of supervision in education.

Chapter 1

Supervision: An Organizational Imperative

Supervision is found in all complex organizations. This is so because organizations are determined to maintain themselves and are sometimes concerned about their improvement or refinement. The connection between supervision and organizations is clear and direct. Organizational resources must be applied to the analysis of efficiency and effectiveness. Therefore, in a general sense, the purpose of supervision is quite simple; it is to promote those conditions which help the organization to achieve its goals.

Supervision in organizations is expressed as both a process and a role. The process concept includes the flow and combination of purpose, philosophy, and component subsystems that comprise supervision. The role concept involves the discrete tasks, the combination of activities and responsibilities that together represent the job of supervisor. The expression of supervisory process and role in combination with the properties of the individual supervisor become the raw materials of supervisory behavior.

In all supervisory efforts there are two major structures that comprise the framework within which supervisory process and roles are expressed. These broad structures are the sociocultural factors and the nature of the particular organization within which the supervisor is to perform.

THE CULTURAL DETERMINANTS OF SUPERVISION

All human efforts, whether individual or group, occur within a social and cultural setting. Supervisory arrangements are no exception. Robert Dubin[1] posed the question: "Do the structures and features of a culture influence modes of production in it as well as the supervision of productive activities?" His anthropologically-based response to this question would ring affirmatively. This response would put heavy emphasis on the belief that phenomena can be most adequately explained in terms of past social conditions, or by influences other than those that are biological or chemical in origin. Cultural determinism is viewed as the force responsible for shaping the pursuits in which humans engage, as well as the particular working behaviors that produce goods and services. The conditions of work in a society are determined by the culture. In like manner, supervisory patterns related to these modes of production are also formed out of the cultural features of the society.

In contemporary American society, the impact of context such as sociocultural forms on management and supervision can be readily discerned. It may be grounded in family ownership and consequently show nepotism in the recruitment of managers and supervisory personnel.

> For example, a managerial system may be grounded in family ownership of enterprises and accordingly display nepotism in recruitment of managers as in portions of Italian industry. The efficiency of supervision under family nepotism rests partly on the manager's loyalty to the owners of the enterprise. But at the same time the knowledge that promotion opportunities are limited influences the responses of rank and file workers to supervisory practices.[2]

However, similar steel industries in West Germany and the United States present different managerial structures. American industries are characterized by a substantially greater proportion of middle management than is found in their German counterparts. Technological differences, it is reported, were not the cause of variation in supervision. German management was concentrated at the top. This managerial pattern may reflect the centralization of decision-making that has been historically prevalent in German government and culture. In the American system, the technological emphasis as well as the professionalism of various occupations in industry is expressed in a higher proportion of staff people to all managers. Similar contrasts may be drawn between productive enterprises under communism and capitalism. The management structures in an American factory and one in the Soviet Union of comparable technology are quite different.[3]

Many facets of a culture influence organizational supervision and productivity. It is important, therefore, to study and assess organizational effectiveness and efficiency *within* a cultural system rather than among national systems. It can be argued, with strong justification, that there has been a reduction of gross differences in the value orientations among organizations throughout the world community. As a result, the perspectives serving as guides to production, including the interaction of the organization and the larger culture, the role of the worker and management, as well as technological development and application, are becoming less varied. Over time the continued synthesis of the values guiding organizations across cultural contexts will reduce differences in patterns of management and supervision. However, prevailing national value orientations presently exist that have a direct bearing upon the arrangements and functions of management and supervision in organizations. The same cultural factors that determine an organization's production system shape the supervisory procedures used in advancing the attainment of the organization's purposes. The relationship between culture and organizational patterns is direct and real.

THE ORGANIZATIONAL CONTEXT FOR SUPERVISION

The characteristics of an organization directly influence the needs and style of supervision. Given a clear set of organizational goals, supervisors and supervisory processes work to make them happen. Stated differently, supervisory services in organizations are directed toward the maintenance and improvement of organizational efficiency and effectiveness.

The goal structure of an organization relies upon the production system of the firm to move the organization toward goal attainment. The production system will be related to the technology being employed by the organization. And in turn it is the supervisory staff that directs the planning, coordination and execution of the production system. These responsibilities are related in their complexity to the organization itself.

Joan Woodward's[4] study is helpful in considering the relationship of the organizational context to supervisory arrangement and process. The study involved 100 British firms, arranged by Woodward into three categories. The classifications were based on the technological character of the firms' production systems. The first group included firms engaged in mass production, the second comprised industries using a continuous process system of production, and the third contained those with unit production.

The mass production system represents those firms wherein the end product of the organization was produced in discrete steps or stages of production. The final step represented the aggregate of the total production processes. The separate steps in the mass production system could be simple or complicated, depending upon the nature of the product and the design of the production process. The supervisors in these mass production enterprises are line supervisors. They are very close to the actual steps in production of the product and, from the point of view of technical knowledge, are interchangeable with the line workers. Their close contact with production processes and responsibility for the successful completion of a particular phase of production require a thorough technical and skill performance level for each supervisor. The supervisor must be familiar with the intricacies of machinery and be a ready hand when and where the production line falters. Clearly the supervisor in a mass production situation is a strategic factor in overall production. He has need of highly efficient technical skills that must be continuously demonstrated as he supervises the work group in a department.

Continuous process production systems provide a different setting for the supervisor. First, there may be a limited number of workmen for whom the supervisor is responsible. The production process is highly technical and of a sophisticated nature. The critical stages in the production process call for the reading, checking, and control of technological devices and procedures predesigned to turn the raw material input into the final product. The production process is itself a complicated expression of science in accord with carefully tested plans. In this kind of organizational setting the supervisor must be a highly trained individual whose preparation includes not only technical ability but also knowledge about the theoretical roots of his production technology. It is also likely that in continuous process production the supervisor functions as much with people at the supervisory level and above as he does with the work force, which is likely to be small in size.

The third category of production systems studied by Woodward was unit production. This system is conceived as involving the constant decision-making and creativity of one or a small group of producers. Unit production can imply as open an approach to production as that expressed in the creation of a work of art. It begins with raw materials. There is an end goal in the mind of the producer, and the movement toward the end in terms of pace and quality is determined almost completely by the unit producer. Whether making special order furniture or devising a new synthetic in the laboratory, it may be his design (certainly to a great extent his skill) that will determine the outcome of his efforts. Skill here suggests a mixture of knowledge, sensitivity and commitment to task in addition to technical know-how. As the product moves toward completion, the unit producer is beset with multiple decisions. Working directly on product completion and controlling related conditions in the production environment are significant concerns of the unit producer. The unit producer, by the nature of his enterprise, is a prime mover of material and conditions, making continual decisions and applying expertise in accord with his production goal. He draws on colleagues and uses the full range of resources available to him in the organization.

The educational system should not be reluctant to be considered in such terms as are commonly used in analyzing production systems. The supervisory problems of promoting quantity and quality of production are the same for highly technical people in research and development activities and for workers in unit production industrial operations. The issue being emphasized in these statements on supervision and technology is that the nature of the production system itself—the organizational culture—which includes its degree of technology, contributes to the determination of supervisory arrangements.

These descriptions of supervision within organizational production systems have implications of significant consequence to the educator engaged in instructional supervision. The school is a production system. The production of knowledge and the stimulation or development of self-reliant and effective human beings is a more complex goal than that of any intricate technical conglomerate such as General Motors or American Telephone and Telegraph. There may be overtones of mass production steps and continuous process arrangements within existing school organizations. However, as a production system the school essentially possesses unit-level production characteristics. Each classroom or instructional mode can be considered a production unit. The ends in mind are the consequences of the curriculum and the instructional system as expressed in the performance of the students. The raw materials consist of the students, with their diversity of needs and dispositions, as well as the behavioral, conceptual and affective outcomes anticipated from the instructional process. The teacher(s) as the unit producer(s) makes decisions to move the students toward the desired effects. Just as important, the teacher is designing the desired effects with the students, since in the most significant way the humaneness of students is related to the expansion of themselves out of a curiosity and need to know. In this sense, the teacher is a unit-level production worker. This is not a mechanical function, nor does it minimize the areas of feelings and human processes. Rather, it is a way of emphasizing the vast room for decision-making and personalizing that falls upon the teacher or teaching team, and in like manner upon the educational supervisor who sees and accepts the responsibility of intervening to make instructional efforts open and positive as related to individual students. The quality of these decisions will be a major variable in determining the outcomes of instruction.

THE PERSONAL PROPERTIES OF SUPERVISORS

The concept of supervision, with its cultural determinants and relationships to an organizational production system, becomes operational through a human agent. A range of personal properties is required for successful supervisory performance. Floyd C. Mann [5] suggests that research supports the need for supervisors to develop competence in three general areas: technical, human, and administrative or managerial. Mann refers to this combination of competence areas as the *skill-mix*. The effective application of the skill-mix will enable the supervisor to link together the different parts of the organization and to integrate the specialized performance of the different units. This supervisory role supports the unity and coherence of the organization. As seen by Mann, the coordinating function is part of the *management* functions of the supervisor. It entails communication and balancing the work of the different divisions or organizational subsystems as well as personalized interaction with individual members of the organization.

Managerial skill needs to be balanced with *human relations* and *technical competence*. In the psychological realm, the results of supervisory behavior are expressed as staff morale and commitment to organizational goals, as well as communication and technical performance. The supervisor in many ways represents the critical link between the management or top leadership level in an organization and the line worker or unit production professional in the production system of the organization.

Leaders in *management* have shown that when work is made simple and rational there is an increase in productivity. Supervisors in any organization are charged with assisting and supporting the work of subordinates. They presumably promote work effectiveness in a positive direction, thereby heightening productivity.

In addition, organizational theorists have concluded that positive human interaction supports motivation of personnel as well as improves their commitment to the organization. This condition affects productivity favorably. The supervisor is typically reported to be a key figure in promoting the condition of "humaneness" within the organizational structure and is therefore crucial in building and sustaining high-level productivity.

It has also been argued in management theory, by proponents of group dynamics, that participation in decision-making related to the worker's welfare promotes commitment and hence the organization's productivity. To augment these human relations concerns, organizations design incentive systems to evaluate the worth of the individual's work in terms of his output. The assumption is that a worker's self-interest will support the other considerations such as "assistance," "humaneness," and "participation in decision-making." The connection between the individual and the organization within which he functions is formulated in accord with the essence of the organization. It is the supervisor who conveys, promotes, and refines the linkage.

Technical competence represents the third dimension of Mann's essentials for the supervisor. He defines it as

> the ability to use pertinent knowledge, methods, techniques, and equipment, necessary for the performance of specific tasks and activities, and for the direction of such performance. Fundamentally, it involves understanding and proficiency with respect to a specific class of functions in the organization. These include not only concrete motor skills, but also the abstract orientations and basic frames of reference that are normally associated with particular professional roles and affiliations. Technical skills may be acquired through formal training in professional schools, informal on-the-job training, or combinations of academic and internship or apprenticeship programs.[6],*

It is the combination of these three clusters of supervisory competence that forms Mann's conceptual framework for analyzing supervisory behavior. Attendant to each are a host of particulars that must be acted upon. The nature of the particulars or the form they take will be determined, to a great extent, by the type of organization that the supervisor serves. Human relations, for example, is clearly necessary in supervision, since modern organizations are human systems as well as production systems. The members of the organization, though they may perform at different levels, still express a complicated interdependency in striving to make their individual and collective contribution to the work of the organization. Where the organization's character is mechanical, to the extent that many of its operations are predetermined with little likelihood of needed adjustments, the human relations skills required of supervisors will be tuned to this condition. It is not that human relations become less important under such conditions, but that the intensity

---

* The supervisory skill-mix was first introduced by Floyd C. Mann at a meeting of the American Sociological Association in 1962. Subsequently he published his paper "Toward an Understanding of the Leadership Role in Formal Organization" (1965). It is interesting to note that Robert L. Katz wrote on the "Skills of an Effective Administrator" in the *Harvard Business Review.*[7] Katz wrote to suggest a more useful approach to the selection and development of administrators. He states that skills are abilities to be developed and demonstrated in performance and not merely potential. Katz presents a trifold definition of effective administration including human, technical, and conceptual skills. Both Mann and Katz interpret technical skills as knowledge, understanding, and complex functions related to particular performance tasks or activities. It may be suggested that Mann's emphasis on management skills relates to the supervisor's direct involvement with the production system. By contrast, many administrators are removed from the production system to the extent that broader conceptualization supplants direct ongoing management concerns as a critical skill performance for administrators.

and form of the human relations contact will correspond to the overall conditions of the organizational structure.

An effective mixture of the three skill areas—administrative or managerial, technical, and human relations—will provide the base for supervisory performance. The definition of the best combination and the ingredients that comprise it is very much a moot question. Mann writes that organizational level, that is, the hierarchical position of the supervisor, and the history of the organization are important variables in contemplating the best "skill-mix" for a particular supervisor. The message rings clear, however, that supervision, the processes engaged in by supervisors, is a reflection of the three dimensions of administration, technical considerations and human relations skills.

It must be recognized that effective instructional supervisory behavior as conceptualized and reported over the years in the professional literature has grossly emphasized the human or interpersonal skills. There appears to be an almost conscious effort to exclude technical competence as a requirement for effective supervisory performance. This exclusion has been the reason instructional supervision has not been recognized as a mature and significant professional role. Supervisory performance that is devoid of demonstrated competence in technical areas is peripheral to instructional development and the support of learning.

Research studies on instructional supervisory performance confirm the priority of technical performance by supervisors. Technical skills are perceived with high priority, while they are typically employed at significantly lower levels of frequency and effectiveness. The reasons for this condition are varied. Some supervisors by virtue of the press of central office considerations find themselves engaged almost totally as managers, as communication links with constant requirements for reports and descriptions. This is a maintenance definition of supervisory activity. Overindulgence in this area, as important as the management function is, dilutes the supervisory role and saps the energy of the supervisor until he is converted to the equation of management as supervision. It is asserted again that supervisors are responsible for the improvement of the instructional system, while recognizing that in reality an overemphasis on management functions and a lack of technical skills have worked to deny this first principle. The consequence, which is so very apparent, is supervision at a conceptual level only, while the school organization moves to reallocate supervisory responsibilities within its structure in different ways.

It is not clear what form supervision will take in the future. However, whether performed by newly designated professionals, by peers, or by teams of specialists, the supervisory process and presence under the press of accountability will continue. Although cloaked in more clinical garb, supervision will move actively and responsibly to pursue its primary intention, the improvement of the instructional system. To do this, supervisory surrogates will need to use more precise technical skills as they work with other professionals on the humanization and effectiveness of instruction for all students.

The ideas reported and interpreted in this chapter focus on supervision as a process found in all formal organizations. It may be that all of the interpretations have a direct connection to supervision and instructional supervisory behavior in education. It may be that all or some of them will be set aside as being unrelated to educational organizations and instructional leadership. Whatever position the reader may assume, it should be taken on a tentative basis while he further probes the concept, supervision, and its implications for the significant responsibilities of instructional supervision.

SUMMARY OF GENERAL PROPOSITIONS

The application of the concept of supervision to an educational setting requires consideration of general propositions regarding the cultural factors within an organizational context and the personal properties of the individual:

1. Supervision as a process is represented in the role performance of supervisors who are responsible for the efficiency and the effectiveness of the organizational system or component to which they are assigned.
2. Supervisors function in formal organizations that are typically complex arrangements for the achievement of particular goals. These formal organizations reflect the larger sociocultural system. Supervisory arrangements and services thereby also reflect the sociocultural conditions.
3. The nature of the organization in which the supervisor performs will have a direct bearing on the combination of supervisory skills and performance that is needed if the supervisor is to guide the organization to its goals.
4. The complexity of a formal organization as well as the production system that characterizes it are factors that contribute to the definition of needed supervisory conditions and services.
5. Supervisors in educational organizations are conceived as being primarily responsible for the improvement of instruction. Their effectiveness in large part must be seen in terms of the overall accomplishments of the students in relationship to the agreed-upon goals of the school program.
6. Supervisors across organizations have need to demonstrate competence in areas of management, human relations, and the technical aspects of the organizational unit within which they work. The correct combination of these competence areas is called the *skill-mix*. This mix can vary, depending upon the cultural setting, the nature of the organization, the production system, and the organization's goals.
7. Supervisory performance in education organizations has tended to concentrate on role expressions that emphasize the human relations and man-

agement dimensions. It is in the technical skill area where educational supervisors have been remiss. This may be the result of a lack of competence in the technical areas or the press and demands of managerial and human relations.

ENDNOTES

1. Robert Dubin et al., "Supervision and Productivity: Empirical Findings and Theoretical Consideration," in *Leadership and Productivity* (San Francisco: Chandler Publishing Co., 1965), p. 7.
2. *Ibid.,* pp. 7–8.
3. *Ibid.,* p. 8.
4. Joan Woodward, *Management and Technology* (London: Her Majesty's Stationery Office, 1958).
5. Floyd C. Mann, "Toward an Understanding of the Leadership Role in Formal Organization," in Dubin, "Supervision and Productivity," pp. 73–77.
6. *Ibid.*
7. Robert L. Katz, "Skills of an Effective Administrator," in *Harvard Business Review,* vol. 33, no. 1 (January-February 1955), pp. 33–42.

Chapter 2

The History of Supervision in Education

The historical development of an organization is a powerful force in the promotion of a philosophy and the condition of an applied style of supervision. The role performance of supervisory leaders requires perspective of the process as it has evolved in the institution of American public education.

In the present context, or more correctly over the past thirty years, the American public school has been called upon to be an active instrument for social change. Educational processes were directed to impact more pervasively upon individuals and communities. For the individual, the educational institution was intended to be a place and an experience that would lift up humanity and cause the release of human potential. For the larger social system, the educational institution was pushed into the arena of social action through the impetus of federal legislation. This action was directed, in its best expression, toward the fulfillment of the American ethic, the realization of equal opportunity, civil rights, and the shared promise of a democratic system. This dynamism within the American culture was aggravated by international developments: the start and end of the great war; the emergence of the nuclear age; the tensions of the cold war; the division of the world into political and economic camps; the alignment of nation states, as well as their surge toward autonomy; the emergence of the third world; wars of liberation; and the continued search for some mechanism of international decision-making that would move nations beyond unilateral expression toward mutual and enlightened problem-solving. Existence and survival were primary motives as nations and individuals worked to control, if not resolve, the issues.

These conditions and factors, among others, illustrate the potent and shifting nature of the forces that confront our institutions and cultural antecedents. Alvin Toffler has vividly portrayed the enormity and complexity of social change as it relates to the challenge of personal meaning, values and social forms. In the midst of these complex forces the educational institution and its subsystem components are called upon to demonstrate educational and social leadership through programs that are consciously and rationally designed. Educational endeavors must promote the rational person who hopefully aspires to serve self and others through reasoned and thoughtful behavior as required in a world of many alternatives. In this sense, schools need to be laboratories of inquiry. As such they need to provide students and others with the tools of intellectual analysis in an environment or context that focuses sharply on the unfoldment of the individual. The basic equation of such education must include the variables of social need, the individual and the multiple factors of operational efficiency forged out of the kind of analysis that aids in the identification and description of the rational society.

As grandiose as a concept of social rationality may seem, it is an ultimate condition toward which the institution of education must direct itself. This attainment in part requires that each school demonstrate the organic commitment, as well as professional and technical competence of an open value stance. This is required by the school's position in the flow of history and its inclusion in the life space of its students and the community it serves.

This is the larger context in which the schools and, consequently, educational supervisors have been functioning. Obviously, it is an environment characterized by fluidity. Change appears, reconstruction starts, when suddenly the momentum of circumstances causes shifts in priorities. These shifts frustrate ideas and actions that but yesterday were nothing less than required. In light of these conditions, William Lucio and John McNeil called for a "supervisory statesman." [1] They wrote:

> A new emphasis is being given the supervisory role. The professional expectation that supervision inspires has been amplified and responsibility for crucial purpose-setting decisions as opposed to routine housekeeping decisions has been made explicit." [2]

In order to implement this perspective, the supervisor seeks to apply tenets of reason and practical intelligence. Given the dynamism and flux in an increasingly complex human existence, schools need supervisors who demonstrate instructional supervisory behavior based upon reason and practical intelligence. This need is more often an expectation than a reality. Indeed, it represents a relatively recent expectation. To better sense the urgency and significance of this expectation, it is helpful to review some of the historical perspectives of supervisory theory and performance.

THE ORIGINS OF EDUCATIONAL SUPERVISION

The early American colonists, particularly in New England, were concerned about the development of adequate educational opportunities. In New England, the Calvinistic heritage demanded that citizens be literate in order that the directly revealed word, the Bible, could be sustained in the faithful. The "priesthood of all believers" was to be perpetuated with educational skills as the vehicle of its maintenance. Legislation in the form of the Massachusetts Bay Law of 1642 and the Deluder Satan Act of 1647 were passed by the colonial legislature. This signal emphasized the high value placed upon education by these people, while functionally prodding reluctant supporters. A measure of concern about supervision was also forthcoming at this time. Generally this concern had to do with the selection of teachers or the moral obligation "to keep school":

> Supervision appeared early in some of the colonies. In 1654 the General Court of Massachusetts Bay Colony directed selectmen of the towns to secure teachers of sound faith and morality and to continue them in office only as long as they met these requirements. Nothing was said specifically about inspection or supervision of schools, but the enactment did imply a felt need for establishing some kind of community responsibility for the success of the school.[3]

The first appearance of supervision in any concerted form appeared in the Boston area in the early eighteenth century. Laymen were given the responsibility of making inspectional tours of the schools in order to evaluate school facilities, upkeep and the progress of pupils. A description of this early supervision through inspection was offered by William Burton and Leo Brueckner:

> Inspection appeared in the early 1700's, specifically in Boston in 1709, when committees of citizens were appointed to visit and inspect the plant, the equipment, and pupil achievement. Specific mention of inspection of teachers' methods did not appear for many years. Committees until about 1714 were made up largely of ministers and learning was qualification for membership. Selectmen increasingly served as inspectors thus marking the beginning of public responsibility for education.[4]

As growth in all aspects of life became part of the colonial scene, the lay committees and teachers were faced with expanding pressures. Increased enrollments and the burdens of organizing and administering the accompanying school responsibilities necessitated the delegation of authority. Someone closer to the educational task was needed to assume additional controls heretofore maintained by the lay committees.

Schools increased in size, as towns grew, until several teachers were working in one building. One teacher was singled out and given certain administrative and managerial duties, thus becoming the principal teacher, later to become a building principal. Supervisory duties, even the meager one of inspection, were not delegated to principals until comparatively modern times. We are even yet struggling to make the principal an important supervisory officer.[5]

It is apparent that educational supervision in the context of seventeenth and eighteenth century colonial America was inspectional in nature, and primarily a function of the lay committee as they exerted their jurisdiction over the educational forms of their creation. The principal, or principal-teacher, was not expected to participate in supervision except as the wishes or demands of the citizenry might be made known to him through the lay committee. Improvement of instruction was not considered, but rather, the enforcement of prescribed instructional exercises including the conditions of learning.

Frank Dickey, some years ago, summarized this early period by stating that "the first attempts at supervision were characterized by three fundamental approaches: 1) authority and autocratic rule; 2) emphasis upon the inspection and weeding out of weak teachers; and 3) conformity to standards prescribed by the committee of laymen." [6]

This conception of supervision is obviously inconsistent with definitions of supervision as democratic, as systems-oriented or as an expression of rational and practical intelligence. Important educational seeds, however, were planted and nurtured. These included the responsibility of the state through the people to organize and maintain schools, and the right of the citizenry to develop and supervise as their schools evolved. It is this heritage, with its implications of local control and decision-making, that confronts and frequently confounds policy-makers at all levels of government in their attempts to meld universal and constitutional rights with the historical and cultural character of state and region.

SUPERVISION IN THE MATURING OF AMERICAN EDUCATION

In the nineteenth century, the principal as "inspector," as keeper of the school and implementor of lay-committee edicts, became more frequently observed. The recognition of the principal as supervisor or instructional leader as defined in his delegated responsibilities accompanied a new period of growth in a maturing educational system. The position of principal began to take its place in the structure of educational organization.

No definite date can be established for the emergence of the principal-ship, but evidently by around 1800 responsibilities began to be central-ized to some extent. Early reports of school systems contained references to the "headmaster, head-teacher or principal teacher." These early "prin-cipals" represented an administration convenience rather than positions of recognized leadership. Maintaining of discipline, administration of plant, regulation of classes, classification of pupils and establishment of rules and regulations were the primary duties of these principals.[7]

In the early years of the nineteenth century turbulent issues faced the common school movement. In many of the large school districts of the country, the future of free public education was in question. The diversified population in expanding urban centers presented severe diffi-culties to those espousing the cause of the free nonsectarian schools. Po-litical factors and prejudice of many types became associated with the battle between forces of the common school and their opponents. This conflict produced elements of strength in that astute planning was necessary if the common school system was to become a reality and survive. In the larger districts the superintendents found themselves in-capable of administering to the many needs of the expanding schools under their jurisdiction. As a result they delegated many new responsi-bilities in governing the individual school:

> The growth of cities was an important factor in the transfer of local supervision from the superintendent to the principal. One of the main functions of the early superintendents was to grade the schools. The growth of cities, which became marked at about 1830, continued at such a rapid pace in the subsequent decades that school enrollments were multi-plied many times. The problems in administration thus created made so many demands on the time of the superintendents that they were unable to give personal attention to the management and supervision of local schools. The logical step was to turn local management of schools over to the principals.[8]

Paul Pierce describes factors other than the growth of cities and increased delegation of responsibility by the superintendent that related to the growth of the principalship:

> Prominent among these were the rapid growth of cities, the grading of schools, the consolidation of departments under a single principal, the freeing of the principal from teaching duties, recognition of the principal as the supervisory head of the school and finally the establishment of the Department of Elementary School and Secondary School Principals within the National Education Association.[9]

It should be remembered that the evolving forces identified by Pierce were slowly appearing during the early national period of Ameri-can history. Full-time school supervision, as carried out by the principal, evolved at the same pace and initially represented the extension of the superintendent's office in the local school. It is not difficult to understand therefore, that supervision in the early nineteenth century was basically managerial. Supervision maintained the inspectional tone previously seen in the supervision of the district schools by the lay committees of the eighteenth century.

An early report from the Cincinnati Public Schools contains the following job description of the elementary school principal. The principal-teacher as the supervisory officer of the school was:

1. to function as the head of the school charged to his care;
2. to regulate the classes and courses of instruction of all pupils, whether they occupied his room or the rooms of other teachers;
3. to discover any defects in the school and apply remedies;
4. to make defects known to the visitors or trustees of ward, or district, if he were unable to remedy conditions;
5. to give necessary instruction to his assistants;
6. to classify pupils;
7. to safeguard school houses and furniture;
8. to keep the school clean;
9. to instruct assistants;
10. to refrain from impairing the standing of assistants, especially in the eyes of their pupils;
11. to require the cooperation of his assistants.[10]

Any recognition of the principal as a supervisor in terms of improving instruction or as a leader in instructional improvement was not, at that time, considered germane or important in terms of the principal's responsibilities. One of the first statements that spoke to the idea of supervision by the principal, as related to the teaching process, was set forth by the Cincinnati School Committee in 1841. It has the significant title of *Improvement in Teaching*.

Resolved, That the teachers in the Common Schools of the City of Cincinnati are hereby authorized to dismiss their respective schools one hour earlier . . . on each and every Wednesday . . . for practical improvement in the various studies, lessons, and qualifications appertaining to their professional duties; under the personal supervision of the principal teachers of each house or district . . . Resolved, That the principal teachers are requested, at the close of the quarter to furnish the Board with a written report as to the effects and probable results of this plan . . . that if found useful it may be continued for a longer period.[11]

School superintendents in the nineteenth century, quite understandably, did little to encourage or recognize the potential of the principal teacher in the area of supervision. By the middle of the nineteenth century, however, the larger school districts did make provisions for the principal to supervise and demanded that he do so. Superintendent William Wells of Chicago, in 1859, wrote:

General Supervision by Principals—In several of the new buildings, the number of teachers and pupils is now so large, that a considerable portion of the Principal's time is consumed in attending to matters of general oversight, and in giving such aid to the other teachers as may be necessary to secure uniformity and efficiency in all the different departments.[12]

In 1856, the Cincinnati Board of Education passed a regulation specifying that principals should devote at least one hour daily for every 200 pupils in attending to the supervision of their schools. Included in these supervisory duties were:

1. supervising and directing the labors of their assistants;
2. seeing that pupils were constantly and profitably employed during school hours;
3. holding examinations once each month to attest to progress in the grades;
4. reporting to directors the degree of effectiveness of teachers;
5. cooperating with the superintendent in advising teachers as to the best modes of instruction.[13]

Other factors contributed to the increased supervisory assignments in the schools. The practice of grading schools started at the Quincy (Massachusetts) Grammar School in 1848 and became more common as numbers of students increased. Also, new and distinct subject matter areas were being included in the curriculum—the elements of science, music, art and physical education were added in the elementary schools. These new subjects and the need for an effective organizational structure made it seem desirable to move the principals out of the classroom completely. This was accomplished in most large systems during the decade of 1860–1870. The importance of the principal's position in developing the instructional program and coordinating a positive functioning unit was referred to in the report of Superintendent Joseph Pickard of Chicago in 1862. He listed the visiting of rooms, examining of classes, conducting model exercises and supervising instruction, as the activities engaged in by the principals. He also attributed the progress he had observed in the Cincinnati schools to the supervision of its principals.[14]

About the same time, Superintendent William Harris of St. Louis engaged in a review of the supervisory practices of principals. He noted the success of Chicago and Cincinnati in placing the primary schools under the supervision of the grammar school principal. It was four years after the adoption of this policy in St. Louis that he stated:

Our principals are rapidly becoming supervisors as well as instructors and the schools under their charge are becoming uniform in their degree of excellence. Close daily supervision is the only method of securing the desired result and one can scarcely believe how great a degree of efficiency may be reached in a corps of teachers of average ability, until he actually sees it as it exists in a large school under the management of a principal who knows how to perform his duty.[15]

At this stage supervisory duties were narrowly conceived with the emphasis upon the inspection of teachers and their adherence to the rigidly prescribed course of study. Principals were the primary supervisors and were to train teachers by acquainting them with new materials and techniques that had been "approved." The teachers in turn were expected to produce a uniform, coordinated school program. Classroom visitation was the accepted method of obtaining testimony concerning the application of the prescribed materials and methods. Such methods, obviously inspectional in character, were consistent with the overall philosophy and purpose of the supervisory program as conceived at this time.

Prior to 1875, supervision consisted primarily of checking on the teachers' activities. "Inspection" is the characterization most often used. Included were making daily rounds, and knowing what each class was doing at any hour during the school day. Subsequent improvement was in the direction of making visitation more concrete in terms of a particular purpose. Superintendent John D. Philbrick of Boston pointed out in 1877 that, "Merely looking on and seeing teachers is not the supervision of instruction which is to be expected of principals." [16] His statement foreshadows the future and represents one of the first statements suggesting a multidimensional role for supervisory concerns. The specific nature of the supervisory role of the principal in the later stages of the nineteenth century, as gleaned from the study of annual reports from twelve major school districts during this era, has been summarized by Pierce:

> New activities added to meetings and conferences with teachers consisted of individual conferences following visits to classrooms (1892), the systematic study of pedagogic works by school staffs (1892), discussions by grade and departmental groups of instructional problems (1895), and demonstrations of teaching for the teachers of various grades (1900). Such procedures marked a great advance in broadening the (supervisory) purposes.[17]

Throughout the seventeenth, eighteenth and nineteenth centuries, supervisory practices perpetuated an orientation to the past. Supervisors acted as administrative inspectors concentrating on the task of auditing teachers, textbooks and pupils. Originally, religious officers and special lay committees had been empowered to visit and to inspect schools. Under this system, the society exercised its right to directly supervise and control education. In some instances official lay committees gave examinations to check student progress. The chief measure of evaluation was the amount of factual recall demonstrated by students in the prescribed areas of study. Where teacher inefficiency was determined it was handled through punitive measure—most often, dismissal. By the turn of the twentieth century, supervisory authority of at least the managerial variety had been delegated to local school personnel.

SUPERVISION IN THE TWENTIETH CENTURY

The trend toward the inclusion of specialized subjects in the school curriculum brought the advent, in limited numbers, of supervisory specialists. These specialists performed as directed in accord with the perspectives of central school administrators. In like manner, it was expected that teachers would exercise little personal judgment but were essentially to do as they were directed. The entire system and set of relationships smacked of a revealed truth and good that, if passed down by those in final authority or through their surrogates, would culminate in efficient schools, classrooms of order and productivity and hence serve well the community and society.

Under the traditional system as it continued to be demonstrated in the early 1900s the supervisor was comparable to the factory foreman. Alvin Toffler comments on the school-factory comparison: ". . . the whole idea of assembling masses of student (raw material) to be processed by teachers (workers) was a stroke of industrial genius." [18] In Raymond Callahan's *Education and the Cult of Efficiency*,[19] the school's administrative hierarchy is defined as constructing itself as an industrial organization with an emphasis on the promotion of efficiency and effectiveness. Students in such conditions marched from place to place under a system of regimentation and rigidity. Authoritarian rule and discipline were enforced by the supervisor. The system was designed to produce a disciplined mentality that was conditioned by the school bell as preparation for coping with the factory whistle. This spirit of regimentation, with unquestioned adherence to procedural and mechanistic codes, has had strong staying power in the process of education.

The emphasis on organizational regimentation early in this century was to reflect efficient planning and the application of scientific methods. It served to further entrench the *inspectional* concept of supervision. The emphasis on scientific management with its stress on empirical research prompted supervisors to aspire to a science of teaching. Implicit in these efforts was the attempt of supervisors to control teacher behavior and its effect on student performance. It is important at this point to take note of two contending interpretations of educational process and organization that were propelled upon the American scene in the early twentieth century. One interpretation was spawned out of the maturation of the discipline of psychology and the larger sociocultural conditions that confronted America. As Lawrence Cremin documented in his work *The Transformation of the School,*[20] the later nineteenth and early twentieth centuries saw the start of some educational experiments founded on principles of psychology, the nature of childhood and the need for schools to promote the democratization of culture. This period demonstrated social, industrial and political problems that somehow had to be harnessed if the American experiment were to continue in accord with the democratic commitments pronounced in the enlightened moments of constitutional construction. In the perception of some, the schools were one of the instruments to be used in offsetting the sociocultural imbalance resulting from the mix of people and their variant values. A deeper sense of individual rights and responsibilities was needed. The relationship between burgeoning industry and its results, including urbanization and the attendant ills of deprived existence, had to be confronted. In turn, political reform in which people were considered partners in the grand experiment was mounting in various forms along the continuum of local and national political activity. Out of these complex factors and conditions some educators were advancing a child-centered, psychologically rooted approach to education. Also witnessed was the stimulation of having the student contend with issues and questions that had meaning in experience for him; consequently, the entire form of education became personalized in that it was related to self, motives, and human needs. In other instances the activity or "learn by doing" framework was applied in the vocational programs that began to be organized. Here the combination of scholastic activity and introduction to various trades and skilled crafts was provided.

It seems reasonable to assert, after a review of the historical record, that the spirit of progressivism in education was part of what Cremin [21] called "progressivism writ large" in the American culture. Progressivism, in other words, was not restricted to the educational scene. In fact, the theories of progressive education never took hold as operational principles within the public schools as some critiques would have the public believe. To this day, innovative and creative schools are struggling to make real the humanizing potential that the early progressives in education, particularly John Dewey, espoused. Dewey, it should be noted, was not an advocate of chaos, mismanagement, or lack of direction. He did, however, have an abiding conviction as to the child's creative spirit, its potential good, and what teachers and other adults do to diminish and nurture this curiosity and creativity. He did not hesitate to register his displeasure with what he thought to be distortions of misguided disciples of the so-called child-centered approach. Dewey wrote:

> Just as, upon the whole, it was the weakness of the "old education" that it made invidious comparisons between the immaturity of the child and the maturity of the adult, regarding the former as something to be got away from as soon as possible and as much as possible; so it is the danger of the "new education" that it regards the child's present powers and interests finally significant in themselves. In truth, his learnings and achievements are fluid and moving. They change from day to day and from hour to hour . . . It will do harm if child study leaves in the popular mind the impression that a child of a given age has a positive equipment of purposes and interests to be cultivated just as they stand.
>   . . . But save as the teacher knows, knows wisely and thoroughly, the race experience which is embodied in that thing we call the Curriculum, the teacher knows neither what the present power, capacity, or attitude is, nor yet how it is to be asserted, exercised, and realized.[22]

As it happened, Dewey was criticized by educational liberals and conservatives. He was accused of recommending a curriculum devoted to the present at the expense of traditional values and truths. At the same time he was accused of betraying the progressive movement in education by those who felt that any social guidance by adults was an unwarranted imposition on children and youth.*

A measure of the general concern over the struggle between contending educational philosophies and the implications of the ideas extending from this struggle is reflected in the reports of several important committees of the National Education Association. *The Committee of Ten On Secondary School Studies* was appointed in 1891 and reported in 1893. This committee was chaired by President Charles W. Eliot of Harvard University. The *Committee of Ten* recommended that the high school program of short courses in many subjects be replaced with relatively few courses to be studied in greater depth.

Another NEA committee, the *Committee of Fifteen on Elementary Education*, was appointed in 1893 and reported in 1895. It was chaired by William H. Maxwell, superintendent of the New York City Public Schools. It produced a report that dealt with school system organization, teacher preparation and the coordination and correlation of elementary school subjects. In addition, in 1895 the *Committee On College Entrance Requirements* was appointed. It reported in 1899. This report dealt with course length, the age at which various studies should begin and standardization of units of credit. This report fixed, for a time, the idea that the high school graduates would go on to college. All of these committees

---

* Dewey responded to these charges and to the singleminded advocates of the conservative or progressive positions in a restatement of his educational philosophy in his work *Experience and Education* (New York: The Macmillan Company, 1938).

were dominated by individuals who had a strong commitment to the more conservative interpretation of education, including the definition of the curriculum as subject matter. As a result, so-called progressive concerns including pupil abilities, social needs, interests, capacities and individual differences were not considered in the NEA committee reports of the late nineteenth century.

As the progressive pronouncements of Dewey became more visible the NEA committee work took a different tack. In 1911 the *Committee on the Economy of Time* was organized. The committee was comprised of professors of education, educational psychologists and practicing schoolmen. Attempts were made to apply scientific methodology to the study of educational problems. This committee engaged in educational research to determine worthwhile instructional materials, their proper grade placement and organization, as well as speculation about which subject matter could be eliminated from the curriculum. The committee made four reports; each one became part of one of the yearbooks of the National Society for the Study of Education. The reports were published in 1915, 1917, 1918, and 1919.

Saul Lavisky summarized the period of heavy NEA committee activity in his comments on the Committee on the Economy of Time:

> In a sense the Committee on the Economy of Time can be said to represent the start of a "scientific approach" to curriculum decision making. The Committee constructed tests to determine instructional efficiency. They reviewed textbooks to see the focus of what was being taught. They studied adult activities to identify socially worthwhile knowledge and skills. They examined the principal institutions and problems of the nation to determine social needs. And, finally, they pulled together the results of all available studies of learning and derived implications for the selection of subject matter and teaching methods.[23]

The NEA also established a Commission on Reorganization of Secondary Education. In 1918 it produced its report, which was entitled *The Cardinal Principles of Secondary Education.*[24] The report cited the primary goals of secondary education in the American society: health, command of functional processes, worthy home membership, vocation, civic education, worthy use of leisure time and ethical character. This report departed drastically from the earlier committee pronouncements of the NEA. The Commission report was labeled utilitarian and anti-intellectual by essentialist critics. Save for the Commission's emphasis on a command of the fundamental processes, critics pointed to the absence of the role of the disciplines in the construction of the Cardinal Principles.

As the development of supervisory services proceeded to the early decades of the twentieth century, there was a contention with conflicting educational perspectives, the impact of industrial development and organization, and general disquiet in the social system. These conditions quite naturally made the introduction and adaptation of supervisory processes extremely complicated.

During the 1920s and extending into the 1930s, supervisory processes in education received ample attention, particularly from the researcher. A host of studies was completed. These studies represented attempts to determine the extent and nature of supervisory services as reflected in the practices and duties performed by supervisors. These efforts provided evidence from which directives for change relative to supervisory practice were announced. In their way these descriptive analyses served well the end of improving supervisory services. The emphasis, however, was still on leading the teacher group and informing them of the findings, including their implications. Typically directives and guidance measures for teachers and supervisory workers were the result. These directives were conceived as precise plans to be applied rather than guidelines for the formulation of more comprehensive approaches to supervisory services.

SUPERVISION IN THE CONTEMPORARY SCENE

The 1930s and 1940s were periods of creativity and refinement in supervision. During this time frame, cooperative-democratic approaches to supervision became actively considered and sporadically applied. The causes for the shift to this mode were many and complex, running from professional maturation to political and economic factors.

The most significant aspect of the shift was the increased emphasis upon the participation and shared responsibility of the teacher in the area of instructional improvement. Lucio and McNeil described the growth of supervision during this period as follows:

> Related to the economic and social transformations of the depression and war years were spirited pleas for a kind of supervison which would embrace the ideals of a democratic order. Instead of emphasis on tradition, the leader and the led, supervision became associated with percepts respecting personality and encouraging wide participation in the formulation of policy.[25]

Gestalt psychology, which emphasized the relationship of the individual to the situation, provided a theoretical base as the Lewin studies provided research evidence for the efficacy of social supervision. Democratic supervision, as defined in George Kyte's *How to Supervise*, published in 1930, stressed "the maximum development of the teacher into the most professionally efficient person she is capable of becoming."

This called for more democratic freedom in the teaching process, reflecting the national climate of the postdepression years. Kimball Wiles indicates that the democratic supervision of the 1930s (kind treatment of the individual) evolved into the cooperative enterprise (group decision-making) of the 1940s, and that the 1950s ushered in the concept of the supervisor as an agent for change.[26]

A corollary of supervision based upon sound human relations and cooperative professional efforts was the attention given to social and perceptual psychology by those concerned with or engaged in supervision. Since supervision was seen as a dynamic process that encouraged the interchange of ideas and the interplay of personalities, the most productive level of human interaction was needed if supervision were to be effective. For this to occur, all participants had to be sensitive to each other as individuals and as professionals. As the required communication level for such sensitive interchange developed, the clearer would be the position and feelings of all involved. The more accurate the perceptions, the greater the organizational opportunity to produce collective approaches to instructional problems including their implementation in the instructional process. In sum, contemporary theory, and hopefully practice, in educational supervision shows a shift from an inspectional authoritative process to one of working with people on problems of mutual concern that are related to the goal structure of the school as an organization. This interpretation of supervisory process requires the identification and contribution of all organizational members if ideas are to emerge as plans of action and be set in motion. Some time ago a contrast of the traditional and so-called modern definition of supervisory services was offered by Burton and Brueckner:

> . . . in the main, traditional supervision consisted largely of inspection of the teacher by means of visitation and conference, carried on in a random manner, with directions imposed on the teacher by authority and usually one person. Modern supervision, by contrast, involves the systematic study and analysis of the entire teaching-learning situation utilizing a carefully planned program that has been cooperatively derived from the situation and which is adapted to the needs of those involved in it. Special help is also given individual teachers who encounter problems that cannot be solved by ordinary group supervisory procedures.[27]

This attempt at contrast emphasizes two views or general types rather than operational givens. Only in isolated cases do such conditions exist in fact; rather, numerous positions exist along a continuum of traditional to modern or contemporary practices in supervision.

The contemporary view of supervision requires that supervisors move ahead with teachers fully involved and not in spite of them. Frequently teachers become prime movers in the identification and analysis of the instructional problem. Teachers are clearly seen as the implementors and the most significant prime movers if any probe toward the resolution of the problem is to be made. Consolidating this dynamism, the supervisor, it is conceived, promotes cooperative social action recognizing that change and growth in people, which is critical to instructional growth, will more likely result when personal involvement and shared responsibility characterize the supervisory program. It is further conceived that cooperative interaction of this type encourages the awareness of variant strengths and needs within the group. Plans for instructional improvement that incorporates diversity signal strength in that a "productive whole" is created out of the complexities of human difference.

Kimball Wiles championed the "supervision as human relations" approach through his writing, leadership, and substantial contributions to professional organizations. He wrote:

> We release the potential of group members by increasing the degree to which each is responsible for his own self-direction. A pupil learns more when he assumes more responsibility for his learning. A teacher is more effective when he is responsible for making the final decision on what constitutes an appropriate teaching procedure for his class. An official leader releases the potential of a teacher when he shares his authority to make decisions with the person who is to take the action.[28]

This sharing of responsibility was never intended to set aside the supervisor's leadership position within the organization. Rather, the leadership effort is directed toward the melding of human resources, particularly those within the formal organization of the school. Waiting for teachers to move toward the issues or to identify them is *not* consistent with the democratic approach to supervision. Momentum, direction, and an ordered framework for the consideration of problems must be provided. Within the framework, however, the opportunity for teachers to clarify the problem area is a priority of the highest order. Thus democratic supervision is not passive or inert, it is in motion and is characterized by vitality.

It may be helpful to consider in chart form the trends and circumstances thus far presented on the development of supervision. This chart (Figure 2-1) suffers from the same difficulties associated with any general overview; it suggests a precision in the occurrence of events that does not truly exist. In particular, trends and developments in American education happen unevenly in terms of time and place. What happens in one section of the country in contrast to another, as well as contrasts within states, such as between urban and rural sectors, testifies to the variability of status and development in American education. The chart portrays the interconnection between periods of educational history, the

27

FIGURE 2-1. *Development of Educational Supervision**

Period	Supervisory "Theory"	Supervisory Personnel	Predominant Practice
Early Colonial to End of 18th Cent.	AUTHORITARIAN INSPECTION	Lay Inspectors Ministers Committees	SCHOOL VISITS TO CONTROL STANDARDS
Early 1800s to Turn of 20th Cent.		Superintendents and Principal Teachers	(EXAMINATIONS)
1920s	SCIENTIFIC SUPERVISION	Principals/ Special Supervisors	CLASSROOM VISITS TO OBSERVE AND RESEARCH
1930s 1940s 1950s	DEMOCRATIC SUPERVISION Group Decision	Principals/ Special Supervisors in Line and Staff Relationships	METHODOLOGY SIGNIFICANT INSERVICE DIMENSION ADDED, WITH <u>FOCUS</u>
1960s	Change Agent	Supervisors and Curriculum Workers	REMAINING ON CLASSROOM VISITS
1970s	ORGANIZATIONAL THEORY – SYSTEMS MANAGEMENT	"PROFESSIONAL" SUPERVISORS, Curriculum Workers, Consultants (TEAM APPROACHES)	DIAGNOSIS, INSTRUCTIONAL SYSTEMS DESIGN, ORGANIZATIONAL EFFICIENCY AND EFFECTIVENESS, ACCOUNTABILITY

Solid Lines = Points of Change
Broken Lines = Overlapping Periods
No Lines = No Change

* Virginia P. Redd, "The Future of Educational Supervision: Change or Extinction?," unpublished paper (December 1972).

prevailing theories or supervisory perspectives, the personnel engaged in supervisory responsibilities, and the practices or procedures that predominated during these time frames. In studying the chart, it is possible to sense at a glance the modification over time of supervisory philosophy, conditions and application.

It has been the intent of this chapter to account for and interpret some of these developments as a prelude to the consideration of processes, concepts and areas of skill that are vital to the expression of instructional supervisory behavior in a multivariate educational scene. In light of these historical perspectives and the nature of supervision as related to organizational efficiency and effectiveness (Chapter 1), what is a valid concept of the supervisor who is needed to advance the work and the impact of the schools upon the individuals and communities?

What is needed is a supervisor who makes a difference, who acts directly and effectively to improve the instructional program.* Such an assertion speaks to the primacy of the supervisor's role in leading organizational efforts in the improvement of teaching and learning. In activating this perspective, the supervisor functions as an analyst of the teaching process, creating supportive conditions so teachers can study and improve instructional behavior. The supervisor is responsible for identifying instructional problems, serving as a resource person, an expert in group dynamics, and more recently as an agent of change within a complex organization. In performing these functions, the supervisor must demonstrate the conceptual and technical abilities required of leaders in any dynamic social system. This is a general statement of the type of supervisor who is needed. It is proposed in light of the historical development and the contemporary setting of supervision in education.

In attempting to achieve this state of supervision, there has been a marked tendency to advance practices based upon the principles of sound human relationships. Drawing upon social psychology, group dynamics, and sociological research, supervisory leaders constructed an interpretation of supervision. If supervisory practices stood as reliable exponents of effective human relationships, hewn from the behavioral and social sciences, instructional growth was thought to be assured.

In too many instances, however, a conceptual framework has not accompanied the development of supervisory programs. That is, a vaguely conceived format of process, roles, and responsibilities can be easily dismissed and replaced by little more than good intentions. Often disillusionment and frustration appear as the power of a lost idea or the momentum for change passes. Old patterns become extremely attractive in such circumstances. Thus an ideal of productivity, growth, and change, through the application of sound human relationships, is subsumed by the need to maintain the system. The symbols, the phrases, the committees, and communication system are retained—more as an expression of hope than reality.

What is needed are supervisors who can transform principles of human relations into substantive programs of action. Making people feel comfortable, creating lines of communication, fostering security—all such concerns are basic but valid only as they contribute to the study and the improvement of teaching. At a given time, for example, disequilibrium rather than comfort or security may be the appropriate condition for instructional growth. To make operational decisions in these areas supervisors must study formal organization, role theory, communication, de-

---

* The ideas expressed in this concluding statement are drawn primarily from Richard F. Neville, "The Supervisor We Need," *Educational Leadership,* February 1968, pp. 414–417.

cision-making, personality theory, the change process and other areas significant to a richer and more functional understanding of the human relations perspective of supervision. The mere offering of pronouncements about the power of the group and of the need for "working together" does not represent a supervisory program.

If pause can be given to incantation and a realistic assessment made of current approaches to improving instruction, needed changes in supervisory behavior may be identified. In particular, the relationship of theory and practice must be reviewed. Where supervision is effective it stands the test of internal consistency; a theory, operational principles and supervisory procedures hold together. Simultaneously there is needed the critical analysis and research of supervision along with the interpretation of the curriculum it breeds. Together, the theory, the operational design and their redefinition as new data are added constitute vital elements of supervision.

In the sections of this book that follow, students of supervisory processes in education are asked to study and consider research and theory in a number of disciplines directly bearing upon the work of supervisors. In these sections general analysis of research findings in these disciplines is provided while propositions for supervision including implications for the educational supervisor are set forth. Out of the combined analysis of research, propositions, and implications, the authors present a construct that synthesizes important theoretical components. These components are set before the reader as guidelines for testing, as well as ideas to be measured against the realities and experience of supervisory efforts.

ENDNOTES

1. William H. Lucio and John D. McNeil, *Supervision: A Synthesis of Thought and Action* (New York: McGraw-Hill, 1962), pp. 36–37.
2. *Ibid.*, p. 12.
3. Mildred E. Swearingen, *Supervision of Instruction: Foundations and Dimensions* (Boston: Allyn and Bacon, Inc., 1962), p. 62.
4. William H. Burton and Leo J. Brueckner, *Supervision*, 3rd Ed. (New York: Appleton-Century Crofts, 1955), pp. 5–6.
5. *Ibid.*, p. 6.
6. Frank G. Dickey, *Developing Supervision in Kentucky*, bulletin of the Bureau of School Services, Vol. XX, No. 3 (Lexington: University of Kentucky, 1948), p. 8.
7. Charles Spain, Harold D. Drummond, and John I. Goodlad, *Educational Leadership and the Elementary School Principal* (New York: Rinehart and Co., 1956), p. 24.
8. Paul Revere Pierce, *The Origin and Development of the Public School Principalship* (Chicago: University of Chicago Press, 1935), p. 7.

9. *Ibid.*

10. Paul B. Jacobson, William C. Reavis, and James D. Logsdon, *Duties of School Principals,* adapted from *Tenth Annual Report of the Common Schools of Cincinnati* (1839) (Englewood Cliffs, N. J.: Prentice-Hall, Inc., 1950), pp. 730–731.

11. *Twelfth Annual Report of the Common Schools of Cincinnati* (1841), p. 51.

12. *Fifth Annual Report of the Board of Education of Chicago* (1859), p. 43.

13. *Thirty-First Annual Report of the Common Schools of Cincinnati* (1860), p. 84. (As adapted from Pierce, *The Origin and Development of the Public School Principalship,* p. 59.)

14. As reported in the *Eighth Annual Report of the Board of Education of Chicago* (1862), p. 37.

15. *Seventeenth Annual Report of the Board of Education of St. Louis* (1871), p. 188.

16. *Annual Report of the School Committee of Boston* (1877), p. 201.

17. Pierce, *op. cit.,* p. 71.

18. Alvin Toffler, *Future Shock* (New York: Bantam Books, 1971), p. 400.

19. Raymond E. Callahan, *Education and the Cult of Efficiency* (Chicago: University of Chicago Press, 1962).

20. Lawrence A. Cremin, *The Transformation of the School* (New York: Vantage Books, 1964).

21. *Ibid.,* p. viii.

22. John Dewey, *The Child and the Curriculum* (Chicago: University of Chicago Press, 1902).

23. Saul Lavisky, "Uncritical Review of the Curriculum Literature, 1955–70," unpublished paper (Alexandria, Va.: Human Resources Research Organization, May 1973).

24. Commission on the Reorganization of Secondary Education, NEA, *The Cardinal Principles of Secondary Education,* U.S. Department of Interior, Bureau of Education Bulletin 1918, No. 35 (Washington, D.C.: U.S. Government Printing Office, 1937).

25. Lucio and McNeil, *op. cit.,* p. 11.

26. Kimball Wiles, *Supervision for Better Schools* (Englewood Cliffs, N. J.: Prentice-Hall, Inc., 1955), p. 151.

27. Burton and Brueckner, *op. cit.,* p. 13.

28. Wiles, *op. cit.*

Chapter 3

The Nature of Instructional Supervisory Behavior

The history of supervision in education records a multitude of roles and responsibilities and a deep belief in the value of supervisory leadership. The instructional leadership motif is an idealized interpretation of the supervisor's role in education, a motif not strongly supported in the light of available evidence concerning supervisory effectiveness. Much attention has been directed toward the tasks that supervisors perform; little has been directed at the critical elements of supervisory behavior. Few professional roles in education have had as little intelligent study done of them.

The profession has consistently identified supervisors in education as instructional leaders. Publications such as those of the Association for Supervision and Curriculum Development have emphasized this attribution. These publications have detailed major elements of the supervisor's role, while recognizing that the sum of those elements converge in the notion of the supervisor as instructional leader. Inherent in this notion is the assumption that the presence and performance of educational supervisors does have a positive impact upon the effectiveness of teachers. It would be more appropriate if this assumption were treated as a hypothesis to be tested instead of a valid description of supervisory behavior. It is frequently stated, for example, that supervisors promote better decision-making by teachers, and that through supervisory efforts curriculum study and articulation of the school's program are better accomplished. These responsibilities are only samples of the anticipated results of supervisory efforts. They are drawn out of what seems to be an unending list of functions and activities for which supervisors, it is claimed, are responsible. Rather than reaffirming or refuting these role interpretations, it is more important at this moment to relate them to a concept of the nature of supervision.

Robert Goldhammer published a significant work in 1969 that has contributed substantially to the professional practice of supervision. It projected detailed images of supervision, including methodological models, while also defining the basis for further theoretical advancement. Commenting on the sorry state of supervisory theory and practice in education, Goldhammer states that supervision often counts for so much, it counts for nothing. Attempting to explain the reason for this condition, he wrote:

> This malady, I suspect, is not simply to be understood as guilt by association, that is, as a result of supervision's adulteration by external issues. The problem is, more seriously, an internal one: that in the absence of some cogent framework of educational values and of powerful theoretical systems, operational models, extensive bodies of case materials to consult, rigorous programs of professional training, and a broad literature of empirical research, supervision has neither a fundamental substantive content nor a consciously determined and universally recognized process—both its stuff and its method tend to be random, residual, frequently archaic, and eclectic in the worst sense.[1]

The study of instructional supervision has historically concentrated on the identification and analysis of supervisory tasks. This approach is weak, because it is largely descriptive and is not drawn from theoretical formulations. An additional weakness of this approach is that the tasks were typically identified and defined by persons other than supervisors. It is also a self-fulfilling prophecy. Because existing supervisory practice is identified and described, it has been treated as appropriate practice.

There is a conceptual and theoretical haze that inevitably settles in as any serious discussion of instructional supervision is undertaken; discussions deal with practice and problems rather than theoretical constructs.

The approach taken in this book to analyzing supervisory behavior represents an attempt to define a theory based upon research findings. In so doing, it completely reverses the tendency to study supervision through direct task analysis. Rather, the organizational phenomenon is investigated through research findings deemed essential to the explanation of instructional supervisory behavior (ISB). From the outset it was anticipated that theoretical guidelines would be developed that could eventually be tested operationally. It was also hoped that a model or series of models would be developed against which supervisory behavior could be studied in a new perspective.

PHASE A: A CONCEPTUALIZATION OF INSTRUCTIONAL SUPERVISORY BEHAVIOR

As anyone acquainted with the literature available on educational supervision realizes, present maxims have been drawn from observation of performance in the field. Virtually all of the textbooks since the pioneer treatise by Barr, Burton and Brueckner deal with supervision in this fashion.[2] The late Kimball Wiles perhaps both epitomized an era of practitioner-oriented supervision and stands as the last spokesman at its climax.[3] A conceptual approach, such as that provided by Ben Harris,[4] provided a new look at instructional supervision in terms of behavior. More recently, attempts are underway to treat supervision through respective client-centered, clinical and sociological system foci.

Any explanations that will make it possible to predict and, therefore, to direct behavior within specified limits first require a preliminary conceptualization of the phenomenon. Such a conceptualization must be sufficiently clear so that independent investigators equipped with similar tools can observe a system and recognize the behavior to be studied with a high degree of reliability.

One way of viewing the educational organization is as a social system.[5] By using the system model, it is possible to study the educational institution as a subsystem of a larger society. The society has certain expectations for the educational institution that are met through interdependent organizational structures. Each organization can be described as a patterning of specialized and interdependent parts created to achieve some common goal or goals. In the case of the educational organization, the common goal is expressed as the facilitation of student learning in certain organizationally defined directions believed to be congruent with both the student's and society's needs and expectations.

In order to achieve its goals, each educational organization must provide for a variety of behavioral systems that have the general functions of contributing to the achievement of organizational goals and maintaining the operation and existence of the organization itself. Examples of some of the behavioral systems in the educational organization would include the administrative behavior system, teaching behavior system, counseling behavior system, and instructional supervisory behavior system. Figure 3-1 illustrates this concept.

As a beginning step in such a conceptualization, instructional supervision is viewed as *one* behavior system within the educational organization. Such a concept presumes the existence of a set of appropriate behaviors that can be identified, analyzed, and that lend themselves to the development of testable hypotheses. The focus of this approach is on supervision, not on the supervisor; on behavior, not on the person and the functional tasks assigned to him by the organizations.

The broken lines in Figure 3-1 indicate that the educational organization is an open system. Its purposes, activities, and values can all be affected by organizations and behavior systems from outside the perimeter of the formal educational organization. As a consequence, not only the organization but the interdependent subbehavior systems within it are impacted upon and affected by external values and behaviors. The unlabeled blocks serve as a reminder that other behavior systems also exist and ultimately must be embraced within a total concept.

This approach focuses on supervisory behavior, regardless of who performs it. It avoids the tedious, unproductive arguments concerning "Who is the supervisor?" and "What is his role?". Many persons engage in supervisory behavior, although they are not all supervisors; just as many may engage in administrative behavior, yet they are not administrators. There are, however, behaviors unique to the performance of each of such gross organizational task elements.

In Figure 3-1, therefore, the various behavior subsystems are circumscribed by broken lines. This indicates not only the open nature of such behavior systems within the organization, but also indicates that members of an organization, although they may operate predominantly within one behavior system, do have access to and move in and out of other subbehavior systems. This concept focuses on behavior, not on role. As a result it is a major departure from traditional approaches to the study of supervision.

Each of the subsystems has a generalizable area of task responsibility within the educational organization; each exists because it is assumed it contributes to maintenance of the organization and to the achievement of its goals. Effective behavior in each of these subsystems requires the performance of organizationally prescribed tasks and the attainment of certain objectives.

It is from such a behavior system that a theoretical base for instructional supervision should be established. Following the development of such a theoretical base, rooted in researchable organizational behavior, the technical skills of supervision can be identified and developed. They can be verified in practice, and the profession can be held accountable for the possession and demonstration of competence.

In order to establish such a theoretical base, however, it is first mandatory that the phenomenon of instructional supervision be isolated and defined as a behavior system. Such a definition must be sharp enough to provide for the isolation and observation of behaviors; it should enable independent observers to judge what is and is not supervision; and it must deal with behavior in such a way that it can lead to testable hypotheses about supervisory behavior. In other words, it must contain the seeds of empirical validation.

Instructional supervision is herein defined as: *Behavior officially*

FIGURE 3-1. *Educational Organization Behavior Systems*

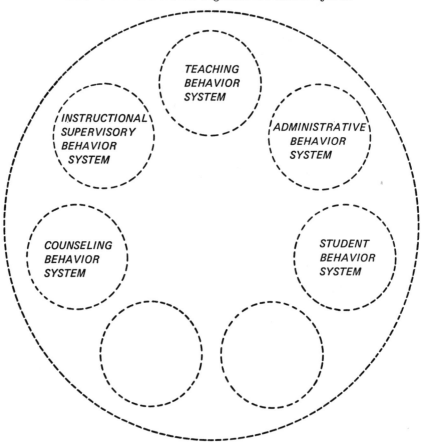

designated by the organization that directly affects teacher behavior in such a way as to facilitate pupil learning and achieve the goals of the organization.[6]

There are three key elements in this definition. First, the behavior exhibited is "officially designated." It is not random, casually determined activity, but it bears the stamp of organizational request and formal authority. Secondly, it "directly influences teacher behavior." This rules out the multitude of tasks performed by supervisors that, while they may be important to the organization, are *not* supervision. It provides a test as to whether one is really engaging in supervisory behavior—does it clearly affect teachers?—the teacher behavior subsystem. Thirdly, it specifies an ultimate outcome tied directly to the reason for the existence of the school: the facilitation of student learning. This element also provides focus for influencing teacher behavior—not willy-nilly, but purposeful change in teacher behavior in order to improve learning.

It is important to note that the entire development of this book from this point on is based on the acceptance of this conceptualization of instructional supervisory behavior, and it is the unifying thread in the entire fabric of this work.

PHASE B: DEVELOPING A RESEARCH-BASED THEORY OF SUPERVISION

Building from the definition of instructional supervisory behavior to a research-based theory requires an understanding of not only the original conception but of the steps taken in moving from a definition, through research findings, to a theoretical model. A review of the phases that occurred prior to the construction of the model or description of ISB constitutes the remaining sections of this chapter. Part II reports a substantial body of empirical findings that make more specific the conceptual base for the formulation of proposals related to performance guidelines and the analysis of instructional supervisory behavior (ISB). Many of the findings are the products of research in a variety of fields as studied in different organizational settings.

A major difficulty is selecting data from research that appear to offer potential clues to the antecedents and consequences of ISB. Review of educational research and empirical studies in the fields usually considered as closely related, notably psychology, sociology and other behavioral or social sciences, fails to uncover a body of theoretical formulations for instructional supervision. Neither does such analysis provide findings that directly serve as a base for deriving such behavior in educational organizations.

Two considerations must then be made. The first is to determine those fields of research that logically would offer information applicable to the educational behavior system generally. The second is to select from among those fields that appear to impinge most appropriately on the instructional behavior system specifically.

Six fields of study were originally assumed to have implications for instructional supervisory behavior. These were leadership theory, communication theory, organization theory, change theory, group dynamics theory and decision theory. The last two were subsequently eliminated from utilization in the initial pursuit of a research approach to ISB when it became obvious that much of the data in group dynamics theory and decision theory appeared in the reports of research in other fields.

Figure 3-2 illustrates the source of data analyzed for generating a theory of instructional supervision. As in Figure 3-1, the empty boxes

FIGURE 3-2. *Educational Organization Matrix and Theoretical Fields Assumed to Have Implications for ISB*

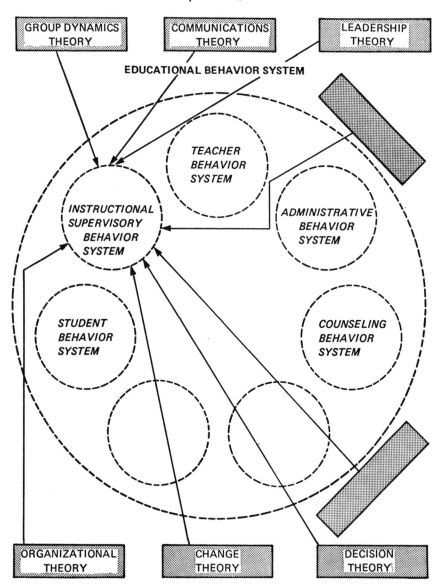

indicate the probability that additional fields not yet covered might also have relevance for ISB.

It is acknowledged that the overlapping of certain fields does not obviate the possibility that the two fields omitted could have provided helpful data. In fact, some may legitimately argue that they might have been more fruitful than one or more of those retained. Nor does the eventual resolution of the process invalidate the possibility that other types of research could have been of assistance.

Of equal importance, the same four fields as well as additional ones may offer research data essential to understanding the other behavior systems illustrated in Figure 3-2. However, the focus of this theoretical development is entirely on instructional supervision without consideration of teaching, management or counseling, except as they are pertinent to ISB.

This approach leads to the categorization of data and findings in a manner that gives sharper focus to the particular area of research. From the formulations a number of basic propositions can then be derived that have general applicability to supervision in organizations. Each proposition can then be examined to determine its specific implication(s) for instructional supervisory behavior.

The use of ISB as a behavior concept through which to select research data to explain it served to produce 106 propositions from research in the fields of leadership theory, communication theory, organization theory and change theory. The implications of these propositions for ISB translate the research studies into viable and structured form.

PHASE C: THE GENERATION OF SUPERVISION THEORY

The propositions themselves codify research findings in a meaningful way for those interested in ISB. Their unique contribution is that they provide some new insight into the phenomenon. Their limitation is that they evolved from analysis of the past but fail to predict the future. Therefore, the theoretical basis for instructional supervision requires such propositions to be submitted to further study.

Preservation of the research approach demanded that the propositions maintain their integrity. The tendency to impose headings or classifications drawn from literature on supervision was avoided. Rather than utilize predetermined categories, the propositions were examined as separate entities without reference to the area of research from which they came. Certain prevailing themes tended to reoccur among the propositions, without regard to the original area of research. Through the utilization of a mix box and the process of interfacing, several different classifications were made. The sorting actually forced revision and clarification of meaning by returning to the original research studies for verification. This evolutionary approach to the clarification of new concepts required that the propositions be consistently sorted into the same categories. Any attempt to label them prematurely was deliberately resisted until the characteristics of the grouping became clear.

Applying this process to the 106 propositions gave rise to the eleven categories that eventually became the critical components of instructional supervisory behavior.

Analysis of the components revealed that they were of three general types. These classifications were named only after this alignment was substantiated. The critical components, as placed in these major categories, became the building units for a model of instructional supervisory behavior. Once assembled, it became apparent that the model possesses dynamic qualities as well as descriptive ones. The major categories are interrelated, as are their internal critical components. Analysis of the relationships between and among the components constituting the model provides a series of theoretical guidelines.

It is anticipated that the application of these guidelines to actual situations will test their value and simultaneously crystalize the nature of the phenomenon called Instructional Supervisory Behavior.

Figure 3-3 illustrates the total process of moving with the original conceptualization, from the determination of the original areas of research studies through the subsequent steps to the building of a theoretical model for instructional supervisory behavior.

The five crucial decisions reached in the execution of this analysis deserve emphasis. At each of these key points, an impasse appeared to have been reached. It would have been far easier to have terminated the operation. Yet, in each case careful analysis provided a possible course of action to be pursued further.

STEP 1: Consensus regarding a preliminary *concept* of instructional supervision as a separate and distinct behavior system.

STEP 2: Agreement on *areas of research* to be included in the project and those to be excluded or given subordinate roles.

STEP 3: Confidence in the *evolutionary nature* of events that suggest new possibilities and potential for further exploration.

STEP 4: Execution of the *interfacing process* with all propositions, while continually reworking them before assigning titles to components and examining relationships among categories.

STEP 5: Development of a *dynamic model* of ISB from which the *theoretical guidelines* are drawn for subsequent empirical testing.

The utilization of a research-based approach requires an understanding of the various steps in the construction of an operational definition for instructional supervisory behavior (ISB). It is intended to provide a basis for further theoretical insight, as well as a possible framework for the design and development of preparation programs, training materials, research and the continuing education of supervisors.

FIGURE 3-3. *Development of Theory of Instructional Supervisory Behavior*

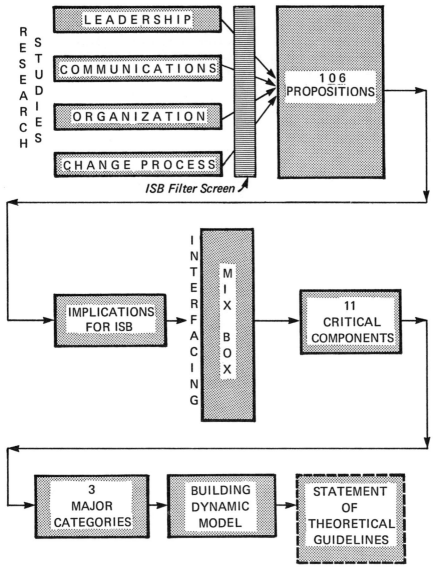

ENDNOTES

1. Robert Goldhammer, *Clinical Supervision* (New York: Holt, Rinehart and Winston, Inc., 1969), p. viii.
2. A. S. Barr, William H. Burton, and Leo J. Brueckner, *Supervision* (New York: T. Appleton-Century Co., 1938).
3. Kimball Wiles, *Supervision for Better Schools* (Englewood Cliffs, N. J.:

Prentice-Hall, Inc., 1950).

4. Ben M. Harris, *Supervisory Behavior in Education* (Englewood Cliffs, N. J.: Prentice-Hall, Inc., 1963).

5. John Lovell, "A Perspective for Viewing Instructional Supervisory Behavior," *Supervision: Perspectives and Propositions* (Washington, D.C.: Association for Supervision and Curriculum Development, 1967), p. 24.

6. Acknowledgement is made to John Lovell for a conceptualization of supervision as a behavior system in his work "A Perspective for Viewing Instructional Supervisory Behavior," *op. cit.* It is from his conceptualization that this definition of ISB is derived.

PART II

A Research Base for Instructional Supervisory Behavior

Previous discussions of instructional supervision have focused largely upon the experiences of those occupying supervisory positions. Seldom was any question raised as to the appropriateness of the activities in which supervisors were engaged. Data was obtained from studies of the practitioners themselves or from those who prepared them for such roles.

The principle is advanced here that supervision as a generic entity should be based on empirical research in other related fields. It states that information so obtained can be utilized to establish the nature of supervision itself and to extract implications for its applications to instructional improvement in schools. The acceptance of such assertions shifts the focus from the reporting of practitioners to experimental studies.

The four chapters of Part II examine the contributions of leadership theory, communication theory, organization theory, and change theory to an understanding of instructional supervision.

The treatment of these areas is somewhat comprehensive, in that a wide range of information is introduced. There is extensive documentation of research. At the same time, it is recognized that an in-depth interpretation of the reported research and theory and their implications for ISB is not undertaken in this text. It is hoped that individuals interested in the phenomenon of ISB will use the leads contained herein as a starting point in the study of leadership, communication, organization, and change for the insights these fields of research have to offer to an understanding of ISB.

Chapter 4

Leadership Theory: Implications for Instructional Supervisory Behavior

The concept of leadership is both powerful and puzzling—powerful because it contains the implication of direction or redirection of people's lives, actions and aspirations, yet puzzling because the determinants of effective leadership still remain so poorly understood. It is impossible for any social structure to long endure if there is continued absence of leadership.

Leadership is often defined as behavior that causes individuals to move toward goals they find to be important and that create in the followers a feeling of well-being. Tannenbaum, Weschler and Massarik define leadership as ". . . interpersonal influence, exercised in situation and directed, through the communication process, toward the attainment of a specified goal or goals." [1] It could be argued that to the extent to which such a situation does not exist there is in fact no leadership in an organization. When such occurs, atrophy and decline have begun, and unless new leadership emerges the organization will ultimately die. This applies no matter what the nature of the organization may be—a social club, a nation, a military organization, or a school.

In a formal organization such as a school, the study of and the provision for leadership become particularly important. The pertinence of investigating leadership as a means of providing insight into the essential character of instructional supervisory behavior is immediately evident. Supervision as defined in Chapter 3 makes clear the responsibility for leadership that accrues to a person who desires to engage in supervisory activity. By assuming the position of supervisor, one indicates willingness to exert leadership and to be held accountable for affecting the behavior of teachers in such a way that the goals of the organization are achieved. Successful instructional supervisory behavior cannot exist in the absence of effective leadership behavior.

In this chapter, the concept of leadership is developed as a significant segment of instructional supervisory behavior. A large body of research and theory exists concerning leadership. From this extensive body of knowledge those theories and empirical findings are examined that appear to hold particular relevance for understanding instructional supervisory behavior.

THE STUDY OF LEADERSHIP

Man has long been fascinated by the study of leadership. While it is only within this century that the sophistication of research has been applied to leadership in any extensive and systematic way, the study and analysis of leadership and the behavior of leaders is probably as old as the history of mankind. In the earliest written records of the history of man the nature of leadership and the assessment of leaders is a recurring theme. In fact, the history of the world could well be written by exploring the behavior of the leaders who have guided society's destinies.

Interest in the phenomenon of leadership is universal and permeates all levels of society. Analyses of the phenomenon range all the way from almost supernatural explanations on one hand, in which leadership is viewed as a particular kind of "gift" over which man has little or no control, being something he is born with, a unique combination of elements and powers that enables him to influence others, to the other end of the continuum, which holds that leadership can be reduced to a small number of identifiable and perhaps even quantifiable elements that are discrete, available for investigation, and can be acquired or developed in some systematic way. The research, however, is not quite so clear and one's own casual observation finds effective leaders behaving in quite different ways and possessing very different personal characteristics.

Why is one president able to rally a nation behind him while another fails? Why is one school superintendent able to bring about extensive change in the curriculum and obtain the support of the faculty and the community while doing so, while another superintendent in the same system is an utter failure? What is it that enables a manager or a player in the sports world to provide the key ingredient of leadership that can spur a team to victory? What is it that makes human beings willing to follow or be influenced by one person and not by another? Even among young children the phenomenon of leadership and followership is evident.

While much attention has been given in recent years to the formal education and preparation of leaders, it is interesting to note that such efforts have not as yet resulted in significant success and that, in fact, attempts at the "processing" of potential leaders in such a way that it would result in a highly similar set of behaviors have been largely rejected. Business has gone through the evolutionary process of "rugged individualism" as a dominant theme of leadership to the "processing" of the organization man and the Madison Avenue man in the 1940s and 1950s. The complexities of leadership and influence are now rather generally recognized.

This is not to say that there is less concern about leadership today than there once was. Quite the contrary, the increasing degree of organization and bureaucracy in modern society has made the need for effective leadership more critical than ever before. In addition, the interfacing of a wide variety of organizations and societal concerns has also heightened the need for responsive, sophisticated leadership that is attuned to organizational objectives *and* to societal and human concerns as well.

And so it is with school organization. As in all formal organizations, leadership is an absolutely essential ingredient in the structure, operation, and achievement of purposes. It is the task of the instructional supervisor to directly influence the behavior of teachers in order to achieve the goals of the organization. Without leadership, without influence, it is highly unlikely that any instructional supervisory behavior can really take place. It is important to note that organizations do not remain stationary, nor do teachers remain so in their own teaching behavior. Either there is influence, positive change, and forward progress, or an institution or an individual falls into decline.

Supervisors bear a special responsibility for providing leadership and becoming students of the process of effective leadership. A supervisor's world is one of influence. He wishes to help a teacher modify his behavior in such a way that his effectiveness as well as his own sense of well-being are enhanced.

These are two important dimensions in the leadership process: 1) influencing people to behave in ways that will ensure the attainment of goals the organization has deemed to be important, and 2) increasing the feeling of importance and dignity on the part of the persons being influenced. Surely, a supervisor needs to be concerned about both of these dimensions. The first one is clear. The school has an obligation to provide for the learning of children and youth, and it ought to be held accountable for the achievement of this. The school, however, is also a uniquely "human" organization. The dynamics of its interpersonal relationships and influence are particularly identifiable yet complex. The "product" of the school is human behavior, and the whole process through which that human behavior is determined and molded is one of influence, the impact of one human being upon another. Therefore, a systematic study of influence and leadership is of great significance to the supervisor or to anyone who seeks to understand and to affect the organization and achievement of the schools.

For centuries man has sought to find explanations for effective leadership and the search has led to a wide variety of different approaches to the study of leadership. Many early investigations turned on the "great man" theory of Thomas Carlyle. Later investigations looked at the personal traits of successful leaders, both physical and psychological, while other studies focused on styles of leadership (the way in which influence was exerted), the analysis of cultural and societal factors as an explanation, and investigations into situational factors and their effect on successful leadership. Most of these approaches have been quite disappointing, and recent studies have turned toward investigating leadership on a more empirical and scientific basis with special emphasis on group interaction theory. It would be difficult as well as impractical to attempt to summarize all of the research and theorizing in the area of leadership. For the purposes of this analysis, those findings that appear to be especially helpful in understanding the essential elements of instructional supervisory behavior will be grouped under three major categories: individual dimensions of leadership, group dimensions of leadership, and organizational dimensions of leadership. It is recognized that these are rather arbitrary groupings and that not all the research fits neatly into these categories. Following this summary, there will be developed more specific implications of this research and theorizing for instructional supervisory behavior.

INDIVIDUAL DIMENSIONS OF LEADERSHIP

Research summarized in this area deals with the personal characteristics and traits of leaders and with leadership behavior styles. A basic approach of the investigations of individual styles and behavior of leaders was to identify those characteristics or patterns that were unique to leaders as contrasted with nonleaders and to correlate these personality, physical, or behavioral traits with leader effectiveness. Obviously, if such traits could be singled out and behavioral styles verified, the task of identifying and training potential leaders would be made both simple and highly successful.

Personality Characteristics. Most of the research in the area of leadership traits and personal characteristics has been quite disappointing. While it has been found that on the average those holding leadership positions are a little bit taller and a little bit brighter than nonleaders, the evidence is nonconclusive. Nor has any consistent pattern of personality characteristics been found; in fact, persons with a wide range of personality traits occupy leadership roles. Moreover, most of the research has failed to distinguish among successful and unsuccessful leaders in its investigation of traits of leaders.

It was reported by McGrath and Altman,[2] for example, that leaders tend to have a higher degree of intelligence, general and task ability, and a higher level of formal education. In addition they found them to be more extroverted, assertive, and socially mature. Similar conclusions were reached earlier by White,[3] who found them practically oriented extroverts rather than holders of radical ideas, and by Nelson,[4] who found leaders high in self-confidence, alertness, job motivation, emotional control and aggressiveness.

Ross and Hendry [5] have enumerated desirable characteristics illustrating what the leader must "be." In their definition they include as a leader both the one who leads by designation and the one who emerges as a leader. They cite the following as important: empathy, consideration, group membership (to a degree), talkativeness, cheerfulness, expressiveness, emotional stability. While they also cite intelligence, competence, self-confidence, and consistency as important attributes, they note that while leaders are more intelligent than followers, they cannot be too *much* more intelligent.

During the period of time when research interest in leadership traits was probably at its highest, Stogdill [6] did a thorough survey of the literature, synthesizing the findings of over 120 studies dealing with personal factors associated with leadership. These studies covered a wide spectrum of different occupational types and leadership roles, as well as investigating child and adult leadership behavior. While there was some relationship found between child and adult leadership behavior, some factors appear only in certain age and social groups. The evidence is contradictory and chronological age cannot be regarded as a factor in leadership. The survey turned up a low positive correlation for height and weight as well as for health and athletic ability. While evidence was weak, there appeared to be a relationship between leadership and personal appearance. More strongly positive correlations were found with fluency of speech, intelligence—as long as not *too* intelligent—specialized knowledge, judgment, initiative and ambition, self-confidence, cooperation, sociability, popularity and prestige. In fact, correlations between leadership and sociability and popularity were among some of the stronger ones found. Mixed results were found on such traits as introversion and extroversion, originality, dominance, and social and economic status, these last two tending to be higher than in followers although not significantly different.

It was Stogdill's conclusion that patterns of leadership traits differ with the situation and that they are "likely to vary with the leadership requirements in different situations." [7] Such a finding suggests that leadership is strongly affected by the nature of the group and by their needs and that group factors may be a significant element in the understanding of leadership behavior.

Cowley,[8] in a study of three types of "face-to-face leaders"—criminals, noncommissioned officers, and student leaders—found that all of these had several leadership traits in common: self-confidence, motor impulsion, finality of judgment and speed of decision-making.

Wolfenstein [9] has been able to identify some traits of "crisis leaders." They have ideological commitment and a related well-developed superego, emotional independence, they see things in two camps—good (his) and evil—and are single-minded—they can work devotedly at a task. In a study of business, Henry [10] concluded that all executives had in common a personality pattern consisting of achievement desire, upward-mobility drive, desire for authority (see it as helpful), decisiveness, aggressiveness, reality-orientation, and apprehensiveness related to the fear of failure. Among other traits noted were good interpersonal relationships, although less responsive to subordinates than to superiors.

Fiedler's [11] studies measuring psychological distance between a leader and coworkers, using an assumed-similarity among opposites measure (ASO scale), found that the ability of a leader to perceive discrepancy between his most and least preferred coworkers as a personality attribute or trait related to leadership effectiveness. High ASO scores indicate a tendency to accept coworkers in a relatively uncritical and, moveover, unreserved manner. Fiedler's research, which was done on basketball teams, small combat units, and open-hearth steel crews, points up the need for a leader to maintain some kind of psychological distance between himself and coworkers, and to be analytical and critical of their abilities. The leader who tends to see all workers as relatively similar is less effective than the leader who perceives discrepancies between his most and least preferred coworkers.

The conclusion one inevitably reaches, given the research evidence available at this point, is that there is simply no trait or pattern of characteristics common to all leaders. While certain characteristics recur frequently, their positive correlation is low and in themselves they cannot be held to be significant determinants or predictors of one's ability to lead. At present it is not possible to predict leadership on the basis of personality traits, although it is possible that the likelihood of effective leadership would be enhanced if leaders were selected who at least possessed some of the personality traits commonly found among leaders.

Leadership Styles. It is not surprising that researchers, disappointed by their inability to identify leadership traits more definitively, turned their attention instead to the way leaders behaved, in an effort to identify leadership styles as a possible clue to discovering effective leadership and thus making it possible to isolate the phenomenon and identify and train potential leaders. It was hypothesized that perhaps the clue to leadership effectiveness was not to be found in personality, but in the particular behavior pattern or leadership style employed. While some interesting aspects of leadership style were uncovered, the results were no more significantly helpful than the studies of personality traits. The focus of many such studies was to look at permissive versus directive leadership style and to explore the relationship in terms of group productivity and morale of autocratic, laissez-faire, and democratic styles.

The early Lewin, Lippitt and White [12] studies were pioneering works in this area, and other work by Lippitt,[13] White and Lippitt,[14] and Bavelas [15] confirmed the findings of Lewin *et al.* that groups operating under different leadership styles develop different patterns of achievement and different group emotional climates. The White and Lippitt studies found certain outcomes that could be predicted for certain leadership styles. While autocratically led groups produced slightly more work, they were also characterized by less motivation, more aggression, discontent, and a greater dependency among the members. Groups under a laissez-faire leader produced less work, played more, were poorly motivated and were very discontent. Groups under democratic leader behavior produced slightly less work, but of higher quality, had greater originality, higher motivation and were more group-minded.

These findings were confirmed by Baumgartel [16] in an investigation of leadership style in the administration of twenty research laboratories. He found that compared with those under directive leadership, "scientists under participatory leadership 1) are somewhat more motivated toward research orientation, 2) have a markedly high sense of achievement in research, and 3) hold generally more favorable attitudes toward their director."[17] It was found that laissez faire leadership related to lower commitment to research orientation, lack of a sense of progress toward goals, and less favorable evaluation of the director of the laboratory. Baumgartel concluded that "even a research organization, where autonomy is highly valued, needs performance of certain essential leadership functions for effective operation." [18] He also found that laissez-faire leadership had more negative effects among larger laboratories than among the smaller ones.[19]

Argyris came to a similar conclusion in his study of organizational leadership, noting that under an autocratic leader there is a tendency for "subordinates to become dependent, submissive and leader-centered, to be in competition against one another which at times results in interpersonal rivalry and hostility; to be productive when the leader is present, to lose a high degree of productiveness when the leader departs." [20]

Kahn and Katz,[21] in a review of industrial research, found four variables of supervisory leadership related to group productivity. It was found that the more effective supervisors as compared with the less effective were more able to play a differentiated role, were better at delegating authority, were more supportive of their subordinates and checked up on them less, and were better able to develop group cohesiveness.

In a study of group atmosphere in democratically and autocratically led groups, Lippitt [22] found that there was very little to distinguish the two so long as the leader was present, but that when the leader absented himself from the group—even for a short time—the autocratically led group stopped work and waited, while the democratically led group continued to work in essentially the same way as when the leader was with them.

Barnes,[23] however, points out the relationship between leadership style and the competence of the group, in findings related to those of Baumgartel. Barnes's study showed that people of low political competence can be mobilized just as effectively and perhaps more so by nondemocratic style as by democratic leadership. It was his conclusion that leadership style needed to be in keeping with the political competence of those to be led: ". . . it seems unreasonable to expect people of low political competence, authoritarian family patterns, authoritarian work and social relations, and marginal politicization to respond as well to democratic as to undemocratic styles of leadership. Such people are likely to be mobilized quite effectively by non-democratic styles, just as people of high competence respond well to democratic styles." [24]

Many studies have investigated leadership style that can be characterized as task or organization oriented, as contrasted with leadership that is relationship or interaction oriented. Bass notes that "permissive leadership, group decision making, and permission to interact prior to reaching such decisions produce more effective groups and more satisfied members," but he cautions that exceptions may occur if the members of a group are of low ability or are under severe stress.[25] Bass also concluded that the "self-oriented" leader is really detrimental to group effectiveness; that the "task-oriented" leader tends to lead only when the tasks and the rewards for task completion are attractive; and that the "interaction-oriented" leader leads only when he perceives that interaction has broken down. While ability in the particular task helps, it was not found to be a significant factor.[26]

In a study of shipboard leadership in the navy, Campbell [27] discovered that men who described themselves as giving major emphasis to procedure and to organization headed up units that in turn described themselves as having low morale. It was found that "the enlisted man would most like to see in command those who are perceived as high on integration, communication down, initiation, recognition, organization, communication up, and representation." [28] Campbell did not find that responsibility correlated significantly with leadership behavior as described by subordinates, but it was found that authority and delegation—and especially delegation—did bear a relationship to the leadership behavior as perceived by their subordinates.[29]

Investigations of consideration behavior as an aspect of leadership style clearly demonstrated its effect on employee morale. Shartle [30] states that the effectiveness of an organization is enhanced when supervisors keep subordinates informed, give them the opportunity to express opinions, are willing and able to help with job problems, and when they are sympathetic to employees' personal difficulties. Halpin and Winer [31] identified "consideration" and "initiating structure" as major dimensions of leader behavior and found that these two behaviors accounted respectively for 50 percent and 34 percent of the common variance in the behavior of fifty-two aircraft commanders. By consideration is meant interpersonal relationships of warmth and trust, while initiating structure refers to behavior that establishes group goals, operations, and social control.

It is important to note that effective leadership was found to consist of high performance behavior in both consideration and initiating structure, although it was found by Halpin [32] and Gibb [33] that subordinates and superordinates evaluate such styles differently, with subordinates placing greater value on consideration behavior and superiors placing a high premium on initiating structure. Such a finding reflects the preoccupation that many employees have with personal need versus the concern of management with goal attainment. Gibb also confirms the need for consideration as well as initiation behavior, stating that ". . . leadership which shows consideration of the needs of followers, while also insisting on discipline and emphasizing task achievement, is most successful in achieving the twin criteria of superior performance and high morale." [34]

Low consideration and high structure by foremen correlate with high grievance and high turnover, according to Fleishman and Harris.[35] These factors increased markedly at the extreme ends of low consideration and high structure. Consideration was found to be the dominant factor in interaction effects. Among groups whose foremen rated medium to high on consideration behavior, grievances and turnover were the lowest. It was also found that foremen who were high on consideration could put increased emphasis on structure behavior with only a very small increase in grievances and no increase in turnover.

Fiedler [36] has also investigated differences in relationship-oriented and task-oriented leaders. He found that his ASO scale measure (reported earlier in this chapter) appeared to be a motivational measure and that a high ASO score indicated relationship orientation and a drive to get personal recognition, while a low score indicated task orientation. High

ASO score leaders get their self-esteem from relationships, while low scores indicate that it comes from the satisfaction of working on and achieving a task.

The informal leaders of teams judged as successful tended to be task-oriented, while the informal leaders of less successful teams—although more pleasant and happy—tended to be relationship-oriented. Fiedler also concluded that groups in which there were good leader-member relations performed better under task-oriented leaders, while groups in which leader-member relations were poor performed more effectively under a relationship-oriented leader.

A major conclusion of Fiedler's [37] is that the nature of a task (including the nature of the group) determines leadership style and that neither a relationship- nor a task-oriented leader is effective in all situations. Task-oriented leaders perform better in either highly favorable or unfavorable situations, while relationship-oriented ones perform better in "intermediate" situations in which they have only moderate influence or acceptance. (It is less clear, however, whether one can actually "select" his own leadership style. While one can behave in both ways, he probably has a dominant motivation.) Conditions of low stress require leaders who are oriented toward managing and control, while situations of moderate or interpersonal stress seem to call for leaders who are considerate and permissive. Fiedler [38] states that "group performance can, therefore, be improved either by modifying the leader's style or by modifying the group-task situation."

In a comparison of behaviors of successful and unsuccessful leaders it was shown by Fiedler [39] that successful leaders "decrease in the intensity of their interaction with group members, that they become less directive, less involved and structuring, and less considerate in unfavorable group situations." This finding is directly related to the need for maintaining some degree of "psychological distance" as reported earlier in this chapter.

It was the conclusion of numerous research studies that effective leadership style is a result of many factors, including the nature of the task, the leader-member relations, the leader's position power, and the expectations and needs of the group to be influenced. Not only appropriateness but consistency and predictability of leader behavior become important factors in leadership attempts. Furneau,[40] for example, found that the effectiveness of a consultant in three patterns of consultant relationships is not merely a function of the consultant role or "style," but that it is dependent on the expectations of those for whom the consultation is provided. To the extent that there is greater congruence between leadership style and group expectations the leader will be more effective. It is not sufficient in analyzing leadership to focus entirely on the leader and on his personality traits and behavior patterns. The nature of groups to be influenced and the interaction between leaders and groups must also be studied.

GROUP DIMENSIONS OF LEADERSHIP

The research summarized in this section deals with the relationship between the leader and the group and the dynamics of the interaction between a group and the leader, either formal or informal. Researchers who failed to find the answers they were searching for in investigating the styles of leaders looked at the influence of groups on leadership styles and the way in which leadership behavior had to concern itself with the performance of functions needed by the groups. It is also a way of looking at the extent to which traits and behavior styles are useful, needed, and accepted by group members. The needs of the group and group interaction in order to meet those needs become major concerns in this approach to the study of leadership. This contemporary approach has much of its basis in the study of group dynamics and in theories of human interaction. Viewing leadership as meeting group needs inevitably leads to the study of such leadership functions regardless of who performs them, whether it be the designated leader or an emergent leader, even if a temporary one, from within the group.

Bellows [41] sees leadership as a group process: "Leadership stems from the interaction of the group members out of which group goal-seeking behavior emerges"; Campbell,[42] as ". . . the contribution of a given individual to group effectiveness, mediated through the direct efforts of others rather than himself"; Fisher,[43] as ". . . the function of a group in investing authority in its agent for a specific task"; Bass,[44] as ". . . the observed effort of one member to change the other members' behavior by altering the motivation of the other members or by changing their habits"; Lippitt,[45] as discovering ". . . what actions are required by groups under various conditions if they are to achieve their objectives and how different members take part in these actions"; and Hemphill,[46] generally, as ". . . the behavior of an individual who is involved in directing group activities." A more comprehensive yet specific definition is offered by Cartwright and Zander [47]: ". . . leadership consists of such actions by group members as those which aid in setting group goals, moving the group toward the goals, improving the quality of the interaction among the members, building the cohesiveness of the group, or making resources available to the group."

The participation of group members in setting goals and in reaching decisions has been extensively researched, and the overwhelming conclusion is that decisions made by the group are more effective than decisions made externally and then imposed on the group. Saunders, Phillips and Johnson [48] state that while the ". . . status leader may have superior knowledge, his decisions are not likely to be effective until the decisions become group decisions." Similar findings were made by Maier,[49] Preston and Heintz,[50] Bass,[51] Newcomb, Turner, and Converse,[52] and many others.

Tannenbaum, Weschler and Massarik [53] see the following benefits as likely to derive from participation: higher rate of output and increased quality of product; a reduction in turnover, grievances, absenteeism and tardiness; greater readiness to accept change; greater ease in management of subordinates; and improved quality of managerial decisions. Maier [54] reports that group satisfaction is more dependent on the process through which a decision is reached than on the decision itself. Bass [55] states, "A great deal of evidence suggests that permissive leadership, group decision-making, and permission to interact prior to reaching such decisions produce more effective groups and more satisfied members." Bass does note, however, that exceptions to this research conclusion are likely to occur at a time when a group is under severe stress or is of low ability. Such a finding suggests the need to consider factors such as time, emotional stress, and competence level before engaging in participatory leadership behavior.

Lippitt and Seashore[56] describe the major functions of a leader in group effectiveness as *task functions* and *maintenance functions*. Task functions are comprised of initiating, opinion-seeking, information or opinion-giving, clarifying, summarizing, and consensus-checking. They see maintenance functions as encouraging, expressing group feelings, harmonizing, gate-keeping, compromising and setting standards. Both functions are viewed as essential to group participation and effectiveness.

Preston and Heintz,[57] in researching the effects of participation on group judgment, found that participatory leadership is significantly more effective than supervisory leadership in situations that focus on attitude change. Group participation and consensus have a strong impact on group member attitude. It was found that the subjects withstood the impact of group opinion under supervisory leadership, which probably indicates that a strong group opinion is not formed under such leadership. Maier [58] notes that in researching group versus leader decision in problem-solving, solutions suggested by the leader are seldom properly evaluated. Members tend either to accept or reject the leader's solutions but not to analyze and weigh them.

Among other benefits from group participation in leadership, Bass [59] found that more changes occur in the behavior of members when interaction is possible, that such changes take place faster, and that such interaction brings rewards to individuals that are not possible in isolation. In addition, ". . . increased effectiveness accompanies increased interaction among members." [60] The following were found by Newcomb, Turner, and Converse [61] to be leader behaviors that facilitate interpersonal relationships and participation:

1. Providing warmth, friendliness.
2. Conciliating, resolving conflict, relieving tension.
3. Providing personal help, counsel, encouragement.
4. Showing understanding, tolerance of different points of view.
5. Showing fairness, impartiality.

A strong relationship exists between managerial and peer leadership characteristics. It is the conclusion of Bowers and Seashore [62] that managerial leadership behavior begets similar behavior among peer groups. If, for example, a leader wishes to increase the extent to which subordinates demonstrate support for each other, he must increase his support and his own emphasis on goals; or if he increases his attempts to facilitate interaction, subordinates will increase interaction among themselves. The best "predictor," therefore, of peer leadership behavior is the behavior of its managerial "opposite number."

In deciding how to lead and the extent of participation to be allowed, Tannenbaum, Weschler and Massarik [63] point out the need to consider 1) the forces in the manager and 2) the forces in the subordinate. In making a leadership decision the manager must first consider his own value system, the degree of confidence he has in his subordinates, his own leadership inclination and his feeling of security. Similarly he must assess the forces in his subordinates and he can generally permit them more freedom if they have high need for independence, are ready for the reponsibility of decision-making, are highly interested in the problem, can tolerate ambiguity, understand and accept the goals of the organization, have the knowledge and experience to deal with the problem, and if they have had an opportunity to and have learned to participate in decision-making. It is the conclusion of Tannenbaum et al.,[64] that if the above conditions do not exist, "the manager will tend to make fuller use of his own authority."

While the potential benefits of subordinate participation are clear, it is also evident that not all attempts at participation are successful and some are probably counterproductive, damaging the possibility of a change being made rather than enhancing it. A finding of Tannenbaum, Weschler and Massarik points to the need for intelligent involvement of subordinates rather than a blind commitment to participation and an almost religious belief that everyone wants to be included and that, when they are, everything is bound to turn out all right. To achieve the advantages that can come from participation these researchers specify four conditions that must exist: [65] 1) The subordinate must be able to become psychologically involved in the participation activity; that is, he must have no blockages but see it as reality and an activity that calls for intelligence; 2) the subordinate must himself believe in participational activity; 3) the subordinate must perceive that the issue being considered is relevant to his own personal life style; and 4) the subordinate must be able to express himself, his point of view, to his own satisfaction in respect to the issue under consideration.

Bowers and Seashore [66] provide the following summary of the need for both formal and peer leadership:

> . . . leadership, as described in terms of support, goal emphasis, work facilitation, and interaction facilitation, may be provided by anyone in a work group for anyone else in that work group. In this sense, leadership may be either "supervisory" or "mutual"; that is, a group's needs for support may be provided by a formally designated leader, by members for each other, or both; goals may be emphasized by the formal leader, by members to each other, or by both; and similarly for work facilitation and interaction facilitation.
>
> This does not imply that formally designated leaders are unnecessary or superfluous, for there are both common-sense and theoretical reasons for believing that a formally acknowledged leader through his supervisory leadership behavior sets the pattern of the mutual leadership which subordinates supply each other.

Researchers have also investigated reasons for a group accepting a leader and for a person attempting leadership. Hollander [67] notes that which person in a group attains and retains leadership is dependent on the perceptions of group members based in ongoing social interaction. He concludes that there is a high relationship between competence and group acceptance of leader influence.[68] Also, it was found that the higher the status of the person the less likely his attempts at initiation would be disapproved by the group. Such a finding was also supported by Brown,[69] who found that a leader "must represent a region of high potential in the social field," meaning prestige, esteem, and status. Leaders who perform highly structured tasks were found by Fiedler [70] to be given higher power by members. Other important considerations are his personal relations with group members, and the power and authority of his position. Laird and Laird [71] state that ". . . the successful leader appears to be a person who gets things done *and* whose interpersonal relations with his crew are such that the members accept him as a person as well as a technical man." Bass [72] also found that the higher the status or rank the greater the likelihood that a person will successfully lead those lower in status; such leadership, however, has to become "potentially rewarding" to them or the success will drop off. He also found esteem, the perceived worth of the individual, as a factor in successful leadership, while mutual esteem contributed to group effectiveness. The work of Fiedler, Bass and others indicates that leadership is a function of both power and ability. Successful leadership results in increased power and esteem, which make attempted leadership, in turn, both increasingly possible and more effective.

Four experiments reported by Hemphill [73] endeavored to explain why people attempt or do not attempt to provide leadership for a group. The positive motivations were found to be:

1) large rewards promised by accomplishing the group's task, 2) reasonable expectancy that by working at the task it can be accomplished, 3) acceptance by other members of the group for attempting to lead, 4) a task that requires a high rate of group decisions, 5) possession of superior knowledge or competence relevant to the accomplishment of the task, and 6) previously acquired status as the group's leader.

On the negative side, reasons found for not attempting leadership were:

1) low task reward, 2) low expectancy of task accomplishment, 3) rejection by group members for attempting to lead, 4) a task that sets requirement for only a few decisions, 5) low competence in the task or little knowledge relevant to it, and 6) respect for leadership status of another group member.

Leadership is sought and exists where groups have needs, where problems need to be resolved. Bass [74] found that leadership is more likely to be accepted in a time of crisis and that the more difficult the problems the more necessary a leader and, correspondingly, the greater the chance for success. Bass [75] cites the following conflicts that may cause leadership to be rejected: preceding events; the task may require more energy than rewards; it may require an unequal distribution of rewards; it may threaten loss of esteem or status; self-esteem may be higher than that which the group accords him; the potential leader is a high status member but is not esteemed; there is an incongruence between ability-esteem and ability-status.

Emergent leadership, that which comes not from the designated leader but from a group member in response to a particular need, has received much study. In some respects participation deliberately gives to subordinates the opportunity to engage in leadership acts and for leadership to emerge in response to the situation. Hollander,[76] in his research on emergent leadership, describes how a task-competent leader whose behavior conforms to the expectations and needs of the group at a particular stage may become the leader at the next stage as well and that, correspondingly, the leader who fails to measure up to the group's expectations for his position of influence will lose credits with his followers and be replaced by one of them. One cannot continue to lead and maintain group support without demonstrating competence and conforming to the expectations of the group.

Newcomb, Turner and Converse,[77] in investigating leadership rules, found that leaders emerge within a group and are perceived as facilitators of goal achievement if they are task-knowledgeable, imaginative, hardheaded, realistic, persuasive; if they can formulate problems and summarize discussions; if they have skills of planning, coordinating and organizing; and if they can be depended on to carry through to completion. The status leader within a group has special functions. Gorman [78] found that this person is looked to as an aid to the group in its effort at satisfying its needs, and his special functions include liaison between the group and status superiors and the development of group members in specific leadership functions.

Research also shows that a leader's effectiveness is evaluated by a group on the basis of the extent to which he performs needed group functions. These are often identified in two broad categories: achievement of group goals and maintenance of the group. Hemphill [79] defines adequate leadership behavior as "behavior indicative of his ability to advance the purpose of the group. He exhibits behavior indicating competence in administrative functions. His behavior is characterized by the ability to inspire the members of the group to greater activity . . . relatively free from activity serving only his own interests." Bean,[80] researching self-concept and leader performance, found no relationship between the way in which a leader perceives his performance as a leader in a group and the way in which his performance is perceived by other members of the group. Campbell,[81] however, in a study of naval officer leadership, concluded that the "striking" find of his study was the strong degree of agreement on leadership as evaluated by a leader's subordinates and superiors.

ORGANIZATIONAL DIMENSIONS OF LEADERSHIP

Leadership behavior does not take place in the abstract. Much of the research in small group leadership and in interaction, however, has been done with informal groups or with formal work goups that, in some cases, are divorced from the impact of the larger organization. Nevertheless, running throughout the research are findings that relate to the significant impact of a particular situation, the general setting or the nature of the organization.

Organizational style, priorities, power structure and the nature of some work tasks or environments all have a bearing on the form and effectiveness of leadership. It has been noted earlier in this chapter that leadership style has to be adapted to the nature of the group and the task. The goals, expectations and form of the organization are also determinants of leadership. It must be consistent with the expectations of the organization, and it must contribute to goal attainment for the organization as well as meet the human needs of subordinates. There are times when the two may be in conflict.

Gibb,[82] for example, indicates that within organizations leadership is evaluated differently from above and below. A superior expects the leader to insist on strict discipline, follow operating procedures very closely and emphasize production. Subordinates, on the other hand, expect him to mingle with them, consult with them on decisions, be socially sensitive, and show consideration for them and their needs. Fleishman, Harris and Burtt[83] state that ". . . the kind of leader the subordinates like is not necessarily the one who is most efficient in getting results." They found that in production departments, while considerate leadership behavior by a foreman is very good as judged from the standpoint of morale, it is not very effective for proficiency as judged by the foreman's boss. Conversely, foremen who were high on initiating structure were rated high by their own boss, but had a negative relationship to employee morale. This situation was most marked in production departments that operated under very tight, demanding time schedules. In nonproduction departments, foremen who were rated high by their own superiors engaged in more consideration behavior with only minimum emphasis on standards, regulations, and structuring of work activity. In a study of leadership in Anglo-American democracies, Hargrove[84] found that the choice of leadership styles is restricted and that ". . . leaders must work within the national style of authority available to them."

Organizational status and esteem also affect leadership attempts, style, and effectiveness. In a study by Pelz[85] of the effectiveness of influential and noninfluential leaders it was found that influential supervisors (high salary, autonomy, a voice in their own group) were more successful in helping employees achieve their goals and employee satisfactions rose. The lower status supervisor had the opposite results. Bass[86] states that "power provides successful leadership but it is not as likely to be effective as far as the coerced members are concerned." He also points out that the higher the status or rank of a leader the greater the possibility that he will successfully lead those who are lower in status, but unless it is "potentially rewarding" for them his success will diminish.

Applewhite[87] defines leadership in terms of "acts issued from a formal or informal position in the organization by someone with power and the ability to act." The organization may or may not have conferred such status. Gibb[88] distinguishes between "leadership" and "headship." Their source of authority differs; in the former it is accorded him by followers, while under headship his power over a group derives from extragroup power. The group accepts his domination out of fear of punishment. In other words, the organization confers the legal right to act, but behavior within the organization is a determinant of leadership.

Leadership also takes place in respect to and is affected by certain "givens," situations that exist within the organization, the nature of the task, the degree of stress in the situation, and the social, structural, and goal conditions of the organization. Tannenbaum *et al.*[89] conclude that "effectiveness of leadership is a function of the dynamic interrelationship of the personality characteristics of the leader, the personality characteristics of the follower, and the character of the situation within the field of each individual." They note that leadership is always exercised in a situation that includes such influential elements as physical phenomena, other persons, the organization, the culture, and a complex of goals —personal, group and organizational.[90]

Gibb [91] also identifies one of the three most important principles of leadership as being that it is "always relative to a situation" and that the nature of a leadership role is determined by the goal of the group. Gibb [92] also notes that research shows "convincingly" that an authoritarian style is both expected and effective when a situation is either highly favorable or unfavorable to leadership, but in moderately favorable situations a democratic style is more effective. Fiedler[93] found that structured tasks such as characterize production management in the daily supervision of unskilled work groups calls for task-oriented leadership, while relationship-oriented leadership is more appropriate for less structured, second level or higher management functions such as in planning, policy-making or research units of organization. Selvin,[94] however, also found out in a study of army trainees that the "impact of a leadership climate does not fall equally on all followers."

Ross and Hendry[95] identify the size of a group as affecting leadership, in that larger groups require an emphasis on formal concerns rather than personal ones. Such a finding suggests that leadership behavior must be geared to the size of the group for which it is intended, and a primary focus on more personal concerns will result in less influence in large groups than a focus on structure and formal concerns. The way in which an organization is structured, the span of control, and the leader-subordinate ratios are givens that affect leadership behavior. Conditions within the organization contributing to effective authority were found by Guest[96] to be the leeway to act, which must be granted by his superiors; the condition of time perspective, the freedom to engage in future planning rather than just meeting each crisis; horizontal workflow interaction; an enlarged span of cognition for both the leader and his subordinates, understanding their place in the organization and possessing relevant information; and group interaction.

Leadership is situational; it is not abstract; it is exercised at a point in time, in a particular organization, in a particular culture, and in response to a particular need. Research makes clear the need to perceive, study, and prepare for leadership in recognition of organizational and situational expectations and restraints. Fleishman, Harris, and Burtt[97] are critical of some human relations training for leaders, noting that "such training conducted in isolation from the practical situation falls short of its objective . . . It is necessary to involve the social situation in which the person is trying to operate."

Organizations must provide for the needs of their members. In every organization there is some kind of a reward system. Stout and Briner[98] conclude that people subordinate themselves to leaders in an organization "in order to gain satisfaction of needs they might not otherwise have been able to satisfy." The theories of Blau,[99] Homans,[100] and Simon[101] suggest that influence involves an exchange between persons, that one allows another to have prestige or approval and is willing to submit to authority in order to have his needs satisfied. The influencer, in a sense, also uses up some of his resources in exerting influence, but it may result in an actual increase in his influence resources because of the increased prestige he gains through successful influence attempts. Much of the leader's influence, therefore, derives from his ability to provide sufficient rewards in such an exchange and from making possible the satisfaction of the needs of subordinates.

Leadership continues to be researched; it is still not possible to predict leadership behavior, or to control it, or to provide programs that guarantee the emergence of skilled leaders. Much of the mystery of leadership still remains, but great strides have been made and the research evidence, while very helpful, also shows the complexity of the concept of leadership.

IMPLICATIONS FOR INSTRUCTIONAL SUPERVISORY BEHAVIOR

A review of selected research in the area of leadership provides ample evidence of the wealth of research in this field and the potential it holds for contributing to an understanding of instructional supervisory behavior. A supervisor who is seriously concerned about his own behavior and influence attempts should seek a deeper understanding of the phenomenon of leadership.

Obviously, the above review of research on leadership is neither comprehensive nor definitive. It is selected out of the many hundreds of research studies and theoretical formulations available because it appears to be particularly helpful in understanding supervisory behavior in education. It has been grouped under these categories for that same purpose. Based on this selection the following propositions, along with their implications for instructional supervision, have been formulated.

Individual Dimensions

PROPOSITION 1: *Successful leadership is not a result of, and cannot be predicted on the basis of, any known single personality trait or pattern of traits.*

Since there are no personality traits common to all leaders, school systems must exercise extreme caution in making conclusive judgments concerning who has or does not have the potential to be a supervisor on the basis of factors related to intelligence, personality, and appearance. While it is necessary that supervisors be selected whose personality traits conform to the nature and expectation of the group to be led, special attention must be given to demonstrated leadership ability and the evidence of competence. Personality characteristics might best be assessed not as generalizable predictors, but rather in relation to a particular set of persons and circumstances. In addition, opportunities must be given to individuals to participate in leadership activity in order to provide some evidence of supervisory potential.

PROPOSITION 2: *The traits that characterize effective leaders are at least partly related to the nature of the situation and the perceived needs of the group.*

Instructional supervisory behavior, to be effective, must take into account that different groups and different situations will require varying patterns of characteristics. The research suggests that expectations and needs of the group ought to be major determinants of who is selected to provide leadership, and that in situations where multiple staffing is possible a range of personality traits should be represented on the supervisory staff. Whether a given personality trait contributes to effective supervision may depend less on the trait than on whether it is in keeping with the needs and expectations of the teacher group. While supervisors cannot alter their basic personality structure, they should realize that they will elicit different reactions from different groups and their effectiveness will be partly a result of the interaction of personality traits and the environment in which it takes place.

PROPOSITION 3: *The probability of successful leadership will be increased if the leader maintains some degree of psychological distance from his subordinates.*

A supervisor is likely to be more effective if he does not become an integral part of the teacher group. While obviously joined to them and responsible for them, a sense of psychological distance is necessary. This is not to suggest that a supervisor needs to be aloof, undemocratic or a "company man," but rather that his relationship to teachers permits psychological freedom and objectivity. While writing in supervision has often suggested a close relationship, research indicates that maintaining some degree of psychological distance enhances a supervisor's ability to make discriminations between teachers and to assess their ability and effectiveness more clearly and objectively. Supervisors need to maintain the delicate balance that enables one to operate freely as a member of a group while still retaining a recognized degree of psychological detachment.

PROPOSITION 4: *A leader is likely to be more effective if he recognizes that democratic and autocratic leadership styles generate different and predictable responses and patterns of achievement among followers.*

Leadership style exists along a continuum. Even though each has a dominant leadership motivation, few supervisors would be totally democratic or totally autocratic in all situations. The literature in supervision gives almost exclusive attention to the virtues of democratic and participatory leadership. A supervisor must recognize that his style will produce quite predictable results, and he should—to the extent possible—select and modify his style in keeping with the nature of the task, the group, and the anticipated outcomes. Authoritarian leadership breeds dependence, while democratically led groups tend to be able to work independently. Yet, democratically led groups produce less work and make slower progress than autocratically led groups.

It is essential for a supervisor to assess a situation carefully and utilize a leadership style that is congruent with the expectations of his followers. Moreover, he needs to become a student of his own leadership behavior—whether democratic or autocratic—and analyze the consequences of it for teacher morale, productivity, group cohesiveness, and goal attainment.

PROPOSITION 5: *Leadership will be more effective if it considers the needs of human beings as well as providing for the initiation of structure.*

A supervisor needs to give attention both to consideration behavior and to the tasks to be achieved—establishing goals, maintaining discipline, emphasizing operations and achievement. An effective supervisor needs to develop good interpersonal relationships, but he also needs to give equal attention to the initiation of structure and process. If a supervisor is concerned about both morale *and* performance he needs to engage heavily in both kinds of leadership behavior. While teachers may place greater value on consideration behavior—a dominant theme of supervision during the past twenty years—the needs of the organization, as a production system, require equal attention to the initiation of structure. A supervisor may find it much easier to initiate structure, however, if he is perceived as caring about and providing for the welfare of teachers.

PROPOSITION 6: *The possibility of successful leadership will be enhanced when a leader is aware of his dominant leadership motivation style and plans his activities in light of it.*

A supervisor needs to be a student of his own behavior and his own leadership motivation. While one cannot change his basic personality structure, he can become more intelligent and sensitive about the nature of his behavior. Clearly, a supervisor should build on his strengths and not on his weaknesses, and his total range of instructional supervisory behavior should be planned in keeping with his own leadership style. He can modify his behavior and has the responsibility to do so, but by such careful assessment he can avoid planning and strategy that requires leadership behavior not within his grasp.

PROPOSITION 7: *Leadership will be more effective when the style employed is consistent with the nature and expectations of the group to be led.*

There is much research evidence available to indicate that no single leader is evaluated as effective in all situations, but that certain kinds of situations—and the group expectations that derive from them—call for different kinds of leadership. This research suggests that a single supervisor operating throughout a system and with all sorts of tasks, groups, and settings will face unavoidable difficulty and the demands on his leadership skill will be almost impossible to meet.

While the research makes clear the desirability of attempting to match one's supervisory behavior with teacher expectations, it also highlights the desirability and the possibility of bringing about better linkage of style and expectations where supervisory teams exist, rather than individual, autonomous supervisors.

Group Dimensions

PROPOSITION 8: *A leader is likely to be more effective if he sees and provides for the possibility of leadership coming from any member of a group.*

A supervisor will find much support for his influence attempts if he recognizes the potential for leadership that exists within teacher groups. Only with such a conviction can he really engage in democratic, participating leadership. Given the staffing ratios of most school systems, a supervisor must almost always depend on leadership to emerge from within a group if change efforts are to have permanence. A supervisor's behavior can be strengthened and made more effective by broadening the base of leadership acts and by deliberately providing the opportunity for teachers to exert leadership. Research indicates that effective leaders delegate authority; supervisors, because of the nature of school organization and because of the professional nature of the teacher group, are in a unique position to increase their effectiveness by delegating authority and by providing for leadership from group members.

PROPOSITION 9: *Leadership will be more effective when it provides for the active participation in decision-making of those to be affected.*

The evidence from a wealth of research studies over a period of many years is clear: supervisors must systematically and conscientiously include teachers in the determination of decisions that are going to affect them. Such involvement must be active and genuine and carry with it the expectation of influence. Passive involvement or "window-dressing" representation is a hollow mockery of democratic participation, which may well have more negative consequences than a total lack of involvement. At the same time, supervisors should guard against a blind belief in participation that can lead to involving teachers in deciding issues that are not appropriate and are of little importance for them.

PROPOSITION 10: *A leader will be more effective if he recognizes that follower behavior is at least partly a function of leader behavior.*

If a supervisor is concerned about the behavior of teachers he must recognize that his own behavior will have a powerful effect on theirs. The supervisor, then, needs to demonstrate through his instructional supervisory behavior, those qualities and patterns that he desires teachers to demonstrate. The kind of peer leadership that exists among teachers may be a direct reflection of the kind of leadership behavior demonstrated by the supervisor. A supervisor will be more effective, therefore, if his behavior contributes to the development of desirable patterns of leadership behavior among teachers. By so doing, his influence is extended and supported.

PROPOSITION 11: *Participatory leadership will be more effective when it is based and planned on intelligent assessment of the value system of the leader and the nature, ability and perceptions of the group.*

The extent and the limit of participation that a supervisor makes available to teachers should be a result of an assessment of his own personality and value system as well as the nature of the teacher group. Both the supervisor and the teachers must be psychologically committed, professionally secure, and have the knowledge and experience to cope with all potential problems if participatory leadership is to be effective. Such a finding implies that a supervisor needs to become a student of the organization and of human behavior, and be able to deal intelligently and honestly with his own values. In addition, such analysis must be a prelude to planning for teacher participation.

PROPOSITION 12: *Leadership is more likely to be accepted and effective when the leader has status and power in the organization.*

While supervisors may sometimes have to align themselves with teachers rather than with administration, the research indicates that their leadership will stand a vastly greater chance of being both acceptable and influential if they represent organizational status and power. Such attributes give validity and authority to acts. Without such status, supervisors have been too often reduced to an influence based almost solely on their own persuasive powers.

If instructional supervisory behavior is to be effective, the organization must confer on supervisors those prerogatives of authority and the visible symbols of power and status that provide credibility and leverage in affecting the behavior of others. To maintain supervisors in positions of low or indeterminate positions of power is to render them much less effective. The effectiveness of supervisors can be enhanced by organizationally conferred status; supervisors can increase their status within the informal system by virtue of their own effective behavior. If a supervisor is to be held accountable for directly influencing teacher behavior and for achieving the goals of the organization, he must be given the power and status consistent with his job responsibility.

PROPOSITION 13: *Esteem contributes to the possibility of successful leadership, and successful leadership enhances the leader's esteem.*

Successful leadership attempts are at least partly a result of the esteem followers hold for the leader. An organization cannot confer esteem on a supervisor; he must earn it. A supervisor does not consciously seek esteem; rather, he works at providing successful, effective leadership through which esteem is gained. Once having earned esteem, the supervisor is in a better position to engage in a wide variety of supervisory behaviors. The cycle moves on: the supervisor's effectiveness begets esteem, which begets more successful leadership, which begets more esteem. It is unlikely, for example, that a new supervisor will have esteem, although he might have power. Without esteem, he must be more dependent on power until the time when his own effective leadership brings him esteem.

PROPOSITION 14: *Leadership attempts are partly determined by favorable or unfavorable conditions existing at the particular time.*

Before leadership is attempted, some weighing of the conditions—whether favorable or unfavorable for the prospective leader—usually takes place. People tend not to attempt to lead when rewards are low, when successful achievement is doubtful, or when they feel less than knowledgeable or competent. Such a finding suggests that supervisors should not expect leadership to come from teachers unless favorable conditions exist; to force such leadership in the face of restraining factors will be counterproductive. While the supervisor himself must often exert leadership in spite of unfavorable conditions, he must assess these conditions, analyze his own reluctance in the light of them, devise an appropriate strategy, and attempt to modify circumstances in order to make them more favorable to a leadership attempt.

PROPOSITION 15: *Leadership emerges from within a group when a member fulfills the needs and expectations of the group or when the formal leader does not measure up to the group's expectations.*

A supervisor will be more effective if he recognizes and allows emergent leadership in response to the needs of a group. Part of his leadership responsibility is to stimulate such leadership among teachers. He must also recognize, however, that a consistent and demonstrated inability on his part to measure up to the expectations of teachers will cause an ultimate rejection of his leadership attempts and a dependence instead on leadership that has emerged from within the teacher group. In such a case emergent teacher leadership, instead of being a valued adjunct of supervisory behavior, becomes substitute leadership.

PROPOSITION 16: *A leader will be effective, as evaluated by a group, if if he is perceived as performing needed group functions.*

A supervisor must recognize that his effectiveness as judged by teachers will be based on the extent to which they perceive him as performing activities they feel to be essential. If a supervisor is concerned that teachers see his efforts as being effective, it is important that he direct his energies toward solving problems and performing tasks that teachers see as vital for their own survival and well-being. Occasionally, in order to develop "social capital," a supervisor may need to give special attention to the functions teachers perceive as essential, rather than working exclusively on concerns of less consequence to teachers though of major importance to him.

Organizational Dimensions

PROPOSITION 17: *A leader will be more effective if he recognizes that his leadership will be evaluated and perceived differently by subordinates and by superiors.*

A supervisor must be aware of the fact that activity valued and desired by his superiors may be perceived as inappropriate by teachers, and vice versa. The superintendent, for example, will place more value on task-orientation, initiating activity, and goal attainment—the production concerns of school systems. Teachers will tend to see as effective the supervisor who demonstrates more concern for their needs, rather than those of the school system. Almost unavoidably, then, a supervisor is placed in the predicament of receiving different evaluations of the same behavior.

The supervisor must recognize this disparity of judgment. His first responsibility is to assist in achieving the goals of the organization. Research does not suggest that such a responsibility automatically brings about negative evaluations from teachers. Rather, it is a matter of emphasis and a recognition that both the personal concerns of teachers and the achievement concerns of the system must be addressed; to the degree that major emphasis is given to one or the other, evaluations of effectiveness will differ. These research findings suggest care in reaching quick conclusions on effectiveness of supervisory behavior based solely on the judgments of either teachers or administrative superiors.

PROPOSITION 18: *Leadership and its effectiveness is a function of the dynamic interrelationships of numerous conditions within an organization.*

A supervisor needs to see the effectiveness of his leadership behavior as deriving from and being affected by many different givens within the organization. He must see his own instructional supervisory behavior as existing in a particular setting, in relationship to a particular group of people, at a given point in time, an expression of his own personality, and in dynamic interaction with the social, structural and achievement conditions of the school system. Supervisory behavior is not solitary and fragmentary. It is more effective when viewed in the context of and planned in keeping with all the shifting components in the human/organizational mix. The setting in which ISB takes place is complex. The supervisor will be more effective if he deals with that complexity in the design and selection of his behavior.

PROPOSITION 19: *Leadership will be more effective if the organization provides conditions that support such behavior.*

Effective leadership is not likely to occur within an organization unless the conditions exist that support such activity and unless it is made demonstrably clear to all that leadership is expected and valued. If supervisors are to provide genuine leadership they must be given not only status support but authority, time for planning, material and human resources, a reasonable span of control, and access to relevant information.

Even more important, their behavior and responsibilities must be seen as strongly supported by the major administrators in the system. Unless both philosophical and organizational support are evident to teachers, the authority and potential influence of the supervisor will be severely decreased. In both subtle and tangible ways, a school system communicates the strength of its support for supervisory leadership. The burden of providing effective instructional supervisory behavior, therefore, must be shared in a considerable measure by a supervisor's superiors, who control the conditions essential to organizational support.

PROPOSITION 20: *Leadership will be more effective when it is a consequence of careful analysis and planning in the light of the nature of the organization and the task to be achieved.*

Clearly, leadership cannot be a random, unplanned, and unsophisticated endeavor. Yet, too often supervisory behavior has not been characterized by detailed, systematic planning and analysis. It is unlikely that such casual supervisory effort can ever yield a rich harvest of change in teacher behavior; it lacks focus, it lacks direction, and it is impossible to evaluate. Leadership does not just happen; nor is it a product of a dynamic personality or the result of an acquired style. Where effective leadership exists it is the result of detailed and intelligent planning and analysis. Supervisors must give far more time to the planning of their activity, rather than merely serving the crisis of the day. The effectiveness of supervision could be significantly increased if it were less immediate and reactionary and, instead, were the culmination of extensive planning and the development of detailed strategies for effecting change.

PROPOSITION 21: *The potential for effective leadership will be increased through the provisions of rewards and satisfaction of the needs of subordinates.*

71

One of the ways through which a leader in any organization solidifies his position of leadership is through the provision (or withholding) of rewards. Obviously, to be effective a supervisor must satisfy the needs of teachers; he must be able to provide professional skill for them. A supervisor's leadership and influence will be increased if he has some control over the reward system of the school, if he has some capability to recognize and reward improved teacher performance. If teachers are to submit to the leadership of a supervisor, they will need to know that their willingness to accept his influence is rewarded in some way. Conversely, through his ability to provide recognition and reward, a supervisor's prestige increases—a development that also increases his ability to influence teacher behavior.

As staff personnel, as consultants who could suggest but not insist, as evaluators of teaching who could offer commentary but not official censure, and as observers who could speak words of praise but could confer no formal organizational recognition, supervisors have been denied a valuable source of potential influence. Such a finding raises serious questions about organizational status, line and staff relationships, and the prerogatives of power and authority in relation to effective supervision. The capacity to meet needs and have some control over a reward system would provide a supervisor with a degree of leverage he seldom possesses.

ENDNOTES

1. Robert Tannenbaum, Irving R. Weschler, and Fred Massarik, *Leadership and Organization: A Behavioral Science Approach* (New York: McGraw-Hill, Inc., 1961), p. 24.
2. Joseph E. McGrath and Irwin Altman, *Small Group Research: A Synthesis and Critique of the Field* (New York: Holt, Rinehart and Winston, 1966).
3. Kinnard White, "Personality Characteristics of Educational Leaders: A Comparison of Administrators and Researchers," *School Review* 73 (1965), pp. 292–300.
4. Paul D. Nelson, "Similarities and Differences Among Leaders and Followers," *Journal of Social Psychology* 63 (1964), pp. 161–167.
5. Murray G. Ross and Charles E. Hendry, *New Understandings of Leadership* (New York: Association Press, 1957), pp. 43–61.
6. Ralph M. Stogdill, "Personal Factors Associated with Leadership: A Survey of the Literature," *Journal of Psychology* XXV (1948), pp. 35–71.
7. *Ibid.*, pp. 60–61.
8. W. H. Cowley, "The Traits of Face to Face Leaders," in *The Study of Leadership*, ed. C. G. Browne and Thomas S. Cohn (Danville, Ill.: Interstate Printers and Publishers, 1958), p. 233.

9. E. Victor Wolfenstein, "Some Psychological Aspects of Crisis Leaders," in *Political Leadership in Industrialized Societies*, ed. Lewis J. Edinger (New York: John Wiley and Sons, 1967), pp. 158–180.
10. William E. Henry, "The Business Executive: The Psychodynamics of a Social Role," in *The Study of Leadership*, ed. Browne and Cohn, pp. 236–241.
11. Fred E. Fiedler, "Leadership and Leadership Effectiveness Traits: A Reconceptualization of the Leadership Trait Problem," in *Leadership and Interpersonal Behavior*, ed. Luigi Petrullo and Bernard M. Bass (New York: Holt, Rinehart and Winston, 1961), pp. 179–186.
12. Kurt Lewin, Ronald Lippitt, and Ralph White, "Patterns of Aggressive Behavior in Experimentally Created 'Social Climates'," *Journal of Social Psychology* 10 (1939), pp. 271–299.
13. Ronald Lippitt, "Field Theory and Experiment in Social Psychology: Autocratic and Democratic Group Atmospheres," *American Journal of Psychology* 45 (1939), pp. 26–49.
14. Ralph White and Ronald Lippitt, "Leader Behavior and Member Reaction in Three 'Social Climates'," in *Group Dynamics: Research and Theory*, ed. Dorwin Cartwright and Alvin Zander (New York: Harper and Row, 1968), pp. 318–334.
15. A. Bavelas, "Morale and the Training of Leaders," in *Civilian Morale*, ed. G. Watson (Boston: Houghton Mifflin Company, 1942), pp. 143–165.
16. Howard Baumgartel, "Leadership Style as a Variable in Research Administration," in *Administering Research and Development*, ed. Charles D. Orth (Homewood, Ill.: Richard D. Irwin and Dorsey Press, 1964), pp. 86–98.
17. *Ibid.*, p. 95.
18. *Ibid.*, p. 93.
19. *Ibid.*, p. 96
20. Chris Argyris, "Organizational Leadership," in *Leadership and Interpersonal Behavior*, ed. Luigi Petrullo and Bernard Bass, p. 326.
21. R. L. Kahn and D. Katz, "Leadership Practices in Relation to Productivity and Morale," in *Group Dynamics: Research and Theory*, ed. Dorwin Cartwright and Alvin Zander (New York: Harper and Row, 1960), pp. 612–628.
22. Ronald Lippitt, "An Experimental Study of the Effect of Democratic and Authoritarian Atmospheres," in *University of Iowa Studies in Child Welfare* 16, no. 3 (1940), pp. 164–165.
23. Samuel H. Barnes, "Leadership Style and Political Competence," in *Political Leadership in Industrialized Societies*, ed. Edinger, p. 78.
24. *Ibid.*
25. Bernard M. Bass, *Leadership, Psychology, and Organizational Behavior* (New York: Harper and Brothers, 1960), p. 455.
26. *Ibid.*, p. 451.
27. Donald T. Campbell, *Leadership and Its Effects Upon the Group* (Columbus: Ohio State University Bureau of Business Research, 1956), 53, p. 62.
28. *Ibid.*, p. 64.
29. *Ibid.*, p. 68.

30. Carroll L. Shartle, *Executive Performance and Leadership* (Englewood Cliffs, N. J.: Prentice-Hall, Inc., 1956), p. 126.
31. Andrew W. Halpin and B. James Winer, *The Leadership Behavior of the Airplane Commander*, Technical Report III (Columbus: The Ohio State Research Foundation, 1952), mimeographed.
32. Andrew W. Halpin, *Theory and Research in Administration* (New York: The Macmillan Co., 1966), pp. 92–98.
33. Cecil A. Gibb, "Leadership," in *The Handbook of Social Psychology*, 2nd Ed., Vol. IV (Reading, Mass.: Addison-Wesley Publishing, 1969), p. 272.
34. *Ibid.*, p. 273.
35. Edwin A. Fleishman and Edwin F. Harris, "Patterns of Leadership Behavior Related to Employee Grievances and Turnover," in *Leadership: Selected Readings*, ed. Cecil A. Gibb (Hammondsworth, Middlesex, England: Penguin Books, 1969), pp. 355–356.
36. Fred E. Fiedler, *A Theory of Leadership Effectiveness* (New York: McGraw-Hill, 1969), p. 60.
37. *Ibid.*, p. 108.
38. *Ibid.*, p. 151.
39. *Ibid.*, p. 196.
40. Elmer F. Furneau, "Role Expectations in Consultation" (Doctoral dissertation, University of Chicago, 1954).
41. Roger Bellows, *Creative Leadership* (Englewood Cliffs, N.J.: Prentice-Hall, Inc., 1959), p. 49.
42. Campbell, *op. cit.*, p. 1.
43. Margaret Barrow Fisher, *Leadership and Intelligence* (New York: Teachers College, Columbia University, 1954), p. 122.
44. Bass, *op. cit.*, p. 447.
45. Gordon L. Lippitt, "What Do We Know About Leadership?," *National Education Association Journal* (December 1955), pp. 556–557.
46. John K. Hemphill, *Situational Factors in Leadership*, Research Monograph no. 32 (Columbus: Ohio State University, 1949), p. 96.
47. Dorwin Cartwright and Alvin F. Zander, eds., *Group Dynamics: Research and Theory* (New York: Harper and Row, 1968), p. 304.
48. Robert L. Saunders, Ray C. Phillips and Harold J. Johnson, *A Theory of Educational Leadership* (Columbus, Ohio: Charles E. Merrill Books, 1966), p. 106.
49. Norman R. F. Maier, "An Experimental Test of the Effect of Training on Discussion Leadership," in Browne and Cohn, *The Study of Leadership*, p. 463.
50. Malcolm G. Preston and Ray K. Heintz, "Effects of Participatory versus Supervisory Leadership on Group Judgment," in Browne and Cohn, *The Study of Leadership*, p. 322.
51. Bass, *op. cit.*, p. 455.
52. T. M. Newcomb, R. H. Turner, and P. E. Converse, "Leadership Roles in Goal Achievement," in Gibb, *Leadership: Selected Readings*, p. 322.
53. Tannenbaum, Weschler, and Massarik, *op. cit.*, p. 93.
54. Norman R. F. Maier, *Problem-Solving Discussions and Conferences: Leadership Methods and Skills* (New York: McGraw-Hill, 1963), p. 41.

55. Bass, *op. cit.*, p. 455.
56. Gordon L. Lippitt and Edith Seashore, "The Leader Looks at Group Effectiveness," in *Looking Into Leadership* (Washington, D. C.: Leadership Resources, Inc., 1961), monograph.
57. Preston and Heintz, *op. cit.*, p. 322.
58. Maier, *op. cit.*, p. 251.
59. Bass, *op. cit.*, pp. 449–450.
60. *Ibid.*, p. 458.
61. Newcomb, Turner, and Converse, *op. cit.*, p. 326.
62. D. G. Bowers and S. E. Seashore, "Predicting Organizational Effectiveness with a Four-Factor Theory of Leadership," in *Leadership: Selected Readings*, ed. Gibb, pp. 378–379.
63. Tannenbaum, Weschler, and Massarik, *op. cit.*, pp. 73–75.
64. *Ibid.*, p. 75.
65. *Ibid.*, p. 96.
66. Bowers and Seashore, *op. cit.*, p. 368.
67. E. P. Hollander, *Leaders, Groups, and Influence* (New York: Oxford University Press, 1964), p. 29.
68. *Ibid.*, p. 204.
69. J. F. Brown, *Psychology and the Social Order: An Introduction to the Dynamic Study of Social Fields* (New York: McGraw-Hill, 1936), p. 342.
70. Fred E. Fiedler, "A Contingency Model of Leadership Effectiveness," in *Advances in Experimental Psychology*, ed. Leonard Berkowitz (New York: Academic Press, 1964), p. 159.
71. Donald A. Laird and Eleanor C. Laird, *The New Psychology for Leadership* (New York: McGraw-Hill, 1956), p. 204.
72. Bass, *op. cit.*, pp. 455–456.
73. John K. Hemphill, "Why People Attempt to Lead," in *Leadership and Interpersonal Behavior*, ed. Petrullo and Bass, pp. 213–214.
74. Bass, *op. cit.*, p. 450.
75. *Ibid.*, p. 457.
76. E. P. Hollander, "Emergent Leadership and Social Influence," in *Leadership and Interpersonal Behavior*, ed. Petrullo and Bass, p. 45.
77. Newcomb, Turner and Converse, *op. cit.*, p. 322.
78. Alfred H. Gorman, *The Leader in the Group: A Conceptual Framework* (New York: Teachers College, Columbia University, 1963), p. 12.
79. Hemphill, *Situational Factors in Leadership*, p. 99.
80. Mabel Gladys Bean, "Self-Concept and Group Leadership Performance" (Doctoral dissertation, University of Michigan, 1970).
81. Campbell, *op. cit.*, p. 42.
82. Gibb, *op. cit.*, p. 272.
83. Edwin A. Fleishman, Edwin F. Harris, and Harold E. Burtt, *Leadership and Supervision in Industry*, Research Monograph no. 33 (Columbus: Ohio State University, 1955), pp. 103–104.
84. Erwin C. Hargrove, "Popular Leadership in the Anglo-American Democracies," in *Political Leadership in Industrialized Societies*, ed. Edinger, p. 218.
85. D. C. Pelz, "Leadership in a Hierarchical Organization," in *Leadership:*

Selected Readings, ed. Gibb, p. 344.

86. Bass, *op. cit.*, p. 454.
87. Philip B. Applewhite, *Organizational Behavior* (Englewood Cliffs, N. J.: Prentice-Hall, Inc., 1965), p. 111.
88. Gibb, *op. cit.*, p. 213.
89. Tannenbaum, Weschler, and Massarik, *op. cit.*, p. 31.
90. *Ibid.*, pp. 26–27.
91. Gibb, "The Principles and Traits of Leadership," in *The Study of Leadership*, ed. Browne and Cohn, p. 74.
92. Gibb, "Leadership," in *The Handbook of Social Psychology*, p. 273.
93. Fiedler, *A Theory of Leadership Effectiveness*, p. 246.
94. Hanan C. Selvin, *The Effects of Leadership* (Glencoe, Ill.: The Free Press, 1960), p. 169.
95. Ross and Hendry, *op. cit.*, p. 91.
96. Robert H. Guest, *Organizational Change: The Effect of Successful Leadership* (Homewood, Ill.: The Dorsey Press, 1962), pp. 128–131.
97. Fleishman, Harris, and Burtt, *op. cit.*, p. 102.
98. Robert Stout and Conrad Briner, "Leadership," in *The Encyclopedia of Educational Research*, 4th Ed. (Macmillan, 1969).
99. Peter F. Blau, *Exchange and Power in Social Life* (New York: John Wiley and Sons, 1964).
100. G. C. Homans, "Social Behavior as Exchange," *American Journal of Sociology* 63 (1958), pp. 597–606.
101. H. A. Simon, *Models of Man* (New York: John Wiley and Sons, 1957).

Chapter 5

Communication Theory:
Implications for Instructional
Supervisory Behavior

The word "communication" is derived from the Latin "communis" and might be literally interpreted as an attempt to achieve mutual understanding. Whether or not it maintains this affective connotation or is reduced to the physical phenomena of transmitting and receiving messages, there can be little doubt that communication represents one of the most fascinating and least understood areas of investigation.

Its relevance for education and its implications for learning stagger the imagination. The school itself may be considered as "a great communication laboratory where students receive information and learn to organize and evaluate it as well. Also, when the new media are recognized as art forms worthy of study and analysis, we may penetrate even further in understanding human cognitive and creative processes." [1] Likewise, the learner may be viewed as "an information-processing, organizing open energy system, in constant transaction with his changing environment." [2]

All organizational behavior depends upon communication. The major problems facing an organization—summarized by Weiss as allocation, adaptation and coordination—require the sharing of information between and among individuals. [3] Moreover, the making of decisions, which is essential for attainment of organizational objectives, requires the assembling of information regarding alternatives from various sources. Once reached, a decision must be communicated to become operational.

In this chapter, a concept of communication is developed as a vital facet of instructional supervisory behavior. Selected theories of communication behavior and empirical findings have been identified and examined to determine their relevance for instructional supervisory behavior.

THE STUDY OF COMMUNICATION

Since a supervisor must, by definition, achieve instructional objectives through the actions of others, communication is central to his effectiveness and essential to his very existence. There can be no instructional supervisory behavior in the absence of communication.

It follows, then, that the supervisor is concerned about communication from a number of foci. He must help the teacher to understand the nature of communication as a psychological process in which the supervisor engages with teachers, they with the students, and the students with the program. He must comprehend the unique characteristics of communication in small and large groups, particularly as the latter pertain to mass media. Moreover, the supervisor must identify, define and design the study of communication problems relating to the learning situation and assist the teacher in gaining proficiency with similar skills. He must apply relevant techniques of communication to education in general and to the instructional enterprise in particular. Finally, the supervisor must discriminate between adequate and inadequate research findings.

In its simplest form, communication involves a sender, who encodes a message into a symbol system, and a receiver, who decodes the transmitted message. The process is then repeated, with the communicators reversing their previous roles. It is essential to maintain constant reference to this model, illustrated below.

To the extent that the two message figures are congruent—the receiver interprets the symbols in accordance with the meaning intended by the sender—the communication is accurate. To the extent that the message figures are not congruent—the receiver interprets the symbols in such a way as to derive a meaning different from that intended by the sender—the communication is inaccurate.

A number of approaches have been taken in exploring communication. Crystallizing the varied and complex factors in the broad spectrum of communication theory is extremely hazardous. One possible approach involves the analysis of the various parts of the process itself—

FIGURE 5-1

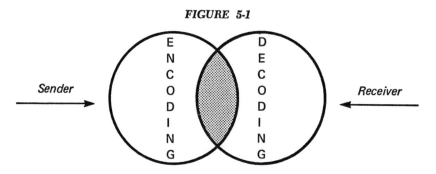

information source, transmitter, channel, receiver and destination. Another deals with the objectives or purposes for types of communication, such as directing, persuading, informing and the like.

For this book, an analysis that included the basic components of communication as a total entity appeared most appropriate. Therefore, this investigation is aimed at the influences exerted on both the sender and the receiver as they interact within the communication process. This focus is retained irrespective of the objectives of those involved.

Under such a schema, the factors that affect communication between sender and receiver may be classified under six major headings. First among these is the nature of the communication process itself, particularly the language symbols upon which so much depends. The relative positions of sender and receiver within a network or organizational hierarchy are also important. Then, there are the results of group membership upon both sender and receiver as well as that of their own personal qualities. The properties of the message being transmitted have their effect. Finally, the situation or environment in which communication occurs must be taken into account. Therefore, the findings substantiated by research, which appear to offer some implications for instructional supervisory behavior, are reported as general characteristics, communication network characteristics, group characteristics, individual characteristics, message transmission considerations, and situational conditions.

GENERAL CHARACTERISTICS

Communication involves problems at three levels. *Technical* problems are those that involve the accuracy of transference of information from sender to receiver. *Semantic* problems occur in the interpretation of meaning by the receiver as compared to the intended meaning of the sender. *Influential* problems are those concerned with the effectiveness or success of meaning that leads to desired conduct on the part of the receiver.[4]

It is quite possible, even probable, that many of these problems occur simply because so many individuals take such a large portion of the communication process virtually for granted. Debt is owed to Earl Kelley for insisting that attention be devoted to communication as one of the crucial and difficult problems of human life: "This is the process by which one human being can to a degree know what another thinks, feels or believes. It is the means by which an individual's need for others can be satisfied. It is the source of all growth except body building, and the key to human relatedness. Communication is not so easy as has been assumed. We have assumed that if we told another something, he knew it; if we showed him something, he saw it. We now know that nothing could be more uncertain or unreliable. . . . Because of the nature of perception, no two individuals can have precisely the same perception or make the same use of it. We have no given common world with any other being, but only the possibility of achieving one to a degree through improved communication." [5]

Much of his concern arose from Kelley's personal observations of light and sight experiments in the Hanover Institute at Dartmouth College during the summer of 1946. Realizing that perception is the stock-in-trade of educators, Kelley emphasizes that perceptions do not come from the things around us; instead, perceptions come from within us. "Since they do not come from the immediate environment (the present), and obviously cannot come from the future, they must come from the past." [6] Thus, states Kelley, perceptions are based upon our experience.

From this study of vision, behavior and habit, Kelley deduces the cause of much of the difficulty in relations between human beings. "No one can ever completely understand another person. This is true because we can never fully get the other person's point of view—that is, we can never be precisely where he is. Added to that, we cannot appreciate his own experiential background, nor his unique purposes. . . . In order to be effective social beings, we have to approach the other person's point of view. This can only be done through better and better communication." [7]

He adds, however, that the process will always be impaired. "To attain complete communication with another human being would mean to occupy the same space he does and to have the same purposes and experience. This of course cannot be. But our success as social beings depends upon the degree to which we can attain communion with our fellow men. This calls for an understanding of practical reality, and why an object cannot be the same to you as it is to me." [8]

Kelley also points out that language, although the most useful and universal means of communication, is far from the perfect instrument. Misinterpretation of words is a matter of common experience. Spoken language is preferable to written language because it generally elicits two-way communication. The written word has some inherent weaknesses that reduce its effectiveness as a communication tool. The most notable limitation is in the one-way communication. Kelley indicates that other forms of communication, which involve such clues to meaning as body position, facial expression and gesture, may often be more accurate than language, since much human feeling cannot be brought to the surface for verbalization. [9]

COMMUNICATION NETWORK CHARACTERISTICS

The research in this area includes the effects on sender and receiver of such factors as the communication patterns, organizational systems and member positions in the hierarchy. "Communication nets or networks refer to the arrangement of communication channels in an organization. An organizational chart depicting the hierarchy of supervision is also a formal communication network showing how information 'should' be communicated among the hierarchical levels. Often, of course, the established 'chain of command' is not followed. The organizational structure is identical to the communication network." [10]

Although much research has been conducted on organizational structures, rigorous laboratory experimentation regarding communication patterns stems from the studies of Bavelas in 1950. He sought to determine significantly better performance among several logically adequate networks and proposed the communication networks shown in the accompanying figure.[11] Each circle represents one of the persons involved, while the lines connecting them indicate the communication channels. Communication among the five persons in each net could take place only through the channels indicated. Networks with four persons subsequently utilized by Shaw are also illustrated.[12]

A common set of network descriptions are: "all-channel," in which each individual can communicate in any direction; "circle," in which each individual can send and receive in two directions; "chain," in which an individual can receive from one direction and send in the other; "wheel," in which each individual can send and receive with a single particular person but not with any other; and "Y," in which three individuals can send and receive with a single particular person but no other, while the remaining two central individuals can send or receive with two or three persons.

Leavitt attempted to discern the influence of various types of interaction connections on communication. He found that major behavioral differences are attributable to communication patterns. The latter affect accuracy, satisfaction, leader emergence, organizational differences, solution speed, self-correction and group durability.[13]

Leavitt found that the wheel, "Y," chain, and circle (in that order) promoted the greatest speed for organizing in performing tasks.[14] These results were verified by Guetzkow and Simon using wheel, circle, and all-channel arrangements. They, too, found that the wheel groups needed the least time to organize for effective problem solution since the most central member automatically became the leader. The greatest difficulty in organizing was experienced by those in the circle nets because they had to choose a leader and establish relays to him. The all-channel net was intermediate in difficulty. While the members had to decide on a leader, they did not have trouble in establishing relays since full communication among members was possible.[15]

Smith, using only the circle and chain structures, found that the person in the most central position is usually seen as the "leader" of the group. The chain net was more efficient, with fewer errors in solving the problem. Leavitt, using all four networks, also found the chain to

FIGURE 5-2. *Selected Communication Networks*

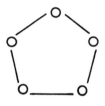 *Circle*

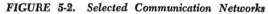

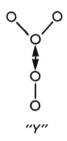 *Chain*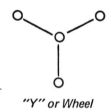

"Y" *"Y" or Wheel*

Wheel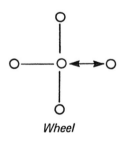

All-Channel

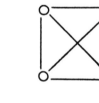

SHAW

BAVELAS

have less errors than the circle. The "Y" net had fewer errors than the chain and the same number of average errors per group as the wheel. It appeared, then, that the network with the least centralized structure (circle) had the most errors and that the errors decreased as the structure became more centralized ("Y" and wheel). As the centralization increased, so too did the agreement on who was the leader (the most central person) and the satisfaction with the group. Those persons most satisfied were the ones who had the highest centrality index in their particular network, while those in peripheral positions with limited independence of action were unsatisfied.[16]

Using the wheel, "Y," and chain nets, Goldberg found that those people in the more central positions were influenced less in their judgment than those in the peripheral ones and were also more often chosen as leaders.[17]

The all-channel network has usually been associated with a higher level of group satisfaction, but such satisfaction is related to centrality in the network. The all-channel communication network has usually produced a solution in a shorter time with fewer errors than any other network.[18]

Therefore, one's position in the network influences behavior, including opportunity for leadership, degree of satisfaction and amount of contribution. The most important single factor in the communication pattern is closeness to the most participants. This concept of "centrality" refers to the position nearest to all other positions of the pattern. In this sense, *distance* is measured by the number of communication links from one position to another, while *centrality* is a measure of the availability of information needed to complete a given task. According to Bavelas, it is a function of size as well as of structure.[19] The likelihood of emerging leadership is related to centrality, even helping make a leader out of a person who possesses "low ascendence." [20]

Centralized communication patterns, with one person in a controlling position, are evolved quickly by groups with specific tasks to perform. Bavelas found that these patterns are stable and efficient, but that they develop lower levels of satisfaction and morale on the part of members. Dispersed, decentralized patterns are less efficient but engender more satisfaction on the part of members.[21] The main procedural difference between group-centered and leader-centered structures is the amount of verbal interaction.[22]

Change can be brought about more readily in systems with many communication channels than in systems with few. Thus, change can take place more readily in a two-way interaction situation than in a one-way situation.[23]

Another important characteristic of communication networks involves the status of both sender and receiver in the organizational hier-

archy. The status system helps to establish authoritativeness of communications. When it is desired to attach the authority of legitimacy to a
communication, it need only be signed by a person of appropriate hierarchical or functional status and be transmitted through the legitimate
channels of the formal organization.[24]

An effective organization presumes that its members are aware of
their positions, their responsibilities and their authority. Therefore,
ambiguity of authority interferes with communication, increases the
internal tensions and reduces the satisfactions that members obtain from
belonging to the organization. However, the absence of ambiguity also
can cause difficulties, for stagnation sometimes results from a rigid
authority-power structure within an organization. "As communication
channels become increasingly complex, as more and more group members
get involved in decision-making or approving and relaying messages
that were sent to someone else, the efficiency of the organization is reduced."[25] At times, authority and power have to be reallocated and
ambiguity increased temporarily so that innovations can be made.

Once again, centrality also plays an important role; it influences
behavior insofar as placing limits on independent action. Where centrality and independent action are evenly distributed, the situation that
results has the following characteristics: no leader, many errors, high
activity, slow organization and high satisfaction.[26] While members more
centrally located in a group's communication pattern show higher satisfaction than do those in peripheral positions, the former do not differ in
this regard from those in intermediate positions. Also, centrally located
members do not view their positions as having any more status than
peripheral members.[27]

Attempts to gain power are a function of the communication network of a group. For example, more attempts are made in an all-channel
pattern than in a circle, and more are made in a circle pattern than in a
chain. Burdick, Ekartsberg, and Hiroshi found that, "The results support
the hypothesis that power is a function of control over pleasant or aver-
sive stimuli and further raise some interesting questions concerning the
situations leading to attempts to alter the given power structure."[28]

There is a tendency for a single individual to avoid expression of
hostility toward a central group member, although the latter may be
safely attacked by the entire group. A peripheral member, on the other
hand, may be attacked by a central member.[29]

The organizational structure—the way in which information is
handled—may put even more severe limits on communication efficiency
than those imposed by personalities.[30] Restricted channels of communication that shut out members breed low morale on the part of members.[31]
Worthy indicates that too many controls, or restrictions on all forms of
communication, can hinder self-reliance and initiative, lead at best to

misunderstanding between hierarchies, or at worst to no understanding at all.[32] The communication hierarchy creates restraints against criticism about others at the same level, both face-to-face and to others.

According to Argyris, in organizations where structures do not allow individuals to have sufficient growth in their work, employees set up informal structures unsanctioned by the organization, decrease their efficiency and become apathetic toward their work.[33]

It is often said that information flows up the hierarchy and orders flow down, implying one-way communication between superior and subordinate. This vertical communication is often inversely proportional to horizontal communication within a particular hierarchial level.[34]

People tend to prefer communicating with one of higher status than themselves rather than with one of lower status, except when a person of higher status has supervisory responsibilities for those of lower status. The fact that superiors and subordinates fail to agree on the problems facing subordinates can actually constitute a communication breakdown. Having formerly held the subordinate's job does not improve communication between that superior and his subordinate. In fact, management tends to neglect facilitating upward communication.[35]

People tend to restrict communication content that would lower status. Ambitious workers refrain from communicating with superiors, particularly when little trust is present, because it may be perceived as a threatening admission of inadequacy.[36] Communication with a superior may often be made merely to become better acquainted and thereby increase possibilities for success. Mellinger reports that a person "may try to put himself in a more favorable light (with a superior) by minimizing actual disagreement" in communication between them,[37] while Read found that information communicated up the hierarchy is screened or filtered, particularly "when the information content is of a type which might reflect negatively upon the competence and thus, indirectly, upon the security of progress of members of the subordinate level." [38] He discovered a negative correlation between the upward mobility aspirations of persons and "the accuracy with which these members communicate upward in the hierarchy."[39] A low trust of superiors also results in filtering information that is destined to go up, but high trust (i.e., when there are high mobility aspirations) does not reduce this filtering.[40] Mellinger found similar results if communication is with a distrusted person, for then the "primary goal of communication . . . becomes the reduction of one's own anxiety, rather than the accurate transmission of ideas." [41] Cohen contends that where persons of high rank in an organization mediate the upward movement in the hierarchy of low ranking members by passing judgments on their performance, the latter may be expected to be exceedingly careful in their relations with those of high rank.[42]

People tend to communicate upward in a hierarchy as a substitute for actual movement to higher positions.[43] Thus, communication serves in place of actual upward mobility for low status individuals who desire to but have no chance of moving up.[44] Cohen also found that those persons considered mobile (i.e., able to move up the hierarchy) were communicating more task-relevant information to the upper levels of higher ranking personnel than to nonmobile persons, who communicated only with each other. Presumably persons in low and undesirable positions who are unable to fulfill strong desires to locomote upward communicate task-irrelevant information upward.[45] As would be expected, the nonmobile groups are often hostile toward their superiors. And those who are mobile express hostility toward each other to some extent, since they represent a threat to each other.[46] Hurwitz, Zander and Hymovitch report that people in the low status positions behave in such a way as "to reduce the feelings of uneasiness experienced in their relations with highs . . . to like highs, to overrate the extent to which highs like them, to communicate infrequently and, when they do talk, to talk mainly to highs." [47] Little communication will flow down the line due to their low status. Low nonmobile and high mobile status conditions are more detrimental to total cohesiveness than other combinations.[48]

Low status individuals communicate more negative attitudes and express more confusion about their jobs than high status individuals and they also tend to criticize at their own level more than high status. High status individuals are freer to criticize lower stratas.[49]

Downward-directed communication results in: insufficient information penetrating to lower levels of management and action, levels of management acting as obstacles to rather than vechicles of communication; discrepancy of perception of situation appearing in top and bottom levels; and communication of information occuring without change of attitude or performance.[50]

It has been found that the poorer the downward communication, the lower the morale of the lower levels, and employees become most threatened and anxious when communications are unclear or messages are inconsistent.[51] Blau and Scott indicate that work pressures increase the frequency with which colleagues consult each other (horizontal communication) about their professional problems. They point out that requesting assistance from a peer changes their informal status relationship and repeatedly receiving advice creates social obligations, since the individual thereby acknowledges that the other's expertise is superior to his own.[52] That is to say, the esteem in which the individual holds his coworker due to his greater competence in similar tasks results in the according of informal status to that coworker within the organizational hierarchy.

The ratio of lateral communication among rank-and-file members remains about the same regardless of unit size.[53] The maximum size of an effective unit, however, is limited by the ability of the unit to solve its problems of internal communications.[54]

GROUP CHARACTERISTICS

Research in this area includes the effects on both sender and receiver of such factors as group behavior, attitudes and beliefs concerning communication. There can be no doubt that human beings function differently as members of groups than they do as individuals. Several important group characteristics influence, and in turn are influenced by, communication.

The general consequences of communication are in the direction of increasing consensus and serve as stabilizing mechanisms to the group and to its members.[55] Groups become more orderly as members perceive the consensus of group opinion, which is far more powerful in affecting individual agreement than expert opinion. Persuasive communications are more likely to be rejected if they are not in accord with the norms of the group; a speaker cannot gain a hearing if he deviates too far from the group norms.[56] The more openly, directly or actively the group identifications are brought into play, the more these identifications determine the responses.[57]

The sender has more influence on an audience if he first makes opportunities to express opinions congruent with the receivers' opinion but on another subject.[58] Acceptance is increased when a sender at first asserts views corresponding with those of the receivers, even if he is ultimately advocating an opposing view.[59]

The more extensive the preexisting information or interest, or the more firmly held the prior attitudes, then the more receptive an audience will be to compatible communications and the more resistant to incompatible communications. Similarly, the greater the receivers' involvement and interest, the greater will be the acquisition of information and skills.[60]

When there is a wide range of opinion in a group, communications tend to be directed to members whose opinions are at the extremes of the range. The more pressure toward conformity and the greater the perception of group homogeneity, the stronger the tendency to communicate to those extremes and the greater the actual change toward uniformity.[61] Communications in opposition to group norms tend to be accepted when they are less significant to the group or when group membership is not highly valued. Individuals who do not conform to group patterns and, as a result, are rejected, will receive fewer communications.

But if they do not conform and are not rejected, then the communications are unaffected.[62]

If a sender can persuade the receivers that the majority opinion is different than it really is, the group will tend to accept the alleged majority opinion.[63] The attribution of a position to majority opinion is itself effective in changing attitudes when the audience respects the group from which the majority is taken.[64] Communication affects attitude change as well as behavioral change; thus, consideration of that part of attitude change that relates to organizational behavior is important in a review of communication.

The size of a group can affect the communication structure of its members. Even a group of three can dissolve into a pair and an isolate who becomes the scapegoat. Numerous researchers have found that as group size increases, the roles and communication behavior of members become formalized and differentiated, with the result that the most frequent contributor gains an increasingly dominant part in the communication. [65,66,67] An increasing gap is then created between the frequent and infrequent contributors to the discussion. Group size also influences change in attitude. Rath and Misra found maximum change of attitude in groups of seven members. Apparently three people do not produce enough points of view to influence attitude change, while eleven members produce too many and perhaps confuse the issue.[68]

Lewin's early experiments found that changes in group behavior are accomplished more successfully by group discussion methods than by a lecture. His explanation was that lectures are passive activities while a discussion "is likely to lead to a much higher degree of involvement."[69] Group discussion is as effective in changing attitudes as in changing behavior. Pennington, Haravey, and Bass found increased agreement on the solution to the task when there was discussion; the change of opinion was signficantly greater for groups which were permitted either discussion or decision, and the greatest change occurred when both were permitted.[70]

The decision-making role apparently serves essentially the same function as a discussion in allowing personal involvement in the decision to change behavior. This implication was drawn by Levine and Butler,[71] Lawrence and Smith,[72] Coch and French,[73] and Morse and Reimer.[74] Moreover, Maier has stated, "The experimental evidence of group decision thus far indicates that a solution worked out by a group is more acceptable to the group than one imposed on the group by an authority."[75]

As group norms are perceived to change, opinions of the members change in the same direction.[76] Members tend to conform to the beliefs and actions of fellow members even to the point of expressing judgments known contrary to fact but accepted by the majority.[77] When the impact of communication produces a shift in opinions, the tendency exists for them to regress to the preexisting position unless they are reinforced by events, other communications or group pressures.[78]

When two people perceive themselves as positively interdependent and each is oriented toward some third entity, they will tend to develop similar orientations towards that entity. Dissimilar orientations in an interdependent pair or group tend to increase the frequency of communicative acts in an attempt to reduce the dissimilarity of the orientations. The strength of these "strains toward symmetry of orientation" are partly determined by the strength of the bond between the people and the strength of their attitudes toward the third entity.[79]

Because audience attention is self-selective, exposure to communications of different media tends to be supplementary rather than complementary; that is, "those who read about a topic also tend to listen, and those who pay attention at one time also tend to pay attention at another."[80] Barnouw terms those with predispositions "focused," and those lacking predispositions "unfocused." The "focused" receiver is far easier to reach and affect than the "unfocused."[81] Even in extreme cases, self-selection of communication exposure in line with predispositions is far from complete. There is usually a sizeable minority of people who read and listen to material that is contrary or indifferent to their prior position—out of curiosity, accident, lack of predispositional strength or, importantly, simple accessibility of materials.[82] Berelson and Steiner note that:

> The more that people receive communications on a given issue, especially in a concentrated fashion, the less undecided they become; the more interest they develop, the more information they acquire; the more consistent their perceptions are with the messages being communicated, the more partisan they become; the more closely they reflect the media emphasis on the sub-issues, the more likely they are to act.[83]

Those receivers whose confidence in a belief has been weakened by exposure to opposing propaganda prefer to speak and listen to arguments from their own side in order to bolster their confidence. Given free discussion, they tend to listen preferentially to those who agree with them and ignore those who oppose their arguments, with the result that confidence in their original opinion tends to return to the initial level. As a result, participation in free group discussion after a persuasive communication tends to counteract the influence of the communication.[84] The category of "other people" is frequently identified as an important persuader in adopting innovations. It is an undeniable fact that interpersonal communication is a major agent of social and technological change.[85]

Rumors spread when there is uncertainty or lack of knowledge about an important issue that is common to all or most members of a group. In fact, there is far more transmission of rumors and speculation of new rumors when the issue is important than when it is relatively unimportant. The amount of distortion of a rumor is related to its complexity and detail.[86]

INDIVIDUAL CHARACTERISTICS

Research in this area includes such factors as the influences of the attitude, status, personal capabilities and/or educational level of the sender and/or receiver on the communication process. While an organization confronts an individual functionally as a contrived communication system, the individual member of an organization likewise intersects with it functionally as a whole operative communication network. He brings this personal network with him, and it is the central node or nub.[87]

Thayler states, "An individual's behavior may be conceptualized as some function of the manner in which he processes present information and relevant information from storage. Thus, work or performance skills may be viewed as a function of the degree of organization of task-relevant information." [88] The content of memories, according to Deutsch and Rieselbach, "often determines which messages will be recognized and transmitted with speed and attention, and which other messages will be neglected or rejected. The consonance or dissonance of messages, of memories and of projected courses of action is thus decisive for behavior.[89]

Communication problems frequently occur because of differences between and among individuals, yet communication is seldom random—a definite audience is usually in mind. When lack of understanding or breakdown in communication occurs, it is caused by: differences in experience relative to the initial situation; differences in perception, apperception, motivation, intelligence, ability and/or inclination to deal in abstracts; linguistic ability; varying experience with specific word or expression meanings; personality differences; sensory defects; and neurological or speech defects.[90]

A receiver exposed to a persuasive communication from a reputable source reacts in one of the following manners. If it is a previously accepted view, confidence in the opinion is reinforced or unchanged. If it is a previously opposed view, opinion may change to the other side.[91] Experience with a subject creates interest in it. Experience in accord with existing frames of reference promotes better learning than experience involving conflict; therefore, individuals may respond quite differently to an initial situation based upon varying experiences.[92]

People tend to receive communications that are favorable or congenial to their predispositions. They are more likely to receive compatible communications than neutral or hostile ones. The more interested the "focused" individuals are in the subject, the more likely such selective attention is to occur.[93] Communications will be most effective in gaining desirable responses when they are in accord with audience predispositions, that is, when they tell receivers what most of them *want* to be told.[94] "Existing beliefs and prejudices are intensified when listeners hear both sides of a fairly academic controversy, but there is more openmindedness or a lessening of the intensity of belief when the receiver feels the issue is closer to reality." [95]

Also, individuals "tend to misperceive and misinterpret persuasive communications in accordance with their own predispositions, by evading the message or by distorting it in a favorable direction." [96] When clear incompatibility exists between the sender's message and the approval he holds with his receivers, the latter tend to misperceive the actual content and distort it in a direction favorable to their own prior position.[97]

A person needs and seeks to maintain consistency between elements in his cognitive system. A change in attitude is one way in which he regains consistency if his equilibrium has been disturbed.[98] Cognitive dissonance arises, assert Allyn and Festinger, when a person is exposed to a communication that differs in opinion from his own. To reduce the dissonance between his and the other's opinion, "he can change his opinion to a position closer to that advocated . . . or he can reject and derogate the communication and the communicator." [99] This provides an explanation for most of the effects encountered in the area of attitude change. Moreover, a person faced with increasing dissonance will seek out "consonant" information to reduce dissonance and avoid "dissonant" information that might increase it.[100]

An individual is likely to distort his own attitudes in communicating with people he distrusts or doesn't know. Distortion or concealment is accomplished by evasive, compliant or aggressive communication. As a result, a distrustful individual may be led to overestimate agreement in others.[101]

When the distance between a receiver's opinion and the opinion advocated in the communication is small, the communication is judged favorable, fair, and factual. With increasing distance, favorable reaction is sharply reduced and the communication is perceived as propagandistic and unfair. Receivers whose opinions differ widely from the communication tend to perceive the message as further from their own feelings than it is (*contrast effect*); receivers whose opinions are close to the communication tend to perceive the message as closer than it is (*assimilation effect*). Persons whose opinions widely differ from the communication are less likely to change initial attitude than persons in moderate positions. It may be deduced, therefore, that relative distance of opinions from the one advocated and the latitudes of acceptance and rejection for various stands on the issue provide bases for predicting reaction to communication and susceptibility to change.[102]

Interpersonal attraction is associated with and possibly derived from group member perceptions of their own and each other's status, power, and attitudes and an increased communication rate is one result of high member attraction toward each other or toward the group. A basis of interpersonal attraction may be a desire for identification with those in favored positions or with those who possess desirable task- and situation-related characteristics.[103]

Several researchers have found that receivers tend to accept ideas from one who wants more or is afraid of losing the authority he has. High status speakers were readily distinguished from low status speakers by "the way they talked" and were consistently rated more credible, according to Harms.[104] Persons having general speech competence are perceived by receivers as prestigious.

It is important to note that it is the expectations, not the prescriptions or descriptions that people have about authority, that control their behavior. Further, the power of an individual and the authority of his position do not necessarily coincide. When the power is less, he becomes dissatisfied; when it is more, others become dissatisfied. An individual likes to be perceived by others as having the authority he perceives himself to have. One who is satisfied with his authority behaves differently from one who wants more or is afraid of losing the authority he has. Bypassing certain positions is perceived as an attack by the persons who occupy those positions, and when individuals feel their positions are under attack, they will react negatively.[105]

According to Berelson and Steiner, "The more trustworthy, credible, or prestigious the communicator is perceived to be, the less manipulative his intent is considered to be and the greater the immediate tendency to accept his conclusions." [106] When there is reason to be suspicious of a sender's motives, the receiver believes the speaker to be one-sided, but the same speech elicits a fair and honest rating when the receiver believes the sender not to be seeking personal gain.[107]

The results of a potentially persuasive piece of communication often can be affected by forewarning. Kiesler and Kiesler found that a warning preceding the communication nullified the propagandistic intent, whereas a warning after the content had been read had no effect.[108] Similarly, Allyn and Festinger found that subjects forewarned of the nature of a communication changed their opinions less and rejected the communication as biased. While it appeared that each individual believed at least part of everything he read unless previously warned, individuals with litttle concern about a topic were influenced more than those who had initial opinions about it.[109] Regardless of initial opinions, however, high anxiety people changed their opinions more than those low in anxiety.[110]

Berelson and Steiner state, "The communication of facts is typically ineffective in changing opinions in desired directions against the force of audience predispositions; the stronger the predispositions, the less effective the communication of facts." [111] Lund found a strong correlation of over + .80 between belief strength and desirability.[112]

Berelson and Steiner also note, "The use and perhaps the effectiveness of different media vary with the educational level of the audience: the higher the education, the greater the reliance on print; the lower the education, the greater the reliance on aural and picture media. The better educated are more likely than others to pay attention to serious communications dealing with aesthetic, moral or educational issues." [113] To put it another way: "The higher a person's level of intelligence, the more likely it is that he will acquire information from communications." [114]

The content of interaction is only slightly related to the personality characteristics and task abilities of members; patterns of interaction are slightly related to general abilities of group members, and are highly related to task abilities. Perceptions of other members' task abilities, however, are not consistently related to discussion behavior. "Group members who are more active in discussion learn and retain more knowledge of the topic than do less active." [115]

Sincerity and poise rank highest as essential qualities of a speaker if he is to gain the greatest effect and influence.[116] Other factors that influence listening comprehension are a real interest in the topic, an ability to see significance in the topic, and a curiosity about the topic.[117]

Research has found that communicative differences exist between the middle and lower classes. These include the number and kind of perspectives utilized in communication, ability to take a listener's role, handling of classifications, and frameworks and stylistic devices that order and implement the communication.

The communications of a person identified as lower class typically exhibit the following characteristics: a single perspective—his own; an insensitivity to perspectives of others—assumes others share his viewpoint; a disinclination to think or talk in terms of classes and/or organizations, a tendency to speak in concrete, individual terms; a habit of using frameworks that are segmental, limited in scope and personal; a lack of organization in communication, with events reported in narrative progression or as recollected; and a use of crude, chronological connectives such as "then" and "so."

The communications of a person identified as middle class also typically exhibit particular characteristics: an ability to speak from other viewpoints; a recognition that others have a different viewpoint, so that a context for his own perceptions must be supplied; a less concrete pattern of speech; a greater use of abstract terms; more frequent use of classes, organizations, and categories, and a variety in frameworks and stylistic devices.[118]

The greatest change in opinion through communication is found in people showing social inadequacy, inhibition or aggression, and depressive tendencies.[119] Individuals whose social behavior has been changed by the communication of information tend to relay this information to others.[120] Individuals with the self-perception of having power attempt to influence others more.[121] People who most influence other people are least likely to be influenced by others.[122] People with low self-esteem are more likely to be influenced by persuasive communications than are those with high self-esteem.[123]

Early acceptors of innovation are most likely to have been influenced by formal and/or impersonal sources.[124] The orientation of these people is an openness to rational evaluation and a willingness to contact the world outside their community. Confidence in one's own abilities, however, is not related to an active or a passive discussion role.[125] The people most likely to utilize, for example, the external entertainment opportunities furnished by mass media tend to be those least able to rely on their own resources, or at least used to relying on them.[126]

The competitive individual is less likely to produce material of common significance to the group than is the cooperative individual, and he is less likely to participate in a common appraisal of communications than the latter.[127] Fewer communication difficulties occur among cooperating individuals than among competing individuals because much greater distortion of content occurs among the latter. When the amount of communication is perceived as a means of advancement, the competitive individual will talk more than the cooperative individual; however, when progress toward the task solution is perceived as possible through the discussion of ideas, the cooperative individual will produce more ideas than the competitive one.[128]

Perceptions of intensity, frequency and distortion differ markedly with individuals. Personal needs can distort sound patterns, while attention spans can be brief and sporadic, with their duration depending on the intensity of the stimulus. The clarity of perception appears to be greatest when stimuli are clustered in focus, with the practical limits of five to eight seconds for auditory stimuli, and four to five seconds for visual stimuli.[129]

Factors that possess attention value for the receiver include change, intensity, striking quality, repetition, definiteness of form, organic condition, social suggestion, and predisposition. Factors that affect the interest of the receiver include animation, vitalness, familiarity, novelty, conflict, suspense, concreteness, and humor.[130]

The determination of the particular messages that will be recognized and transmitted quickly and attentively, and those that will be neglected or rejected, is related to the content of memory recalled to recognize items in current messages. A disassociation of items from old memories and a recombination of these into new patterns are essential in processes of initiative, innovation and human freedom.[131] Under the pressure of communications, people tend to use changes in their own opinion, however recent or immediate, as blocks against further modification of that opinion.[132] In view of this, it is no surprise to find that there appears to be a decline in the effect of suggestibility with increasing age; individuals preserve their beliefs as they grow older, with the result that such beliefs become stronger and are less likely to be relinquished.[133]

MESSAGE TRANSMISSION CONSIDERATIONS

The effects of verbal and nonverbal expression, of significant language factors, of kinds and rates of interactions, and of content organization all figure importantly in the research related to message transmission. Gerbner points out that communication can be defined as "social interaction through messages." [134] Such interaction requires that the receiver of a stimulus discriminate to determine the meaning intended by the sender. In doing so, attention to the nature of the stimulus and the clues it provides is essential.

Gerbner states, "The ways we reflect on things, act on things, and interact with one another are rooted in our ability to compose images, produce messages and use complex symbol systems. A change in that ability transforms the nature of human affairs." [135] Moreover, "Communication channels do have an influence upon the composition of message flows and memories and hence on the content of their ensembles, but the content of messages in turn may change the operating preferences and practices—that is, the values—of the systems." [136]

Three basic information systems exist within any organization: operational, regulatory and maintenance-development. Likewise, three kinds of information distortion can be identified in this process: "stretch distortion," in which no information is lost, but is changed slightly; "fog distortion," in which some information is lost because of the inability to respond to all level ranges of input (random error); and "mirage distortions," in which extra, unwanted information is given and a message is seen that really isn't there.[137]

Message originators should achieve an ability to construct messages that take into account systematically human errors in information-processing and, at the same time, protect against "noise" through minimum channel or message redundancy to eliminate many of the so-called people-problems in communication.[138]

The grammar of a language is not just an index of ideas but in itself constitutes a determinant of the person's ideas.[139] Verbal patterns bind thinking just as thoughts shape language.[140] Words can be used either to express thoughts or to disguise them. The verbal behavior of a speaker is the product of a number of different types of psychological processes.

Communication means have been ranked by Dahle from the most to the least effective in the following sequence: combined oral and written, oral only, written only, bulletin board, and grapevine.[141] A significant stylistic signal in a communication situation exists when a person strives with great regularity to use precise, literary words and constructions despite different standard colloquial usage in his environment.[142] This is modified when one adds to it Leavitt's [143] observation that the ability to express oneself vocally and facially are positively related. Furthermore, Leavitt contends that the processes of expressing and receiving emotional messages are positively related, as are sensitivity to vocal and facial expression, according to Davitz and Mattis.[144] Speech behavior, then, involves both a verbal or content component and a vocal or sonal component. The verbal component carries potential semantic information, while the vocal component carries potential affective information.[145]

Attitude and behavior are themselves forms of communication. Therefore, it is of more value to know about each other's emotional states through the latent forms of communication than to give precise information to each other.[146]

Most research in communication theory has centered either on verbal acts or the influence of verbal behavior. As a result, the status of nonverbal communication remains indeterminate and presents a fertile area of study. Recently an increasing number of investigators, including Davitz,[147] Efron,[148] Galloway,[149] Hall,[150] and Ruesch and Kees,[151] have explored this obvious but elusive realm.

Nonverbal clues are vital signs for both sending and receiving. These include facial expressions, movements, postures, mannerisms, and vocal tones. Even silence itself can be most effective in communicating meaning. By reacting to nonverbal cues, the receiver obtains information by which he determines his next action and his appropriate role. Moreover, to play a role, it is important to communicate the nonverbal cues that are consonant with its performance. This is because the expressive state of an individual is taken as symptomatic of his inner feelings and attitudes. Although such cues are not usually accepted at face value, inferences typically are made from them.

All of this activity is so natural and spontaneous that most individuals overlook the fact that they influence and are influenced by others through nonverbal cueing. Nonverbal reactions are especially significant for the formation of attitudes, since they stem from automatic responses. Individuals unwittingly may reveal feelings that are not in their own best interests. A receiver assumes that nonverbal cues more nearly approximate actual thoughts; therefore, he accepts them in preference to the sender's verbal behavior if a contradiction is detected between the two types of signals. Incongruity between the verbal and the nonverbal troubles the receiver, who attempts to see through the sender's real self. The verbal message will make little impact if the sender fails to understand the image of self being projected nonverbally.

On the other hand, nonverbal expressions can be deliberately used to give an impression or to convey an attitude to a receiver. These cues may be calculated to achieve a desired effect by convincing others of the way in which the sender wishes to be viewed. In many instances, the sender eventually believes his own performance to be authentic.

The ability to recognize emotions in speech, gesture, or facial expressions is not considered dependent on common experience. Patterns of facial expressions for emotions, especially unpleasant ones, are highly variable, and posed or simulated emotions appear to be more reliably recognized than spontaneous, true ones. Certain facial features are more expressive than others; for example, the mouth gives more emotional cues than the eyes. Accuracy of identification of emotions increases according to the number of expressive cues to which the observer may respond, such as voice and gesture.[152]

All such cues are learned in the cultural setting; gestures, communications and motions are learned systems of behavior differing greatly from culture to culture. These systems are learned informally, by imitation, with little or no consciousness of learning. Gestures differ in meaning from person to person and despite little systematic teaching, everyone learns to react to nonverbal communication and to rely on the consistent symbolic value of gestures.[153]

It is important to note that receivers tend to respond to and evaluate senders by overall impressions rather than by separate elements in the process. In addition, credibility and extent of persuasiveness correlate highly with effectiveness of delivery; receivers tend to make stereotyped responses to sterotyped stimuli, and receiver comprehension is positively related to vocal skill.[154]

Listeners tend to respond to the emotional connotations of words. Homogeneity of native language among speakers and listeners is not related to the accuracy of their nonverbal communication, and interpersonal sensitivity is not linearly related to the compatibility of language patterns.[155] Pittenger and Smith[156] have identified the following effects of various vocal qualities in the American culture:

1. Increasing softness indicates displeasure, disappointment.
2. Increasing loudness indicates alarm, annoyance; it is often accompanied by raised pitch.
3. Raised pitch is used when adults address children and animals.
4. Low pitch indicates emphasis or incredulity and is often accompanied by openness or drawl.
5. Spread register is used to call someone at a distance or not visible.
6. Squeezed register and rasp indicates lack of interest and weariness.
7. Openness and hollow, booming acoustic tone is associated with clergy, politicians, undertakers; this can indicate a lack of sincerity to the receiver —a feeling that the speaker believes he enjoys a superior status and possesses all the answers.
8. Rasp and loudness indicate extreme annoyance and no interest.
9. Drawl implies sarcasm, a contradiction of word meaning.
10. Clipping words indicates a desire to talk, often seen in interjections.
11. Increased tempo signals emphasis or annoyance and anxiety about being heard or interrupted.
12. Decreased tempo indicates emphasis on certain phrases or ideas; uncertainty is also communicated this way.
13. Breaking of speech accompanied by overloud, overslow, open pronunciation indicates deep emotional involvement.
14. Laughing and crying, although among the most common communication patterns, are arbitrary and differ in meaning from culture to culture.

The interaction rate of an individual is related to the rates of others in the group as well as to his own personality. This rate increases with an increase in activity in the content areas and with attempts to control a deviant member. It is high when task success is high, but it can vary while the content remains stable.[157]

Types of communication acts in social interaction are classified by Bales into four categories: positive reactions, problem-solving attempts, questions and negative reactions. His studies of patterns of interaction in discussion situations indicate that a speaker's first remark is likely to be a reaction if his communication continues for any length of time; moreover, probability is high that his second remark will be a problem-solving attempt. On the average, of seven problem-solving attempts, four are opinions, two are offers of information and one is a solution suggestion.

Bales further identified rates for the types of communication acts involved in social interaction. When meeting length was divided into thirds, he made the following observations: information-giving ranks highest in the first third, with a decline in the second and third thirds; opinion-giving ranks highest in the second third; and suggestion-giving ranks low in the first and second thirds, highest in the final third. Positive and negative reactions tend to increase during a meeting, and they are more frequent in response to suggestions than to facts. When a decision is reached, the negative reactions decrease, while the positive reactions increase.[158]

An analysis of types of communication during conferences indicates that 56 percent of the communicative acts engaged in are problem-solving attempts, while 44 percent are positive or negative reactions and questions. The positive reactions outnumber the negative reactions two to one. It appears that after each negative reaction a problem-solving attempt must be made that meets with a positive reaction. Progress is secure only when a repetition of problem-solving attempts has unopposed acceptance. So it would seem that communication in groups tends to depend on error and correction for guidance.[159] There is a tendency for persons, once they have gained the floor, to complete several communicative acts in succession due to a need to provide inferences or to check facts. This is done to gain the acceptance of the group in preparation for the succeeding steps in making a suggestion.[160]

A conversational, relaxed, informal type of delivery has more influence on attitude shift than a dynamic, rapid, dramatic, enthusiastic one. Extemporaneous speaking gains better attention and retention than reading from a manuscript or notes, but humorous and nonhumorous speeches on a topic appear to have equal effect in interest and persuasiveness.[161]

In the speech situation, the delivery impact, or stimulus potency, exhibits certain noticeable characteristics. Intensity increases potency, and this potency is related to duration. A longer stimulus is more effective than a shorter one increased by reinforcement, by vigorous gesture, and by a third and fourth repetition (beyond four, there is no proportionately greater effect). Repetition is more potent when spaced over intervals of time to strike at attention spurts, and the greater potency of a specific stimulus in a series occurs when it is placed first or last. This potency is increased when reinforced by the social facilitation of others making similar responses.[162]

Over short periods of time inequality of participation exhibits side effects in the social organization of the group. The person ranked as having the best ideas usually does most of the talking and gives many suggestions and opinions. Those rated "best liked" have high rates of tension release and agreement. Those rated as having the "best ideas" are seldom rated, however, as the "best liked"; in fact, the persons "best liked" are usually second or third in the participation hierarchy.[163]

No superiority has been found regarding the relative effectiveness of rational or emotional appeals of messages in the changing of attitudes. Janis and Feshbeck found that a fear-arousing appeal causes the most worry, but the "greatest amount of conformity to the communicator's recommendations was produced by the minimal appeal," which rarely refers to unpleasant consequences.[164] A strong fear appeal is not very effective in maintaining attitude change over an extended time period. In fact, strong fear arousal shows less change in behavior than minimal arousal.

Communications designed to affect acceptancy should include certain characteristics: the organization of communication should be apparent early in the communication process; any "fear" appeals should be kept to a minimum; the conclusions should be drawn by the communicator rather than by the audience; the presentation of one-sided arguments is effective with the lesser-educated listener; and the presentation of both sides of a question is more effective with the better-educated one.[165]

For the more highly-educated listener, and those opposed to an issue, it is better to introduce both arguments opposed to the issue and evidence for it, because this induces the feeling that the speaker is being fair. For the lesser-educated listener, and those favorable to an issue, it is better to offer only evidence for the issue.[166] Replication with more sophisticated audiences indicates that arguments for and against the issue aid in better retention but are not more persuasive.[167]

Greater attitude change occurs when the desirable features of a proposed change are presented before the undesirable ones. Also, need arousal followed by information is more effective in producing change than the reverse sequence.[168]

There is no significant difference or advantage in any particular kind of organizational or structural pattern of a speech; however, a well-organized speech in which conclusions are succinctly drawn is clearly more effective than a poorly organized one. A greater shift of opinion occurs when speeches are built on evidence rather than on assertion or generalization; however, an expansion of evidence through the citing of sources does not lend still more credibility. In speaking to inform, citing quotations and assertions provides more effective support than giving specific instances; in speaking to persuade, quotations are the most effective support, assertions are less effective, and analogies are relatively ineffective.[169]

Fine found that articles containing a definite conclusion were more effective in changing attitudes than articles that did not.[170] In some cases, conclusions to arguments are often all that is presented. In such an occurrence, the communicator must be able to reconstruct the entire argument and assure its validity, or predict the extent to which the receiver will be able to reconstruct the argument for himself or accept the conclusions without doing so.[171]

When relevant issues are discussed certain results are evident. Communications become larger and interruptions and pauses become less frequent. Also, the incidence of personal references increases. Irrelevant issues induce reverse results, because they produce shorter communications, more interruptions, more pauses and fewer personal references. Relevant issues are characterized by slow, even-paced, long, well-considered discussion and more personal involvement. Irrelevant issues are characterized by fast, brief, clipped, sporadic, more glib, and more super-ficial discussions.[172]

SITUATIONAL CONDITIONS

There are a number of other characteristics of the situation in which communication occurs that affect the interchange between sender and receiver. These pressures include those toward uniformity, movement within the social structure and reaction to existing emotional states. They involve important specific aspects of the environment, such as distance, feedback, atmosphere and mass media.

Pressure to communicate to any one member increases with an increase in the perceived discrepancy of the individual's opinion with the total group opinion. It also increases with an increase in the relevance of the opinion or item to the functioning of the group. An increase in group cohesiveness will increase this pressure, while a rejection of the ideas proposed will decrease it. If the perception that communication will change opinion becomes evident, the force to communicate will increase.[173]

Neither primacy nor recency effect is immediately evident in a situation where two communications on a single topic, one affirmative and one negative, are presented successively. A *primacy effect* is one in which the communication presented first is more effective in changing opinion, while a *recency effect* is one in which the communication presented second or last is more effective in changing opinion. The recency effect is evident when there is little or no familiarity with the topic. Increasing familiarity with the topic is directly related to an in-creasing primacy effect in producing attitude change. However, neither primacy nor recency operates with total familiarity.[174]

Full feedback has a significant effect on communication because it increases the accuracy of information transmission and the mutual under-standing of the participants.[175] According to Hare, the less or slower the feedback, the lower will be the degree of reality. The lower the degree of reality, the more the response is determined by internal features and tensions in the individual or group.[176] Feedback on self-response and on a combination of self and teammate response is more significant as to accuracy and learning rate than feedback on just the teammate's response. Redundancy or repetition, like feedback (error-correcting mechanism) assists in overcoming ambiguity or uncertainty.[177]

As one would expect, high member attraction increases communi-cation rate. Members show less aggressiveness, less defensiveness, fewer communication difficulties, and more attentiveness when they are mutually attractive. Interpersonal attraction, interpersonal communication and perceptions of task-success vary independently, but manipulation of one brings correlated changes in the other two.[178] Members of groups operating under success conditions see less discrepancy between their own and others' opinions.[179]

In determining rates of interaction, distance is the most important factor.[180] Lack of intimate friendship restrains communication, as does the perception of the existence of a hierarchy.[181] Knowledge of such existence restrains the upward communication of hostility because valid change takes place more readily in interactions where there is valid, unconstrained, easy, emotionally expressive communication than where there is not.[182] The effect of hostility can be lessened, however, according to Thibaut and Coules, if the overt aggression directed toward the instigator of hostility is expressed. The opportunity to communicate hostility will ensure less loss of friendliness for the instigator than if there is no chance to communicate. The amount of change in friendliness is a positive function of initial friendliness.[183] Familiarity facilitates communication.

Frequent communication among employees makes working for an organization more or less attractive, depending on whether communicating persons value each other's contribution to the organization.[184] Overcommunication can result in the frustration of knowing too much, but supplying more information to employees creates the desire for still more.[185]

Attention and assent constitute reinforcement and increase the frequency of self-reference statements. Withdrawal of attention and of assent not only decreases the frequency of self-reference statements, but also causes the subjects to show emotional disturbance, anger and hostility.

Subtle communication, such as an overheard conversation, can influence individual attitudes. Attitude change in such circumstances may be effective because defenses against new ideas will presumably be weaker and the gratification of hearing something not intended for the receiver offers certain psychological advantages.[186] Moreover, the speaker cannot possibly be seen as intending to influence the listener.[187]

Mass media can be influential in the early phases of decision-making, but personal influences are more effective in the later deliberation/decision phase.[188] There is a high correlation between urbanization, literacy, participation in government and the use of mass media; wherever one is present the others are present, and vice versa. Whenever these factors are present, mass media must operate as part of the general cultural setting.[189] Even when it does operate, however, whether in an urban or a rural setting, mass media is less effective than personal influence in changing popular opinion.

Whatever its effect may be, some principles of mass persuasion influence behavior and are a necessary part of the communication process. They include the creation of a particular cognitive, motivational, and behavioral structure. To modify cognitive structure, the message must reach the sense organs of the individual and be accepted as part of the cognitive structure. The total stimulus situation is selected or rejected on the basis of the impression of general characteristics. The categories used in characterizing such a stimulus situation tend to protect the process from unwanted changes in cognitive structure. The receiver is inclined to accept or reject on the basis of the general categories to which the message appears to belong. When such categories are inconsistent with the existing cognitive structure, the message will be rejected, be distorted to fit or cause a change in the structure. The exact outcome will depend upon the strength of the forces that maintain the cognitive structure and the force of the message.

The action induced by mass persuasion must be seen as a path to a goal if motivational structure is to be modified. It will be accepted as a path if the connections fit the cognitive structure. The more goals seen attainable by the path, the more likely that the path will be accepted or taken; however, actions seen as leading to a goal will not be taken if other actions are seen as easier, cheaper or more desirable.

To modify behavioral structure, an action must be induced in an appropriate cognitive and motivational system that gains control of behavior at a point in time. The more specifically defined the path of action to the goal, the more likely that the structure will gain control of behavior. The more specifically the path of action is located in time, the more likely that it will gain control. A motivational structure may be set in control of behavior by placing an individual in a situation requiring a decision to take or not to take a step of the action.[190]

IMPLICATIONS FOR INSTRUCTIONAL SUPERVISORY BEHAVIOR

It should be clear by now that research in the field of communications and communications theory yields significant and substantial promise for instructional supervisory behavior. The exact nature of these implications may await further study and empirical experimentation. Even in their embryonic stage of development, however, some aspects perhaps deserve more than cursory consideration.

In some instances, the available data appear to substantiate and reinforce perceptions regarding the role of supervisory personnel formulated long ago on the basis of common sense. In others, the converse is suggested. Perhaps long-established precedents must undergo modification or even drastic change as additional information is obtained.

Realizing that much more awaits to be crystallized, the following tentative hypotheses may be warranted from the present review of the literature in communication:

General Characteristics

PROPOSITION 1: *Communication will always be inaccurate because sender and receiver can never share common perceptions.*

Supervisors often operate on the assumption that communication is perfect. Instead, they should function on the basis that communication is imperfect and must always be so. Since perceptions are drawn from the past, the importance of experiences similar to those of the teachers with whom a supervisor must communicate cannot be overemphasized. It follows that supervisors should have extensive and varied backgrounds upon which to draw in communicating with teachers. Unless the supervisor is able to perceive a situation in terms that closely mirror the perception by a teacher, he is unlikely to achieve accurate communication.

This perhaps adds support to the common expectation that supervisors must themselves be effective teachers. Also, it provides support to evidence from typical practice that teachers do not seek or accept assistance from supervisors who do not have substantial and appropriate classroom experience.

PROPOSITION 2: *The effectiveness of language as a symbol system will be improved by two-way (verbal) rather than one-way (written) communication.*

Supervisory behavior that builds upon discussion and conversation rather than upon written materials will reduce the limitations to communication imposed by language itself. The supervisor must recognize the possible and probable variations of interpretation inherent in the symbol system. Moreover, he must be alert to all forms of nonverbal communication as clues that support, contradict or substitute for written and oral expression.

Communication Network Characteristics

PROPOSITION 3: *Communication will be affected by the nature of the network and the channels it provides for interaction between sender and receiver.*

Evidence indicates that an individual charged with purpose-oriented behavior will communicate in a more efficient manner with greater satisfaction to himself and others, depending upon different types of networks. The supervisor should have free movement and access to teachers, administrators, other supervisors and supporting staff personnel. Therefore, an all-channel communication pattern is most likely to allow for the effective exercise of ISB.

PROPOSITION 4: *Communication will be affected by the respective positions occupied by sender and receiver, particularly in regard to centrality.*

It may be that a supervisor who makes infrequent visits to each of the various school buildings for periodic observations of particular individuals operates contrary to the concept of centrality. Viewed as a member of the administrative hierarchy, the supervisor may have considerable difficulty establishing rapport with the teachers to really be included in their communication network. However, viewed as an ancillary service rather than a peer assignment by members of the administrative hierarchy, the supervisor often is not included in the communication network through which important decisions affecting teachers are made. By attempting to achieve the best of two worlds, the supervisor may inadvertently obtain communication with neither.

While proximity does not necessarily serve the same function, evidence suggests that supervisors must be on the communication links of many staff members having varied assignments. Whatever the physical location, it is clearly important to establish a communication network in which the supervisor is central to both teachers and administrators. Otherwise, ISB is unlikely to achieve a high degree of success.

PROPOSITION 5: *Communication will be more effective in promoting change if the sender utilizes many communication channels rather than a few.*

The simplest example of this can be seen in the greater effectiveness of a two-way interaction situation as opposed to a one-way situation. As more communication channels are opened, the danger of misunderstanding or misinformation due to personal dislike or perception interference is minimized.

It is important, then, that the supervisor who desires change in teacher behavior take advantage of all the channels of communication available to him. Change will be more likely to occur if he does this than if he attempts to gain support for new ideas through a one-to-one or a one-to-many communication network.

PROPOSITION 6: *Communication effectiveness of an individual occupying an official position will be at least partially a function of the authority of that position.*

A high positive correlation exists between communication and authority. Unless the individual engaged in ISB possesses sufficient power to change the situation in which the teachers operate, there is little reason for them to communicate with the supervisor.

Moreover, administrators respect authority; principals whose concurrence and/or support are essential to changing an instructional situation may place the recommendations from a supervisor at a lower priority while responding to individuals perceived as vested with authority.

This may suggest the creation within the school organization of supervisory positions quite at variance with most of those currently in existence. Rather than dealing with the specious issue of line or staff assignments of supervisors based upon their acceptance by teachers, it may well be necessary to determine the nature and degree of authority for individuals involved in instructional supervisory behavior to ensure that communication with teachers and administrators will be achieved.

PROPOSITION 7: *Communication will be more effective if it is recognized that messages will differ in kind with a person perceived as having higher status than with one perceived as having lower status.*

There can be little doubt that the amorphous nature of supervisory assignments complicates the communication processes in many school situations. The unwillingness of human beings to communicate problems to those in positions of superior status in order to avoid feelings of inadequacy cannot be ignored. However, perhaps of equal significance is the reluctance of individuals to betray inferior status by requesting assistance from a colleague. This points up the curious situation that has long plagued even the most devoted supervisors, in that they must at one and the same time preserve their peer relationship with teachers while establishing communication with administrators. This schizophrenic characteristic of the supervisory role is a deterrent to recruitment, since many individuals prefer to identify clearly with either one group or the other.

Perhaps a reasonable compromise is possible with a procedure that permits supervisors to have certain prerogatives of status while eliminating the rating of teacher performance.

Evidence also indicates the need for allowing teachers to move to higher status if communication is to be accurate. Role differentiation for teachers may offer important advantages for communication effectiveness.

PROPOSITION 8: *Communication will be more frequent and in greater amount with a peer whose expertise is accepted as superior.*

This suggests that collegial status for an individual engaged in ISB is possible only if the teachers perceive him as possessing competence greater than their own. The role of the supervisor must logically be diagnosis, planning, assessment and the like so that the teacher may improve his teaching skills, rather than presentation of a particular teaching model for imitation.

PROPOSITION 9: *Communication will be less precise and accurate if it proceeds in an upward direction through the hierarchy than if it proceeds in the downward direction.*

A person in a subordinate position in a hierarchy may conceal, disguise or alter communications that are sent upward in the hierarchy because he believes that they may threaten his present position or hamper his upward mobility if they reflect views opposite to those above him. Those with aspirations to rise in the hierarchy are more likely to practice such caution than are those who expect to remain at their present level.

Since in many instances teachers who desire upward mobility are among those who may be the most competent to contribute valuable suggestions, it is particularly important that the supervisor learn to minimize the feeling of possible threat that these persons tend to experience.

Group Characteristics

PROPOSITION 10: *Communication will be more effective when the views of the sender and the receiver(s) are in harmony.*

This supports the contention that supervisors should begin to focus attention on problems of teachers as the latter perceive them to exist. Teachers are unlikely to support efforts of the supervisor that are not viewed as important by them.

PROPOSITION 11: *Communication verifies group norms, which in turn determine the nature of internal communication and receptivity to external communication.*

The new supervisor who is unaware of existing norms should obtain evidence from the type of communication that takes place in respective groups. He should seek many and varied opportunities to listen to such discussions in determining the expectations of the teachers regarding their own behavior and that of ISB. The supervisor also can ascertain the potential acceptance of particular ideas, the manner of presentation and the type of audience that will achieve maximum favorable consideration, and the priority order for dealing with several topics or operations.

PROPOSITION 12: *To be effective in modifying individual behavior, communication must achieve a comparable change in the norms of the group to which the individual belongs.*

This would seem to bolster the view that the supervisor must work with and through the entire staff. He must be able to alter the total school environment in which a teacher operates if the supervisor hopes to help a particular teacher achieve a change in himself. It also indicates the futility and frustration that must inevitably result in seeking extensive and lasting change through approaches to "a teacher at a time" by "a subject at a time" in "a school at a time."

PROPOSITION 13: *Communication will cause change by providing both ample preparation and continuous reinforcement.*

It seems clear that teachers seek supportive communications, particularly during periods of change from previously accepted norms. Moreover, they tend to regress to the previous norms unless continuous communication provides reinforcement of their actions. Therefore, group discussion that offers support of innovative efforts would seem to be an important factor of ISB.

PROPOSITION 14: *Communication will be more effective in influencing group behavior and attitudes when it utilizes discussion and decision-making.*

The supervisor must realize the nature, range, and depth of views held by members of a group, the type of information that is most likely to achieve the desired change in group norms, and the available channels of communication that can be utilized. The supervisor must be able to bring varied and supportive communications to bear on group situations in order to effect change. He will obtain a more appropriate and acceptable solution to a situation if he assists the teachers in reaching it rather than imposing his own views. However, the supervisor also must realize that the size and composition of a group can be controlled to determine the effectiveness of communication in changing norms. In similar fashion, ISB can void the frequently negative effects of rumor.

Individual Characteristics

PROPOSITION 15: *Communication will be more effective when the sender and receiver are dealing with situations in which both have obtained previous experience.*

Since supervisors focus upon concerns of teachers, broad experience in relation to these problems should be a basic attribute for those engaged in ISB. Evidence of such compatibility of experience should be explored at the outset. In its absence, measures should be taken to equip the supervisor, the teacher, or both, to deal in consonance with a particular situation. The communication process itself should seek to obtain a basis of common experience by sharing information between teachers and supervisors.

PROPOSITION 16: *Communication will be more effective if the message from the sender indicates compatibility and common basis of interest with problems confronting the receivers.*

While the supervisor often obtains directions for desired instructional improvement from the administration or from the community, he must begin with the interests of the teachers. To be viewed as service and resource personnel, individuals engaged in ISB must communicate with teachers regarding problems to be confronted by them within their spheres of influence. Communication stemming from central office plans or public pressures is unlikely to develop ISB unless it meets the other criteria. The supervisor who induces ideas through teacher participation and suggestion, rather than through a direct introduction by some member of the upper power structure, will more likely gain acceptance of those ideas so that change can be initiated.

PROPOSITION 17: *Communication will be more effective if the message is perceived by the receiver as within acceptable limits of possibility and/or the distance from his own opinion is not considered excessive.*

The supervisor must be able to build communication on the basis of existing views of the staff. He must deal with teachers of varied background, experience, motivation and insight in terms they can accept. Innovative ideas or suggestions for creative change beyond the limits of the staff will not be communicated and may lead to confusion, frustration and fear of supervision.

Any attempt to change opinion toward a distant state of operations from that currently in effect should be approached through communication techniques that function on the basis of successive approximations toward the state sought. A too rapid progress toward a very different operational or behavioral framework may cause resistance on the part of teachers, whereas a steady progression through discussion is more likely to be acceptable.

PROPOSITION 18: *Communication will be more effective if the style and techniques selected by the sender are consistent with the expectations of the receivers.*

109

The supervisor must be able to adapt his manner of communication to his audience. This is complicated by the range that extends from beginning staff to seasoned veterans, from modest preparation of an earlier day to recent study that exceeds in both content and extent that of the supervisor himself. The operation of ISB may depend upon the facility with which the supervisor is able to recognize the nature of a particular audience and to adapt his communication style and/or technique.

PROPOSITION 19: *Communication will be more effective if the sender takes into account social and educational similarities and differences between himself and his receivers, as well as those among his receivers.*

The development of skills that can assist teachers with many differences in social factors and in preparation to communicate with the supervisor and with each other is perhaps the hallmark of ISB. The supervisor who is able to remove barriers between himself and the teachers whom he serves is far more likely to influence them. His achievement will be enhanced to the degree that he can eliminate isolation and move toward cooperative activities with teachers as groups.

Such ethnic and educational differences may require a qualified supervisor from outside the social situation who can assist the inservice development of the teacher, special provisions to develop leadership personnel from within the situation who are cognizant of the needs to be met through ISB and/or perhaps the establishment of teams that accentuate the strengths and minimize the limitations of the other options.

In any case, it is equally important that those responsible for ISB recognize not only the similarities and the differences between the supervisor and the teachers, but those among the teachers themselves as well.

PROPOSITION 20: *Communication will be more effective if the sender takes into account his own personality characteristics and those of his receivers.*

It is important that the supervisor seek acceptance from the teachers of his own personality. This may not always be possible, but ISB will be enhanced in proportion to his success in achieving such acceptance. The supervisor may do a great deal in this regard by presenting himself to the teachers as an accepting, perceptive person who desires them to share ideas rather than to be a silent audience. He should enlist the help of the teachers to pursue collectively a common goal that all can support. The supervisor will have a far better opportunity to exert influence *as one of them* than as an isolate seeking to impose his own ideas.

Evidence is clear that the nature of the supervisor as a person, as well as the characteristics of the respective teacher, may have a profound effect on communication. It follows that ISB requires an understanding on the part of the supervisor regarding the personalities of the teachers. Even more important, perhaps, is an understanding of his own personality. The supervisor also must realize the influence that personal differences exert in order that he may transmit and respond in the communication process to improve ISB.

Message Transmission Considerations

PROPOSITION 21: *Communication will be more effective if verbal messages and nonverbal cues from the sender reinforce each other.*

A supervisor must weigh the effects of nonverbal behavior. Eyes and facial expressions may communicate, unintentionally, messages at variance with those that the supervisor would have preferred. No matter what is said, if manner, gesture or appearance indicate an opposite view, the value of the communication will be considerably reduced. The danger here is that the supervisor may be completely unaware that he is sending signals at variance with each other to the teachers whom he is seeking to influence. The teachers will be particularly sensitive to lack of enthusiasm, apparently deliberate omission of crucial factors in the discussion process, or evasion of points they consider important. The supervisor must develop a sensitivity to that which he omits to say as well as to his physical facial expression, mannerisms and bodily gestures, if he wishes to utilize nonverbal communications to his greatest advantage.

PROPOSITION 22: *Communication will be more effective if the sender considers the connotative value of language to the receiver.*

The factors of semantics as well as those of positional emphasis influence the inferential meaning that a listener gains in any communication process. Ignorance of regional mannerism or usage in speech patterns may inadvertently obscure or color not only the speaker's message but also the interpretation of that message by the listener.

Since teachers in any system may come from widely diverse geographical areas, the supervisor cannot be completely aware of all possible chances for misunderstanding through misinterpretation; however, he can become particularly aware of specific connotations that might be unacceptable to the geographical area of the particular system, for it is with the group of teachers native to this system that he may encounter the greatest chance of negative reaction, since they see the "community" as "theirs" in a very personal sense.

111

PROPOSITION 23: *Communication will be more effective if the sender considers the rates and kinds of interactions that his message promotes or discourages with the receivers.*

The supervisor should have a knowledge of the kinds of communication acts in social interaction that are positive, problem-solving, questioning and negative in type. If a supervisor is to utilize communication acts to advantage, he needs to be aware of the types of elicited responses that certain techniques are likely to induce. Different lengths of communication will elicit different responses from the teachers involved. If the length of a communication is extensive it is more likely that the teacher's response will be merely a reaction, whereas if the length is short the response will more likely be an addition to the topic under discussion. Knowledge of response patterns to kind and rate of initial communication can be of great assistance to a supervisor who wishes to elicit positive contributory responses from the teachers with whom he works. A further understanding of relative rates of effectiveness is necessary if he is to take advantage of cues for the effective initiation of messages as the communication interaction progresses toward a decision.

PROPOSITION 24:   *Communication will be more effective if the sender organizes the content of his message to maximize receptiveness by the receivers.*

The supervisor will achieve more success in communicating with teachers if the content of the message is organized to elicit the most favorable reaction possible. A too early introduction of controversial ideas, without preliminary indentification with the speaker and the problem to be considered, will tend to produce a negative reaction to the position the supervisor wishes to promote.

Situational Conditions

PROPOSITION 25: *Communication will be more effective if the sender takes account of factors that tend to apply pressures for increased interaction among receivers.*

Certain pressures within groups can be utilized effectively in ISB. The tendency to move toward uniformity and movement within the social structure can be effectively harnessed by the supervisor to achieve the consensus desired. The emotional predisposition of the individual members or of the group as a whole can also exert a pressure that may facilitate or obstruct the communication process. A knowledge of these pressure factors can be of great assistance to the supervisor in facilitating goal-directed action.

The supervisor can afford to spend some time in the initial stages to promote a friendly atmosphere—not by glossing over possible hostilities but by allowing a certain amount of hostility to be expressed and re-solved. Any attempt on his part to stifle initial communication attempts will be detrimental to the free flow of ideas he is seeking to encourage. Initial friendliness is important, but not at the expense of pretending it exists when some discord is present.

PROPOSITION 26: *Communication will be more effective if the sender utilizes feedback from receivers to enhance the accuracy of the message.*

The significance of feedback should not be underestimated. Proper use of this technique strengthens the degree of reality in the communica-tion situation. It can increase the accuracy of information being generated as well as the intermember understanding through which a climate for communication can be facilitated.

A supervisor must not only continually employ techniques to en-sure feedback so that he is aware of the reception that ideas are receiving by the teachers, but also to ensure feedback to the teachers concerning the value of the ideas contributed by them. Feedback in either instance has a reinforcement value as well as a diagnostic one—the former prob-ably being the greater in importance.

PROPOSITION 27: *Communication will be more effective if the sender employs factors that increase interaction rate and reduce hostility among receivers.*

Certain factors that can facilitate an increase in the rate of com-munication, such as personal attractiveness and intimate friendship, are not always possible to ensure; however, the knowledge that members who are less aggressive, less defensive and more attentive toward the sender are more acceptable to the group can assist the supervisor in planning a course of action. Just as some characteristics facilitate ac-ceptance, so others induce hostility. One of these is the real or imagined belief that the speaker exists in a higher level of the power hierarchy than the listener. Even when such a belief exists, the supervisor who is aware of how to direct this hostility has at his disposal the means to reduce its hindrance to a minimum.

He will be more personally effective if he can minimize his appear-ance-of-authority status. Many factors can contribute to such a view; lack of dogmatic attitude, willingness to listen to suggestions, and reluc-tance to make hasty decisions are just as important as personal accepta-bility.

PROPOSITION 28: *Communication will be more effective if the sender utilizes the capabilities of mass media for appropriate message transmission to receivers.*

The advent and continued development of educational television opens up enormous opportunities for utilization of mass media in supervision. Those responsible for ISB must learn the characteristics of these media for their effectiveness with teachers. As schools expand in size and diversity of programs, supervisors may extend their range of activity and multiply their coverage through mass media communication. Perhaps he who can persuade most effectively from afar can revolutionize the time-honored personal approach through classroom visitation. Observation can easily be extended to teachers and supervisors, as can diagnosis and planning for instructional improvement.

The supervisor would do well, however, to precede such mass media approaches with a more personal, participatory one. Once the desire to change has been initiated, mass media can serve the purpose for which it is suited. Few individuals can accomplish through mass media that which a less knowledgeable person can accomplish more adequately and congenially in a more intimate situation. Because of this, the role of media should be a supportive rather than a replacement one.

ENDNOTES

1. Robert E. Shafer, "The Communication Revolution and Learning," in *Learning More About Learning*, ed. Alexander Frazier (Washington, D.C.: Association for Supervision and Curriculum Development, 1959), p. 54.
2. Ira J. Gordon, "New Conceptions of Children's Learning and Development," in *Learning and Mental Health in the School*, 1966 Yearbook, ed. Walter B. Waetjen and Robert R. Leeper (Washington, D.C.: Association for Supervision and Curriculum Development, 1966), p. 68.
3. Robert S. Weiss, "A Structure-Function Approach to Organization," *The Journal of Social Issues* 12, no. 2, p. 64.
4. Warren Weaver, "The Mathematics of Communication," in *Communication and Culture*, ed. Alfred G. Smith (New York: Holt, Rinehart and Winston, 1966), pp. 15–16.
5. Earl C. Kelley and Marie I. Rasey, *Education and the Nature of Man* (New York: Harper and Brothers, 1952), p. 78.
6. Earl C. Kelley, *Education for What Is Real* (New York: Harper and Brothers, 1947), p. 25.
7. *Ibid.*, pp. 54–55.
8. *Ibid.*, pp. 55–56.
9. Kelley and Rasey, *op. cit.*, p. 83.

10. Philip B. Applewhite, *Organizational Behavior* (Englewood Cliffs, N. J.: Prentice-Hall, Inc., 1956), p. 100.
11. Alex Bavelas, "Communication Patterns in Task-Oriented Groups," *Journal of Acoustical Society of America* 22 (1950), pp. 725–730.
12. Marvin E. Shaw, "A Comparison of Two Types of Leadership in Various Communication Nets," *Journal of Abnormal and Social Psychology* (1955) 50, pp. 127–134.
13. Kimball Young, *Social Psychology*, 3rd. Ed. (New York: Appleton-Century-Crofts, 1956), p. 230.
14. Harold J. Leavitt, "Some Effects of Certain Communication Patterns on Group Performance," *Journal of Abnormal and Social Psychology* 46 (1951), pp. 38–50.
15. Harold Guetzkow and Herbert A. Simon, "The Impact of Certain Communication Nets Upon Organization and Performance in Task-Oriented Groups," *Management Science* 1 (1955), pp. 233–250.
16. Applewhite, *op. cit.*, p. 101.
17. S. C. Goldberg, "Influence and Leadership as a Function of Group Structure," *Journal of Abnormal and Social Psychology* 51 (1955), pp. 119–122.
18. Roger Brown, *Social Psychology* (New York: Free Press, 1965), p. 681.
19. Leavitt, *op. cit.*, pp. 38–50.
20. Leonard Berkowitz, "Personality and Group Position," *Sociometry* 19 (1956), pp. 210–222.
21. Edward C. Glanz and Robert W. Hayes, *Groups in Guidance* (Boston: Allyn and Bacon, Inc., 1967), p. 90.
22. Everett W. Bovard, Jr., "Group Structure and Perception," in *Group Dynamics: Research and Theory*, ed. Dorwin Cartwright and Alvin Zander (Evanston, Ill.: Row, Peterson and Co., 1956), p. 184.
23. Harold J. Leavitt, "Applied Organizational Change in Industry: Structural, Technological and Humanistic Approaches," in *Handbook of Organizations*, ed. James G. March (Chicago: Rand McNally, 1965), p. 1162.
24. Harold Guetzkow, "Communications in Organizations," in *Handbook of Organizations*, ed. March, p. 541.
25. David K. Berlo, *The Process of Communication* (New York: Holt, Rinehart and Winston, 1960), p. 157.
26. Leavitt, "Some Effects . . . ," p. 50.
27. Joseph E. McGrath and Irwin Altman, *Small Group Research: A Synthesis and Critique of the Field* (New York: Holt, Rinehart and Winston, 1966), p. 118.
28. H. A. Burdick, Rolf Von Ekartsberg, and Ono Hiroshi, "Two Experiments in Social Power," in *Dimensions of Social Psychology*, ed. W. E. Vinacke, W. R. Wilson, and G. M. Meredith (Chicago: Scott, Foresman and Co., 1964), pp. 342–346.
29. John Thibaut, "An Experimental Study of the Cohesiveness of Underprivileged Groups," in Cartwright and Zander, *Group Dynamics: Research and Theory*, p. 117.

30. Applewhite, *op. cit.*, p. 93.
31. Glanz and Hayes, *op. cit.*, p. 90.
32. James C. Worthy, "Organizational Structure and Employee Morale," *American Sociological Review* 15 (1950), p. 174.
33. Chris Argyris, "The Individual and Organization: Some Problems of Mutual Adjustment," *Administration Science Quarterly* 2 (1957), pp. 22–23.
34. Applewhite, *op. cit.*, p. 94.
35. N. R. F. Maier, L. Richard Hoffman, and William H. Read, "Superior-Subordinate Communication: The Relative Effectiveness of Managers Who Held Their Subordinates' Positions," *Personnel Psychology* 26 (Spring 1963), pp. 1–11.
36. Phillip K. Tompkins, "Organizational Communication: A State-of-the-Art Review," in *Conference on Organizational Communications*, ed. Gary M. Richetto (Washington, D.C.: N.A.S.A., 1967), pp. 12–13.
37. Glen D. Mellinger, "Interpersonal Trust as a Factor in Communication," *Journal of Abnormal and Social Psychology* 52 (1956), p. 304.
38. William H. Read, "Upward Communication in Industrial Hierarchies," *Human Relations* 15 (1962), p. 3.
39. *Ibid.*, p. 4.
40. *Ibid.*, p. 13.
41. Mellinger, *op. cit.*, p. 304.
42. Arthur R. Cohen, "Upward Communication in Experimentally Created Hierarchies," *Human Relations* 4 (1951), p. 40.
43. Harold Kelley, "Communication in Experimentally Created Hierarchies," *Human Relations* 4 (1951), p. 40.
44. *Ibid.*, p. 48.
45. Cohen, *op. cit.*, p. 40.
46. Applewhite, *op. cit.*, p. 96.
47. Jacob Hurwitz, Alvin F. Zander, and Bernard Hymovitch, "Some Effects of Power on the Relations Among Group Members," in Cartwright and Zander, *Group Dynamics: Research and Theory*, p. 491.
48. H. Kelley, *op. cit.*, pp. 55–56.
49. *Ibid.*
50. Tompkins, *op. cit.*, p. 6.
51. *Ibid.*, p. 7.
52. Peter M. Blau and W. Richard Scott, *Formal Organization* (San Francisco: Chandler Publishing Co., 1962), pp. 134–135.
53. Guetzkow, *op. cit.*, p. 541.
54. H. A. Simon, D. W. Smithburg, and V. A. Thompson, *Public Administration* (New York: Knopf Publishers, 1950), p. 131.
55. Theodore M. Newcomb, "The Study of Consensus," *Sociology Today*, ed. R. Merton *et al.* (New York: Basic Books, 1959), p. 106.
56. Jon Eisenson, J. Jeffrey Auer, and John V. Irwin, *Psychology of Communication* (New York: Appleton-Century-Crofts, 1963), p. 290.
57. Bernard Berelson and Gary A. Steiner, *Human Behavior: An Inventory of Scientific Findings* (New York: Harcourt, Brace and World, 1964), p. 539.

58. Eisenson, Auer, and Irwin, *op. cit.*, p. 290.
59. *Ibid.*
60. Berelson and Steiner, *op. cit.*, p. 542.
61. Leon Festinger and John Thibaut, "Interpersonal Communication in Small Groups," *Journal of Abnormal and Social Psychology* 46 (1951), pp. 92–99.
62. Young, *op. cit.*, p. 229.
63. Eisenson, Auer, and Irwin, *op. cit.*, p. 290.
64. Berelson and Steiner, *op. cit.*, p. 538.
65. R. E. Bales, F. L. Strodtbeck, T. M. Mills, and Mary Roseborough, "Channels of Communication in Small Groups," *American Sociological Review* 16 (1951), pp. 461–468.
66. F. F. Stephan and E. G. Mishler, "The Distribution of Participation in Small Groups: An Exponential Approximation," *American Sociological Review* 17 (1952), pp. 598–608.
67. George Castore, "Numbers of Verbal Interrelationships as a Determinant of Group Size," *Journal of Abnormal and Social Psychology* 64 (1962), pp. 456–458.
68. R. Rath and S. K. Misra, "Change of Attitudes as a Function of Size and Discussion Groups," *The Journal of Social Psychology* 59 (1963), p. 256.
69. Kurt Lewin, "Group Decision and Social Change," in *Readings in Social Psychology*, ed. Eleanore E. Maccoby, Theodore M. Newcomb, and Eugene L. Hartley (New York: Holt, Rinehart and Winston, 1958), p. 202.
70. D. F. Pennington, Jr., Francois Haravey, and Bernard M. Bass, "Some Effects of Decision and Discussion and Coalescence, Change, and Effectiveness," *Journal of Applied Psychology* 42 (1958), p. 407.
71. Jacob Levine and John Butler, "Lecture Versus Group Decision in Changing Behavior," *Journal of Applied Psychology* 36 (1952), p. 32.
72. Lois C. Lawrence and Patricia C. Smith, "Group Decision and Employee Participation," *Journal of Applied Psychology* 39 (1955), p. 336.
73. Lester Coch and John R. French, Jr., "Overcoming Resistance to Change," *Human Relations* 1 (1948), pp. 512–532.
74. Nancy C. Morse and Everett Reimer, "The Experimental Change of a Major Organizational Variable," *Journal of Abnormal and Social Psychology* 52 (1956), p. 120.
75. Norman R. F. Maier, "The Quality of Group Decision as Influenced by the Discussion Leader," *Human Relations* 3 (1950), p. 156.
76. Joseph T. Klapper, "What We Know About Effects of Mass Communication: The Brink of Hope," *The Public Opinion Quarterly* 21 (1957-1958), pp. 453–474.
77. Eisenson, Auer and Irwin, *op. cit.*, p. 283.
78. Berelson and Steiner, *op. cit.*, p. 543.
79. Morton Deutsch and Robert M. Krauss, *Theories in Social Psychology* (New York: Basic Books, 1965), p. 35.
80. Berelson and Steiner, *op. cit.*, p. 532.
81. Erick Barnouw, *Mass Communication: TV, Radio, Film, Press; The Media and Their Practice in the United States of America* (New York: Rinehart, 1956), p. 94.

82. Berelson and Steiner, *op. cit.*, p. 531.
83. *Ibid.*, p. 543.
84. May Brodbeck, "The Role of Small Groups in Mediating the Effects of Propaganda," *Journal of Abnormal and Social Psychology* 52 (1956), p. 170.
85. Elihu Katz, "Communication Research and the Image of Society: Convergence of Two Traditions," *American Journal of Sociology* 65 (1959), pp. 439–440.
86. Stanley Schachter and Harvey Burdick, "A Field Experiment on Rumor Transmission and Distortion," *Journal of Abnormal and Social Psychology* 50 (1955), pp. 370–371.
87. Lee Thayer, "Communication and Organization Theory," in *Human Communication Theory*, ed. Frank E. X. Dance (New York: Holt, Rinehart and Winston, 1967), p. 98.
88. *Ibid.*, p. 96.
89. Karl W. Deutsch and Leroy N. Rieselbach, "Recent Trends in Political Theory and Political Philosophy," *The Annals* of American Academy of Political and Social Science 360 (July 1965), pp. 150–153.
90. Eisenson, Auer, and Irwin, *op. cit.*, pp. 139–140.
91. Brodbeck, *op. cit.*, p. 166.
92. Eisenson, Auer and Irwin, *op. cit.*, p. 291.
93. Berelson and Steiner, *op. cit.*, p. 529.
94. *Ibid.*, pp. 540–541.
95. R. L. Schanck and Charles Goodman, "Reactions to Propaganda on Both Sides of a Controversial Issue," *Public Opinion Quarterly* 3 (1939), pp. 107–112.
96. Berelson and Steiner, *op. cit.*, p. 536.
97. *Ibid.*, p. 538.
98. Jack M. McLeod, "The Contribution of Psychology to Human Communication Theory," in *Human Communication Theory*, ed. Frank E. X. Dance (New York: Holt, Rinehart and Winston, 1967), p. 211.
99. Jane Allyn and Leon Festinger, "The Effectiveness of Unanticipated Persuasive Communications," *Journal of Abnormal and Social Psychology* 62 (1961), p. 35.
100. McLeod, *op. cit.*, p. 213.
101. Mellinger, *op. cit.*, p. 304.
102. C. I. Hovland, O. J. Harvey, and Muzafer Sherif, "Assimilation and Contrast Effects in Reactions of Communication and Attitude Change," *Journal of Abnormal and Social Psychology* 55 (1957), pp. 251–252.
103. McGrath and Altman, *op. cit.*, p. 120.
104. L. S. Harms, "Listener Judgments of Status Cues in Speech," *Quarterly Journal of Speech* 48 (1961), pp. 164–168.
105. Berlo, *op. cit.*, p. 156.
106. Berelson and Steiner, *op. cit.*, p. 537.
107. C. I. Hovland and Wallace Mandell, "An Experimental Comparison of Conclusion-Drawing by the Communicator and by the Audience," *Journal of Abnormal and Social Psychology* 47 (1952), pp. 581–588.
108. Charles A. Kiesler and Sara B. Kiesler, "Role of Forewarning in Per-

suasive Communications," *Journal of Abnormal and Social Psychology* 68 (1964), p. 549.

109. Allyn and Festinger, *op. cit.*, p. 40.
110. Bernard J. Fine, "Conclusion-Drawing, Communicator Credibility, and Anxiety as Factors in Opinion Change," *Journal of Abnormal and Social Psychology* 54 (1957), p. 374.
111. Berelson and Steiner, *op. cit.*, p. 543.
112. F. H. Lund, "The Psychology of Belief," *Journal of Abnormal and Social Psychology* 20 (1925), pp. 63–112, 117–224.
113. Berelson and Steiner, *op. cit.*, p. 533.
114. *Ibid.*, p. 548.
115. McGrath and Altman, *op. cit.*, pp. 109–115.
116. Eisenson, Auer, and Irwin, *op. cit.*, p. 288.
117. *Ibid.*, p. 291.
118. Leonard Schatzman and Anselm Strauss, "Social Class and Modes of Communication," *American Journal of Sociology* 60 (1955), pp. 329–338.
119. Klapper, *op. cit.*, pp. 453–474.
120. Young, *op. cit.*, p. 229.
121. McGrath and Altman, *op. cit.*, p. 120.
122. R. H. Simpson, "A Study of Those Who Influence and of Those Who Are Influenced in Discussion" (New York: Teachers College Bureau of Publications, 1938), p. 87.
123. Berelson and Steiner, *op. cit.*, p. 533.
124. Katz, *op. cit.*, pp. 439–440.
125. McGrath and Altman, *op. cit.*, p. 115.
126. Berelson and Steiner, *op. cit.*, p. 533.
127. Morton Deutsch, "The Effects of Cooperation and Competition upon Group Process," in *Group Dynamics: Research and Theory*, eds. Dorwin Cartwright and Alvin Zander (Evanston, Ill.: Row, Peterson and Co., 1953), pp. 414–448.
128. *Ibid.*
129. Eisenson, Auer, and Irwin, *Psychology of Communication*, pp. 237–242.
130. *Ibid.*
131. Deutsch and Rieselbach, *op. cit.*, p. 49.
132. Berelson and Steiner, *op. cit.*, p. 541.
133. C. H. Marple, "The Comparative Susceptibility of Three Age Levels to the Suggestion of Group Versus Expert Opinion," *Journal of Social Psychology* 4 (1933), pp. 176–186.
134. George Gerbner, "Mass Media and Human Communication Theory," in *Human Communication Theory*, ed. Dance, p. 43.
135. *Ibid.*, p. 42.
136. Deutsch and Rieselbach, *op. cit.*, p. 152.
137. John R. Kirk and George D. Talbot, "The Distortion of Information," in *Communication and Culture*, ed. Smith, pp. 308–321.
138. Thayer, *op. cit.*, p. 96.
139. B. Wholf, "Science and Linguistics," *Technology Review* 44 (1940), pp. 229–248.
140. Joost A. M. Meerlo, "Contributions of Psychiatry to the Study of Human

Communication," in *Human Communication Theory*, ed. Dance, p. 152.

141. Tompkins, *op. cit.*, p. 8.

142. Robert E. Pittenger and Henry Lee Smith, Jr., "A Basis for Some Contributions of Linguistics to Psychiatry," in *Communication and Culture*, ed. Smith, p. 170.

143. Leavitt, "Some Effects . . . ," *Journal of Abnormal and Social Psychology* (1951), pp. 38–50.

144. Joel R. Davitz and Lois Davitz, "The Communication of Feelings by Content-Free Speech," *Journal of Communication* 9 (1959a), pp. 6–13.

145. John A. Starkweather, "Content-Free Speech as a Source of Information About the Speaker," in *Communication and Culture*, ed. Smith, p. 189.

146. Meerlo, *op. cit.*, p. 156.

147. Joel R. Davitz, *The Communication of Emotional Meaning* (New York: McGraw-Hill, 1964).

148. David Efron, *Gesture and Environment* (New York: Kings Crown Press, 1941).

149. Charles Galloway, "Teacher Non-Verbal Communication," *Educational Leadership* 24 (1966), pp. 55–63.

150. Edward T. Hall, *The Silent Language* (New York: Doubleday and Co., 1959).

151. Jurgan Ruesch and Weldon Kees, *Nonverbal Communication* (Berkeley: University of California Press, 1956).

152. David Krech and R. S. Crutchfield, *Elements of Psychology* (New York: Knopf, 1958), p. 261.

153. Pittenger and Smith, *op. cit.*, p. 181.

154. Eisenson, Auer, and Irwin, *op. cit.*, pp. 283–305.

155. Joel R. Davitz, "The Communication of Emotional Meaning," in *Communication and Culture*, ed. Smith, pp. 477–478.

156. Pittenger and Smith, *op. cit.*, pp. 177–179.

157. A. Paul Hare, "The Dimensions of Social Interaction," in *Communication and Culture*, ed. Smith, p. 93.

158. Robert F. Bales, "How People Interact in Conferences," in *Communication and Culture*, ed. Smith, p. 99.

159. *Ibid.*, p. 96.

160. *Ibid.*, p. 101.

161. Eisenson, Auer, and Irwin, *op. cit.*, pp. 299–304.

162. *Ibid.*, pp. 250–251.

163. Bales, *op. cit.*, p. 99.

164. Irving Janis and Seymour Feshbeck, "Effects of Fear-Arousing Communications," *Journal of Abnormal and Social Psychology* 48 (1953), pp. 91–92.

165. Berelson and Steiner, *op. cit.*, pp. 551–553.

166. C. I. Hovland, A. A. Lumsdaine, and F. D. Sheffield, *Experiments on Mass Communication* (Princeton, N.J.: Princeton University Press, 1949), pp. 201–227.

167. Eisenson, Auer, and Irwin, *op. cit.*, p. 288.

168. W. S. McGuire, "Order of Presentation as a Factor in 'Conditioning' Per-

suasiveness," *The Order of Presentation in Persuasion,* ed. C. I. Hovland *et al.* (New Haven, Conn.: Yale University Press, 1957).

169. Eisenson, Auer, and Irwin, *op. cit.,* pp. 299–305.

170. Fine, *op. cit.,* p. 374.

171. Berlo, *op. cit.,* p. 248.

172. Stanley Schachter, "Deviation, Rejection, and Communication," *Journal of Abnormal and Social Psychology* 46 (1951), pp. 190–207.

173. Leon Festinger, "Informal Social Communication," *Psychological Review* 57 (1950), pp. 271–282.

174. Robert E. Lana, "Familiarity and the Order of Presentation of Persuasive Communications," *Journal of Abnormal and Social Psychology* 62 (1961), pp. 573–577.

175. Harold J. Leavitt and Ronald A. H. Mueller, "Some Effects of Feedback on Communication," in *Communication and Culture,* ed. Smith, pp. 352–353.

176. A. Paul Hare, *Handbook of Small Group Research* (New York: Free Press, 1962), p. 268.

177. Seymour Rosenberg and Robert L. Hall, "The Effects of Different Social Feedback Conditions Upon Performance in Dyaoic Teams," *Journal of Abnormal and Social Psychology* 57 (1958), pp. 271–277.

178. McGrath and Altman, *op. cit.,* p. 61.

179. *Ibid.,* p. 120.

180. Harold Guetzkow, *op. cit.,* p. 536.

181. Festinger, *op. cit.,* pp. 271–282.

182. Harold J. Leavitt, "Applied Organizational Change . . . ," p. 1162.

183. John W. Thibaut and John Coules, "The Role of Communication in the Reduction of Interpersonal Hostility," *Journal of Abnormal and Social Psychology* 47 (1952), pp. 770–777.

184. Jay M. Jackson, "Reference Group Processes in a Formal Organization," *Sociometry* 22 (1959), pp. 307–322.

185. Guetzkow, *op. cit.,* p. 540.

186. Bernard Berelson, "Communication and Public Opinion," in *Reader in Public Opinion and Communication,* ed. Bernard Berelson and Morris Janowitz (New York: The Free Press, 1950), pp. 448–462.

187. Elaine Walsten and Leon Festinger, "The Effectiveness of 'Overheard' Persuasive Communications," *Journal of Abnormal and Social Psychology* 65 (1962), pp. 395–402.

188. Katz, *op. cit.,* pp. 439–440.

189. Daniel Lerner, "Communication Systems and Social Systems: A Statistical Exploration in History and Policy," in *Communication and Culture,* ed. Smith, pp. 563–564.

190. Dorwin Cartwright, "Some Principles of Mass Persuasion," *Human Relations* 2 (1949), pp. 253–267.

Chapter 6

Organization Theory: Implications for Instructional Supervisory Behavior

Organizations are plentiful in this society. They are contrived designs and arrangements that reflect practical intelligence. Organizations may be uncomplicated or very complex systems. They are attempts to manage and satisfy the needs of the larger society that produced them. Seemingly the determination of man to survive, to create and to assist in ordering human existence gives rise to organizational structures.

Although organizations are usually conceived in terms of social needs and as mechanisms to advance human conditions, they may actually produce stricture rather than structure, and demean rather than advance humanity. It would appear that many organizations in the American cultural system have pushed a concept of effectiveness to the detriment of humanization and social consciousness. This may be a necessary risk if society is to reach the level of technical efficiency needed for all to share the good life. A momentary pause, however, is enough to verify the extant and growing dissatisfaction over the complex ordering of institutions, organizations, systems and subsystems that confront individuals as they try to harmonize their personal needs and aspirations within and through an organizational society.[1] Unless organizations reconstruct their performance in light of intended goals and the needs of their constituents, they are faced with the promise of change from without, of new structures designed to respond to the needs of the people. It is doubtful that continued support will be provided for organizations emphasizing efficiency or the profit motive as their primary incentives.

The study of organizations is a rather new discipline. There already exists, however, a substantial amount of written commentary and a constantly expanding body of research reports. There is a continuing effort to shape concepts and theoretical constructs as tools in the study of organizations.

This state of things does not diminish the significance of the discipline. The analysis of organizations will become an increasingly critical area of study as social scientists attempt to construct a foundation for organizational behavior that promotes a society based on human rationality. Introducing a statement on the requirements for a science of organizations, Hills has written:

> Although there has been a vast amount of research done in organizations, and about organizations, there has been little study of *organization* as such. We study leadership, morale, decision-making, communication, bureaucracy, and role conflict, but not organization. More frequently than not, a particular role, e.g., that of superintendent of schools, has been studied in isolation. It is as though the chemist selected a single element of a compound for examination and never got around to investigating how that element interacted with other elements *to form the compound.* In the field of educational organization and administration we have had innumerable studies of the roles of superintendent, principal, teacher, trustee, etc., but we know very little about *organization.* We cannot even say, in any precise way, what there is about an educational organization that makes it different from a business firm.[2]

There are a number of reasons why the study of organizational theory is important to the educational supervisor. First, there is great confusion about the role of the supervisor in education. Although numerous role studies have been made, little emphasis has been given to the study of the supervisory role in terms of the formal organization of the school. Second, the school is a critical part of the network of institutions and organizations that pervade society. In its potential for societal growth the school may be the most critical of social organizations. And third, formal educational organizations are now being carefully assessed in terms of their goals, structure, and effectiveness. The school was once aloof from such scrutiny, a result of public indifferences or traditional privilege. Today the public school is not so sacred, for through importance and organizational complexity it is competing for needed attention and support. In some instances alternatives to public education are being created. These areas are significant concerns for supervisors.

When educational supervisors behave so as to provide leadership, to improve communication, or to initiate change, they do so within the organization of the school or school system. It is critical, therefore, that proposals and hypotheses about effective supervisory behavior be developed in light of existing knowledge, research, and theory on organizations. This chapter offers a rudimentary introduction to a critical and rapidly developing field of study.

Areas to be considered are: the relationship of organizations to the social institution; an interpretation of organization; organizational goals; authority in organizations; formal and informal relationships, and organizational analysis. It should be noted that many of the ideas presented are of an interpretive nature, as opposed to prescriptions derived from research.

ORGANIZATIONS IN SOCIAL CONTEXT

This section attempts to clarify the relationship between society as the overarching social system, and the institutions and organizational forms derived from society. This interpretation suggests that the interrelationship of these elements is critical and that change in society pressures organizations to continually review their purpose and structure.

Organizations are products of society. They are significant parts of the culture created by men. They are means of accommodating human needs while transmitting the values of the past.

If a society is to promote the common good, it must create and be served by units of control, production, and maintenance. Such conditions cause people to sense the support of structure while providing the means for growth and change. People tend to strive for the equilibrium provided by these arrangements.

The structures created to provide society with balance and direction are its institutions. These are broadly conceived systems that evolve out of the heritage and values of a nation. They represent deeply ingrained ideas.[3, 4] Government, formalized religions, businesses and educational institutions serve as illustrations. Institutions are represented by the complex organizations established to apply and pass on the accepted way of living and behaving. Culver has written:

> It is important to note this distinction between the institution, which is an abstract nucleus of values centering around some segment of human life, and the specific organizations and groups through which institutions are actually expressed.[5]

Institution, as an abstract term, represents the patterns of belief and value that are shared by members of a society. The form of institutions, of their nature, represents the ideas to which society is committed. In American society this patterned description is challenged by the stress of cultural pluralism. The conflict of ideas, coupled with the search for individual and group identity, sets a dynamism in motion that is both a problem and a source of strength.[6,7] In periods of ferment, institutional and organizational forms must constantly probe their traditions and relationship to the larger social system.[8]

The values and institutions of this nation were formulated out of dissent. This nation has known dissenters, but has been capable in searching their messages for fallacy and vision. This discernment is the task of leadership, for it is in ordering the process of social change—as a means of elaborating and refining our values—that makes up the challenge of our existence.

Institutions, however, seldom undergo dramatic changes in a short time span.* The apparently unchanging face of social values and institutions suggests a design set in motion with great calculation. Social forces tend to cause a hard institutional core, a rigidity, as a defense against conflicting ideas. The emergence of new arrangements within the core of social values happens grudgingly. Tradition has created social institutions within a firmly established code or set of perspectives. Change, when it does occur, will be found expressed in the organizations that reflect the institutions at large. As institutional commitments change, organizational goals, structures, and procedures are vulnerable and subject to pressures for change.

In more practical terms the relationship between the cultural order and organizational productivity is very real. Dubin states that:

> The anthropological viewpoint gives heavy emphasis to cultural determinism of working and productive behaviors by its attention to 1) the kinds of pursuits that engage human energies for the production of goods and services, and 2) the particular working behaviors that produce the goods and services. Working behaviors in a society are determined by the culture which characterizes that society.[9]

In proceeding with his discussion of culture and organizational productivity Dubin emphasizes the importance of viewing organizational efficiency *inside* a system rather than among national systems.[10] In relation to supervisory practice he suggests that cultural relativity cautions us against the generalization of "one best supervisory structure." [11] Extending this thinking about the cultural impact upon organizational structure and supervisory performance, reference can be made to Woodward's study,[12] which analyzed the relationship between the technological system of the organization and its management components. Woodward determined that the production technology of the organization was a

---

* Daniel Bell, writing in *Daedalus*, states: "The problem of any science is to understand the sources of change. And in this respect social science is fairly recent. The great intellectual barrier was that men always thought they knew the sources of change, which were also the sources of power, namely the personal will of kings, lawgivers, and prophets, those who governed states, drafted laws, and established or reinforced religious beliefs. But only gradually did men realize that behind these visible sets of acts were such intangible nets as customs, institutions, and cultures, which subtly constrained and set the boundaries of social action. At the same time came the slow realization that there were 'social forces' which generated change, whether they be impersonal processes such as demographic pressures, technology, and science, or conscious striving such as the demands of disadvantaged groups for equality or social mobility."

determinant of managerial (supervisory) structure. Hence, the nature of an organization's management system will be determined by both the larger sociocultural system and the organizations production technology.*

The preceding statement was intended to indicate the background, the interchange of history with the present and the idea of overarching social systems that generate the social and institutional pressure that groups and individuals seek to balance and reconcile. This struggle perhaps becomes most intense as individuals operate as members of formal organizations.

ORGANIZATIONS DEFINED

This section offers interpretations of the concept of formal organizations. Reference is made to various definitions provided by students of organization over a wide span of time. The dynamic nature and characteristics of formal organizations are also cited.

Society is replete with schemes for getting things done. Such is the essence of the concept of organization. It implies that purpose is more efficiently attained when energy is directed in a meaningful, goal-oriented way. Many people admit to the presence and power of organizations within society. Our society has been interpreted by Presthus [13] as an *Organizational Society*. Social critics such as Mills [14] have made pointed observations and offered purposeful commentaries on the nature of man's attempts to control his existence through formal organizations.

Many scholars have considered the concept of organization.† Talcott Parsons wrote the following:

> An organization is a system which, as the attainment of its goal 'produces' an identifiable something which can be utilized in some way by another system; that is, the output of the organization is, for some other system, an input. In the case of an organization with economic primacy, this output may be a class of goods or services which are either

* See Chapter 1 for a discussion of Dubin's position and Woodward's research as they relate to the nature of supervision.

† James G. March, ed., *Handbook of Organizations* (Chicago: Rand McNally & Co., 1965), p. ix. "The study of organizations has a history but not a pedigree. This distinction is simple. A pedigree suggests a series of casually connected events in time; history (in the present sense, at least) consists in a temporal ordering of events. The names associated with interest in the problems and phenomena of organizations are impressive. There is scarcely a major philosopher, historian, or biographer who has overlooked the management and perversities of organizations. The church, the army, and the state had to be managed. Aristotle, ibn-Khaldun, Thucydides, Caesar, Marsilius, Aquinas, and Bentham, were not reluctant to solve such problems in the course of determining the ultimate destiny and primordial nature of man."

consumable or serve as instruments for a further phase of the production process by other organizations. In the case of a government agency the output may be a class of regulatory decisions; in that of an educational organization it may be a certain type of 'trained capacity' on the part of the students who have been subjected to its influence.[15]

Barnard [16] emphasized the organization as a system of cooperation: "A cooperative system is a complex of physical, biological, personal, and social components which are in a specific systematic relationship by reason of the cooperation of two or more persons for at least one definite end." Gaus [17] defines organization as "the arrangement of personnel for facilitating the accomplishment of some agreed purpose through the allocation of functions and responsibilities."

More recently, Etzioni* offered this statement:

Organizations are social units (or human groupings) deliberately constructed and reconstructed to seek specific goals. Corporations, armies, schools, hospitals, churches, and prisons are included; tribes, classes, ethnic groups, friendship groups, and families are excluded. Organizations are characterized by: a) divisions of labor, power, and communication responsibilities, divisions which are not random or traditionally patterned, but deliberately planned to enhance the realization of specific goals; b) the presence of one or more power centers which control the concerted efforts of the organization and direct them toward its goals; these power centers also must review continuously the organization's performance and re-pattern its structure, where necessary, to increase its efficiency; c) substitution of personnel, i.e., unsatisfactory persons can be removed and others assigned their tasks. The organization can also recombine its personnel through transfer and promotion.[18]

Etzioni's exclusion of classes, ethnic groups, friendship groups and the like from his interpretation of organizations is based upon the limited extent to which these social units are "consciously planned, deliberately structured and restructured, with a membership which is routinely changed." Hence, he sees formal organizations as being more in conscious control of their nature and destiny.

It is within the formal organization, the "consciously coordinated activity toward identified goals," that the individual behaves and contributes to the larger social system.[19] An organization is also a context for attaining the personal support and gratification that help make work worthwhile and comprehensible. It is the intent of formal organization to bring together knowledge and skills in addition to the needed arrangements, equipment, and technologies that will enable the organization to

* Amitai Etzioni, *Modern Organizations*, p. 3. In this section Etzioni refers to Talcott Parsons, *Structure and Process in Modern Societies* (Glencoe, Ill.: The Free Press, 1960), p. 17. Etzioni notes: "Some minimal amount of such construction and reconstruction will be found in all social units, but it is much higher in organizations."

accomplish its purpose. Beyond knowledge, skill, and contrived supports, the organization must encourage emotional or psychological commitment. This requires more than the mere ritual of behavior compliance from workers, be they professional or mass production workers. An ideal state for an organization would express the blending of purpose, knowledge, skill, production requirements and emotional/psychological input. If organizational arrangements do not foster the development of these elements, then they are limiting and self-defeating.

Gross states: "In positive times, a formal organization may be regarded as a group or cooperative system, with the following characteristics:

1. An accepted pattern of purposes
2. A sense of identification or belonging
    Both the directors and the workers of a telephone company regard themselves as part of an organization. This sense of identification is heightened by the felt distinction between in-group and out-group. Despite their crucial importance to the organization, the people who merely talk on the telephone are outsiders.
3. Continuity of interaction
    The members of an organization interact with each other with some minimum degree of regularity and continuity. Members leave an organization by falling below the required minimum—as when a factory worker does not appear on the job any more or when a union member stops paying dues.
4. Differentiation of function
    The activities of members of organizations are based upon some minimum amount of formal differentiation of roles. In small organizations, this differentiation may be rudimentary. In larger organizations, it becomes elaborate.
5. Conscious integration
    The divided parts of an organization are held together not only by spontaneous cooperation but also by the conscious efforts of certain members responsible for bringing or holding them together. These, of course, are the administrators themselves, who bring people together for the formulation and achievement of an organization's purposes." [20]

These characteristics are an attempt to communicate the dynamic nature of an organization. As Gross implies, it is the role of the administration or leadership group within the organization to shape the quality of human interactions by setting conditions and gathering the resources required for the organization to attain its goals.

Applewhite [21] states that there is a difference between studies of organizations and organizational behavior. The former suggests that the total organization, its history, goals, structure, and relationship to other organizational systems can become a profitable focus of study. It is also important to study the behavior of people within an organization. Individuals and groups become the embodiment of the organization. Analysis of human activity within organizations is required if an organization is to be really understood in both a structural and qualitative sense. Both of these areas, the study of organizations as complex, goal-seeking systems, and the behavior of individuals and groups within organizations, are important areas of analysis for those interested in advancing organizational effectiveness.

ORGANIZATIONAL GOALS

This section emphasizes that organizational purpose or goals is part of the vital substance of a formal organization. Here recognition is given to the need for clearly established organizational goals, the relationship of goals to the work and structure of the organization, the evolving character of goals, and research on the relationship of organizational goals to morale and productivity.

Organizations, as already stated, are social units that pursue the attainment of specific goals.[22] The goals of an organization are the source of its activities and the reason for its existence. If an organization is to survive, it must reach the goals specified for it; the problem of goal attainment has primacy over all others.[23, 24]

In accordance with the characteristics of organizations previously cited, the process of goal fulfillment is set in motion by: a) establishing a set of offices; b) assigning responsibilities for individual tasks (parts of a division of labor); and c) creating a stable system of coordinative relationships, i.e., a structure.[25] An office is a position within the organization about which there is general agreement as to responsibilities and duties. Elements of status are assigned to an office, and hence to the person occupying the office. Elements of status include title, rank, duties, and privileges, along with concomitant support from other offices within the organization. The tasks assigned to each office become the responsibilities of whoever fills that office. In this sense, the tasks are the functional activities of the office.[26]

Formal organizations do not exist without goals*:

---

* Goals, depending upon the writer or the nature of the organization itself, may be referred to as purpose, primary objectives, tasks, functions, or mission. Gross and Grambsch have written on the primacy of organizational goals:

"In a communal relationship, persons are met for the pleasure intrinsic to the relationship itself, as in the case of a group of friends, a clique, a gang, or a family. Such a group may indeed develop goals (e.g., attacking another group, having a baby), but it does not disband if it fails to attain those goals. It breaks up only when hostilities and cleavages mean that persons are no longer at ease with one another. On the other hand, in an associational relationship, persons are met in order to pursue some goal and their meeting is a means toward that end.

We will find no organization without goals, but it is of interest to speculate on what such a social form might be like. Franz Kafka's inventions probably capture the essential elements: an organization which strives for nothing, where there is no reason for one activity to be preferred to another, except perhaps tradition. The total effect is of unbearable pointlessness.[27]

It is common to refer to an organizational goal as "a desired state of affairs which the organization attempts to realize."[28] Once realized, however, these "states" are no longer goals; they represent an accomplishment, which requires that the goals of the organization be redefined. This is because the originally defined state of things or organizational goal, once achieved, no longer serves as the end toward which energy and activity are directed. Clearly, the maintenance of the accomplished goal state can require a substantial amount of the organization's resources. At the same time, the definition of new organizational goals, or the refinements of accomplished goals, induces organizational vitality by making demands upon the capacities and creative talents of the system's human resources. New or redefined goals result from the interchange of the organization with the larger social system and the various interpretations of the participating individuals, divisions, and leadership as to the best direction or response for the organization to make the larger environment.

It is not unusual for an organization to express a disparity between its stated goals and its real goals. Although the stated goals of the organization may be those to which the membership has committed itself, there may be numerous factors that cause the stated goals to be set aside in favor of a more reasonable expectation as determined by the existing market and resources available within the organization. This is not a critical state of affairs, as long as the members of the organization realize that for the time being priorities in goals have undergone realignment— and for what reasons. When the difference between stated and real goals is not understood or planned for, the organization can suffer a serious morale problem and a lack of willingness to strive for the established goals.[29, 30]

The importance of clarity in organizational goals as a factor in the morale of the membership has been stated by Katz, Maccoby and Morse: "Morale is a condition of congruent motivation among members of a group resulting in relatively high levels of energy expenditure toward

They need not like one another or indeed have feelings any more positive than what is minimally necessary for them to work together to attain the common goals. It is the presence of such goals and the consequent organization of effort to attain them which characterize modern organizations and leads to such accomplishments as healing the sick, attacking an enemy, producing a high standard of living, incarcerating the criminal, organizing the distribution of goods or administering the affairs of an empire." (Edward Gross and Paul Grambsch, *op cit.*, p. 4.)

common goals." [31] Blum [32] defined industrial morale "as the possession of a feeling . . . of being accepted by and belonging to a group of employees through adherence to common goals and confidence in the desirability of these goals." Organizational goals, stated and real, serve to communicate the meaning and identity of the organization as well as to help clarify the individual's role within the organization as expressed in his work and productivity.

Misunderstanding about the goals of an organization prompts indecision and ambivalent reactions from the membership. This results in cautious if not misdirected organizational behavior. When goals are not made clear, or when the environment in which the organization functions does not support its stated goals, adjustment or adaption of goals is likely to occur. A number of studies have been made in this area.

Sills [33] reports on goal succession, through his work on the changing goals of voluntary organizations. One organization studied was the National Foundation for Infantile Paralysis. The Foundation, after reaching its major goal, sought to determine its future. Rather than disband, the goal structure was adjusted. This was possible due to the commitment of the membership of the organization, beyond the single goal of fighting polio.[34, 35] Other volunteer organizations have followed the same pattern.[36] They have adjusted, reinterpreted, or added new goals based upon their own internal capabilities and as a response to changing conditions within the larger cultural matrix.[37]

Clark writes on the relationship of the value system to organizational goals.[38] Reporting on an adult education program, he illustrates how the value incongruence between the organization and its clientele produces a pragmatic response, resulting in an approach that is almost entirely "other directed," thus making the goals of the adult education program precarious. The lack of defined goals legitimized by the community places the organization within a hostile environment and makes it vulnerable to the pressures, real or potential, brought to bear by the larger community.

Some authorities have seen organizational goals as linkages to the larger environment.[39] When defined in this way, members within organizations have reduced freedom in setting goals—or are challenged to persuade outsiders of the acceptability of their organization's goals.[40] Thompson and McEwen[41] viewed organizational goal-setting as a dynamic and recurring situation. They focused on the interaction of the organization with its environment. They prescribed four modes of interaction; one mode was competitive, while the other three were of a cooperative nature.

Competition (rivalry) exists when society causes the disbandment of an organization that refuses to consider social needs or fails to efficiently manage its activities. The cooperative interactions take the form of bargaining (agreement between organizations for the exchange of goals and services), cooperation (absorbing new elements into the leadership or policy-making structure) and coalition (the combination of two or more organizations for common purposes). The Thompson and McEwen analysis describes this process in organizations in terms of organization and client-system relationships, including other organizations with which there is competition or cooperation.

Etzioni points out that organizational goals, in addition to guiding or directing the work of the system, can also serve as measures of efficiency (in-put) and effectiveness (out-put). All organizational leaders are faced with the responsibility of adjusting internal structure so as to better achieve goals and thereby increase effectiveness. When goals are not clearly stated or understood, they are precarious. . . . "Moreover, goals serve as standards by which members of an organization and outsiders can assess the success of an organization—i.e., its effectiveness and efficiency."[42]

On organizational effectiveness, Argyris has written:

An organization increases in effectiveness as it obtains: a) increasing outputs with constant or decreasing inputs, b) constant outputs with decreasing inputs, and c) is able to accomplish this in such a way that it can continue to do so.

We have also said that an organization manifests three core activities: achieving its objectives, maintaining itself internally, and adapting to its external environment. If this is related to the foregoing definition, we may suggest that as an organization's effectiveness increases, it will be able *to accomplish its three core activities at a constant or increasing level of effectiveness with the same or decreasing increments of inputs of energy.*[43]

In this section the emphasis has been on the centrality of goals within organizations. The following caution should be noted:

Paradoxically, an organization must do more than give attention to goal attainment in order to attain its goals. It is noteworthy that in one attempt to state a set of conditions necessary to system survival, the categories of adaptation, integration, pattern maintenance, and tension management, as well as goal attainment, are named. A good part of any system's energies must be spent on activities that do not contribute directly to goal attainment but rather are concerned with maintaining the system itself.[44]

In other words, the efforts of the organization in working toward its goals cannot continue, the work of the organization cannot be effective, unless the ongoing demands of maintaining the organization are also satisfied.

Obviously, organizations succeed in attaining their goals through the efforts of people. Hence, when an organization's members share a sense of purpose their performance is more likely to be in accord with the goals to be attained. A study by Katz, Maccoby, and Morse [45] on productivity, supervision, and morale showed that pride in work group was the only measure of job satisfaction that evidenced a distinct relationship with productivity. High production groups showed greater pride in their work than did low production groups. It was also indicated that the supervisors of the low production groups supervised their work force more closely.

Applewhite [46] presents an overview of another study in office work productivity. This was a study done by Morse,[47] who found that those groups in the organization who were most satisfied with their jobs were not necessarily the most productive. Morse's study suggests the need to look at job satisfaction in terms of the reduction of tension level within an individual or group. The higher the tension level, the stronger the need system that is operating. The amount of job satisfaction experienced by the individual is a function of: 1) how much his needs are fulfilled by being in a particular situation, and 2) how much his needs remain unfulfilled. When tension is lowered, when needs are being met, satisfaction is likely to result. Apparently there is an interactive relationship between job satisfaction, tension or degree of need satisfaction, and worker productivity. The constitution of the correct balance of these conditions in support of the organization's work remains difficult to specify.

Likert [48] proposes an approach he identifies as "participatory management." Here organizational members share in various phases of decision-making typically reserved solely to management people. Action in this area must be more than an administrative technique, however, for leadership behavior that is inconsistent with "pronouncements" about participatory management can produce serious morale problems. The definition of organizational purpose and the effective management of its manpower are two major issues inherent in any analysis of a formal organization. To promote a clear understanding of the organization's purpose(s), philosophically and operationally, is a main function of leadership. This process of clarification will require the judicious use of the leaders' legitimate authority:

> The high ranking executives of an organization do have a special role in relation to the organization's goals. They are responsible for the development of a program, a plan of action for the organization, by which the goal may be achieved. This program should not be thought of as setting the goal in any way. Instead, it interprets it—operationalizes it—and sets the means.[49]

AUTHORITY IN ORGANIZATIONS

Organizational leaders use and conceive of authority differently. Hence, consideration is given to the sources and types of authority, power and influence, and the bureaucratic system as a mechanism for distribution of organizational power and authority.

A complex organization performs numerous tasks and exhibits varied levels of responsibility. Differentiation of tasks and levels requires decisions that help coordinate the various parts or subsystems of organizations. To spawn such coordination, they rely on the use of legitimate authority.*

The intent of using authority in organizations has been described by Cartwright:

> To give further assurance that the system will work properly, rules, regulations, and policies are promulgated as guides to the behavior of the participants. Finally, a control mechanism is established whereby the various positions are linked together by a chain of command so that the authority and responsibility of each position is unambiguous.[50]

Barnard [51] offered a distinction between the "authority of the position" and "authority of leadership." The former suggests authority based upon organizational role or office, while the latter, the authority of leadership, depends upon personal ability. The authority of leadership can be expressed by various members of a formal organization, and is not restricted to those holding formal offices. Through the expression of the leadership of authority, esteem is gained. Esteem provides a significant lever in the performance of leadership responsibilities.

Authority, and the responsibility that accompanies it, is an essential ingredient of organization. Weber's [52] work on bureaucracy, formal organization, and authority structures provided a seminal work for present scholars in many of these areas. He defined authority as "the probability that certain specific commands (or all commands) from a given source will be obeyed by a given group of persons." [53] The group will obey when the authority source is seen as legitimate (power and justification). Blau and Scott [54] make a distinction between authority and persuasion, considering persuasion the process whereby one person influences another's decisions or actions, whereas in an authority relationship the subordinate "holds in abeyance his own critical faculties for choosing between alternatives and uses the formal criterion of the receipt of a command or signal as his basis for choice." [55] Two criteria of authority are voluntary compliance with legitimate commands and suspension of judgment in advance in order to follow the directives of the superior. This results largely from the influence exerted by the organization's members or the social control (rewards/punishment) present in formally organized systems.[56]

Three major aspects of the influence process include: a) the person

---

* Etzioni, writing on bureaucracies and authority, refers to legitimization as "the power to control and ability to justify." (*Modern Organizations,* p. 50.)

exerting influence; b) the method of exerting influence; and c) the person subjected to the influence.[57] When a person exerts influence through some act of communication with another person, and when that act of communication results in some change by the person subjected to the influence, it may be said that the initiator has power.

Expressions of power and influence may be related to the properties of the person. Levinger [58] brought together previously unacquainted people. They took part in tasks that required a series of joint decisions. At the outset one subject was informed that his knowledge about the task was either superior or inferior. It was observed that those who believed they had superior knowledge expressed more assertiveness and thought they had more influence over decisions.

Cartwright,[59] and French and Raven [60] have argued the difference between "opposition to attempted influence" and "resistance resulting from an influence attempt." If, for example, a worker refuses to do an assigned task because he dislikes the assignment, his behavior is in opposition to the task. He might also refuse to comply with the assigned task because he does not think that the supervisor has the right to make such an assignment. This is resistance. When opposition to the prescriptions of a supervisor is in evidence, it may result from the nature of the task or change. Resistance tends to emanate from confusion as to the worker's perceptions concerning the legitimacy of the supervisor's authority or ability.

Authority requires the support of shared value perspectives as the basis for its legitimation. The degree of compliance accorded organizational decisions will be related to the perceived legitimacy of the decision-maker's authority. Weber [61] saw three main sources of legitimate authority. He considered legitimate authority as being based on tradition, legal enactments, or charisma. Traditional authority finds its way by cultural transmission from one generation to the next. Charismatic authority rests on the affection and dedication of the people to the qualities and person of the leader. Perceived as powerful and right, the charismatic leader will gather the devotion of those he leads. This authority rests on the leader and his continued expression of those qualities that project his image. Legal authority stands on the regulations and enactments of the group. Officials occupying positions of authority have their roles defined in order for the limits of their authority to be known. This authority is accepted as long as it reflects the prescribed limits and is accompanied by the competencies or skills required of the office.

Authority exerted by the various levels of officialdom within organizations is rational-legal authority.[62] Such authority is supported by laws or documentation that describe various roles, and the interrelationship among the levels and "offices" that comprise the organization. This dispersion of authority and responsibility is thought to be beneficial to the organization. It is, after all, only reasonable that a large, complex system define for itself the distribution and limits of control necessary to mold a collection of individuals into a cooperative, productive system. Large bureaucratic organizations are based upon rational-legal authority.

Numerous research and organizational theorists indicate that difficulty arises when authority is used for the aggrandizement of the office-holder rather than for the benefit of the organization. When this or other dysfunctions in the use of authority occur, they are reacted to strongly as illegitimate. In such circumstances, authority is rebuked or reacted against, the organization is disturbed and its services or production interrupted. The legitimacy of organizational authority, along with its consistent and appropriate application, are vital to the well-being of the system.

Power and authority held different meanings for Weber.[63] He defined power as "the probability that one actor within a social relationship will be in a position to carry out his own will despite resistance"; in authority, the response of persons to the command is voluntary. Lutz and Iannacconne offer the following interpretation of power:

> The expression social power, or the word power used alone, will have as its referent behavior directed toward influencing others whether successful or not. Social power here is conceived as more tangible, more manifest, than potential power. It is the behavior or relationship that exists between two individuals, groups, or other social entities in which one is seen producing an effect on the other.[64]

Power as an organizational mechanism has been described somewhat differently by Etzioni.[65] He posits three classifications of power: coercive, utilitarian, and identitive. Using physical force in order to control is classified as coercive power; rewards of a material or service nature are considered utilitarian power; while using symbols of prestige or esteem for control purposes is identitive power. It is suggested that identitive power generates more commitment than utilitarian, and utilitarian more than coercive.[66]

It is also suggested that organizations use various kinds of power in fostering compliance and identification among the membership. Coercive power would more than likely be the threat of physical restriction. When used, it would be directed at the lower status levels of membership; higher-working members would be rewarded, and when change in behavior is thought necessary, persuasion would be used. Warnings and persuasion are not apt to be found in exercising power among the lower levels of organizational membership.[67] The need for the exercise of authority and power within organizations is stated by Etzioni:

> Most organizations most of the time cannot rely on most of their participants to carry out their assignments voluntarily, to have internalized

their obligations. The participants need to be supervised, the supervisors themselves need supervision, and so on, all the way to the top of the organization. In this sense, the organizational structure is one of control, and the hierarchy of control is the most central element of the organizational structure.[68]

The conditions and use of power and authority within an organization purportedly make it more effective (control is organizational structure), more rational, and less subject to the detriments of internal dysfunction and external pressures. An organization must, as a first principle of its existence, survive and to do so it should operate rationally. One of the basic properties of the formal organization is its logical foundation, "or as it has been called by students of administration, its essential rationality."[69]

The bureaucratic system, as an ideal type, tends to establish relationships that legitimize authority. Bureaucracy, classically conceived, is a method of arranging an organization in order to ensure its success or to provide a design that will promote the accomplishment of purpose.[70]

The method of arranging an organization in order to ensure its success and to provide a conscious design that will promote the accomplishment of purpose was central to the work of Max Weber. According to Weber,[71] a bureaucratic system has the following characteristics:

1. Fixed and official jurisdictional areas, which are regularly ordered by rules, that is, by laws or administrative regulations.
2. Principles of hierarchy and levels of graded authority that ensure a firmly ordered system of super and subordination in which higher offices supervise lower ones.
3. Administration based upon written documents; the body of officials engaged in handling these documents and files, along with other material apparatus, make up a "bureau" or "office."
4. Administration by full-time officials who are thoroughly and expertly trained.
5. Official activity demands the full working capacity of the official.
6. Administration by general rules that are quite stable and comprehensive.

The codification of an organization's structure is often summarized in a line-staff chart. This chart attempts to portray the decisions the organization has made regarding the division of responsibility and levels of authority. Line-staff charts usually reflect an ideal, a conceptualized plan of ordering the work of the total organization and the interaction of its various subsystems. Generally, organizations attempt to clarify these relationships as a means of helping members adjust to the work of the organization.[72] Official action, the decisions of the organization, occurs within a framework of these preexisting rules and regulations. Knowledge of an organization's internal characteristics, rules, regulations, role relationships, task expectations, communication lines, and work of the various subsystems is requisite for an effective contribution to its work.

When members of an organization experience difficulties in adjusting—but when job performance skills are present—the problem may result from the lack of knowledge of internal arrangements. When an individual experiences such difficulty, his problem is frequently labeled "human relations." In many such cases, the problem may be caused by inadequate understanding and knowledge about the organization.[73] It may also indicate a dissonance between the formal design of the organization and its other reality as expressed through the informal relationships of people and offices.

The pervasiveness of the bureaucratic model is readily established by a quick look at existing events and conditions. From the various agencies of the federal government to the neighborhood school—and innumerable stops in between—bureaucracy abounds.[74] Bureaucratic concepts in organizations have had ready acceptance. They were quickly transferred because they were seen as measured attempts to use the technical dimensions of organizations as an aid to production, to reduce waste and inefficiency and, in general, to provide a more reasoned approach to the construction of a successful organization. In this sense bureaucratic structures are meant to promote the efficiency and effectiveness of organizations. In the face of such a statement the individual may reflect upon personal experience, recalling an impression that is far from efficiency and effectiveness. A columnist, writing on a teacher strike in New York City, turned for a moment to responsibility, and quoted the head of the teachers' union as refusing "to permit . . . teachers to be used as scapegoats for the failures of a system for which we are not responsible." "Who is responsible," inquired the writer, "if not the teachers, the supervisors, and the bureaucracy-logged Board of Education?" This is a small example, yet it reflects a growing resentment against "bigness" in the bureaucratic system—a system that breeds anything but rationality and efficiency. Many claim it is this system, the bureaucratic model or the establishment, that causes inefficiency and organizations that are anything but models of goal-attaining, purpose-fulfilling enterprises. This is one of the conditions and challenges of organizational society.

FORMAL AND INFORMAL RELATIONSHIPS

This section views aspects of the interaction of men with the formal structure of an organization. Consideration is given to the regulatory nature of organizations, the idea that men modify the formal structure, and proposals on integrating formal and informal organizational systems.

Men at work express their desires, motivations, and ingenuity in various combinations. It is anticipated that the behavior of an organization's members will support the work to be done. Today, however, work is done less and less by an individual in isolation. Working in the dynamics of groups, large and small, people affect the organization. They modify the formally prescribed system and, consequently, contribute to or hinder its work.[75] In turn, supervisors and other functionaries of the organization may demand disciplined worker behavior or a conformity with bureaucratic regulations, sometimes for sheer compliance. The result is a ritualistic behavior that suggests the primacy of the rule or procedure over that of organizational purpose. This problem is a vexing one. It is as much a concern for supervisors, foremen, and middle management people as it is for line workers—or, in the case of the school, for the teacher. If the character of the organization as it is translated from the higher echelons down focuses on control, on attention to "the" prescribed way with a heavy emphasis on conformity, there will be few opportunities for supervisors to perform as relevant adjuncts to the production process. In such circumstances, supervisors are quickly "institutionalized"; they are encumbered by the organization they are supposed to serve. A highly regulated, bureaucratized system can breed inflexibility; it can make imagination, resourcefulness and the pursuit of meaning within organizations suspect qualities. When the bureaucratic system trods on such expressions, it is pushing behavior into preconceived forms. If there is no opportunity to modify an organization's structure and if encouragement in this direction is not provided, the organization has ordered its own eventual failure. This is the confrontation of the man and the organization. The grating of man against the system is a constant source of disequilibrium within organizations and can become very harmful, depending upon the reaction of organizational leadership.

When a formal organization exists, an informal system will follow. The task of leadership is to develop action programs based upon sound theories and research, which will turn the informal expression of the organization into a positive force.

Blau and Scott describe the situation as follows:

> The fact that an organization has been formally established, however, does not mean that all activities and interactions of its members conform strictly to the official blueprint. Regardless of the time and effort devoted by management to designing a rational organization chart and elaborate procedure manuals, this official plan can never completely determine the conduct and social relations of the organization's members. . . . In every formal organization there arise informal organizations. The constituent groups of the organization, like all groups, develop their own practices, values, norms, and social relations, as their members live and work together.[76]

In order to lessen this problem, one view calls for the elimination of the bureaucratic form in organizations. Another view asks for a continued analysis of organizational arrangements within the bureaucratic scheme with emphasis on the application of concepts, such as participatory management.[77,78] Likert's management concepts move to modify the rigidity of communication and extend involvement in the decision-making processes of the organization. This is expressed most effectively in Likert's overlapping form of organizational structure, in which each group or subsystem of the total organization is linked to the others by individuals who hold overlapping subsystem membership. Likert writes:

> These individuals who hold overlapping group membership are called "linking pins." The interaction and decision-making relies heavily on group processes. Interaction occurs also, of course, between individuals, both between superior and subordinates and among subordinates. At each hierarchical level, however, all subordinates in a work group who are affected by the outcomes of a decision are involved in it.

Diagrammatically, Likert presents his "linking pin" concept below.

Likert's work suggests that the "linking pin" concept as a modification of the bureaucratic system is not intended to make light of authority and responsibility. The linking pin does open the organization's communication network. It may, therefore, offset the perception of psychological distance between levels or subsystems within the total organization. It has the advantage of stressing meaningful involvement in the decision-making process of the organization while maximizing the utiliza-

FIGURE 6-1.   The Linking Pin (from Rensis Likert, New Patterns of Management. New York: McGraw-Hill Book Company, 1961. By permission of the publishers.)

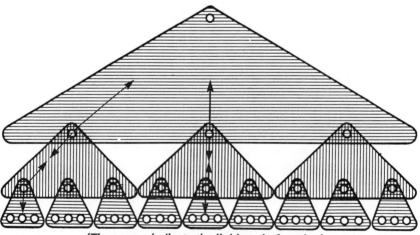

(The arrows indicate the linking pin function)

tion of knowledge and expertise possessed by the membership.* The purpose of a design such as Likert's "linking pin" is to make organizations more effective by emphasizing the use of human inputs, energy, and ideas in their work. The bureaucratic system need not be limited in such respects but does, when rigidly applied, become less efficient than its potential idealized form would suggest.

The resolution of the problem may be found in the proposition that men (personalities) can be harmonized with organizations and that by working toward such equilibrium the organizations' purposes will be served.

> To put this another way, we believe that organizations and personalities are discrete units with their own laws, which make them amendable to study as separate units. However, we also believe that important parts of each unit's existence depend on their connectedness with the other. We hypothesize that one cannot fully understand the individual without understanding the organization in which he is embedded, and vice versa.[79]

Argyris[80] earlier reviewed the impact of the organization upon the individual. In clear-cut fashion he cited the inconsistency between the mature adult personality and what is typically expected in most organizations:

> In effect, therefore, formal organizations are willing to pay high wages and provide for adequate seniority if mature adults will, for eight hours a day, behave in a less mature manner.

This is not always the case, but by assuming the extreme Argyris highlights a deleterious condition common in modern organizations. He summarized his findings by formulating three propositions:

1. There is a lack of congruence between the needs of healthy individuals and the demands of the formal organization.

    Again, the emphasis is on the distance between the mature individual and what the organization demands. An organizational disturbance will be created in proportion to the degree of incongruence.

2. The results of this disturbance are frustration, failure, short-time perspective and conflict.

    If the organization's members are mature and self-actualized they will experience frustration and failure because they will not be permitted to define their own goals and paths; they will see the future as uncertain; the consequence of these conditions will be conflict.

3. The nature of the formal principles of organization causes the subordinate, at any given level, to experience competition, rivalry, intersubordinate hostility, and a focus toward the parts rather than the whole.

---

* It is interesting in the analysis of educational organizations, particularly universities, how little use is made of the vast resources of the faculty in tackling the problems confronting it. There seems to be a mutually accepted distance based on the concept of differentiated formal roles.

These conditions in organizations cause subordinates to see themselves in competition with each other, breeching hostility and a narrow perspective of the nature of the organization. The system becomes "pieces" or "parts" -oriented, demanding ever-increasing levels of coordination and authority.

It is the contention of Argyris and others* that attempts to improve organizational efficiency should include a reduction of dependence, subordination, and submissiveness. "It can be shown that job enlargement and employee-centered (or democratic or participative) leadership are elements that, if used correctly, can go a long way toward ameliorating the situation." [81]

Mann[82] states that "the first-line supervisor is constantly confronted with the task of making organizational objectives compatible with the needs and goals of his subordinates." To do this, and simultaneously contribute to the organization's goal attainment, Mann[83] declares that the supervisor must possess a skill-mix consisting of administrative competence, human relations competence, and technical competence. Technical competence, as used by Mann, refers to "the ability to use pertinent knowledge, methods, techniques, and equipment necessary for the performance of specific tasks and activities, and for the direction of such performance."

Neville[84] and Stewart,[85] analyzing supervisory behavior in education through factor analysis studies, confirmed the relevance of Mann's skill-mix for educational supervisors. Existing supervisory behavior in educational settings studies was characterized by major clusters of behavior including human relations, management (administrative) and technical functions. These studies suggested that educational supervisors have need, in terms of the perceptions of teachers, to express concern with both the human and the technical dimensions of their responsibilities if they are to assist teachers to greater instructional effectiveness and job satisfaction.

---

* In addition to Argyris there are other scholars who advance the organic or non-structuralist position on organizational theory and effectiveness. Argyris, in *Integrating the Individual and the Organization* (1964), offers this summary: The organic organization is variously called "participative group" (Likert), "problem-solving" (Bennis), "open system" (Barnes), "human relations" (Litwak), and "Theory 'Y'" (McGregor). The "organic organization" is characterized by:
1. decision-making widely done throughout the organization,
2. an emphasis on mutual dependence and cooperation based on trust, confidence, and high technical or professional competence,
3. a constant pressure to enlarge tasks and interrelate them so that the concern for the whole is emphasized,
4. the decentralization of responsibility for and use of information, rewards and penalties, membership,
5. participants at all levels being responsible for developing and maintaining loyalty and commitment at as high a level as possible, and
6. an emphasis on status through contribution to the whole and intergroup and interindividual cooperation.

One approach to the problem requires that the supervisor act as leader of both the formal and informal systems.[86] It is recommended that the supervisor be democratic (permissive, nondirective, group centered). This position was based on early Lewinian studies in which production of groups under autocratic and democratic supervision were essentially the same. Quality of production in the democratic groups was judged superior, workers had a greater interest in their work and work effort in the absence of the supervisor was higher; in addition, democratic groups had more enthusiasm and satisfaction in their work.

McGregor[87] refers to organizations (General Mills, General Electric) that have been experimenting with programs which permit workers to set "targets" or objectives for themselves, and involve the individual in his own evaluation. It is interesting to note that supervisory competence must be more substantial here than in conventional processes of standard-setting and evaluation. Bennis[88] refers to an "essential problem of the Western tradition—the relationship of the individual and his fulfillment to the demands and constraints of some supra-individual entity." Bennis further states, "effective leadership depends primarily on mediating between the individual and the organization in such a way that both can obtain maximum satisfaction." Leavitt,[89] however, argues that the human relations or participative theory is insufficient as a basis for managing the effective organization. He contends that human relations is too narrow a view and seeks to examine "participative beliefs." He sees these as a great advance but asks that they be placed in perspective.

Hopkins [90] studied the comparative positions of Weber and Barnard in interpreting bureaucratic structure. He views Weber as stressing power structures that operate in a quasi-judicial fashion, rational values that legitimate these structures, experts who run them and a hierarchy that prescribes the relationship between a unit and its power. Barnard is viewed as concentrating on the bureaucratic structure as a "communication system"—interrelated lines of authority where—"individuals are able to exercise authority only when they are acting officially." Barnard also introduced another important property of authority in organization: "Objective authority is only maintained if the positions or leaders continue to be adequately informed."

Hopkins concludes his analysis of Weber's and Barnard's interpretations of bureaucratic authority work by stating:

Current studies of formal organizations tend to fall into two groups, those in which the authority system is viewed as a power structure and those in which it is viewed as a communications process, a division which this essay has tried to show is neither useful nor necessary. The principal theorists for each view, Weber on the one hand and Barnard on the other, converge in their ideas about the nature of bureaucratized systems of authority, and their explanations of effectiveness are mutually supporting, not mutually exclusive.[91]

ORGANIZATIONAL ANALYSIS

There is a great demand that organizations be held accountable for the services they provide or products they produce. This brings us to proposals concerning the study and analysis of formal organizations. Reference is made to system analysis and functional-structural analysis as two ways of looking at the present state of an organization. These methods have the potential for generating significant information pertinent to organizational decision-making.

Organizations will continue to evolve in complexity. Mainly, this trend will reflect events in a burgeoning, technocratic society. One consequence will be a highly specialized environment. The emergence of restrictive specialization is less of a threat, however, when leadership is conceptually and technically equipped to analyze problems and shape organizational action. It is doubtful whether participants will accept or support as legitimate, organizational leadership that acts to constrain members from working on the problems of the organization. In other words, perspectives provided by theories of leadership, communication, organizations, and change processes will have to be applied. Since these areas of study are themselves developing, organizations must also exist in a continuous state of self-renewal. This requires the continuing analysis of goals, procedures, context, and human resources as a basis for decisions.

"System analysis" represents one model or approach to organizational study and decision-making. Definitive statements on the nature and procedures of system analysis are still being constructed. Pfeiffer[92] discusses the general features of the system approach. The first phase calls for shaping a "design for action." Working with a problem requires problem definition and the statement of organizational objectives in operational terms. This phase also entails establishing criteria to help determine when—or to what extent—the objectives have been met. Secondly, Pfeiffer suggests that *alternatives*—a variety of approaches—be constructed for each objective. This is crucial in a system approach, since no one method of attack on a problem may be completely satisfactory in all aspects. The decision to guide the work of the organization is then made through an evaluation of the alternatives. This is the point at which the system concept is most visible. "A full-fledged analysis will attempt to evaluate a combination of alternatives by maximizing the benefits or utility to be attained for a given cost, or by minimizing the price which must be paid to achieve specified changes."[93] Evaluation continues as the alternatives making up the plan become operative. Modification of procedures, in process, occurs as evaluation is made of the movement of the organization toward its objectives.

System analysis studies of organizational problems often evoke the accusation of dehumanization. That is, organizations, particularly educational systems, applying "systematic" principles may be seen as remote and mechanistic. Hamreus [94] suggests that this thinking has emerged because the system approach has been employed in military and industrial settings, and the use of flow charts with quantitative interpretations may convey something cold and formidable. Hamreus [95] also thinks the dehumanizing fear to be unfounded. He states that a system approach provides the means to enhance human interaction and that without employing some system format, educational organizations will fall short of their goals.

Industry, business, and governmental institutions have made great strides in the application of decision-making and system models.

Coombs [96] also makes a strong plea for application of "system" procedures to the problems of education.* He cites various conditions of the educational environment to support this plea. Such conditions include:

> . . . sharp increase in popular aspirations for education; and the inertia of societies themselves—the heavy weight of traditional attitudes, religious customs, prestige and incentive patterns, and institutional structures— which has blocked them from making the optimum use of education and of education manpower to foster national development.

Although Coombs is considering the international scene, his ideas are not disassociated from conditions and issues facing many of our national, state and local educational agencies. To make the intent of system analysis more precise, it is helpful to consider an additional statement from Coombs:

> A "systems analysis" of education resembles, in some respects, what a doctor does when he examines the most complicated and awe-inspiring "system" of all—a human being. It is never possible, nor is it necessary, for the doctor to have complete knowledge of every detail of a human being's system and its functional processes. The strategy of the diagnosis is to concentrate upon selected critical indicators and relationships within the system and between its environment. The doctor, for example, is concerned especially with correlations between such critical indicators as heartbeat, blood pressure, weight, height, age, diet, sleeping habits, urinary sugar content, white and red corpuscles. From these he appraises the way the total system is functioning, and prescribes what may be needed to make it function better.[97]

The following charts present a clearer definition of the areas of study or data categories that would be studied as discrete and then as interrelated components of an educational organization.

* See the Coombs system analysis charts following.

FIGURE 6-2. *The Major Components of an Educational System*

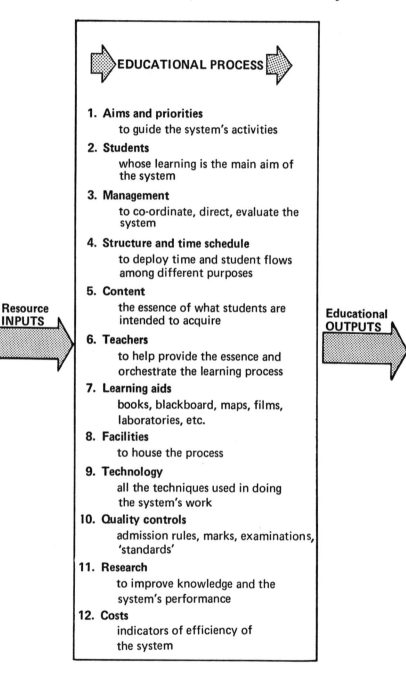

Resource
INPUTS

EDUCATIONAL PROCESS

1. **Aims and priorities**
   to guide the system's activities

2. **Students**
   whose learning is the main aim of
   the system

3. **Management**
   to co-ordinate, direct, evaluate the
   system

4. **Structure and time schedule**
   to deploy time and student flows
   among different purposes

5. **Content**
   the essence of what students are
   intended to acquire

6. **Teachers**
   to help provide the essence and
   orchestrate the learning process

7. **Learning aids**
   books, blackboard, maps, films,
   laboratories, etc.

8. **Facilities**
   to house the process

9. **Technology**
   all the techniques used in doing
   the system's work

10. **Quality controls**
    admission rules, marks, examinations,
    'standards'

11. **Research**
    to improve knowledge and the
    system's performance

12. **Costs**
    indicators of efficiency of
    the system

Educational
OUTPUTS

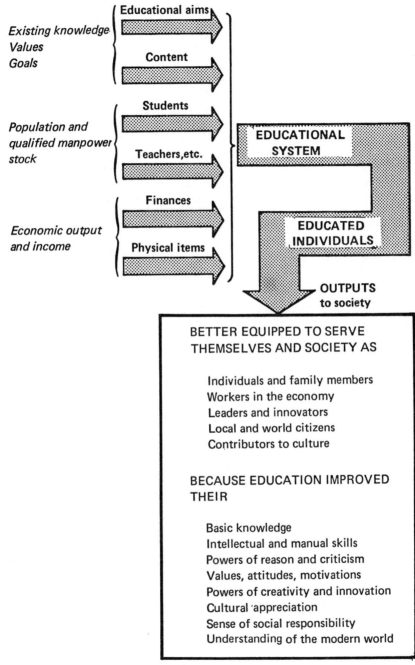

FIGURE 6-3. *Interaction between an Educational System and Its Environment*

INPUTS from society

Educational aims

Existing knowledge
Values
Goals

Content

Students

Population and
qualified manpower
stock

Teachers, etc.

Finances

Economic output
and income

Physical items

EDUCATIONAL
SYSTEM

EDUCATED
INDIVIDUALS

OUTPUTS
to society

BETTER EQUIPPED TO SERVE
THEMSELVES AND SOCIETY AS

Individuals and family members
Workers in the economy
Leaders and innovators
Local and world citizens
Contributors to culture

BECAUSE EDUCATION IMPROVED
THEIR

Basic knowledge
Intellectual and manual skills
Powers of reason and criticism
Values, attitudes, motivations
Powers of creativity and innovation
Cultural appreciation
Sense of social responsibility
Understanding of the modern world

147

Coombs [98] considers Figure 6-2 to deal with the internal aspects of an educational organization. Figure 6-3 depicts the "external linkages." Determining the meaning of internal components along with the qualitative interaction of them is necessary to an understanding of the organization. From here the internal dimensions are viewed in relation to its external links. Coombs writes:

> If external conditions lead to change in the inputs available to the system —as when a national manpower shortage and an unfavorable salary structure result in a shortage of teachers—the effect within the system may be a decline in the size and quality of its outputs. On the other hand, the input stringency may conceivably provoke a change in "technology" and in the use of resources calculated to avert a decline in the size and quality of the outputs. The system analysis thus shows that there need be no rigid pattern of internal responses to which an education system must adhere in meeting external stringencies. Aided by such an analysis, the system is in a position to choose its own response, and the choice it actually makes can have a considerable influence on the quantity and quality of its output, and on its internal efficiency and external productivity. [99]

A more generalized approach to the study of organization is functional-structural analysis. This approach assumes an organization to be defined as previously developed in this book: individuals in offices; distributed responsibility for definite tasks—the functional activities; the existence of organizational goals; and a stable system of coordinative relationships—a structure. [100] When such structure exists in an organization, it is then possible to analyze the state of the system by collecting information for analysis. This method suggests that organizations have certain needs, particularly with regard to internal orderliness and outside interference. These needs are related to the overarching concern of self-maintenance as a reaction to external conditions. Dimensions that could be studied as a part of functional-structural analysis have been identified by Selznick. [101] These include:

1. The security of the organization as a whole in relation to social forces in its environment.
2. The stability of the lines of authority and communication.
3. The stability of informal relations within the organization.
4. The continuity of policy and of the sources of its determination.
5. A homogeneity of outlook with respect to the meaning and role of the organization.

These factors, suggests Selznick, are general characteristics of formal organizations. They are vital structural concerns. They are derived from the "organizational need" to maintain and preserve the system. Attempts to go beyond maintenance, toward the refinement of the organization, would be guided by study applying Selznick's dimensions. It is imperative that organizational leadership include the conceptual and technical skills required to systematically study organizational effectiveness.[102, 103, 104]

As organizations strive to perpetuate themselves there will be the need for rigorous analysis of the existing level of organizational effectiveness. In the present environment this process is called *accountability*. Measures of accountability should be used to suggest refinements in the internal state of the organization, not to attach some gross label such as "good," "bad," or "high/low" productivity. Through the systematic study of organization, there is the potential of substantive benefits for the organization, the people it serves, and the total society.

IMPLICATIONS FOR INSTRUCTIONAL SUPERVISORY BEHAVIOR

The school as a formal organization has much in common with other complex organizations. Schools provide significant service, develop products, are increasingly characterized by differentiated functions, and have planned structures to promote their work. The school, however, has yet to be studied definitely as a formal organization. Despite this, the concepts and research in organizational analysis do represent valid areas of consideration for supervisors. As organizational leaders, supervisors should be alert to the implications of organizational study. The educational supervisor needs a variety of concepts with which to sharpen his view of his role and the organization he serves.

The propositions that follow, along with the implications derived from them, are presented as principles to be tested against the reality and constraints of organizations in action. They are meant to prompt supervisors, and supervisors in preparation, to construct personal knowledge of the school as a formal organization. This knowledge may offer helpful guidelines to supervisory behavior in education.

Organizations in Social Context

PROPOSITION 1: *If an organization is to operate effectively and make a significant contribution to social purpose, its services and/or products must be consistent with the values of society.*

Organizations are formed under particular circumstances and conditions. As these conditions change, organizations must be ready to modify their operations in terms of the new social needs. In the case of educational organizations, a conscious effort must be made to keep the school close to its constituents. It is a responsibility of ISB to contribute to the mutual understanding and efforts of community, home and school. This implies that supervisors must help teachers to grasp the main patterns of community needs and values, while also helping to explain the school, as a rational system, to the community it serves. In addition to explanations, ISB must also provide opportunities for community representation as educational policies and programs are shaped. Efforts in this area were once conceived as good "public relations." Today it is a requirement stemming from the reasonable expectation that people will contribute to the construction of the systems and organizations designed to serve them.

PROPOSITION 2: *The nature of a particular organization, along with its stage of historical and technical development, are factors that determine the system's supervisory and managerial requirements.*

The purpose of an organization, as well as the makeup of its production system, have a great deal to do with the organization's needs in the realm of supervisory and management services. Hence, as our existence shows increased specialization, educational organizations tend to move in a similar direction. As school programs become more specialized, there will be an increasing demand for more specialized ISB. There is a great need for supervisors to define more precisely the components (human, technical, and management) of effective ISB if supervisory services are to make any substantive contribution to the school's effectiveness.

PROPOSITION 3: *An organization will effectively contribute to the needs of people to the extent that it maintains an open and responsive posture.*

The universality of the public school opens educational organizations to the pressures of many groups and ideas. This situation creates a new dimension for the supervisor. ISB must promote understanding and mutual respect between school and community. ISB is charged with the responsibility of promoting new role relationships between teachers and administrators, and between community and school. The suggestion here is that ISB needs to extend beyond the description of what *is*, with its inherent gatekeeping activities, moving toward a more active role as mediator in the area of instruction and program development. ISB must also seek ways of establishing relationships between the school and other agencies working on pressing matters of social need.

Organizations Defined

PROPOSITION 4: *An organization will be more effective when its structure and designed modifications are consonant with the cultural milieu within which it exists.*

If an organization is to exist and perform effectively, it must be consistent, in its purpose, structure, and mode of production, with the social context. The supervisor who proposes changes must reflect beyond the idea to the environment and people served by the school organization. The relative merits of a proposed change should be examined in terms of community needs and standards. As the relationship between community and the organization is analyzed, constraints may appear. Supervisors, however, are responsible for identifying and designing changes within organizations. This requires an approach to ISB that pushes the refinement of the instructional system with reference to the makeup of the cultural system.

PROPOSITION 5: *An organization will be more effective when there is a conscious effort to blend the resources needed for production and the psychological commitment of the membership.*

An effective organization will have to meet the physical demands required for production. In addition, the organization should be served by members with the diverse skills required by its nature and purpose. In schools, beyond these conditions, ISB must stimulate the instructional staff to identify with the school organization as a system that requires human ingenuity and creative input if it is to accomplish its purpose. Unless there is a behavioral commitment to these purposes, the school may become a place where "rules" are played out and authentic human concern is a stated, rather than a real, goal.

PROPOSITION 6: *Organizations will be more effective if the membership understands the organization's structure and uses this understanding as a basis for contributing to its work.*

ISB should promote a working understanding of the organization of the school among the instructional faculty. The faculty should be apprised of the roles played by various individuals and offices within the system. Such understanding will enable instructional personnel to use the organizational system to best advantage in working through their job responsibilities. To a great extent the efficacy of supervisory efforts within school organizations is related to the clear-cut understanding of the purpose of supervisory efforts and how these efforts support the work of administrators and instructional personnel. Existing evidence indicates that the role of supervisors in education is not clearly perceived.

PROPOSITION 7: *The effectiveness of an organization will be increased when there is provision for continuity of interaction and structural integration.*

As organizations increase in size and complexity the problems of communication and intraorganizational relationships are accented. ISB can work to promote effective working relationships among the parts of the total organization. In a real sense, instructional supervisors represent links among the levels and parts of the school organization. The supervisor having access to teachers and responsibility for instructional efficiency can gain firsthand knowledge of the needs of the organization. These needs, along with the concerns of teachers and support personnel, can be considered in the decision-making process. When productive interaction between the levels and parts of the organization is lacking, there will be a concomitant divisiveness that will thwart its work.

Organizational Goals

PROPOSITION 8: *Organizations will be more effective when there exists a clearly understood definition of goals or purposes.*

Schools, as organizations, have no shortage of statements of overall purpose. It is important that ISB give direction to the careful development of an operational interpretation of the general purpose posed for an educational organization. It is through careful study at the individual school or district level that general educational purposes can be transformed into plans of action. This is a function of ISB. In turn, it is through such work that teachers can build a measure of identity with the school. The suggestion here is that the struggle with "What we are all about" has seldom been subjected to the scrutiny necessary for making purposes clear and important to the people who serve the organization. When there is only a casual interest in purpose and a rejection of this pursuit as theory-building, then the organization will suffer accordingly. Working toward the effective organization requires continuing examination of purposes in relation to what actually happens; this is a basic guideline for ISB, and for the analysis of the school as an organization.

PROPOSITION 9: *When there are changes in the goal(s) of an organization, continued effectiveness will require accompanying changes in the organization's internal structure and in the distribution of its resources.*

ISB must be ready to provide the conditions and the technical support necessary for the redirection or expansion of the school's program. This includes helping teachers to gain necessary skills and assisting in the definition of needed structures and resources. It is also vital that supervisors provide opportunities for teachers to become conscious of the facts and principles upon which any changes are based.

PROPOSITION 10: *An effective organization will continue to examine its stated goals in relation to its real goals as defined in the behavior of its membership.*

It is a constant struggle in organizations to determine the relationship between stated goals and the goals toward which different groups and individuals are working. ISB can aid individuals as they try to clarify their personal or group expectations in relation to those of the organization. This process can aid the professional identity of the participants while also contributing to the realization of how the individual or group contributes to the primary goals of the larger unit. In some cases the supervisor may find it appropriate to stimulate divergent approaches to organizational goals as a means of setting processes in motion. What is required here is a balance between supporting individuality and analyzing these factors in relation to the school's primary goals of student fulfillment. There is nothing so empty as a school in which statements of intent are not matched by the reality of teacher performance and leadership behavior.

PROPOSITION 11: *The morale of an organization will be enhanced when its goals are understood and perceived as important.*

ISB has as a major responsibility the clarification of the school's goals. This means that the supervisor must communicate and interpret the goals of the school organization as well as those of the instructional program. This task can be done formally, through planned programs, and through informal interactions among supervisors and faculty. It is critical that organizational goals be accepted so the energy of the staff member will be applied in working toward these goals. If an individual is to derive satisfaction from his work and in turn contribute to the satisfaction of others within the system, he must know and be oriented to the goals of the system. This is a prerequisite of good morale. Since morale is an important aspect of productivity, ISB must plan for the integration of individual goals with those of the organization.

Authority in Organizations

PROPOSITION 12: *In an effective organization, leadership behavior will be distributed between maintenance activity and more creative, goal directed activity.*

Organizations strive to maintain themselves. Supervisors play an important role in the maintenance of an organization. Typically it is their responsibility to see that activities as defined by the organization are carried out efficiently in its various departments or subdivisions. This requires a great deal of management behavior and communication by the supervisor. ISB in its leadership capacity carries heavy management functions. However, when the management aspects are not balanced by leadership activity that stimulates the growth or refinement of the organization's work, ISB becomes perfunctory. Any dynamic and professional sphere of responsibility, such as teaching, requires ISB that stimulates the analysis of problems as a way of provoking refined insight about all instruction-related concerns. ISB, therefore, serves the organization by helping to maintain its internal efficiency and by challenging the system in an attempt to keep it open and responsive.

PROPOSITION 13: *The nature of supervisory structure in organizations should be directly related to their production systems.*

When an organization reflects a mass production system there will be a great many supervisors at a variety of levels. In humanistic enterprises, such as schools, the supervisory staff will be few in number and will assume a colleagual relationship. ISB derives its strength from the ability of the educational supervisor to work with teachers in the redefinition of goals and instructional processes. Although the educational supervisor cannot relinquish his formal authority within the system, his ISB should be constructed out of professional ability rather than official status.

PROPOSITION 14: *Effective organizations will indicate lines of responsibility and the authority upon which they are based.*

It is critical that organizations convey to their members the definition of organizational roles. In addition to role clarification, the rational-legal basis for different roles should be provided. ISB frequently suffers from role conflict. In one instance, educational supervisors may be defined as staff people; in another, as line authorities. The staff designation implies an advisory function, while a line designation indicates a prescribed area of direct control. Organizational theory generally supports the supervisor as a line position, particularly when he has direct responsibility for quality of production. In any case, ISB as an official status must be supported by leadership competence.

Formal and Informal Relationships

PROPOSITION 15: *Effective organization is a function of the integration of formal and informal systems.*

It has already been proposed that ISB include efforts to communicate the formal structure of the educational organization. This includes its internal structure and goals. It is also important that supervisors contribute to the development of a positive informal organizational system. This includes the quality of communication among its members and the creation of a positive tone throughout the system. It is imperative that supervisors contribute to the nonformal, human aspects of the organization as a goal in itself, and also a supporting factor to its formal aspects.

PROPOSITION 16: *Organizational effectiveness will be expressed in attempts to modify the existing structure as a response to changing conditions and circumstances.*

Organizations cannot be static. They will be less inclined to be so if ISB establishes the conditions whereby risk-taking and creative thinking are encouraged. This requires that supervisors foster an open climate. It also requires that supervisors and instructional personnel stay in close contact with the major issues through their work with people. It is through the direct knowledge of problems and concerns that the need for restructuring or modification can be recognized. School organizations that do not maintain their relevance become misunderstood and suspect. Supervisors can and should behave so as to make the system more modifiable.

PROPOSITION 17: *Organizational effectiveness will be enhanced when leadership behavior is characterized by interpersonal strength, technical skills and management ability.*

The supervisor has need of a variety of conceptual skills if his performance is to have any impact on the work of the organization. ISB should be founded on effective human relations and the technical skills needed in the analysis of teaching and curriculum development, along with managerial ability that enables the organization to continue steps toward improved operation. Without the breadth of such areas of competence, ISB is extraneous to the development of effective instructional systems.

The basic approach of many supervisors has been unidimensional. The emphasis has been on effective human relations and the communication systems required to support such a condition. The primacy of good human relations in any cooperative endeavor must be recognized. In educational systems this need is particularly acute. Cooperative systems also need leadership that encompasses in-depth knowledge of the processes involved in production. The organization must be served by leaders who evidence the competence(ies) required of the system. In many cases, the burden of maintaining the system pressures supervisors to dwell on management functions, while failing to advance the system through the application of technical competence with teachers. For a supervisor to be truly effective, he must demonstrate the best combination of skills and related competencies.

PROPOSITION 18: *An organization will be more efficient when it seeks to reduce human submission and alienation of persons within it.*

Supervisors should promote the worth and independence of the individual staff members. This is a critical psychological concern in organizations, since the vitality of any organization depends on the individual and collective efforts of its membership. The promotion of self-actualization, as opposed to submission, will require supervisory personnel who are ready to accept the challenges of leading by competence rather than by official position. By providing for the advancement of competence and professional decision-making among teachers, the supervisor promotes organizational effectiveness.

Organizational Analysis

PROPOSITION 19: *The assessment of an organization's effectiveness should include its analysis as a total complex structure and as a laboratory of human interaction.*

Leadership personnel in organizations must constantly study the organization as a complex network of structural elements. These elements have identity and perform strategic functions in the work of the total system. ISB can promote the understanding and beneficial interaction of the organization's structure. Structure becomes real, however, only as people work within the organization. It is appropriate that ISB contribute to the analysis and interpretation of the school as both a structural entity and a system of human interactions. It is felt that more effective supervisory services result when organizational structure and behavior have been studied in terms of some mutually planned model or design.

PROPOSITION 20: *An organization should construct and use mechanisms for the analysis of its efficiency and effectiveness.*

ISB should reflect the reality that educational systems are constantly under pressures to modify. These pressures are produced by ideas in the larger society. There are also pressures for change within the organization. It is vital that supervisors be able to lead or contribute to the study of the school's effectiveness. If changes are to occur and if the school is to be responsive to social and individual needs, there must exist data helpful in assessing present performance as a basis for rational change.

ENDNOTES

1. Robert Presthus, *Organizational Society* (New York: Alfred A. Knopf, Inc., 1962).
2. R. Jean Hills, *Toward a Science of Organization* (Eugene, Ore.: Center for the Advanced Study of Educational Administration, 1968), pp. 1–2.
3. Amitai Etzioni, *Complex Organization* (New York: Holt, Rinehart & Winston, Inc., 1961).
4. R. C. Angell, *The Integration of American Society* (New York: McGraw-Hill, 1941), pp. 25–27.
5. John F. Culver, *Sociology*, 3rd Ed. (New York: Appleton-Century-Crofts, Inc., 1955), p. 439.
6. Max Lerner, *America As a Civilization* (New York: Simon and Schuster, Inc., 1957).
7. Jules Henry, *Culture Against Man.* (New York: Random House, Inc., 1963).
8. Robert M. Hutchins, "Permanence and Change," *The Center Magazine.* Center for the Study of Democratic Institutions (September 1968), pp. 2–6.
9. Robert Dubin *et al.*, *Leadership and Productivity* (San Francisco: Chandler Publishing Co., 1965), p. 7.
10. *Ibid.*, p. 9.
11. *Ibid.*
12. Joan Woodward, *Management and Technology* (London: Her Majesty's Stationery Office, 1958). As interpreted by Dubin, *op. cit.*, pp. 10–14.
13. Presthus, *op. cit.*
14. C. Wright Mills, *White Collar: American Middle Classes* (New York: Oxford University Press, Inc., 1956).
15. Talcott Parsons, "Suggestions for a Sociological Approach to the Theory of Organizations," *Administrative Science Quarterly* I (1965), pp. 63–85.
16. Chester I. Barnard, *The Functions of the Executive* (Cambridge, Mass: Harvard University Press, 1938).
17. John M. Gaus, "A Theory of Organization in Public Administration," in *The Frontier of Public Administration* (Chicago: University of Chicago Press, 1936).
18. Amitai Etzioni, *Modern Organizations* (Englewood Cliffs, N. J.: Prentice-Hall, Inc., 1964), chap. 1.
19. Peter M. Blau and W. Richard Scott, *Formal Organizations* (San Francisco: Chandler Publishing Co., 1962).
20. Bertram M. Gross, *The Managing of Organization* (New York and London: Free Press of Glencoe, Inc.; Collier-Macmillan Ltd., 1964).
21. Philip B. Applewhite, *Organizational Behavior* (Englewood Cliffs, N. J.: Prentice-Hall, Inc., 1965), p. 1.

22. Etzioni, *Complex Organizations,* p. 5.
23. Edward Gross and Paul Grambsch, *University Goals and Academic Power* (Washington, D.C.: American Council on Education, 1968), pp. 4–13.
24. Talcott Parsons, "A Sociological Approach to the Theory of Formal Organizations," in *Structure and Process in Modern Societies* (New York: Free Press of Glencoe, Inc., 1960), chap. 1.
25. Robert S. Weiss, "A Structure-Function Approach to Organization," in *Studies in Organizational Behavior and Management,* ed. Donald Porter and Philip Applewhite (Scranton: International Textbook Co., 1964) pp. 3–10.
26. *Ibid.,* pp. 4–5.
27. *Ibid.,* p. 5.
28. Etzioni, *Modern Organizations,* p. 6.
29. Douglas McGregor, *Human Side of Enterprise* (New York: McGraw-Hill, 1960).
30. Morris S. Viteles, *Motivation and Morale in Industry* (New York: W. W. Norton & Company, Inc., 1953).
31. Daniel Katz, Nathan Maccoby, and Nancy C. Morse, *Productivity, Supervison and Morale in an Office Situation* (Ann Arbor, Mich.: University of Michigan Press, 1950).
32. Milton L. Blum, *Industrial Psychology and Its Social Foundations* (New York: Harper & Row, Publishers, 1956).
33. David L. Sills, "The Succession of Goals," in *The Volunteers* (New York: Free Press of Glencoe, Inc., 1957), pp. 253–268.
34. Etzioni, *Complex Organizations,* pp. 143–144.
35. Etzioni, *Modern Organizations,* pp. 13–16.
36. Sills, *op. cit.*
37. Peter M. Blau, *The Dynamics of Bureaucracy* (Chicago: University of Chicago Press, 1955).
38. Burton C. Clark, "Organizational Adaptation and Precarious Values," *American Sociological Review* 21 (1956), pp. 327–336.
39. Parsons, *op. cit.*
40. Gross and Grambsch, *op. cit.,* p. 6.
41. James D. Thompson and William J. McEwen, "Organizational Goals and Environment," *American Sociological Review* 23 (1958), pp. 23–31.
42. Etzioni, *Modern Organizations,* p. 5.
43. Chris Argyris, *Integrating the Individual and the Organization* (New York: John Wiley & Sons, Inc., 1964), p. 123.
44. Gross and Grambsch, *op. cit.,* p. 8.
45. Katz *et al., op. cit.*
46. Applewhite, *op. cit.,* p. 12.
47. Nancy Morse, *Satisfactions in the White Collar Job* (Ann Arbor, Mich.: University of Michigan Press, 1953).
48. Rensis Likert, *New Patterns of Management* (New York: McGraw-Hill, 1961).
49. Weiss, *op. cit.,* p. 5 .
50. Dorwin Cartwright, "Influence, Leadership, Control," in *Handbook of*

Organizations, ed. James G. March (Chicago: Rand McNally & Co., 1965), pp. 1–2.

51. Barnard, *op. cit.*

52. Max Weber, *The Theory of Social and Economic Organization*, ed. Talcott Parsons (Glencoe, Ill.: Free Press and Falcon's Wing Press, 1947).

53. *Ibid.*, p. 324.

54. Blau and Scott, *op. cit.*, p. 28.

55. Herbert A. Simon, *Administrative Behavior*, 2nd Ed. (New York: Macmillan Co., 1957), pp. 126–127.

56. Blau and Scott, *op. cit.*, pp. 28–29.

57. Cartwright, *op. cit.*, pp. 4–41.

58. G. Levinger, "The Development of Perceptions and Behavior in Newly Formed Social Power Relationships," in *Studies in Social Power*, ed. D. Cartwright (Ann Arbor, Mich.: University of Michigan, Institute for Social Research, 1959), pp. 83–98.

59. D. A. Cartwright, "A Field Theoretical Conception of Power," in *Studies in Social Power*, ed. Cartwright (Ann Arbor, Mich.: University of Michigan, Institute for Social Research, 1959).

60. J. R. P. French, Jr., and B. Raven, "The Bases of Social Power," in *Studies in Social Power*, ed. Cartwright (Ann Arbor, Mich.: University of Michigan, Institute for Social Research, 1959), pp. 150–167.

61. Weber, *op. cit.*, pp. 324–386.

62. Etzioni, *Modern Organizations*, pp. 51–53.

63. Weber, *op. cit.*, p. 152.

64. Frank Lutz and Laurence Iannacconne, *Understanding Educational Organizations: A Field Study Approach* (Columbus: Charles E. Merrill Books, Inc., 1969), p. 10.

65. Amitai Etzioni, "Organizational Control Structure," in *Handbook of Organizations*, ed. James G. March (Chicago, Ill.: Rand McNally, 1965), pp. 651–652.

66. E. Banfield, *The Moral Basis of a Backward Society* (Glencoe, Ill.: Free Press, 1958).

67. Etzioni, "Organizational Control Structure," p. 651.

68. *Ibid.*, p. 650.

69. Chris Argyris, "The Individual and the Organization: Some Problems of Mutual Adjustment," *Administration Science Quarterly* II (1957), pp. 1–24.

70. Hans Gerth and C. Wright Mills, "Bureaucracy," in *From Max Weber* (New York: McGraw-Hill, 1964).

71. *Ibid.*

72. William R. Van Dorsal, *The Successful Supervisor in Government and Business*, 2nd Ed. (New York: Harper & Row, Publishers, 1968).

73. Ian C. Ross and Alvin Zander, "Need Satisfaction and Employee Turnover," *Personnel Psychology*, 10 (1957), pp. 327–338.

74. Presthus, *op. cit.*, chap. 3.

75. Robert K. Merton, "Bureaucratic Structure and Personality," in *Social Theory and Social Structure* (Glencoe, Ill.: The Free Press, 1957), pp. 195–206.

76. Blau and Scott, *op. cit.*, pp. 5–6.
77. Likert, *op. cit.*
78. Rensis Likert, *The Human Organization* (New York: McGraw-Hill, 1967).
79. Argyris, *Integrating the Individual* . . . , p. 13.
80. Argyris, "The Individual and the Organization . . . ," pp. 1–24.
81. *Ibid.*, p. 59.
82. Floyd C. Mann, "Toward an Understanding of the Leadership Role in Formal Organization," in *Leadership and Productivity*, ed. Dubin *et al.* (San Francisco: Chandler Publishing Co., 1965), pp. 72–73.
83. *Ibid.*, p. 73.
84. Richard F. Neville, "Factorial Analysis of Supervisory Behavior in Education," unpublished research report (College Park, Md.: University of Maryland, 1967).
85. Bob R. Stewart, "The Relationship of Teacher, Supervisor, and Principal Perceptions of Supervisory Behavior," unpublished Doctoral dissertation (College Park, Md.: University of Maryland, 1968).
86. Robert T. Salembiewski, "Small Groups and Large Organizations," in *Handbook of Organizations*, ed. March, pp. 113–114.
87. McGregor, *op. cit.*
88. Warren G. Bennis, "Revisement Theory of Leadership," *Harvard Business Review* 39 (1961), pp. 26–36, 146–150.
89. Harold J. Leavitt, "Unhuman Organizations," *Harvard Business Review* (July-August 1962).
90. Terence Hopkins, "Bureaucratic Authority: The Convergence of Weber and Barnard," in Etzioni, *Complex Organizations* (New York: Holt, Rinehart & Winston, Inc., 1961), pp. 82–98.
91. *Ibid.*, p. 98.
92. John Pfeiffer, *New Look at Education* (Poughkeepsie, N.Y.: Odyssey Press, 1968).
93. *Ibid.*, p. 5.
94. Dale G. Hamreus, *The Systems Approach to Instructional Development.* Teaching Research. A Division of the Oregon State System of Higher Education, U.S. Office Contract, Bureau of Research, pp. I–9, I–10.
95. *Ibid.*, p. I–10.
96. Philip H. Coombs, *The World Educational Crisis: A Systems Analysis* (New York: Oxford University Press, 1968).
97. *Ibid.*
98. *Ibid.*, p. 13.
99. *Ibid.*
100. Weiss, *op. cit.*
101. Philip Selznick, "Foundations of the Theory of Organization," in Etzioni, *Complex Organizations* (New York: Holt, Rinehart & Winston, Inc., 1961), pp. 18–32.
102. Neville, *op. cit.*
103. Mann, *op. cit.*
104. Stewart, *op. cit.*

Chapter 7

Change Theory:
Implications for Instructional
Supervisory Behavior

In Chapter 3, ISB was conceptualized as a behavior system that directly influences—or changes—teacher behavior. Chapters 4, 5, and 6 explored research and theory in the areas of leadership, communication, and organization to derive their implications for instructional supervisory behavior. The final area to be explored is that of "change," a field of study that is rich with implications for understanding systems of human behavior. The appropriateness of investigating change as a tool in analyzing effective ISB is immediately obvious.

Change exists. It is a condition of human existence. But all change is not carefully planned nor is it necessarily orderly; and change may be either good or bad, moving a social system either forward or backward. Moreover, it is a truism that a social organization must value and provide for change if it is to retain any vitality as an organization. Those individuals with leadership responsibilities in organizations bear a special responsibility for the stimulation, planning, and direction of change.

In this chapter, the concept of change is developed as a crucial element of ISB. Out of the vast amount of research in the area of change, those theories of change and empirical findings that appear to be particularly relevant for ISB have been identified and examined.

THE STUDY OF CHANGE

Concern for change in individuals, in society, and in organizations is a part of the history of man. Concern for change takes on quite different dimensions, however, in the present age. Man in the latter half of the twentieth century has an overwhelming sense of the need for change.

There is an urgency, a compulsion about it; there is a belief that our survival as a society and as civilized man depends on our willingness to initiate and accept change.

Such a conviction as this places a special responsibility on those who have been selected or who desire to provide leadership in our society. It is no longer possible to hang out a "business as usual" sign. But the recognition of the need for a change does not lead automatically to its rapid and easy adoption. Change almost never comes easily. The concept of change, which implies leaving the tested and trying the new, forsaking the comfortable and familiar in favor of an unknown quantity, leads to resistance and insecurity. One knows he ought to change but he resists; there are constantly opposing forces affecting a person's willingness to change. Lewin's "quasi-stationary equilibrium" theory describes those driving forces that on one hand impel one to change his behavior and those restraining or counter forces of equal strength that inhibit change.[1]

One of the myths that society lives by is that there is something called a "little" change or a "minor" change. This probably is not so. A change that appears minor to the change agent can be a major one to some of those to be affected by it. Change, even a presumed "little" one, is almost always threatening in some degree, because it forces one out of his former ways of behaving; it calls for new responses, new skills, new modes of thinking; it is a disruptive element in the established flow of human and institutional activity. This is not meant to imply that there is a human predisposition in favor of the status quo. On the contrary, as Watson points out, almost everyone prefers excitement to a humdrum, monotonous existence and is eager for some kind of change in his life and situation.[2] The conclusion one comes to, then, is that if people and organizations do not change it must be because the human desire for change is held in check by some counterbalancing factors. Factors that are external to a change are equally and sometimes more crucial to its acceptance than the change itself.

Change operates at several levels. Some of these are largely concerned with the organization and its operation, while others are focused on the behavior and belief systems of individuals within the organization. Such levels are clearly related, and a change in one affects the others. Organizational change, either in purposes or structure, does affect the ways in which individuals are expected to behave. Conversely, changes in the ways individuals behave, in the ways which they perceive themselves, their purposes, and their relationship to the organization also work to bring about organizational change. These interrelationships of change origin and affect might be conceptualized as: individual→ organization; organization→ individual; individual→ other individuals; individual→ and himself.

If the purpose of ISB is to directly influence teacher behavior in such a way as to facilitate the achievement of the goals of the educational organization, it is axiomatic that a supervisor must be concerned about the nature and the processes of change. The school itself is involved in the simultaneous and delicate process, on the one hand, of seeking to transmit and sustain our culture while, on the other hand, seeking through educating the young to bring about change in that culture. It is a delicate balance. And so, with the supervisor there exists such a duality of purpose: to maintain, but also to change.

If the study of change has not yet produced a generally accepted theory, it has, nevertheless, provided a rich and extensive body of research, experimentation, and theoretical investigation. It is a field of study abounding with implications for supervisory practice. One can only describe as astounding the lack of systematic study given to the processes of change by persons who are charged with the specific responsibility for bringing about change in individuals and in institutions.

Explorations in change have dealt with two general categories: change in individuals and change in social systems. Within these two broad divisions there have been numerous foci of investigation. For the purposes of contributing to an understanding of ISB, the investigations selected for summarization here will be categorized as: planning and strategy of change, content factors and change, resistance and rejection of change, conditions for acceptance of change, influence of group membership on change, the change agent, and maintaining and sustaining change.

THE PLANNING AND STRATEGY OF CHANGE

Research in this area involves the processes of planning, problem-solving, and the strategy of organizing people and groups to plan, attack, and accomplish objectives of change.

Two idea-systems concerning methods of change have been observed in the contemporary scene by Bennis, Benne, and Chin [3]—one the idea of nonintervention, and the other the idea of radical intervention. They propose an alternative to the doctrinal extremes of laissez-faire or conflict; the alternative is "planned change" in which social technology is used to solve the problems of a social system. Planned change is defined as "a conscious, deliberate, and collaborative effort to improve the operations of a system, whether it be self-system, social system, or cultural system, through the utilization of scientific knowledge."

Bennis [4] distinguishes between "planned change" and seven other types of change: indoctrination, coercive change, technocratic change, interactional, socialization, emulative, and natural.

It has been found through an examination of hundreds of schools and school board philosophies, that local schools seldom have realistic or well-thought-out statements on educational philosophy, nor are they aware of general or specific educational objectives.[5] When shortcomings are identified and change is desired, it then becomes necessary first to establish goals or objectives in order to solve the problems.

Hansen comments on the inherent difficulties of planning for change when purposes and policies of the organization are simply not clear or consistent, stating, "If change is to have any real thrust, it must have both force and direction. That is, the change must come out of the constellation of forces that necessitate or demand change, but it must be given the direction that only clear-cut goals can provide." [6]

Huefner implies that often the consideration of goals is an isolated and academic exercise and is not really used to direct a given plan. He states: "The goals should provide the common objectives by which the merits of alternative programs are weighed and by which conflicts between programs are resolved." He makes the point that goals must be more than statements of platitudes in order to make them worthy of involvement and consideration within the change process.[7]

The analysis of problem-solving and planning for change that has most influenced educators is Dewey's "scientific method," which consists of the following steps: becoming aware of the problem—a felt difficulty; clarifying and defining the problem; evaluating proposed solutions, and experimental verification.[8] A plan devised by Hansen, which encompasses many existing patterns, is: identification of problems; diagnosis of the problem-situation; clarification of the diagnostic findings; search for solutions; mobilizing for change, and making the actual change decisions.[9] This plan closely resembles the familiar "scientific method"; however, Hansen concludes that a systematic method of problem-solving should be used, and if one does not exist that meets the needs of the problem-solver, then one should be developed and followed.

H. A. Simon, researching participation in planning, concluded that "significant changes in human behavior can be brought about rapidly only if the persons who are expected to change participate in deciding what the change shall be and how it shall be made." [10] The importance of participation in planning has also been established by Guest,[11] who reports that planning of changes in response to specific needs that have been identified is to "adapt" rather than "adopt." Such a process avoids change motivated by the desire to "change for the sake of change or to conform to unfocused pressures from higher management, parents, or universities." Such a process is also supported in the work of Shepard and Blake.[12]

Change processes, according to Rogers,[13] involve five stages following the design of innovations: awareness, learning of the existence of an innovation; interest, in which a person seeks more data and considers the innovation; evaluation, in which the merits of the innovation are weighed; trial, whereby the individual actually tries out the innovation— perhaps on a small scale; and adoption, whereby he accepts the innovation for continued use. These five steps might also lead to a decision to reject an innovation.

Another proposed formulation of stages suggested by Mackenzie includes: criticism of existing programs; proposal of changes; development and clarification; evaluation, review, and reformulation of proposals; comparison of alternate proposals; action on proposals; and implementation of action decisions.[14]

Numerous researchers, Benne,[15] Lewin,[16] and Jenkins,[17] among others, have used force field analysis as a tool for diagnosing situations and developing a change strategy. A classic piece of work in this area is Kurt Lewin's theory of quasi-stationary equilibrium, which holds that individuals and systems are held in equilibrium by a balance of driving forces on one hand and restraining forces on the other.[18] Lewin found that levels of quasi-stationary equilibrium can be altered by either of two methods, by increasing the strength of the driving forces or by decreasing the strength of the restraining forces. The first method is more likely to be tension-inducing. Jenkins states that "changes will occur only as the forces are modified so that the level where the forces are equal is changed."[19]

Chin suggests the following as to what strategy includes:

Strategies of change is interpreted as including, but not limited to, dissemination and provisions for utilization of pertinent information regarding all aspects of the proposed plan; ways of identifying and dealing with internal and external (environmental) constraints as well as facilitating influences; ways of identifying potential opposition, conflicts and tensions and of resolving them advantageously; appropriate means of helping individuals, organizations and agencies to effect needed change in their perspectives; and procedures (guidelines) for implementing proposed change.[20]

Miles cites certain characteristics of strategies that have been asserted to be most effective:

1. comprehensive attention to all stages of the diffusion process,
2. creation of new structures, especially by systems outside the target system,
3. congruence with prevalent ideology in the target system, such as beliefs about the importance of "local control,"
4. reduction of pressures on relevant decision-makers, and
5. use of coalitions or linkage between existing structures, or between old and new structures.[21]

An accepted general strategy is to approach change in such a way that there results a climate hospitable to continuous adaptation and change.[22] Approaches are weak if they have been planned and directed toward one single change. Howsam states "This approach is dysfunctional in any long-term view since it tends to lead to an attitude of 'we innovated last year'." [23]

Watson found that change strategies may deal with attitude and value change, with social structures, or with processes occurring within the structures. His conclusion is that structural approaches appear most productive. In his S–P–A formula he theorizes that an effective change sequence usually involves structures first, altered interaction processes as a result, and attitudes last.[24] In schools, Miles finds that the one-teacher-in-a-classroom model makes it extremely difficult to create the kind of interdependency and contact that encourages diffusion of new practices.[25]

Within any strategy of change, there will probably exist many possible approaches to the solution of a given problem. In the Western States Small Schools Project, "entry" to the problem was sought at many points: upgrading teachers, reorganizing class schedules, using new instructional materials, providing new grouping patterns, and encouraging interschool cooperation. Hansen refers to the need to get a handhold or a toehold, a spot with "leverage enough to get something moving." Finding these places, he says, is "not so much a matter of formal research or even rational analysis as it is a matter of thorough understanding of the situation and the people involved in the educational issue. . . ." [26]

A survey by Grenier found seven approaches in frequent use in organizational change:

1. The decree approach—a person or group in authority orders a change to be made;
2. The replacement approach—a new person is brought in, or at least someone is removed from his position;
3. The structural approach—reorganizing the required relationships in the organization, changing the roles and job definitions, the contracts and organizational variables;
4. The group decision approach—members of the organization or group decide on a plan and elect to do it together;
5. The data discussion approach—wherein data about the organization and its functioning are brought to the members for review (in general, the feedback procedure);
6. The group problem-solving approach—whereby internal groups diagnose and collect relevant data about the problem; and
7. The T-group approach—wherein the emphasis is upon the nature of the relationship of the organizational and interpersonal environment, the quality of trust, openness, power balance, and other such factors.[27]

Bennis [28] classifies change processes into mutual goal-setting types (planned, indoctrinational, interactional, and socializational), and non-mutual goal-setting types (technocratic, coercive, emulative, and "natural"). Walton[29] classifies change strategies as those based on love and trust, and those based on problem–solving. Chin's grouping of change strategy falls into three major types: empirical-rational, normative-re-educative, and power.[30]

Howsam concluded that the strategies and processes of change must include at least as much attention to the development of professional and human competence as they do to the other supportive and enabling aspects.[31] And Hansen, in the same vein, states that only people within an organization have psychological reactions; therefore, it is "with the people and not the organization itself that we must concern ourselves." [32]

Chin discovered that the preference for a particular strategy for effecting change seems to lie in our biases, depending on whether we see the educational system as "people processes, technical processes, or processes centered around things and materials." [33]

Miles concluded that certain types of strategies are less effective: those that attempt to use only existing structure, and are thus hamstrung by the status quo; those self-initiated by the target system, since they fail to see broader problems; and those that rely on arousing a high degree of conflict.[34]

What happens, according to Lionberger's studies,[35] beyond the point when adoptions of a new practice begin to occur at an increasing rate, is primarily a result of people interacting with people and not a direct result of any change-agent efforts. Stone, too, found that most of the effort expended by change agents was highly concentrated in the early stages of the diffusion process.[36]

Lionberger also reports that researchers have suggested that there is a point, somewhere between 3% and 25% adoption level, at which diffusion becomes more important than "selling." [37] Research indicating that physicians share new ideas with each other while restaurant owners almost never share new ideas about the restaurant business, led Lionberger to conclude that in a competitive endeavor ideas are not readily shared.[38]

CONTENT FACTORS AND CHANGE

Research in this area investigates the effect that the content or the nature of the change has on the ease with which a proposed change can be achieved. The less complicated the change, the more easily it can be adopted. Changes whose basic content is technological rather than value-based require less effort to achieve.

Studies by Mort[39] and Forsdale[40] indicate that the "cost" of an innovation, not only in terms of money but also in time and energy, affects adoption. The higher the cost, the more slowly the change progresses.

If changes can be "divisible," that is, made in part, the obstacle of cost may be reduced.[41]

Technological factors were also found to affect willingness to adopt. While a change that is primarily a technological one is relatively easy to make, it was found by Eichholz and Rogers,[42] and by Jennings[43] that such changes are also easy to reject or discontinue. Miles[44] concluded that the opinions of a small technological elite may exert a "disproportionate influence" in the acceptance of a change. Both Forsdale and Marsh[45] found that direct experience with a technological device seemed essential for an adoption decision.

The more difficult or complex an innovation, the more slowly it will diffuse. Miles[46] points out that the potential of technological changes in a classroom depends on implementation factors such as availability, ease of use, and skill of the operator. Changes with built-in implementation supports should be adopted and should diffuse more quickly than those without supports.

The work of Forsdale [47] and Wayland [48] indicates that a change is more likely to be accepted if it appears to be an addition to an existing practice and not a threat to it. Wayland also found that changes which were relatively easy to institutionalize were more likely to be accepted than those which required continued creativity and were not subject to routine.

Forsdale [49] also found that if the content of the change is perceived as not too different from existing procedures, it may be in danger of rejection as "not being worth the trouble." Numerous writers (Miles [50]) have found that when the content of a change requires a value change, it will encounter much more difficulty than change not affecting values.

Atwood [51] discovered that changes will be resisted if they appear to require increased dependence on others, decrease personal initiative, or violate important values. Changes that cause the reverse of these conditions are more likely to be accepted, especially if they appear to increase autonomy.

A study by Carlson found that the varying rates of diffusion of education innovation could be *partially* accounted for by the characteristics of the innovations themselves. The five factors identified as partially controlling the fate of an innovation are: relative advantage (superior to former idea); compatibility (consistent with values of adopters); complexity (difficulty of use); divisibility (can be tried on a limited basis); and communicability (degree to which the results can be indicated to others).[52]

RESISTANCE AND REJECTION OF CHANGE

Research in this area deals with the reasons why individuals and organizations resist change. Some of the factors leading to resistance are related to human personality, the nature of social systems, and perceived effects of change; still others derive from the initiation and the process of the change. Resistance to change may be individual or it may be organizational, in which a segment of the larger system resists a change effort.

Resistance in Personality

By resistance to change is meant that behavior intended to protect the person or persons against the consequences of a change. Zander [53] distinguishes between "resistance" and opposition to a change that is perfectly logical and based on some well-supported reasons.

Cannon has described the stabilizing forces within individuals as "homeostasis" [54]; Lewin's "quasi-stationary equilibrium" theory describes a similar condition.[55] Raup generalized the reversion to complacency as the most basic characteristic of the psychological as well as the physiological behavior of man,[56] yet there is also considerable research to indicate the human organism's desire for change. Thomas [57] proposed the "desire for new experience" as one of the four basic wishes underlying human behavior, and Lilly's [58] experiments showed that lying quietly awake in a comfortable bed, free from disturbing stimuli, soon becomes intolerable. People need to interact with a changing environment.

Some researchers have concluded, therefore, that opposition to change, which would appear to indicate satisfaction with existing conditions, may actually be the result of insufficient adaptation to them.[59]

Zander has found six conditions that contribute to resistance to change: 1) nature of the change not made clear; 2) people see different meanings in a proposed change; 3) people caught between strong forces asking them to change and equally strong prohibiting forces; 4) people pressured to change, having no "say" in the change themselves; 5) change based on personal grounds rather than impersonal ones; and 6) change that ignores established customs and norms of the group. Zander suggests the following principle in decreasing resistance to change: "Resistance will be prevented to the degree that the changer helps the changees to develop their own understanding of the need for the change and an explicit awareness of how they feel about it, and what can be done about those feelings." [60]

There is some evidence to indicate that in the face of considerable resistance, new attitudes can be accepted by a person only if he has a chance to completely vent his original attitude. A kind of catharsis may be necessary; the air is cleared after a gripe session and new understandings can be developed.

Research indicates that what is commonly referred to as "habit" also causes resistance. A particular response, Stephens [61] postulates, once having been learned, will continue to operate in a fixed fashion. Once a habit is established, its smooth operation becomes satisfying to the organism, and forces that would alter this operation are resisted.[62] The way in which the organism first successfully meets with a situation sets an unusually persistent pattern. Watson [63] observed that teachers, despite inservice courses and the efforts of supervisors, will continue to teach in about the same way as they were taught. Once an attitude has been set up, a person responds to other suggestions within the framework of his established outlook.[64] Levine and Murphy [65] conducted experiments with materials designed to bring about changes in attitude. The experiments revealed that subjects did not hear clearly, nor remember well, communications with which they disagreed.

Watson[66] found that children tend to incorporate the values, attitudes, and beliefs of those who care for them. Although there may be some instances of rebellion in adolescence, the typical adult still agrees far more than he disagrees with his parents on such basic items as language, religion, politics, child rearing, and the purpose of schools.

Watson refers to the "illusion of impotence," in which an individual feels trapped, enmeshed in a system that he can do nothing about. As a result, he resists the opportunity to contribute to or accept change, not believing that his involvement can really be of much use. Another personality factor identified by Watson as causing resistance to change is the "superego": the moral standards acquired in childhood from authoritative adults, a powerful tradition-serving factor. An individual needs considerable ego-strength in order to be able to cope with changing life situations and to disregard unrealistic, perfectionistic demands of his superego that were acquired in childhood. Watson states further that "organisms resist change because, as a consequence of childhood dependence and the stern authority of the tradition-oriented voice of the superego, children quickly learn to distrust their own impulses. Each says, in effect, 'What I would really want is bad! I should not want it!'" Guilt, he states, is mobilized against change—to be good is to accept the status quo.[67]

The fear of losing status, or that submitting to a request to change involves a kind of personal defeat, becomes a major factor in resistance. Frank[68] found that change would be resisted if it involved what seemed to be submitting to another's arbitrary personal demand, which was the equivalent of a personal defeat. Numerous researchers have pointed out the difference between resisting a proposed change on the grounds of opposition to the change and resisting because of the personality of the change agent or because of antipathy generated by the influence attempt.

Much research has been done to show that participation can modify individual resistance to change. It has also been found, however, that individuals with a strong need for independence or with authoritarian personalities respond less favorably to the opportunity to take part in decision-making.[69]

Lippitt believes that, in education, most of the significant changes in practice imply and require changes in attitudes, skills, and values of the practitioner if the proposed change is to be a successful adoption and adaptation.[70] Although learning a new skill or using a new mechanical device is a relatively easy change, the altering of attitudes and values requires far more time to accomplish.

Some pioneering research done by Neugarten [71] in the area of personality change among adults has implications for the study of change. She found that in middle age there is a sense of expertise, a feeling that past experience makes quick decisions possible. In middle age there is a consciousness that accomplishment is to be *expected*. Reflection, introspection, and stock-taking are characteristic of middle age. The middle-aged adult processes new information in the light of past experience.

Neugarten found that forty-year-old men see their environment as one that rewards risk-taking and boldness, while sixty-year-olds view the world as complex and dangerous. As they grow older men seem to cope with their world in more abstract and cognitive terms, women in more affective and expressive ones. In both sexes she found that older people become more egocentric, more concerned about the control and satisfaction of personal needs. A type of "social timetable" says that there are certain times in life when it is "best" to do certain things.

Social age definitions are important in conceptualizing adult change. Society's expectations create a system of norms that govern interaction. The concept of "age status" guides our interaction with other people. We adjust our behavior, Neugarten concludes, to fit the age status of a person. The child defers to the adult, the adult to the aged. Age status provides the legitimization of influence. If a person in authority is younger than his subordinates, there may be some discomfort about the mismatch between age status and institutional status, and such discomfort may exist until the younger person "proves" himself.

Strauss [72] discusses what he calls "regularized status-passage," an elaborate way that systems have of preparing one for status positions and of regularizing one's conduct in terms of what is appropriate behavior. The attainment of status may require that one has had certain experience and demonstrated certain kinds of conduct. Strauss, like Neugarten, finds there are time-status rites that govern one's entry and acceptance; he comments on those in a new position who "commit the indelicate error of taking a formal promotion too literally, when actually there exist intervening informal stages that must be traversed before the full prerogatives of the position are attained."

Resistance arises when demands are made by one who has not yet passed through the rites of time-age status. An overeager person can be kept in line by all kinds of controlling devices, and he will find that the changes he had planned will take longer to initiate than he expected. A person raised in rank or status must still "prove" himself before he can move about with ease in his new postion. Strauss refers to the special language of rankings: "He's a *new* lieutenant," or, "That board member is one of the old-timers."

Resistance in Social Systems

Mann and Neff cite examples of change resisted because of "side effects" that are perceived as destructive in related areas of an organization.[73] Lippitt, Watson, and Westley [74] also cite presumed advantage for another group as a reason for resistance; a technical change that enabled piece-workers in a factory to earn more than the supervisors had to be abandoned. Dimock and Sorenson conclude that advance in one sector cannot proceed far ahead of change in other sectors.[75] Cartwright reports that "changes in one part of a group produce strain on the other related parts which can be reduced only by eliminating the change or by bringing about readjustments in the related parts."[76]

Starbuck observes that change is resisted because of the pleasure one receives from performing familiar tasks and associating with familiar people; organizational tasks are molded to personal values and goals. Change in an organization often brings with it different salaries, statuses, personnel, methods, and goals. Those who stand to loose by such an unbalancing of the system resist the change, even though the effect of it may be only temporary.[77]

A threat to the vested interests of a powerful individual or group is one of the most obvious sources of resistance in social systems. A change may be a threat to vested interests of prestige, status, or power; it may also threaten economic interests. The vested interests and the influence of power groups in a community was documented many years ago by Hollingshead.[78]

Morison [79] illustrates how a change was resisted in the Navy, not because of the change itself but because of the social consequences of the change. The change was resisted because of the "status disequilibration" among officers that it would have wrought. Research by Bavelas and Strauss,[80] Mann,[81] Morison,[82] and Marrow and French [83] indicates the limitation of facts as the sole lever to bring change. Man does not behave as a rational being; if he did, resistance to change would be less. Bennis, Benne, and Chin [84] note that reason and rational arguments have little appeal, given the forces arrayed against change—especially if the proposed change has important and uncertain consequences that might entail loss to the interested groups.

Anthropologists have repeatedly noted that, within any culture, some activities are easily changed, while others are highly resistant to innovation. Generally, technology is receptive to new ideas and procedures. The greatest resistance to change concerns matters connected with what people hold to be sacred.[85] Spicer reports that the introduction of improved technology in underdeveloped countries runs into obstacles if it seems to impinge on religious superstitions, beliefs, or practices.[86] Cultures also strongly resist alterations that enter the realm of morals and ethics. Anthropologists have repeatedly found that even when few people in a society live by the traditional code, it is still defended as "ideal."

Griffiths reports that the major impetus for change comes from outside rather than inside an organization.[87] Suspicion and hostility toward outsiders, however, is almost universal; Kohler even observed this kind of behavior among chimpanzees on the Island of Tenerifa.[88] Jung has found that organizational rejection can be lessened if the outside agent can be linked to internal change agents. He must first find a point of entry to gain acceptance in the organization.[89]

Several researchers have noted that the existence of an innovation elsewhere is not sufficient basis for a change in one's own organization. Watson [90] notes that the history of experimental demonstration schools is that though they were often observed, such schools were seldom replicated. Observers were not convinced that the fine practices they saw would work in their own systems. Agricultural agents long ago discontinued model farms run by state colleges, and instead developed demonstration projects within the local neighborhood. Farmers would accept what they could observe being done within their own county, while they were reluctant to import new practices from far away.

Research in rural sociology indicates that even after a trial period some farmers eventually become rejecters.[91] Eichholz formulated a theory of rejection paralleling the more familiar theory of acceptance. His five stages in the rejection process are awareness, disinterest, denial, trial, and rejection.[92] When it is felt that change will alter production, and it is not readily apparent whether the output will increase or decrease, resistance is likely.

In an effort to identify some of the reasons for teacher rejection of innovation, Brickell, in a study relating to change, stated this principle:

> A school, like any other institution, tends to continue doing what it was established to do, holding itself relatively stable and resisting attempts at restructuring. There is a sound reason for this: Stability in the institutional structure makes for maximum output of the results that structure was designed to produce.[93]

Blau and Scott observed that much of the resistance to change in organizations is the result of the disturbance that change produces in the status structure.[94] It was found that older teachers generally held conservative views, while younger teachers were more liberal and permissive. The older teachers thus resisted changes that seemed likely to result in more permissive procedures—thus disturbing status relations between older and younger teachers and forcing the latter to question the wisdom and dominance of the older groups.[95]

Guest states, "There must be some kind of involvement from below which makes it possible for subordinates to accept and even to initiate a certain amount of change themselves." [96] He adds that if errors (which are likely to be made in introducing a major change) result in nonsupport by those at higher levels, a planned change may end abruptly. Obviously, change may be resisted because of lack of information or skill. Resistance to certain curriculum changes (e.g., the "new mathematics") may be based on this ground.[97]

Miles reports that systems tend *not* to change for a variety of reasons:

1. Maximum energy goes into current operations and maintenance; the development and implementation of new programs appear to require the addition of money and staff over and beyond that required for regular operations.
2. The hierarchically arranged subsystems in the overall organization tend, over time, to become progressively segregated and independent from each other.
3. Durable feedback loops tend to develop between individuals and subsystems, and operate to restrict communication in self-confirming, stabilizing ways. Thus, the longer the tenure of individuals—either administrators or those lower in the structure—the more stable the patterns of interaction that develop, and the more difficult change becomes.[98]

Willower points out that the forms resistance to change takes may run from verbal hostility to organizational sabotage.[99] In Gouldner's study in industry, a new manager was harassed by frequent favorable references to a former plant manager.[100] In Willower's school study, a teacher compared the new principal unfavorably to a man who had been principal some thirty years before.[101]

Zander states that once a change has been made, resistance may take the form of sloppy work or apathetic indifference.[102] Willower and Jones support this conclusion: "Indifference represents a safer kind of resistance than more aggressive forms since it is less obvious and less easily detected. . . . In the JHS study, one administrator consistently interpreted what we regarded as teacher apathy to be staff harmony." [103] Rigid conformity is another form of resistance. Rules and instructions are followed to the letter even when reason or the good of the organization clearly dictate a more permissive kind of behavior. A classic example of this is the customs inspector creating chaos by simply enforcing all of the regulations.

CONDITIONS FOR ACCEPTANCE OF CHANGE

Much less appears in the literature about acceptance of change than about resistance or rejection; this is hardly surprising. However, it would probably facilitate the change process if more were known about the causes, sources, and forms of acceptance.

Kelman identifies three processes of attitude change: 1) compliance, the receiving of reward or escaping of punishment; 2) identification, the change agent is an attractive person and the change is made to establish or maintain a satisfying relationship; 3) internalization, one's cognitive field is actually reorganized and he sees the relevance of the new behavior for the issues at hand.[104]

In the field of agriculture and rural sociology the five stages of the process of innovation acceptance are awareness, interest, evaluation, trial, and adoption.[105] Various studies show that omission of any of these five steps makes implementation of any innovation more difficult.[106]

Ross[107] reviewed a number of studies dealing with the diffusion of educational ideas among public schools, and concluded that the wealth factor was the one variable most closely related to adoption of innovations. Rogers,[108] Ross,[109] and Griffiths[110] all report a high relationship between financial resources of a school system and its innovativeness. In fact, outstanding innovative school systems are usually located in particularly wealthy communities. At the same time, Rogers notes, it is important to remember that not all rich schools are innovators and that not all schools that innovate are rich. Research by Carlson, however, does not support school wealth as a predictor of either rate or amount of adoption of educational innovation.[111]

Rogers states that the community's attitude about providing support for school costs is obviously an important intervening variable between community wealth and school innovations.[112] Demeter also indicated that the motives for more innovative schools must necessarily come from the desire of the community for more effective learning by their children. This observation extends beyond the concern of financial support, but it certainly includes it.[113]

Miles notes the effect of involving high-status target-group members:

> If the innovative group draws high-status members from the target system in which innovation is contemplated, it is more likely to have its recommendations accepted, particularly if the group is strongly legitimated by the system, and maintains clear, open communication with it. However, these conditions, if met thoroughly, also mean that the norms and demands of the target system exert a good deal of influence on the innovating group; thus the innovations achieved are likely to be moderate rather than radical in nature.[114]

There is some research to indicate conditions that affect the rate of adoption of a change. The work of Mort,[115] Marsh,[116] and Brickell [117] suggests that innovations which are difficult in form, require much administrative energy, tend to disrupt, or, in a technical sense, are confusing or threatening will diffuse slowly. Innovations with built-in implementation supports, however, such as training as part of the innovation and self-teaching materials, will diffuse more rapidly.

Changes are also more likely to be accepted if they: can be adopted without seriously disturbing other parts of the program; reduce a recognized gap between ideals and practice; reinforce initiative-taking and autonomy; can be routinely managed, rather than requiring continued creativity.

Barnett found that among the early acceptors of an innovation will be the dissident, the indifferent, the resentful, and the disaffected. He concluded that these people have nothing to lose and will readily accept the new. Those who are later acceptors will be influenced by the prestige of those who create, sponsor, or initially accept a change.[118]

In a study by Carlson of innovative school superintendents, early adopters of change were found to have a tendency to be younger, know few peers well, be less sought for advice, get higher professional ratings, have shorter tenure in their positions, and seek advice and information from outside the system.[119]

Studies by Merton,[120] Lazarsfeld,[121] and Berelson and Gaudet [122] emphasized the decisive role of "trusted others" in decisions involving doubt or uncertainty. Studies by Lionberger of the adoption of farm practices point out the important contributions of early adopters.[123] The "first to try" are generally considered innovators, but these people serve as models for later adopters—especially for those who insist on proof. Lionberger also found that those who adopt early tend to learn and get information from direct and authentic sources, while later adopters rely heavily on early or middle-range adopters for both original and additional information and for advice on adoption decisions.

Some individuals in organizations have been found to be more important as legitimizers than others. This condition has been found among many of the social organizations studied. Marsh suggests that the opinions of teachers and observation of classroom situations are important, particularly when the validity of other available information is in doubt.[124]

Lionberger found that in the change process individuals play different roles: some are innovators, risk assumers, quick adopters; others are communicators, who get the word around but are not counted on as advisors; still others are legitimizers, who put the local stamp of approval on a change that makes it acceptable to many others.[125]

INFLUENCE OF GROUP MEMBERSHIP ON CHANGE

The research in this area deals with the effects of group norms and sub-systems on change and with the group as a medium of change.

Although it is often presumed that innovators and change agents are in a good position to influence others, there are numerous studies to indicate that norms operating within the group may act as an important intervening variable. Marsh and Coleman [126] found that in communities where traditional norms prevail, innovative farmers were not looked to by their peers as information or advice sources. Several studies indicate that innovative farmers are looked on as deviant, and a study by Rogers indicates that innovators often perceive themselves as deviant.[127]

Groups exert powerful forces, which are of great importance in understanding individual behavior. Seashore found that members of highly cohesive groups show less anxiety than members of low cohesive groups. He concluded that the highly cohesive groups provide effective support for their members in their encounter with anxiety-provoking aspects of their environment.[128]

Whyte's *The Organization Man* analyzed the way in which a group prescribes the kind of behavior expected of its members, including modes of dress, ambition, participation in community life, time schedules, and indications of loyalty.[129]

Merei points out that the typical individual conforms to group norms, and cannot change them. He may deviate somewhat in his behavior but the norm will persist. Merei's laboratory experiment showed that even a child with strong leadership qualities was required to conform to the established play norms of a small group of kindergarten children.[130]

An experiment by Lewin, Lippitt, and White [131] found that an individual's aggression level depends not solely upon personal traits but upon the social structure and atmosphere of the group he is in. The now classic Western Electric studies clearly demonstrated that groups develop behavior norms for their members and that to be a "good" group member one must adopt those norms as his own. Numerous researchers have shown that group decisions can produce changes in individual behavior that are much larger and lasting than those brought about by individual decision, or through attempts to modify individual behavior.[132]

Lippitt [133] reports that colleagues in a number of fields examined deliberately avoid observing each other at work and frequently are reluctant to adopt new practices because they fear that their deviancy would be negatively evaluated by their peers. A number of situations were found in which colleagues deliberately maintained a collusive ignorance and opposed changing the socialization practices because each employee feared that what he would like to do would be considered deviant by the others.

Festinger and Thibaut[134] describe what happens when a person deviates noticeably from the group norm. The group will first try to alter his attitude; failing in this, they one by one abandon him as hopeless. Contact and communication will decrease; he may be ignored or excluded to the extent that, finally, he no longer "belongs."

Coch and French,[135] Gerard,[136] Kelley,[137] and Kelley and Volkhart [138] found that the more salient or important the group was for the person, the less effective were the attempts to change his attitudes or actions.

Lewin [139] compared the effect of individual decision with the effect of group decision among farm women in a maternity ward. The superiority of group decision-making was clearly established. When using individual procedures, the force field that corresponds to the individual's dependence on a value standard acts to resist changes, but when one succeeds in changing group standards, this force field will tend to facilitate changing the individual and will tend to stabilize individual conduct on the new group level.

An early study by Sherif, [140] as well as more recent research by Asch,[141] Blake, [142] Newcomb[143] and other researchers, has demonstrated that in a situation in which an individual is unable to tell whether his answer is right or wrong, he is almost totally dependent on the group for selecting a response.

Research by Kelley and Volkhart,[144] Argyle,[145] and Raven [146] all indicate that when a person is made to express his opinion publicly rather than privately, he is much more likely to conform to group norms. Raven found that "the greater the possibility of rejection for nonconformity, the greater the pressure to change toward the group norm."

Moeller and Applezweig,[147] and Strickland and Crowne[148] found a relationship between conforming behavior and the need for social approval; individuals with a strong need for social approval will yield more easily to group pressures.

Cartwright and Zander suggest that group pressures are set up for three reasons: to help a group accomplish its goals; to help the group maintain itself as a group; and to help members develop validity or reality for their opinions.[149] Festinger concludes that pressures are exerted, therefore, because a member who behaves in a different way from that approved by the group becomes a threat to the achievement of the group.[150]

Festinger, Schacter and Back,[151] and Coch and French,[152] through field studies, have found that the extent of a group's conformity to its own standards depends on the cohesiveness of the group.

French found that members in long-established groups tend to react more uniformly than members of newly formed groups.[153] Similarly, Back [154] and Festinger [155] discovered that the power a group has over its members—to accept or resist change, for example—is directly proportional to the cohesiveness of the group. The more cohesive the group, the more power it holds over its members. In highly cohesive groups rejection of the deviant was observed. Kelley and Shapiro [156] found that the more accepted a person feels by the other members of his group, the greater the freedom he feels to deviate from group standards. Research by Asch has shown that the presence of a partner for a deviate greatly increases his tendency to be independent.[157]

Maladjustive behavior patterns were found by Lewin to result from "marginality," or an unstable membership situation in which a person stands on the boundary between two groups, belonging to neither. Such a situation results in high tension and behavior extremes; it does not foster individuality but, rather, makes belonging to cohesive high-demand groups appear very attractive.[158] Cartwright and Zander state that when group pressures are so set as to create group standards, the uniform behavior is difficult to change.[159]

The effectiveness of group decision-making in accepting change has been well documented in research by Maier,[160] Lewin,[161] Levine and Butler,[162] and Morse and Reimer.[163] Coch and French [164] have clearly demonstrated in their classic Harwood Corporation experiment how group resistance to change can be modified by involving the group members in making the decision about the change. Their experiment with three groups (no participation, participation through representation, total participation) indicated the high degree of receptivity to change on the part of the group that was heavily involved in the decision-making process; in fact, their productivity rate after the change even surpassed the previous rate!

Miles's work has described the effect on experimental schools and colleges of the larger system imposing its norms, even though these experimental units were set apart and intended to operate by different standards.[165]

Willower and Jones[166] report in their study that norms held by older teachers stressed order, firmness, and social distance in teacher-student relationships. The new teachers learned that if they were not tough in discipline, or if they attempted innovations that resulted in more permissive methods, they were open to the charge of softness. Standards of teacher behavior were communicated in many ways and places. In the study, the informal structure and norms functioned to discourage the proposal and accomplishment of certain kinds of change.

Chesler, Schmuck, and Lippitt [167] divided a small group of schools into four types: schools in which the teachers perceived support for creative teaching 1) from both the principal and staff; 2) from the principal, but not the staff; 3) from the staff, but not the principal; and 4) from neither the staff nor the principal. Data showed that schools of type (1) had the highest average number of innovations per teacher—5.2, while schools of type (4) showed the lowest average number of innovations per teacher —3.5. These researchers concluded that the kinds of interpersonal staff relationships present in a school are important factors that either encourage or discourage the sharing of educational insights and experimentations.

Miles found that the difficulties of group norms acting to resist change ". . . can often be avoided by creating new innovative structures which bypass vested interests. Isolation frees the innovative enterprise from the (usually anti-innovative) norms of the target system. The problem appears to be that of linking new structures with target systems closely enough to aid the construction of innovations."[168] Miles also states that temporary innovative systems have some of the advantages of new systems plus the advantage of not having permanent status that threatens the existing system.

Lewin[169] and Cartwright[170] conclude from their research that the normal gap between practitioner and client could be a real obstacle to the adoption of the suggested conduct. In spite of status differences, it is essential that the influencer and the one to-be-influenced be members of the same group in matters affecting values.

There are also strong pressures for conformity or for acceptance of a change when the change is of appropriate concern to the group. Lippitt and others have demonstrated that the greater the prestige of a group member in the eyes of other members, the greater will be the influence he can exert upon them.[171]

One's acceptance of an influence attempt is affected by the opinion he has of the person attempting to influence him. Osgood and Tannenbaum[172] found that if a highly regarded person holds views that differ from one's own, the result will be either a lower regard for that person or an altering of one's own opinion. The higher the regard one has for the other person, the greater the chance that the opinion will be modified. Merton also concludes that in such a situation, change takes place in the area in which one's values are less strongly held.[173]

Based on numerous research studies, Miles identifies several aspects that are favorable to group survival and effectiveness, including:

> . . . energy devoted to the accomplishment of novel, significant, focused, internalized, shared goals; effective, controllable procedures for achieving the goals; *esprit de corps*, group support, and mutual identification with peers; high autonomy and spontaneity, with freedom for creative experimentation, along with norms actively supporting change itself; higher quality problem-solving via increased communication among participants and fuller use of member resources; active meeting of members' needs

for autonomy, achievement, order, succorance, and nurturance; high involvement and commitment to decisions, followed by group support for implementation after the termination of the temporary group's life.[174]

THE CHANGE AGENT

The research in this area deals with the nature of the change agent, and his characteristics, behavior, and location in respect to the target system.

Research by Rogers has shown that innovative farmers are younger than those who are later adopters. Young people, he concludes, are not so conditioned by cultural traditions.[175] Much research has indicated that after middle age there is less willingness to respond favorably to change—but this does not imply that older adults never change.

Considerable research indicates the importance of external contact and influence in the change process. Coleman et al. reported that innovative physicians were more likely than others to attend out-of-town medical meetings.[176] Ryan and Gross found that the hybrid-corn innovators among Iowa farmers traveled more often to urban centers, such as Des Moines, than farmers who became later adopters of innovations.[177] Carter and Williams [178] found that in innovative industrial firms, there was extensive worldwide travel by their executives, who were interested in progress both at home and abroad; Goldsen and Ralis [179] found that farmers from Thailand who were innovative visited Bangkok, while less innovative ones seldom traveled. Ross reported in his study that teachers in the more innovative schools usually secured new educational ideas from outside their community.[180]

There is abundant research evidence to indicate that change does not take place unguided and haphazardly. "Most innovations appear to be stimulated, triggered, shepherded, and nurtured by some active person or group either external to or within the 'target' system." [181] In most cases, Miles concludes, the initiation for change in an educational system seems to come from outside, while most local changes appear to involve adoption or adaption, rather than direct invention, initiated from within.

Lippitt, Watson, and Westley [182] see the change agent as someone from outside the client system, a person free from intimate involvement with the clients to be served. While recognizing the reality of this view in practice, Bennis, Benne, and Chin contend that the view is too narrow and that client systems have the potential for their own planned change as well as individuals who can and do serve as change agents. They view the change agent as "any agent used by a client system to bring about improved performance." [183] Jung, while agreeing that any individual in a system has some potential to act as a change agent, if only to maintain equilibrium, found that people have vastly differing power and potential power to change a system.[184]

The relative strengths of the external and internal change agents is questioned by Jung.[185] He finds that the external change agent is actually allowed into the system temporarily, so that for a period of time he may be a quasi-internal change agent. In many cases the most rational change strategy may be to unite the efforts of external and internal change agents. Jung states that in most systems few persons see themselves as change agents, but that it would be beneficial for a system to have a role clearly identified and primarily concerned with the phenomenon of change. Such a person would provide the linkage between gaps in a system; these gaps might exist between a group and the resources, either human or material, that would enable them to do their work more effectively.

Bennis and Shepard have found that the success of a catalytic agent in moving a group depends in part on the degree of his freedom from involvement in the dependence and interdependence areas of the group. His power to move the group lies in his "freedom from anxiety based reactions to problems of authority (or intimacy); he has the freedom to be creative. . . ." [186]

There is abundant research evidence, however, of the effectiveness of groups as a medium of change, and Lewin,[187] Cartwright,[188] and Lippitt et al.[189] have demonstrated the effectiveness of change efforts that stem from an accepted member of the group.

Status differences, lack of acceptance, and ideological differences can be obstacles to a change agent's efforts. Lewin's conclusion is that although status differences exist, the change agent and the client must feel like members of the same group in matters affecting their sense of values.[190] This does not necessarily imply that the change agent must come from within the system or from within the client system; it is clear, though, that "linkage" must take place if the change agent is to be effective.

A change agent must win the cooperation of both leadership personnel and other members of an organization before he can experiment. French [191] cites the problem inherent in the need to gain approval of potential change from a top official, for the change agent may then become identified with management in the eyes of the subordinate group. French [192] concludes that a change agent must devote enough time to contact and communication so that people will develop confidence in him, a belief that he will do nothing to hurt them or conflict with their interests.

The importance of the concept of "systemic linkage" in achieving change has been articulated by numerous researchers (including Loomis,[193] Homans,[194] and Parsons [195]). Loomis defines it as a process by which "the elements of at least two social systems come to be articulated so that in some ways they function as a unitary system." [196] In a model of change presented by Loomis,[197] the change agent becomes part of the target system by systemic linkage.

Loomis identifies two broad phases of social change: the first, permissive and supportive; the second, denying and withdrawal. In the first phase, the change agent develops what Loomis[198] calls "social capital": he gains the confidence of members and builds his rank and power in the system, so that later, in phase two, he may deny accustomed satisfactions and may manipulate rewards to bring about change.

Loomis[199] found that in systems with pronounced *Gemeinschaft*-like solidarity, the change agent will experience difficulty in gaining entry. In such a case, his systemic linkage or entry must be achieved through his contributions to the external pattern. He must demonstrate the worth of his performance in the external pattern in order to gain acceptance into the internal pattern. He gains social capital in the external pattern and then effects systemic linkage. In target systems where there is low boundary maintenance, however, leaders or change agents can enter an internal pattern with relative ease, especially if their effort meets an unfilled need of the existing system. Systemic linkage occurs when the change agent is no longer perceived as an "outsider."

MAINTAINING AND SUSTAINING CHANGE

Research in this area deals with the problems of maintaining and sustaining change after the initial impetus dies down. It also deals with the problems of "locking," in which an individual or an organization, having changed, now becomes rigid in this new form.

According to Miles,[200] innovations in education are dropped or retained indefinitely, largely because their effectiveness is never evaluated. Since change is "good," evaluation is superfluous. Barton and Wilder [201] refer to substitute bases for judgment—ideology, sentiment, and persuasive claims by advocates. People's informal reactions are often assessed and their shared wishes for success in a venture are too often taken as evidence of the effectiveness of change.[202] Because evaluation of educational innovations is so infrequently done, Miles states that some innovations may fail for substantive reasons—an inability to achieve the desired results—but that the real reason for failure may go unnoticed.[203]

Mort indicates that for the reasons cited, among others, many promising innovations have been dropped before they have had a chance to "put down their roots," while many other ineffective and implausible ones have persisted for decades.[204]

Lewin [205] describes changing as a three-step procedure: unfreezing, moving, and freezing on a new level. His analysis of the reason for group life returning to a previous level after a "shot in the arm" is that the objective of a planned change was not defined as the reaching of a different level. Freezing on a new level ensures that the new force field is made relatively stable and secure against change or a return to a previous level.

Lionberger states that reinforcement of an adoption decision may be necessary if an idea or new practice is to be continued, particularly if local support of colleagues and significant groups does not occur.[206]

Four steps in effecting change are identified by Jenkins: analyzing the present situation, determining the changes required, making the changes indicated by the analysis, and stabilizing the new situation so that it will be maintained.[207]

Research by Jenkins suggests that one of the reasons for inability to maintain a change is that most often a change was achieved by increasing the driving forces. If the original restraining forces have not been modified, they may eventually push the new condition back to the earlier level. Jenkins points out the need to develop as clear a picture as possible of the forces that will exist after a change is achieved. There must be careful planning to ensure that the forces supporting the new condition are stable.[208]

Parsons notes the importance of the problems of tracing the repercussions of a change once it has been initiated into a system, including what he refers to as "backwash," a modification of the original direction of the change.[209] If change has depended on "compliance," DuBois has found, its permanence is unlikely. Conditions will return to the former level as soon as this influence is withdrawn.[210]

Bradford comments on the considerable difficulty that teachers face when they attempt in the fall to initiate improved teaching practices they have learned about during the summer. He argues for the need to prepare for the problem of maintenance at the outset of the effort: "Change, to be maintained, must be well rooted in the individual and well supported by forces in his external worlds."[211]

IMPLICATIONS FOR INSTRUCTIONAL
SUPERVISORY BEHAVIOR

A review of selected research in the area of change indicates that this field of study has much to contribute to an understanding of ISB. If a supervisor is seriously interested in effecting change in the behavior of teachers, an understanding of the processes of change and their implications for supervision seems essential.

A rich and extensive body of research findings concerning change is in existence; so much material is available that the above review does not pretend to be exhaustive. It is, rather, a selection of research and writings that appears to be particularly relevant to an understanding of ISB. Based on this selection, the following propositions have been formulated:

Planning and Strategy of Change

PROPOSITION 1: *Planning and initiating change will be more effective when the objectives and policies of the organization are clear, realistic, and understood.*

If a supervisor intends to initiate planned change, he must do so in keeping with the objectives of the school organization or of the subsystem with which he is dealing. If organizational objectives are nonexistent or are not clearly understood, there is only the random chance that ISB will be more than an isolated and ineffectual application to a problem existing in one part of the school organization. The supervisor's efforts to bring about change must contribute to the goals of the school and be in harmony with its policies if they are to be effective.

PROPOSITION 2: *Change efforts will be more effective when they are carefully planned, have definite goals, and incorporate some functional method of problem-solving to attain the desired ends.*

This suggests that a supervisor should make a thorough analysis of the change he contemplates and of the means to be employed in accomplishing this change. ISB will not be effective if there is a lack of careful planning or if a supervisor focuses only on the outcomes he desires and fails to develop an appropriate strategy.

PROPOSITION 3: *The effectiveness of change efforts will be enhanced when the people who are to be affected are involved in the planning and decision-making.*

Evidence indicates that if a supervisor wishes to make important changes in the behavior of teachers and to do so with some speed, then teachers must be involved in the process of deciding on the nature and direction of change. To operate without regard for such a principle would not only doom the change effort to unnecessary difficulty and resistance, but it would also deprive the supervisor of the benefit of the ideas and the clarification of needs that those to be affected could contribute. The evidence indicating the desirability of involving teachers in planning for a change is overwhelming.

PROPOSITION 4: *Change efforts will be more effective if they are supported by an appropriate, systematic, and comprehensive strategy.*

There is no single strategy that can be used, but there are characteristics of strategies that do appear to be more effective than others. No matter what strategy a supervisor uses, attention must be given to such concerns as dissemination of information, environmental constraints, potential conflicts and opposition, development and support of technical and human competence, the development of a climate conducive to change, and the identification of a "point of entry." The type of strategy a supervisor selects will depend on his own particular bias and on the way he views the educational system and the people for whom he is responsible, but whatever strategy he chooses, it should be logical, consistent, and considerate of both the nature of the organization and the people within it.

PROPOSITION 5: *Change will be more effective when the choice of a strategy is consistent with the focus of the change effort.*

Changes in school systems may emphasize people, technology, organization, or materials. The supervisor must decide what the focus of his change shall be, and then develop an appropriate strategy. To treat all changes in the same way is to disregard the unique qualities of individuals, organizations, and the nature of the change itself. The strategy employed in introducing a mechanical device in a classroom is quite different, for example, from that which seeks to affect the way a teacher interacts with students.

PROPOSITION 6: *Change will be more effective when, at the appropriate point in the change process, the change agent's efforts shift from "selling" to "diffusion."*

Although a supervisor's initial activity in his change strategy will involve helping people decide what change is desired, once the change has been accepted, his activity should shift to "diffusion." Since evidence indicates that rapid diffusion of an idea is a result of the interaction of people, a supervisor should provide opportunities for teachers who have initiated new practices to interact with others. Once a new behavior has begun, it will be spread more rapidly and effectively by teachers than by the supervisor. Continuing to expend energy in the "selling" endeavor would be a poor use of his time.

PROPOSITION 7: *Change will be more effective within groups that do not see themselves in competition with each other.*

If a supervisor expects teachers to share new ideas with each other, then he must strive to develop an atmosphere that encourages cooperation. If, on the contrary, teachers feel the need to seek an advantage over their colleagues, then they will jealously guard new ideas, materials, and practices, and the diffusion of change will be severely restricted.

Content Factors and Change

PROPOSITION 8: *A change effort will be more effective if it takes into account the demands of time, money, and energy that the change requires.*

A careful consideration of the nature of the change and of the "costs" entailed, will help a supervisor make proper judgments about the allocation of his time and effort, as well as the time he might need to achieve results. An understanding of how these factors affect a teacher's willingness to change will prevent him from making unreasonable demands on teachers and on himself.

The assignment of supervisors to certain change activities must also be based on a realization that their content may require work for an extended period of time.

PROPOSITION 9: *Changes that are primarily technological will be more effective if they are buttressed by direct experience and support in their implementation.*

If a supervisor desires teachers to use technological devices, he can bring this about with much less effort than, for example, something dealing with values; however, adoption will not be easy unless teachers are provided with the opportunity for direct experience with the equipment, and the change will not persist if implementation supports such as availability and ease of use are not built in.

PROPOSITION 10: *A change effort will be more effective if it is perceived as building on existing practice rather than threatening it.*

It will be easier for a supervisor to bring about change if he can show that it builds on current practice and does not discard all that is valued or currently in vogue. A supervisor who indicates by word or deed that the proposed change is a condemnation of current methods of operation creates a situation in which teachers will endeavor to defend current practices rather than welcome new ones.

Resistance and Rejection of Change

PROPOSITION 11: *The effectiveness of a change effort will be increased when one sees the nature of the change as enhancing his own personal relationships and status in the organization.*

In examining a proposed change, teachers will evaluate it not just for content and difficulty but for how it affects them, their autonomy, their prestige and power relationships, and their dependence or independence of certain others in the school. A supervisor must analyze such possible attitudes about a change and provide support for the people involved. This also implies that a supervisor needs to have a much greater understanding of personality theory and of the developmental processes of the adult than has hitherto been common. Such a need contains clear implications for the preparation and continued career development of supervisors.

PROPOSITION 12: *Change will be more effective when it is recognized that change efforts will be perceived differently by different people, as a result of the many forces at work within each individual.*

The clear implication from the wealth of evidence available is that if ISB is to be effective, a supervisor must develop skill in analyzing the reasons that teachers resist certain changes. Teachers' perceptions of a change will be conditioned by factors in their own personality such as habit, value systems, early training, and ego strength. A supervisor must be aware that his change efforts will be perceived in different ways by different teachers; they will not hear clearly, or remember well, communication about changes with which they disagree. A supervisor must seek feedback from a variety of sources, and thus avoid the error of assuming that a single teacher's perception is necessarily the common one.

PROPOSITION 13: *The effectiveness of change efforts will be improved when those restraining factors which inhibit an individual's normal desire for change are recognized and dealt with deliberately.*

Most individuals desire *some* change rather than maintenance of the status quo. Therefore, a supervisor needs to investigate the reasons for resistance to a change, and not assume that it stems solely from the proposed change. The source of resistance may lie in personality factors or in other factors seemingly or actually external to the change. A teacher's normal desire for new experience may be held in check by some counterbalancing force. ISB must deal with this counterforce in order to be successful.

PROPOSITION 14: *Change efforts will be more effective if the change is not perceived as causing a loss of prestige or group esteem.*

The unknown consequences of a change will cause resistance, especially if it is not known whether the change will result in a loss of official status or the esteem of colleagues or superiors. A supervisor needs to build into any change effort the necessary psychological supports that will enable teachers to change. Consequently, ISB must not create situations in which a teacher feels he is being asked to "give in" to the demands of a supervisor; "giving in" is seen as a personal defeat, and will be resisted.

PROPOSITION 15: *A change will be more readily accepted if it is not perceived as requiring a shift in one's attitude or belief system.*

A supervisor will find that a change which requires a teacher to restructure his value system will meet with stiff resistance, yet this is precisely the area in which ISB will have to become involved if he truly intends to influence teacher behavior. A supervisor will need to plan his strategy and his use of time around the resistance that such an attempt may generate. He must not expect changes to come overnight or without skillful planning and execution.

PROPOSITION 16: *Change will be more effective if it recognizes differences in acceptance of change according to the personality fluctuations that occur with age.*

ISB must take into account that age differences affect teachers' attitudes about change, about risk-taking and reward, and about interaction with others. Young teachers and older teachers see their environment differently, and a supervisor's efforts must reflect these differences. A supervisor must become a student of human behavior in order to select the most appropriate method of working with individual teachers.

PROPOSITION 17: *Change will be more effective if it is not perceived as giving advantage to some other group or area within the organization.*

If the result of a change appears to give advantage to one group within the school, it will be resisted by teachers who see themselves being placed at a disadvantage; ISB, therefore, must take into account what effect a change may have on related groups within the school and anticipate any possible resistance early in the change process. To achieve change in one part of a school, it may be necessary for a supervisor to deal with related parts.

PROPOSITION 18: *Change will be more effective if it does not threaten the vested interests of powerful groups or individuals.*

A supervisor must weigh a contemplated change carefully and anticipate just what resistance might occur. This does not mean that no change should ever be contemplated that tends to threaten vested interests, but rather, that a carefully planned strategy will consider such interests and will seek to modify if not eliminate resistance. Little change can occur when the vested interests of power groups cause strong resistance; ISB must deal with this reality.

PROPOSITION 19: *Change will be more effective if it does not appear to disturb the existing organizational structure of status, relationship, and recognition.*

Although at times it may be necessary or even desirable to disturb status relationships during a change effort, the supervisor should anticipate that such an action will encounter considerable resistance. A supervisor may want to plan a change so carefully that such disruption will be avoided; when it sometimes becomes necessary, however, to disturb the existing relationship, he can do so with a clearer analysis of some of the reasons for resistance and build in such supports as may help those affected to accept the change. In either case, ISB should be cognizant of the role that existing status relationships play in one's receptivity to change.

PROPOSITION 20: *Change will be more readily accepted if it can be demonstrated to be practicable in the target system or a close approximation of it.*

Supervisors should make a greater effort to provide a demonstration within the system of the practicality of an innovation. The common practice of providing information or a film about an innovative school system "somewhere else" may serve to spark some interest, but teachers tend to resist any innovation in their own school until it can be proved workable and effective locally. Although teachers have often been taken on visits by supervisors to "lighthouse" school systems as a stimulus to change, such practice is open to criticism. It is probably far more effective to enable teachers to view an innovation in a school system or in classes not too different from their own.

Supervisors should place more emphasis on local demonstration of change, rather than "importing" an idea from the outside. The use of "outsiders" to initiate change in a school system needs careful examination. Outside experts are probably more useful as resource people than as agents for the initiation of change.

Conditions for Acceptance of Change

PROPOSITION 21: *Change will be more effective when the conditions that exist within the target system are those which encourage change processes.*

Although some factors related to the acceptance of change (such as financial resources of a school district) are beyond the scope of ISB, the supervisor, nevertheless, can work to produce the kind of school climate in which change and experimentation are valued, support is given, cooperation is stressed, and quick censure is not brought on those who experiment unsuccessfully. The fear of failure must be removed before teachers will be willing to try new ideas. Supervisors must work deliberately to create a climate for change.

PROPOSITION 22: *The effectiveness of a change effort will be increased when it is recognized that the characteristics of some changes make them easier to accept than others.*

Supervisors must expect and plan to put more effort into achieving some changes than others, hence they can conserve their time and energy by devoting less time to those changes which teachers will accept readily. Built-in implementation supports such as training or self-teaching materials will make acceptance of a change more likely. Changes that close recognized gaps between what teachers believe they should do and what they are actually doing will also be readily accepted. In such cases, a supervisor uses the strength of a teacher's value system to support his own effort.

PROPOSITION 23: *A change effort will be more successful if recognition is given to the different roles that individuals within a system play in accepting change.*

A supervisor must know his teaching staff so well that he can predict with reasonable accuracy which teachers will be early adopters, which will wait for "proof" or for influential others to adopt first, which will spread information, and which will be the legitimizers who make a change acceptable to many others. Only with such knowledge can he devise an efficient strategy.

Influence of Group Membership on Change

PROPOSITION 24: *A change effort will be more effective if recognition is given to the presence and influence of group norms.*

The research evidence is clear: ISB will have serious difficulty when it asks for change that violates the norms of the group in which the teacher holds membership. It is extremely difficult for a teacher to depart from group norms; if he succeeds in doing so, he will be considered deviant and may finally be excluded from membership. Teachers will resist any change that places them in conflict with the group.

> PROPOSITION 25: *Change will be more effective when leadership and acceptance from within the group to be influenced come from an individual with group membership and esteem.*

Although supervisors have traditionally looked to innovative teachers for leadership in bringing about change, a reexamination of such a practice is in order, since innovators are considered (and often consider themselves) as deviant. If teachers violate group norms and participate in deviant behavior, it is unlikely that they will be looked to for advice and information. If a supervisor persists in publicizing the achievements of such teachers, he may in fact lessen the chances of achieving change. On the contrary, he should seek out those teachers who are "key" members of a group and whose influence is the greatest, and utilize the power of these individuals' group prestige as support for his change effort.

> PROPOSITION 26: *The success of change efforts will be affected by the cohesiveness and the longevity of the group to be influenced.*

Supervisors should anticipate that it will be more difficult to bring about change in some individuals than in others because of the great strength of their group membership. The more cohesive a group and the longer its history, the more it tends to act uniformly. Obviously, then, it is almost wasted effort to attempt to persuade senior teachers to make changes that might isolate them from their fellow members. Newer teachers, on the other hand, or those who do not have strong group ties, are more likely to adopt changes that violate group norms.

Such evidence also suggests the possibility of greater change being brought about in new schools in which cohesive groups have not yet formed; these new schools might become models within a system, yet would not require the violation of group norms. Other implications support the desirability of some turnover in staff as well as the reassignment of teachers to different buildings in order to lessen the effect of restrictive group norms.

> PROPOSITION 27: *A change effort will be more effective when it recognizes and utilizes the strength of group norms.*

A supervisor should anticipate that any change effort which runs counter to the established norms of the group to which a teacher belongs will encounter resistance. When the norms of a group support a change effort or when the group decides on a particular change as being desirable, the supervisor should recognize that in these supporting group norms he has an important ally. A supervisor who plans a change effort must carefully analyze the dynamics of the group to which those to be affected belong.

The power of group norms can also be *used* by a supervisor to achieve change. When a decision is made by a group, the change will diffuse more quickly and will more likely become permanent. If a supervisor succeeds in changing group standards, a new force field will be set up that will facilitate the change process.

It may be that where there are strong, cohesive groups, ISB needs to be group-centered rather than individual-centered, and so the traditional visits to one teacher in one classroom will be almost completely ineffective.

PROPOSITION 28: *The effectiveness and stability of a change will be enhanced when a cohesive group commits itself to it, thereby setting up a new force field.*

Cohesive groups make strong demands on their members; the more cohesive the group and the greater its longevity, the more stringent are the demands. A supervisor must recognize that such conditions, while often operating to restrict change, can also be a positive force.

When a supervisor is successful in bringing about change in the behavior of teachers in a highly cohesive group and the group commits itself to this change, the powerful norms will work in a supportive way, in that they now demand adherence to this new behavior from those teachers who wish to become or remain group members. This kind of group support provides a supervisor with a significant sustaining force after initiating a change. When a highly cohesive group of teachers endorses a change, the supervisor can expect the change to be "enforced."

PROPOSITION 29: *Change efforts will be more effective when the change agent, as perceived by other group members, has prestige and acceptance within the group.*

It is clear that prestigious group members can have a far more significant impact on group behavior than can an outsider. The greater a group member's prestige, the greater the influence he can exert on that group. It appears essential that the supervisor and the teacher be members of the same group in matters affecting values. This would seem to suggest that, to be effective, a supervisor must identify more clearly with the teachers and less with the school administration; this suggests a careful consideration of where supervisors belong in the current move toward collective bargaining and its tendency to segment rather than unify teachers and central staff personnel.

The Change Agent

PROPOSITION 30: *Change is more likely to occur if there is a recognized role-responsibility for initiating and directing change in the system.*

Supervisors, like any other members of a system, will find it difficult to participate in behavior that is not officially sanctioned by the organization. To be effective, ISB must be clearly recognized in the organization as an activity that exists for the purpose of changing the behavior of teachers. It must further be recognized that supervisors have the responsibility for *initiating* change in keeping with the objectives of the school, not acting solely as middlemen.

PROPOSITION 31: *Change will be more effective when external contact and influence are components of the change process.*

Supervisors need to seek fresh ideas and inspiration outside their system. Since effective change agents demonstrate a strong interest in the world "outside," this is one criteria to be considered when selecting persons for supervisory positions. Supervisors must also seek to provide opportunities for teachers to come into contact with new ideas and with activities outside their own system.

PROPOSITION 32: *Change will be effective and is more likely to occur when it is brought about not by chance, but deliberately, and when it is initiated and guided by some active person or group.*

If change is to occur, a school system must value it enough to give some person or group the responsibility for it, and not leave it to chance occurrence. Supervisors, if they desire change, must make this a priority activity, or else it will not occur. They should not expect to be agents of change unless they devote a significant amount of time, effort, and creative thought to the change process.

PROPOSITION 33: *A change agent will be more effective if he remains free from intimate involvement with the client system.*

Although it appears essential for a supervisor to identify closely with teachers and teaching, it is also essential that he maintain some "psychological distance" and that he not become so inextricably involved as a group member that he loses the leverage of status and of freedom from personal commitment to group norms. It is a delicate but significant balance: a supervisor must have the trust and respect of the teachers, while avoiding the kind of intimate involvement that would hinder his effectiveness.

PROPOSITION 34: *The change agent will be more effective if he has prestige and acceptance in the eyes of those in the client system.*

If a supervisor is to be effective, he must establish a relationship of respect and trust with the teachers he intends to influence. Although the school system cannot confer such a relationship, it can contribute to it to the extent that the supervisory position is recognized, rewarded, and accorded organizational status by the administration. The supervisor will contribute to his prestige and acceptance by virtue of his knowledge, skill, and the effectiveness of his ISB. Where there is little respect or prestige, there can be little ISB.

PROPOSITION 35: *Change will be more effective if linkage occurs between external and internal agents of change.*

If a supervisor wishes to use the services of an outside change agent or consultant, the external agent must be perceived as enhancing the work of the supervisor. If such "linkage" can take place, or if, in fact, the external agent can be at least temporarily joined to the system, the total change effort will be more successful. Simply "importing" a change agent will not assist the supervisor markedly in his work unless teachers perceive such a person as connected to the system or to the supervisor in some acceptable way.

Maintaining and Sustaining Change

PROPOSITION 36: *A change is more likely to be lasting if it receives continued evaluation after initial adoption.*

Once a change has been achieved, supervisors need to evaluate the change to see if it actually achieves the purpose for which it was planned. Since lack of attention to an innovation can cause it to be dropped, supervisors need to provide reinforcement for a change, particularly if anticipated support does not develop.

195

The satisfaction a supervisor feels after bringing about a change must not cause him to fail to evaluate it objectively. The widespread feeling that change is "good" can cause uncritical acceptance, and a sentimental attachment to a successful change can cause a supervisor to maintain one that perhaps should be dropped.

PROPOSITION 37: *Change efforts will be more effective and durable when they are buttressed by supportive forces.*

In affecting change in teacher behavior, the supervisor must give attention, even at the outset of a change effort, to developing the necessary supports—organizational, human, and material—that will stabilize the change once it has been accepted. To initiate a change and then abandon it is to threaten a potentially good change with a short life. Supervisors must help provide the kind of support that will not only enable teachers to attempt new behavior but will make it possible for them to continue in it.

Ideally, the supervisor should seek to develop organizational, environmental, and collegial support for changes in teacher behavior. If this is not forthcoming, the reinforcement may have to come from the supervisor himself, or else the behavior may soon return to the previous level.

ENDNOTES

1. Kurt Lewin, "Quasi-Stationary Social Equilibrium and the Problem of Permanent Change," in *The Planning of Change* by Warren Bennis, Kenneth Benne, and Robert Chin (New York: Holt, Rinehart and Winston, 1961), pp. 235–238.
2. Goodwin Watson, "Resistance to Change," in *Concepts for Social Change*, Cooperative Project for Educational Development (Washington, D.C.: National Training Laboratories, NEA, 1967), p. 10.
3. Warren Bennis, Kenneth Benne, and Robert Chin, *The Planning of Change* (New York: Holt, Rinehart and Winston, 1961), p. 2.
4. Warren Bennis, "A Typology of Change Processes," in Bennis, Benne, and Chin, *op. cit.*, p. 154.
5. Donald C. Orlich and Samuel S. Sheamis, "Educational Philosophy as Mythology: A Critical Analysis of School Philosophies," *Administrator's Notebook* XIV (December 1965).
6. Kenneth H. Hansen, "Planning for Changes in Education," in *Planning and Effecting Needed Changes in Education*, ed. Edgar L. Morphet and Charles O. Ryan (Denver: Publishers Press, 1967), p. 28.
7. Robert P. Huefner, "Strategy and Procedures in State and Local Planning," in *Planning and Effecting Needed Changes in Education*, ed. Morphet and Ryan, p. 20.
8. John Dewey, *Human Nature and Conduct* (New York: Holt, Rinehart and Winston, 1922).
9. Hansen, *op. cit.*, pp. 25–29.

10. Herbert A. Simon, *Research Frontiers in Politics and Government* (Washington, D.C.: Brookings, 1955), pp. 23–24.
11. Robert H. Guest, *Organizational Change* (Homewood, Ill.: Richard D. Irwin, 1962).
12. Herbert Shepard and Robert Blake, "Changing Behavior Through Cognitive Change," *Human Organization* 21 (Summer 1962) (Lexington, Ky.: Society for Applied Anthropology, University of Kentucky), pp. 88–96.
13. E. M. Rogers, *Diffusion of Innovations* (New York: Free Press, 1962).
14. Gordon N. Mackenzie, "Curricular Change: Participants, Power, and Process," in *Innovation in Education*, ed. Matthew Miles (New York: Bureau of Publications, Teachers College, Columbia University, 1964), pp. 420–423.
15. Kenneth Benne, "Deliberate Changing as the Facilitation of Growth," in Bennis, Benne, and Chin, *op. cit.* p. 231.
16. Lewin, *op. cit.*, pp. 235–236.
17. David H. Jenkins, "Force Field Analysis Applied to a School Situation," in Bennis, Benne, and Chin, *op. cit.*, pp. 238–244.
18. Lewin, *op. cit.*
19. Jenkins, *op. cit.*, p. 241.
20. Robert Chin, "Basic Strategies and Procedures in Effecting Change," in *Planning and Effecting Needed Changes in Education*, ed. Morphet and Ryan, p. 40.
21. Matthew Miles, ed., *Innovation in Education* (New York: Teachers College Press, copyright 1964 by Teachers College, Columbia University), p. 648.
22. Robert B. Howsam, "Effecting Needed Changes in Education," in *Planning and Effecting Needed Changes . . .* , ed. Morphet and Ryan, p. 72.
23. *Ibid.*
24. Goodwin Watson, *Social Psychology* (Philadelphia: Lippincott, 1966).
25. Matthew Miles, "Some Properties of Schools as Social Systems," in *Change in School Systems*, ed. Goodwin Watson, Cooperative Project for Educational Development, National Training Laboratories, NEA (1967), p. 12.
26. Hansen, *op. cit.*, p. 29.
27. Grenier, quoted in *Planning and Effecting Needed Changes . . .* , ed. Morphet and Ryan, p. 42.
28. Bennis, *op. cit.*, p. 154.
29. Richard Walton, "Two Strategies of Social Change and Their Dilemmas," *Journal of Applied Behavioral Science* 1 (1965), pp. 167–179.
30. Chin, *op. cit.*, pp. 43–51.
31. Howsam, *op. cit.*, p. 68.
32. Hansen, *op. cit.*, p. 24.
33. Chin, *op. cit.*, p. 53.
34. Miles, *Innovation in Education*, p. 649.
35. Herbert F. Lionberger, "Diffusion of Innovations in Agricultural Research and in Schools," in *Strategy for Curriculum Change* (Washington, D.C.: Association for Supervision and Curriculum Development, NEA), p. 45.
36. John T. Stone, "How County Agricultural Agents Teach" (East Lansing: Cooperative Extension Service, Michigan State College, 1952).
37. Lionberger, *op. cit.*, p. 35.

38. *Ibid.,* p. 36.
39. Paul R. Mort and Francis G. Cornell, *American Schools in Transition* (New York: Bureau of Publications, Teachers College, Columbia University, 1941).
40. Louis Forsdale, "8mm Motion Pictures in Education: Incipient Innovation," in Miles, *Innovation in Education,* pp. 203–230.
41. Paul E. Marsh, "Wellsprings of Strategy: Considerations Affecting Innovation by the PSSC," in Miles, *Innovation in Education,* pp. 249–267.
42. Gerhard Eichholz and Everett M. Rogers, "Resistance to the Adoption of Audio-Visual Aids by Elementary School Teachers: Contrasts and Similarit'es to Agricultural Innovation," in Miles, *Innovation in Education,* pp. 299–316.
43. Frank G. Jennings, "Mass Media, Mass Mind and Makeshift: Comments on Educational Innovation and the Public Weal," in Miles, *Innovation in Education,* pp. 563–586.
44. Miles, *Innovation in Education,* p. 636.
45. Marsh, *op. cit.,* pp. 249–267.
46. Miles, *Innovation in Education,* p. 636.
47. Forsdale, *op. cit.,* pp. 203–230.
48. Sloan R. Wayland, "Structural Features of American Education as Basic Factors in Innovation," in Miles, *Innovation in Education,* pp. 587–614.
49. Forsdale, *op. cit.,* pp. 203–230.
50. Miles, *Innovation in Education,* p. 636.
51. M. S. Atwood, "Small-Scale Administrative Change: Resistance to the Introduction of a High School Guidance Program," in Miles, *Innovation in Education,* pp. 49–78.
52. Richard O. Carlson, *Adoption of Educational Innovations* (Eugene, Oreg.: The Center for the Advanced Study of Educational Administration, 1965), pp. 70–73.
53. Alvin Zander, "Resistance to Change—Its Analysis and Prevention," in Bennis, Benne, and Chin, p. 544.
54. Walter B. Cannon, *Wisdom of the Body* (New York: W. W. Norton, 1932).
55. Lewin, *op. cit.*
56. Robert Bruce Raup, *Complacency: The Foundation of Human Behavior* (New York: The Macmillan Co., 1925).
57. William Isaac Thomas and Florjan Znaniecki, "The Polish Peasant in Europe and America: Monograph of an Immigrant Group" (Chicago: University of Chicago Press, 1918–1920).
58. John C. Lilly, "Mental Effects of Reduction of Ordinary Levels of Physical Stimuli on Intact, Healthy Persons," Symposium on Research Techniques in Schizophrenia, *Psychiatric Research Reports* 5: American Psychiatric Association (June 1956).
59. Peter M. Blau, *The Dynamics of Bureaucracy* (Chicago: University of Chicago Press, 1955).
60. Zander, *op. cit.,* p. 544.
61. John M. Stephens, *The Psychology of Classroom Learning* (New York: Holt, Rinehart and Winston, 1965).
62. Watson, "Resistance to Change," p. 13.

63. *Ibid.*, p. 14.
64. *Ibid.*
65. Jerome M. Levine and Gardner Murphy, "The Learning and Forgetting of Controversial Material," *Journal of Abnormal and Social Psychology* 38 (October 1943), pp. 507–511.
66. Watson, "Resistance to Change," p. 15.
67. *Ibid.*
68. J. D. Frank, "Experimental Studies of Personal Pressure and Resistance," *Journal of General Psychology* 30 (1944), pp. 23–41.
69. V. H. Vroom, *Some Personality Determinants of the Effects of Participation* (Englewood Cliffs, N. J.: Prentice-Hall, 1960).
70. Ronald Lippitt, "Roles and Processes in Curriculum Development and Change," in *Strategy for Curriculum Change*, p. 12.
71. Bernice Neugarten, "The Developmental Processes of the Adult" (Mimeographed) (New York: Conference on Consultation on Adult Learning, Bank Street College of Education, January 9, 1967).
72. Anselm Strauss, "Transformation of Identity," in Bennis, Benne, and Chin, p. 550.
73. Floyd C. Mann and Franklin W. Neff, *Managing Major Change in Organizations* (Ann Arbor, Mich.: Foundation for Research on Human Behavior, 1961).
74. Ronald Lippitt, Jeanne Watson, and Bruce Westley, *The Dynamics of Planned Change* (New York: Harcourt, Brace and Co., 1958).
75. Hedley S. Dimock and Roy Sorenson, *Designing Education in Values: A Case Study in Institutional Change* (New York: Association Press, 1955).
76. Dorwin Cartwright, "Achieving Change in People: Some Applications of Group Dynamics Theory," *Human Relations*, vol. 14, no. 4 (1951), pp. 381–392.
77. William H. Starbuck, "Organizational Growth and Development," in *Handbook of Organizations*, ed. James G. March (Chicago: Rand McNally, 1965), p. 471.
78. August Hollingshead, *Elmtown's Youth* (New York: John Wiley and Sons, 1949).
79. Elting E. Morison, "A Case Study of Innovation," in Bennis, Benne, and Chin, pp. 592–605.
80. Alex Bavelas and George Strauss, "Group Dynamics and Intergroup Relations," in Bennis, Benne, and Chin, pp. 587–591.
81. Floyd C. Mann, "Strategy and Creating Change," in Bennis, Benne, and Chin, pp. 605–615.
82. Morison, *op. cit.*
83. Alfred J. Marrow and John R. P. French, Jr., "Changing a Stereotype in Industry," in Bennis, Benne, and Chin, pp. 583–586.
84. Bennis, Benne, and Chin, *op. cit.*, p. 561.
85. Watson, "Resistance to Change," p. 21.
86. Edward H. Spicer, ed., *Human Problems in Technological Change* (New York: Russell Sage Foundation, 1952).
87. Daniel E. Griffiths, "Administrative Theory and Change in Organizations," in Miles, *Innovation in Education*, pp. 425–436.
88. Wolfgang Kohler, "Zur Psychologie des Shimpanzen," *Psychologische*

Forschung 1 (1922) (Berlin: Zeitschrift für Psychologie, Ethologie und Medizinische Psychologie), pp. 1–45; quoted in Goodwin Watson, *Concepts for Social Change,* p. 21.

89. Charles C. Jung, "The Trainer Change Agent Role Within a School System," in Watson, *Change in School Systems,* pp. 89–105.

90. Watson, "Resistance to Change," p. 22.

91. Donald Johnson and A. van den Ban, "The Dynamics of Farm Practice Changes," paper read before Midwest Sociological Society, Lincoln, Nebr. (April 1959).

92. Gerhard C. Eichholz, "Why Do Teachers Reject Change?" *Theory Into Practice* 2 (December 1963), p. 268.

93. Henry M. Brickell, *Organizing New York State for Educational Change* (Albany, N. Y.: State Educational Department, December 1961), p. 19.

94. Peter M. Blau and W. Richard Scott, *Formal Organizations* (San Francisco: Chandler Publishing, 1962).

95. Donald J. Willower and Ronald G. Jones, "When Pupil Control Becomes an Institutional Theme," *Phi Delta Kappan* 45 (November 1963), pp. 107–109.

96. Guest, *op. cit.,* p. 152.

97. Donald J. Willower, "Barriers to Change in Educational Organizations," *Theory Into Practice* 2 (December 1963), pp. 257–263.

98. Miles, *Innovation in Education,* p. 644.

99. Willower, *op. cit.,* p. 260.

100. Alvin W. Gouldner, *Patterns of Industrial Bureaucracy* (Glencoe, Ill.: Free Press, 1954), pp. 79–83.

101. Willower and Jones, *op. cit.*

102. Zander, *op. cit.,* p. 544.

103. Willower and Jones, *op. cit.*

104. Herbert C. Kelman, "Compliance, Identification and Internalization: Three Processes of Attitude Change," *Journal of Conflict Resolution,* vol. 2, no. 1 (March 1958), pp. 51–60.

105. North Central Regional Rural Sociology Subcommittee on the Diffusion of New Ideas and Farm Practices, *How Farm People Accept New Ideas,* Iowa Agricultural Extension Service Special Report No. 15 (1955).

106. Miles, *Innovation in Education,* pp. 647–661.

107. Donald H. Ross, ed., *Administration for Adaptability* (New York: Metropolitan School Study Council, 1958).

108. Everett M. Rogers, "What Are Innovators Like?" *Theory Into Practice* 2 (December 1963), pp. 252–256.

109. Ross, *op. cit.*

110. Daniel E. Griffiths, "The Elementary School Principal and Change in the School System," *Theory Into Practice* 2 (December 1963), pp. 278–284.

111. Carlson, *op. cit.,* p. 63.

112. Rogers, *op. cit.*

113. Lee H. Demeter, "Accelerating the Local Use of Improved Educational Practices in School Systems," Ph.D. diss., Teachers College, Columbia University (1951).

114. Miles, *Innovation in Education,* p. 643.

115. Paul R. Mort, in Mort and Cornell, *op. cit.*
116. Marsh, *op. cit.*
117. Brickell, *op. cit.*
118. Homer G. Barnett, *Innovation: The Basis of Cultural Change* (New York: McGraw-Hill, 1953), p. 404.
119. Carlson, *op. cit.*, p. 65.
120. Robert K. Merton, "Patterns of Influence: A Study of Communications Behavior in a Local Community," *Communications Research 1948–1949*, ed. Lazarsfeld and Stanton (New York: Harper and Brothers, 1949).
121. Elihu Katz and Paul F. Lazarsfeld, *Personal Influence* (Glencoe, Ill.: The Free Press, 1955).
122. Paul F. Lazarsfeld, Bernard Berelson, and H. Gaudet, *The People's Choices* (New York: Columbia University Press, 1954).
123. Lionberger, *op. cit.*, pp. 33, 43.
124. Marsh, *op. cit.*
125. Lionberger, *op. cit.*, p. 33.
126. Paul C. Marsh and A. Lee Coleman, "Farmers' Practice-Adaption Rates in Relation to Adaption Rates of 'Leaders,'" *Rural Sociology* 19 (1954), pp. 180–181.
127. Everett M. Rogers, "Characteristics of Innovators and Other Adapter Categories," *Research Bulletin 88*, no. 2 (Wooster, Ohio: Ohio Agricultural Experiment Station, 1961).
128. S. F. Seashore, *Group Cohesiveness in the Industrial Group* (Ann Arbor: Institute for Social Research, 1954).
129. William H. Whyte, Jr., *The Organization Man* (New York: Simon and Schuster, 1956).
130. F. Merei, "Group Leadership and Institutionalization," *Human Relations* 2 (1949) (London: Tavistock Publications), pp. 23–29.
131. K. Lewin, R. Lippitt, and R. White, "Patterns of Aggressive Behavior in Experimentally Controlled Social Climates," *Journal of Social Psychology* 10 (1939), pp. 271–299.
132. Dorwin Cartwright and Alvin Zander, eds., *Group Dynamics: Research and Theory* (Evanston, Ill.: Row, Peterson and Co., 1960), Second Edition, pp. 27–29, 165–186.
133. Ronald Lippitt, "Improving the Socialization Process," in Watson, *Change in School Systems*, p. 41.
134. Leon Festinger and John Thibaut, "Interpersonal Communication in Small Groups," *Journal of Abnormal and Social Psychology* 46 (January 1951), pp. 92–99.
135. L. Coch and J. R. R. French, "Overcoming Resistance to Change," *Human Relations* 1 (1958), pp. 512–532.
136. H. B. Gerard, "The Anchorage of Opinions in Face to Face Groups," *Human Relations* 6 (1954), pp. 249–271.
137. H. H. Kelley, "Salience of Membership and Resistance to Change of Group Anchored Attitudes," *Human Relations* 8 (1955), pp. 275–290.
138. H. H. Kelley and E. H. Volkhart, "The Resistance to Change of Group Anchored Attitudes," *American Sociological Review* 17 (1952), pp. 453–465.

139. Dorwin Cartwright, ed., *Field Theory in Social Science, Selected Theoretical Papers by Kurt Lewin* (New York: Harper and Brothers, 1951).
140. Muzafer Sherif, *The Psychology of Social Norms* (New York: Harper and Brothers, 1936).
141. S. E. Asch, "Effects of Group Pressure Upon the Modification and Distortion of Judgments," in Cartwright and Zander, *Group Dynamics: Research and Theory*, pp. 189–200.
142. R. Blake, H. Helson, and J. Mouton, "The Generality of Conformity Behavior as a Function of Actual Anchorage, Difficulty of Task and Amount of Social Pressure," *Journal of Personality* 25 (1957), pp. 294–305.
143. T. M. Newcomb, *Social Psychology* (New York: Dryden, 1950).
144. Kelley and Volkhart, *op. cit.*, pp. 453–465.
145. M. Argyle, "Social Pressure in Public and Private Situations," *Journal of Abnormal and Social Psychology* 54 (1957), pp. 172–175.
146. Bertram H. Raven, "Social Influence on Opinions and the Communication of Related Content," *Journal of Abnormal and Social Psychology* 58 (1959), pp. 119–128.
147. George Moeller and Mortimer Applezweig, "A Motivational Factor in Conformity," *Journal of Abnormal and Social Psychology* 55 (1957), pp. 114–120.
148. Bonnie R. Strickland and Douglas P. Crowne, "Conformity Under Conditions of Simulated Group Pressure As a Function of the Need for Social Approval," *The Journal of Social Psychology* 58 (1962), pp. 171–181.
149. Cartwright and Zander, *Group Dynamics: Research and Theory*, p. 169.
150. L. Festinger, S. Schacter, and K. Back, *Social Pressures in Information Groups* (New York: Harper and Brothers, 1950).
151. *Ibid.*
152. Coch and French, *op. cit.*
153. *Ibid.*
154. Kurt W. Back, "Influence Through Social Communication," *Journal of Abnormal and Social Psychology* 46 (1951), pp. 9–23.
155. Festinger, Schacter, and Back, *op. cit.*
156. H. H. Kelley and M. M. Shapiro, "An Experiment on Conformity to Group Norms Where Conformity Is Detrimental to Group Achievement," *American Sociological Review* 19 (1954), pp. 667–677.
157. Asch, *op. cit.*
158. Kurt Lewin, *Field Theory in Social Science* (New York: Harper and Brothers, 1951).
159. Cartwright and Zander, *Group Dynamics: Research and Theory*, p. 181.
160. Norman R. F. Maier, "The Quality of Group Decisions as Influenced by the Discussion Leader," *Human Relations* 3 (1950), pp. 155–174.
161. Kurt Lewin, "Group Decision and Social Change," in *Readings in Social Psychology*, ed. Maccoby, Newcomb, and Hartley (New York: Holt, Rinehart and Winston, 1958).
162. Jacob Levine and John Butler, "Lecture Versus Group Decision in Changing Behavior," *Journal of Applied Psychology* 36 (1952), pp. 29–33.
163. Nancy C. Morse and Everett Reimer, "The Experimental Change of a

Major Organizational Variable," *Journal of Abnormal and Social Psychology* 52 (1952), pp. 120–129.

164. Coch and French, *op. cit.*
165. Miles, *Innovation in Education.*
166. Willower and Jones, *op. cit.*
167. Mark Chesler, Richard Schmuck, and Ronald Lippitt, "The Principal's Role in Facilitating Innovation," *Theory Into Practice* 2 (December 1963), pp. 269–277.
168. Miles, *Innovation in Education,* p. 643.
169. G. W. Lewin, ed., *Resolving Social Conflicts* (New York: Harper and Brothers, 1948).
170. Cartwright, ed., *Field Theory in Social Science.*
171. Ronald Lippitt, Norman Polansky, Fritz Redl, and Sidney Rosen, "The Dynamics of Power," in Cartwright and Zander, *Group Dynamics: Research and Theory,* pp. 745–764.
172. C. E. Osgood and P. Tannenbaum, "The Principle of Congruity and the Prediction of Attitude Change," *Psychological Review* 62 (1955), pp. 42–55.
173. Paul F. Lazarsfeld and Robert K. Merton, "Friendship as a Social Process: A Substantive and Methodological Analysis," in *Freedom and Control in Modern Society,* by Berger *et al.* (New York: Van Nostrand, 1954), p. 33.
174. Miles, *Innovation in Education,* p. 655.
175. Rogers, "Characteristics of Innovators . . ."
176. James Coleman, Elihu Katz, and Herbert Menzel, "The Diffusion of an Innovation Among Physicians," *Sociometry* 20 (1957), pp. 253–267.
177. Bryce Ryan and Neal C. Gross, "The Diffusion of Hybrid Seed Corn in Two Iowa Communities," *Rural Sociology* 8 (1943), pp. 15–24.
178. C. F. Carter and B. R. Williams, "The Characteristics of Technically Progressive Firms," *Journal of Industrial Economics* 7 (1959), p. 97.
179. Rose Goldsen and Max Ralis, "Factors Related to Acceptance of Innovations in Bang Chan, Thailand," Southeast Asia Program Data Paper 25 (Ithaca, N. Y.: Cornell University, 1957).
180. Ross, *op. cit.*
181. Miles, *Innovation in Education,* p. 639.
182. Lippitt, Watson, and Westley, *op. cit.*
183. Bennis, Benne, and Chin, *op. cit.,* p. 16.
184. Jung, *op. cit.,* p. 89.
185. *Ibid.,* pp. 89–90.
186. Warren Bennis and Herbert Shepard, "A Theory of Group Development," in Bennis, Benne, and Chin, pp. 321–339.
187. G. W. Lewin, *Resolving Social Conflicts,* p. 67.
188. Cartwright, ed., *Field Theory in Social Science.*
189. Lippitt, Polansky, Redl, and Rosen, *op. cit.*
190. G. W. Lewin, *Resolving Social Conflicts,* p. 67.
191. J. R. P. French, Jr., "Experiments in Field Settings," in *Research Methods in the Behavioral Sciences,* by L. Festinger and D. Katz (New York: Dryden, 1953), pp. 98–135.

192. *Ibid.*
193. Charles P. Loomis, "Tentative Types of Directed Social Change Involving Systemic Linkage," in Bennis, Benne, and Chin, pp. 223–240.
194. George C. Homans, *The Human Group* (New York: Harcourt, Brace and World, 1950).
195. Talcott Parsons and Neil J. Smeltzer, *Economy and Society* (New York: The Free Press of Glencoe, Inc., 1956), pp. 257–258.
196. Loomis, *op. cit.*, p. 223.
197. *Ibid.*
198. Ibid., pp. 224–225.
199. *Ibid.*
200. Miles, *Innovation in Education*, p. 657.
201. Allen H. Barton and David Wilder, "Research and Progress in the Teaching of Reading: A Progress Report," in Miles, *Innovation in Education*, pp. 361–398.
202. Henry M. Brickell, "State Organization for Educational Change," in Miles, *Innovation in Education*, pp. 493–532.
203. Miles, *Innovation in Education*, p. 659.
204. Paul R. Mort, "Studies in Educational Innovation from the Institute of Administrative Research: An Overview," in Miles, *Innovation in Education*, pp. 317–328.
205. Lewin, "Quasi-Stationary Social Equilibrium. . . ."
206. Lionberger, "Diffusion of Innovations . . . ," p. 44.
207. Jenkins, "Force Field Analysis . . . ," p. 238.
208. *Ibid.*, p. 243.
209. Talcott Parsons, "The Problem of the Theory of Change," in Bennis, Benne, and Chin, p. 217.
210. Cora DuBois, "The Public Health Worker as an Agent of Socio-Cultural Change," in Bennis, Benne, and Chin, pp. 528–541.
211. Leland P. Bradford, "The Teaching-Learning Transaction," in Bennis, Benne, and Chin, p. 501.

PART III

The Critical Components of Instructional Supervisory Behavior

Systematic organization and the codification of terminology are conspicuous by their absence from most efforts to explore supervision. The eleven critical components of instructional supervisory behavior discussed herein are drawn from a number of controlled investigations in several fields. Taken separately and collectively, these components serve to illuminate aspects of the supervisor's behavior in working through teachers to improve learning.

The principle is advanced here that supervision can be visualized by a matrix consisting of components that intervene on the interpersonal and milieu dimensions. According to this principle, the logical outcomes of alternative actions can be predicted and certain components can be altered by careful selection among possible elements and sequences of intervention.

The two chapters of Part III define the critical components and describe their interrelationships within the matrix, which explains supervision in education.

Chapter 8

Definitions of Critical Components

The analysis of over one hundred propositions drawn from research in the fields of leadership, communication, organization, and change theories suggests that they fall into three major divisions or categories.* The first of these categories contains those components which deal with the relationships of a person with others; the second contains those components which deal with the relationships of a person to the environment in which he functions; and the third contains those which deal with the alternatives available to a person who decides to alter the relationships of people to each other or to their environment. These respective categories have been termed Interpersonal Components, Milieu Components, and Intervention Components.

A study of these categories and the components that comprise them suggests an interactive quality. The component propositions are related, not single threads unattached to a larger and more complex fabric. Efforts to conceptualize the nature and interrelatedness of these research propositions promote a more rational approach to ISB.

INTERPERSONAL COMPONENTS

The Interpersonal Components relate to three general types of relationships among persons. These deal with those relationships of colleagues who participate as members of a group (the *reference* component), those relationships earned by performance (the *esteem* component), and those relationships conferred by the position occupied within the hierarchy (the *status* component).

The *reference* component refers to that relationship between a

* See Appendix for the categorization of these propositions into critical components.

207

person and others existing as a result of his desire to become and remain a member of a particular group. It is confirmed by research in leadership, in communication, and particularly in change. Because certain standards are thought to be normative, this component is imposed as a result of group membership. The significance of this for ISB is enormous. The supervisor must always remember that he is not working with teachers as isolated individuals. The teacher's behavior is affected, even predetermined to some extent, by his relationships with others. In fact, this relationship to his colleagues may be far more important to the teacher than his relationship to the supervisor. If the teacher is forced to endanger his colleagual ties, he may be unable to follow the suggestions of the supervisor, even though the latter action might otherwise appear very appropriate; the teacher may not respond to new possibilities because of the strong bond that the colleagual relationship imposes upon him. Therefore, the supervisor is going to fail if he works only with the teacher as an individual without recognizing that there are all kinds of prohibitions and motivations within that individual.

On the positive side, the supervisor may be able to use norms to convince a teacher who might be reluctant to make a change. Such an individual would be forced to adapt because the norms would require him to modify his behavior in order to maintain his relationship with his colleagues. The supervisor should realize that the reference component exerts both negative and positive effects. Also, the norms themselves are not necessarily negative; they may, in fact, be quite supportive of his endeavors.

The *esteem* component refers to the relationship a person earns within an organization by demonstrating his own competencies. This is not organizationally (formally) ascribed, but derives instead from recognition and acceptance as a result of manifested ability. Esteem can come from any direction. It may be awarded by colleagues and clients alike. It is a multidimensional condition that is gained within a certain environment. Any member of a group may have esteem—the leader as well as a member. Therefore, in terms of ISB, the effectiveness of the supervisor will be enhanced if he is esteemed as an individual by those with whom he functions.

Another part of this concept has to do with the other people in the system who participate in or who are receptive to supervisory activity. Such individuals also have esteem in the organization. They inevitably will influence the total impact of the supervisory endeavor. Supervision will make more impact, and that impact will be extended, if those who are most esteemed are willing to give it the greatest support. This has significant implications for deciding where to place the primary emphasis of supervision. The reverse is also true. A large effort directed at people who have little or no esteem with their associates may be worthless as

FIGURE 8-1. *Critical Components of ISB*

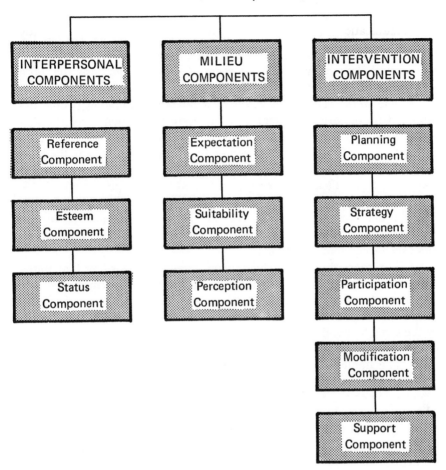

far as changing the total system is concerned. The members of the target-audience are not those to whom others would look for an example. Even though the target-person himself could be changed, there would not be any "spin-off." Not only would the adoption of a change by a person of low esteem fail to convert others, it might in fact have a negative influence. Such a circumstance could produce another tug-of-war for the as-yet uncommitted individual who was sympathetic toward the proposed change. If the person in the operation whom he held in high esteem were not supportive of it, the sympathetic individual might be unwilling to proceed very far; he might be even less willing to do so if a person he held in low esteem elected to champion the change. There are at least these three dimensions to the concept of esteem. A possibility of a fourth implication for the supervisor also merits consideration.

A person who is held in esteem by others recognizes and feels this relationship. He has the opportunity, and conceivably the responsibility, to try some things that others may decline to attempt. He should be more willing to be adventurous because he is more comfortable. He has the feeling of acceptance and may launch out and take some risks, while the person with low organizational esteem is unwilling to lose the little acceptance he has by doing so.

The *status* component refers to a relationship among people determined by the organizational positions they hold. Such a relationship is usually conferred, but not necessarily so. It has to do with some kind of formal or informal hierarchy rather than qualities of the individuals themselves. By definition, therefore, status provides one the opportunity and at least the official power to influence others. The person who holds a position of higher status has greater prerogative to exert his influence than the one with lesser status. Whether his status is conferred by the organization or by colleagues, he still has the kind of leverage to help him cause some movement.

The concept of status differs from esteem in the sense that status operates in a clear, defined orientation and it normally carries with it certain accoutrements of office, such as salary and/or title, which are visible to others. It is possible to have esteem and not really have status; by the same token, it is possible to have status, and not have esteem. But in tandem they provide a very powerful force.

This implies that a supervisor will have greater potential for working with people if his position entails status officially conferred within the organization or the hierarchy in which he operates. A status position is related to the task of supervision officially through organizational definition, or functionally through one's work. In other words, it is impossible for a supervisor to have status when it is not clear that his position within the organization is related to the things he is trying to do. There are also positions of *relative* status, such as those between administrators and supervisors, or among various supervisors, or among various administrators. Because status is relative, the matter of change will be treated differently in a system in which supervisors have greater status than principals, than in a system in which principals have greater status than supervisors. Such circumstances need to be taken into account regarding ISB. The supervisor must anticipate the results that will occur, depending upon the relative status of the type of position.

A still different dimension to be considered by the supervisor is the relative status of the various incumbents despite organizational hierarchy. He must operate differently in a system in which the principal of a particular school has great status by virtue of many years of experience or strong community acceptance. The supervisor also must recognize the status held by his colleagues, his subordinates, and his superordinates or superiors. There are teachers who have status within an organization, both with their colleagues and with their superordinates. The relationship of the supervisor with each of these persons must be guided by his understanding of the status concept.

MILIEU COMPONENTS

The Milieu Components are concerned with the relationships a person has with his environment. Consistent with this concept are three general types of involvement between a person and his surroundings: those which deal with his anticipation of the prospective interaction (the *expectation* component), those which deal with his view of the interaction process (the *perception* component), and those which deal with his assessment of the results (the *suitability* component).

The *expectation* component refers to the manner in which an individual structures his environment—even one with which he is not completely familiar—so as to anticipate the things that will or should happen and the way certain people will or should behave in a given situation. His own conduct and willingness to act or not to act are governed in part by expectations that he carries with him all the time. Some of these expectations even pertain to the individual himself and the way he believes he should behave.

The implications of this component are of importance both to the supervisor and to the teachers. Every sociocultural setting shapes what is appropriate and expected behavior, and a supervisor must function in full recognition of the characteristics of his environment. Expectations of behavior exist for supervisors, teachers, and for the interactions of these persons; and teachers and supervisors, in fact, see certain behavior for themselves as being either expected or inappropriate. In brief, expectation is a personalized response to environment. Undoubtedly there is an expectation on the part of a teacher that he should behave in a particular fashion in his environment; a supervisor who wants a teacher to behave differently meets with difficulty if the expectations of the teacher are quite to the contrary; he may see himself moving counter to his environment. If it is not an appropriate way for him to behave in that environment, the supervisor might attempt to alter the environment. At least, he has to recognize that he may be asking a teacher to behave in violation of his own expectations of himself, or of the environment. While the supervisor may wish to do this, he ought to do it knowingly and not in ignorance. Such a procedure has to be well conceived because of the far-reaching consequences it might entail. The supervisor should understand that he is attempting to alter a very important relationship.

The way a person views the situation in a particular environment may be considered the *perception* component. It embraces the events, actions, and behavior of himself and others. All of these factors are put through the individual's own filter screen of perception and values. In all probability, the very existence of this component is evidence that no two people perceive the same events or behaviors in exactly the same way. There may be some similarities, and the greater these similarities of perception in both number and extent, the more likely an organization will be effective. The converse also applies. To the extent that a particular event or behavior is seen differently by different persons involved in an environment, the desired result is unlikely to occur; in fact, confusion may be caused by the introduction of that event or behavior. In brief, that which is perfectly clear to one individual may be completely confusing to another because their perceptions are entirely different. Perceived behavior and intended or actual behavior may be distinctly different, and often are.

This means that the supervisor must assume that his behavior will not be perceived in the same way by the people with whom he operates. He may in fact be considered at variance with his environment no matter how hard he seeks to avoid it. Obviously, his behavior will not be perceived by everybody in the same way, as this feat is virtually impossible to accomplish. If he assumes that ISB is understood in the same way by all teachers, the supervisor is doomed to difficulties. Instead, he should operate knowing full well that his behavior will be perceived differently by different persons. To the extent that the supervisor is able to discover the way his behavior is being perceived, he will increase his effectiveness Much will depend upon obtaining and interpreting appropriate feedback.

The third aspect of a person's relationship with his environment is the *suitability* component, which refers to the consonance of the behavior or event within the environment, given the expectations and/or perceptions of those involved. The suitability component concerns an existing set within an organization or a group that makes it possible to absorb or accept certain kinds of behavior or events because the environment has a "fitness" for it. In a sense, suitability relates to both perceptions and expectations. If the perceptions of an event are in keeping with its expectations, there is one kind of response; if the perceptions of the event are at variance with the expectations, another kind of response occurs. Whether or not the perceptions or expectations are accurate or inaccurate really matters little. Since this phenomenon does in fact occur, suitability as a factor in relationship to environment has to be taken into account by anyone who operates in that environment. Thus, suitability of events or intentions of behavior is related to the environment and to the people therein. This is consistent with the way in which the concept was originally defined. If such events or behaviors are suitable, in the sense of "fitting" within the appropriate range of acceptability to other people, certain results will accrue, whereas if they fall outside that range, other results will accrue. All of these results are predictable.

The implication for ISB is that the supervisor must know the limits and the nature of suitability in terms of the organization, in both the Milieu and Interpersonal dimensions. He has to anticipate the consequences when he acts within or beyond the established limits. For example, the supervisor who requests that a teacher do something which is at variance with the expectations of the school certainly has to anticipate that the teacher may feel unable to do it. Also, the supervisor must anticipate other reactions when a certain behavior is not only acceptable but highly desirable. This is not an oversimplification; many factors enter into a person's thinking and help him decide if a behavior is suitable or unsuitable. One of the most important of these factors is the element of competition among persons, which often strains other relationships.

INTERVENTION COMPONENTS

The third major category deals with those components involved with Intervention. These are the components which an agent must consider if he seeks to alter either the interpersonal relationships of one individual with others or the milieu components of the individual and the environment in which he operates. These consist of five subcomponents: planning, strategy, participation, modification, and support.

The *planning* component requires deliberate, purposeful, goal-setting activity in which the outcomes, in terms of relationships among people and between people and their environment, are taken into account in view of the objectives of the organization in which the activity takes place.

To the supervisor, this simply means that if there is no plan he cannot proceed in any kind of organized direction. The result is the random, haphazard operation that characterizes the nature of most ISB. The supervisor finds himself working on a project at a time, for a change at a time, in a school at a time, with a teacher at a time, and on a course at a time. There is no long-term consideration of implications for both environment and people, nor any consistent focus of the numerous activities in which he is engaged; hence, there is no cumulative impact. Rather, his efforts are being disbursed over a wide area to no avail.

Moreover, the supervisor is unable to accomplish major changes all by himself or only as a result of his own ideas and philosophy. He has to be in consonance with the larger organization. The supervisor is employed by the organization to achieve purposes that it deems to be im-

portant. Planning must involve both the people who are going to participate in a change and those who are going to face the results of that
change. Planning is more effective when it involves those people to be
affected. Put another way, no effective planning can take place unless
those to be affected are involved from the initial stages. These people
must clearly understand the implications of a change not only for themselves, but for their associates and for the environment in which they
function.

The *strategy* component involves the selection of appropriate procedures and means by which to deal with the relationships of people with
people, or of people with their environment, in such a way as to bring
about the desired results in terms of the defined plan. This component
entails the organization of the procedures, means, or activities by which
one intervenes in the interpersonal or the milieu to influence or to achieve
the change that is considered important or desirable. The strategy concept
means that the person who intends to intervene should have more than
one arrow for his bow, or more than one club in his bag. He chooses from
among the various possibilities that which is best, in keeping with the
amalgam of elements with which he has to deal. The individual does not
commit himself unalterably to one strategy or one method of operation.
Sometimes he must bring to bear different tactics or strategies in order to
accomplish his overall mission. In one situation, he may operate in one
way, whereas in another situation, he will have to operate quite differently.

The implication for ISB is that the supervisor must select a strategy
in keeping with the purpose of the change, the nature of the individuals
involved, the state of the organization, and the nature of the change itself.
He must not assume that because a particular procedure works in school
X one way, it will also work in school Y the same way. Perhaps the distinction to be made between tactics and strategy is that there is a single,
broad strategy, while the tactics utilized to implement it in certain areas
or with certain individuals might differ considerably. The choice of
strategy or tactics depends upon the interpersonal relationships that are
to be changed.

The *participation* component deals primarily with changing human
relationships. It refers to those activities deliberately intended to change
the interpersonal components, usually by involving individuals in a face-
to-face situation and engaging them collectively in some part of the
activity. As a result of altering interpersonal communication, people's perceptions of themselves and of the situation are revised. There is a shift
in their expectations, as well as what they consider to be important or
desirable. In a real sense, the people become suitable for another milieu.
Through change in interpersonal relationships, there is a modification in
the environment in which the people function. Through participation,

they become involved with a new group of people or with a new set. It is almost impossible to avoid a shift. The process of identification then takes place with an activity or with people who are seeking to change.

The implication for a supervisor who wants a change in personal relationships or who expects to influence teacher behavior, is that those to be affected must participate in the making of decisions about the nature of the change and the way in which it should take place. This must be done largely through face-to-face communication. Only in this way are the teachers likely to experience change, because they will be dealing with a problem in a very personal way rather than abstractly or through someone else. Such participation or involvement is a two-way street; it involves more than simply sending information to someone.

The supervisor needs to consider the many ways in which people can be encouraged to participate. This requires a distinction between the usual participation—that between supervisor and teacher—and the kind that occurs between and among the teachers themselves. This may be the major type of participation, rather than the supervisor dealing directly with each individual. This concept is related to the interpersonal relationships, or the reference component, which means that participation between teacher and supervisor alone might not achieve a particular change. The individual *may* modify his behavior, but, again, he may *not* do so unless other people also participate and adopt change as a unified group. The concept of participation has to be a bit broader than typically conceived.

The *modification* component deals primarily, although not exclusively, with changing the relationship between a person and the environment. The distinction between modification and participation hinges on whether the impact is directed toward the people themselves or toward the milieu. In the latter case, change is usually attempted by three types of intervention to create another environment. A group of people may be placed in a situation different from their own so that they will see and function, at least for a brief period of time, in new surroundings. Part of the other environment, or another agent, may be introduced into the existing environment as a catalyst. Or, some item or person may be removed from the present situation, perhaps dismissal or transfer, so as to change the mix. As opposed to participation, in which one is working directly with people, in modification, he is working directly with the environment in which those people function.

As far as implications for ISB are concerned, the supervisor may deal with the problem of environment by having teachers visit another school where they can become aware of new ways of doing things or new types of behavior. Or, he may bring something or somebody to the teachers, so that the new ways can be demonstrated while at the same time altering the local situation. The catalytic agent—be it person, program, event, or whatever—will in fact change the environmental set. In either case, the teachers will be deliberately exposed to what is going on someplace else. Change in the immediate situation can also be achieved by shifting teachers around within the system. The milieu is broken up because the members of a particular group are transferred to another school within the same system, or even to another system. This may be an extremely effective way of modifying the environment. It may encourage some individuals to change, because the old norms will no longer be operating in the same manner. Therefore, the supervisor may introduce new pieces, redistribute existing pieces, or, conceivably, take some of the pieces out. In any one or combination of these procedures, he will be altering the set in which the teachers operate.

This concept also has ramifications for the expectation, perception, and suitability components. If a person does in fact meet an agent or a program from the other setting and deals with it in specific terms, he may realize that he *can* function in that environment. Even for a brief period, teachers can be introduced to aspects of the new milieu and understand that change *can* happen. To the extent that the modification can be made without complete destruction of the existing environment, teachers will be able to make the transition more easily.

It is important to note that the supervisor is responsible for altering the existing environment or creating a new milieu to bring about conditions of change. These things do not just happen; the supervisor must take some overt action to ensure that they do. Therefore, in addition to maintaining equilibrium, the supervisor should also be the agent of disturbance. When something is to be changed because it is no longer relevant, or is to be put back together in different form, it will be necessary to disturb the original structure first. Hence, in addition to being an agent of pacification, the supervisor is charged with modifying the organizational milieu to help teachers gain new insights concerning their behavior.

The *support* component has to do with both the organizational and psychological elements that provide for effective intervention. While intervention is possible in the absence of support, its result is unlikely to endure. Support exists in terms of such tangible items as time, resources, consulting service, and the like; however, there are other items of a more intangible nature that may be of significantly greater importance. Lack of disapproval and overt approval would fall under the latter heading. A "greenhouse" with a controlled environment is essential for a newly evolving program. Only after the new program has been nurtured to a reasonable level, is it ready to undergo an actual field test.

The concept of support involves supporting people, environment, and relationships with psychological and material items. For an activity being initiated or a change being attempted, support factors must be built in, and their need must be anticipated and planned for in advance. Moreover, support factors are needed to keep a change going. These may take the form of resource personnel, inservice training, or physical facilities. Therefore, support is required for the initiation of the idea, but that support must also be continued; otherwise, the idea will collapse of its own weight because there is no protective and supportive environment.

In terms of ISB, one of the reasons ideas haven't flourished is that although support has been given at the beginning, it has not been sufficiently strong to overcome the resistance. Consequently, when support has either been withdrawn or directed elsewhere, with a return to people's earlier sets and environmental expectations, even the best ideas atrophy and die.

One type of common support is really single-dimensional: the supervisor giving support to the teacher. However, other forms of necessary support typically are not present. These involve both the interpersonal relationships and the milieu, from which support also has to come. Nor will one type of support—psychological support, for instance—suffice without the material support that is just as essential, or vice versa. Consider the supervisor who gets many things started in a system but who fails to build in ongoing support elements for the period when his personal involvement ceases. Upon his return a few months later, he finds that nothing has changed; the situation is just as it was in the beginning. In fact, an actual recession may have occurred; the pendulum may have swung the other way due to lack of support. To employ an analogy, the advance party in any exploratory venture depends upon a strong, continuing support system. If the venture goes beyond the capacity of the support system, it is placed in a precarious position and its continued existence is jeopardized. Moreover, a support system not only has to be maintained, but it may have to be strengthened to overcome stiffening resistance. Innovators need to feel (and actually *be*) supported or they are not going to stay in advance positions very long. This is particularly true of pioneer innovators. Such individuals cannot remain unsupported; a decision must be made, either to terminate the venture or to build it into the system on a permanent basis.

This idea is highly relevant to the situation in a school district in which an individual teacher is asked to do something quite innovative. The idea that has been initiated may finally become standard operating procedure, in which case the total operation is going to be moved forward. Or, the decision may be made that this is not as crucial an element as was initially thought, and the project is terminated. Be that as it may, the innovative teacher cannot be left in limbo to his own devices. If support is withdrawn, the teacher may have to get out of the situation, organizationally and psychologically, the best way he can. Not only is this teacher unlikely to become personally involved in any subsequent venture, but other teachers who observed that he was deserted may likewise refuse to undertake any innovation on their part. The supervisor must be careful not to initiate more than he and the organization are capable of supporting adequately. Consolidation of effort is essential. A supervisor should not spread himself too thinly; if he cannot provide adequate support, then the result will be wasted effort and a record of promising ventures ending in failure. It is far better for one to consolidate his effort and use it for the maximum impact.

Chapter 9

Component Relationships

The three major divisions of the components form a matrix in which the interpersonal and milieu components serve as the vertical axis and the intervention components as the horizontal axis. This configuration indicates that effective intervention is in fact a function of the three interpersonal components and the three milieu components.

More specifically, ISB is interpreted as resulting from: the supervisor's personal properties; his interaction with other members of the organization; and the environmental conditions that characterize the organization. Any analysis of supervisory performance, particularly the study of how or to what extent ISB contributes to the effectiveness of the organization, should consider these dimensions. They should be considered as discrete categories. They should also be studied as a total functionally related system. In this way it may be conceived that the total set of research propositions, although falling into three major categories, are best conceived as a matrix or framework against which ISB can be studied.

The interpretations are not complete. It is hoped that the three categories of research components, the empirical and/or logical basis of this arrangement, and the internal order or suggested interrelatedness of these factors will be studied further, in a variety of ways, as a guide to the better comprehension of supervisory behavior in education.

RELATIONSHIPS AFFECTING THE INTERPERSONAL AND MILIEU COMPONENTS

The process of analyzing the relationship of each of the intervention components to each of the other six components indicates that the interpersonal and milieu components are not static but are, in fact, dynamic. The direction of change that occurs is at least partly a function of the utiliza-

FIGURE 9–1. *ISB Critical Components Matrix*

		INTERVENTION				
		Planning	Strategizing	Participation	Modification	Support
I N T E R P E R S O N A L	Reference	2	3	1	✕	4
	Esteem	2	4	3	✕	1
	Status	OFFICIAL *(Formal Organization)*		UNOFFICIAL *(Informal Organization)*		
M I L I E U	Expectation	2	3	✕	1	4
	Perception	2	3	✕	1	4
	Suitability	2	3	✕	1	4

tion of the intervention components. For example, not only is effective support partly dependent on esteem, but either gaining or losing esteem is at least partly a function of the utilization of the intervention components.

Thus, behavior of the instructional supervisor must take into account the possibility that the interpersonal and milieu components may need to be altered in order for the supervisor to successfully influence teacher behavior. Whether or not he chooses to alter these components deliberately, he must recognize that his activity in the intervention component will, in fact, increase or decrease the strength of these various forces.

The following are examples of the ways in which an instructional supervisor may conceivably alter these components. These are general applications that seem warranted in the light of interpretations of the research findings that have been considered. Other areas of study and local circumstances may suggest other applications and priorities in the use of these components.

Reference Component. In order to alter the reference component, the supervisor might seek to change the nature of the existing group norms through the participation component. Once a shift in group norms begins to occur, he can plan with the members and utilize the new norms of the reference group to design and execute an appropriate strategy. Support can now be introduced to bolster this effort. Earlier introduction of support would have served to strengthen the existing group norms, which, under certain circumstances, might be desired; however, evidence indicates that although providing support increases the strength of group norms, the withholding of support does not decrease their strength.

Esteem Component. The intervention component that seems most likely to provide opportunity for the supervisor to achieve esteem in the eyes of teachers is the support component. To the extent that he is able to provide the desired human, technical, and material resources, he will increase or decrease the degree of esteem in which he is held by teachers. His success in the planning and participation components will be partially determined by this degree of esteem. Although his performance in the strategy component runs the greatest risk of decreasing esteem, it is also the very component that offers the richest opportunity for increased esteem. The supervisor will probably venture into this component, then, only after he obtains sufficient esteem, so that if a strategy should fail, it will not seriously impair his effectiveness; obviously, high esteem will increase the likelihood of a strategy being successful.

Status Component. This component exists within both the informal and the formal organization. Since status in the informal organization is often gained through esteem, the support and participation components are more likely to lead to the conferring of status. In the formal organization, where status is officially conferred, high achievement in the strategy component is most likely to result in increased status. The uniqueness of the strategy component as it influences status is that high success will earn increased esteem from both teachers and organizational supervisors. The planning component, while contributing to increased status, offers less opportunity because the results will not be immediately recognizable.

Expectation, Perception, and Suitability Components. To influence teacher behavior, it may be necessary first for the supervisor to alter one or all of the three milieu components. The modification component offers the greatest promise of successful change in expectation, perception, and suitability. After altering these components, the supervisor can move to the planning component, and then to the strategy component to further alter these three components of milieu. As in the reference component, the application of the support component will contribute to additional movement in the direction of the desired alteration. The support component may also be used to strengthen existing expectations, perceptions, and suitability if so desired. While it is possible for the supervisor to directly affect suitability, he is more likely to do so by altering the relationship between the expectation component and the perception component.

RELATIONSHIPS AFFECTING THE INTERVENTION COMPONENTS

We have reviewed the way in which the interpersonal and milieu components may be altered by the appropriate application of the intervention components. It is also important to recognize that the intervention components are in turn affected by the respective interpersonal and milieu components. That is, the expression of supervisory intervention (ISB) is shaped by the quality of human interactions and the nature of the environment in which they occur.

The data and inferences in this approach suggest that supervisors tend to perform sets of action behaviors. Identified as "intervention components," these behaviors are planning, strategizing, participating, modifying, and supporting. These are the actions, or types of intervention choices, available to the supervisor as he formulates the approach he will take in engaging in ISB. Many possible applications exist for each of these intervention components. A supervisor may attempt, through participation, to improve the quality of the interpersonal components. He may, for example, work more directly with teachers; he may listen more; or, he may act in dramatic fashion by taking an administratively unpopular position, but one which is in accord with the views of teachers. Such behaviors, which are consciously expressed, may affect the level of esteem in which the supervisor is held. They may also affect his status or official position, and both of these factors will determine the quality of interpersonal relationships between teachers and supervisors. The exact intervention procedure to be used at a given time and the form that it takes will be determined by the supervisor's knowledge and sensitivity to the interpersonal and milieu components. Effective ISB will be based upon the supervisor's grasp and satisfactory accommodation of the three sets of interacting conditions.

Planning Component. The intent of developing a plan is to guide action or behavior. When a plan exists, goals should be clearly established. Established goals become the end toward which human activity and organizational resources are directed. If supervisory planning is to be effective, consideration must be given to the norms of the teacher(s) reference group. This does not mean that the supervisor has to agree with perspectives that he considers detrimental to effective education. It does suggest, however, that the plans of the supervisor must be constructed in light of the existing state of the attitudes, values, knowledge, and norms of the individual or group with whom he works. Planning that does not express concern for the norms of the teacher(s) reference group is likely to be inconsequential and irrelevant.

If a supervisor has earned the esteem of his colleagues, he will have much greater latitude in drawing plans and leading the goal-setting process. Where supervisor esteem has been conferred informally, in recognition of his abilities—human and technical—he has gained a powerful prerequisite of effective leadership. Status—or a formal position within the organization—also assists in the development of planning. Influence—or the ability to cause people to behave in a particular fashion—is obviously an aid to the hearing and reception that certain plans receive. It is desirable that *status* influence be balanced by *esteem*, which is the informal validation of power and authority. In some situations, supervisors have tended to play down the status aspects of their position. This is not only inappropriate, but a waste of opportunity to promote growth within the organization. Obviously, status authority must be used wisely and to the benefit of the system that conferred it. To deny the status authority of the supervisor is likely to produce confusion as to his legitimate role and reduce his potential effectiveness.

Supervisory planning must also take into account the relationship that the teachers have with their environment, along with the expectations they have for themselves and others within that environment. In large measure, the expressed perceptions of the teachers indicate whether or not their expectations are being met. When teacher perceptions indicate a discrepancy between expected and perceived supervisory performance, the plans of the supervisor, however well intended, become incompatible and rejected. In these circumstances, plans set in motion by the supervisor that do not square with teacher expectations and perceptions may be set aside—probably over a period of time—as teachers withhold compliance and employ other more subtle forms of rejection. This may occur to the point where the plan is finally considered unsuitable to the support of the organization's work.

Strategy Component. It is not enough to formulate a plan for change. Even when plans are precisely developed and communicated, they can be dismissed as the sole property of the administration, a new gimmick to add to the pressures and responsibilities of the faculty. If the planning process has been accomplished in light of the interpersonal and milieu components, it is less likely that plans will be suspect and ineffectual. Beyond the planning stage, the supervisor must move to implement the plan. Attainment of the planned goals will be related to his leadership effectiveness. To implement and attain the purpose(s) of sound plans requires a comprehensive strategy. This strategy must be an important guideline in making decisions relative to those plans.

Strategizing is not to be confused with Machiavellian schemes. There may well be informal meetings or discussions, at which time the best approach to a plan is discussed or analyzed. As an organization has both a formal and an informal structure, such deliberations are quite natural. By considering strategy in this way, the supervisor will seek the opinions or advice of others. That is, he will consider the relationship of the plan to the expectations and perceptions of the people who will be involved and affected by it; he will draw from this study the most potentially successful approach to its implementation. Since each complex of interpersonal-milieu conditions is likely to be different, the strategizing process will continue throughout the change period.

The esteem component is also related to the development of strategy. When a supervisor has been extended the acceptance of the group, his options in the realm of strategy are far greater than would otherwise be the case. It is more likely that the faculty will respond positively to a program development or problem resolution when the supervisor is perceived as competent and strong in his relationships with faculty and other leadership personnel.

If it is desired that a supervisor gain increased esteem, one strategy would be to give him a status position within the organization. By the same token, the status of a supervisory position will be enhanced when the person appointed to that position has already earned the esteem of those he intends to influence. The range of options available to a supervisor for strategizing are similar whether esteem is earned in the informal organization or status is conferred by the formal organization.

It is critical, even with the supervisor's status position and esteem, that he be aware of the range of expectations that the participants have for themselves. The less appropriate the strategy is to the expectations of the teacher, the less likely that those expectations will be changed. However, when the supervisor is sensitive to the expectations and perceptions of the group, the more likely it is that milieu components can be changed in a direction consistent with the plan or the goals being sought.

Participation Component. By definition, participation is affected only by the interpersonal components in the matrix. The greater the participation by members of a reference group, the greater will be the possibility of ISB changing group norms. It must be recognized, however, that existing norms may also define what is currently deemed to be appropriate participation for reference group members. The higher the esteem in which the supervisor is held, the greater will be his ability to promote participation; conversely, low esteem will reduce that ability. Clearly, the supervisor's status (or lack of it) will affect the participation component in similar fashion. When supervisors are established leaders within the organization, when in addition to their official status they have been able to gain the esteem of their co-workers through strong interpersonal effectiveness and technical competence, they will be in an excellent position to run the risks inherent in faculty participation. Through the promotion of faculty participation, it is more likely that prevailing attitudes and other psychological restraints will be altered.

Modification Component. In the matrix, modification is affected by the milieu components only. For example, expectations affect the modification component in two ways: if the attempt to modify is in accord with the expectations within the milieu, then the attempt is likely to be successful; if it is at variance with those expectations, the likelihood of success is decreased. Similarly, the greater the consonance between the attempted modification and existing perceptions, the more success there will be. To the degree that a modification attempt is seen as suitable or appropriate, will the attempt be successful in altering the milieu. Modification or change in the environment, however, cannot be made without considering the relationship of an environmental change to the goals of the organization. In this sense, supervisory decisions to modify the psychological or organizational environment of the school result from decisions about the school's purposes.

The environment within which teachers work greatly affects their efforts. The psychological environment or "organismic" quality of the organization will either support a high level of individual commitment and input, or else it will diffuse human energy to the detriment of the work to be done.

Support Component. If group norms are in accord with the direction of the support the supervisor wishes to provide, those norms will allow him to give greater and more effective support. Conversely, if the direction of the support conflicts with group norms, the support he provides will be less strong and less effective. Therefore, a supervisor should be aware as to whether or not the group norms reinforce his support attempts.

The effects of esteem and status on support are similar in that the higher the status or esteem the supervisor possesses, the greater and more varied will be the kind of support he is able to provide.

The milieu components also affect the support efforts of the supervisor. The more the expectations and perceptions are in agreement with the nature and direction of the support given, the stronger the support effort will become, because it will be reinforced by those powerful environmental factors. Likewise, certain actions will be seen as suitable or appropriate in particular situations. Whether a support attempt is seen as suitable or not will affect not only the strength and effectiveness of the attempt, but also the selection of the support elements themselves.

Support has been defined as relating to both organizational and psychological elements. Organizational support may suggest the application or availability of materials and resources required to do a job. Psychological support pertains to the complex of feelings, the administrative tone, and the open or closed atmosphere that pervades the organization. Each of these kinds of support will be affected by the interpersonal and milieu components, which to some extent will determine the appropriateness, possible direction, strength, and success of support efforts. As with the other intervention components, the support component must be developed with full realization of the possible effects—both positive and negative—of these impacting interpersonal and milieu components.

UTILIZATION OF THE MATRIX

The ISB matrix places the tasks of the supervisor in a new perspective. In some respects, it affirms beliefs long cherished by educators. In others, it focuses attention on limitations that have heretofore appeared as symptoms rather than causal factors.

The interpersonal components of reference, esteem, and status substantiate the need for supervisors to deal carefully with human conditions and concerns. Likewise, the milieu components of expectation, perception, and suitability testify to the critical importance of the environment in which the supervisor functions. These interpersonal and milieu components, however, are the static dimensions of the matrix; the altering of interpersonal relationships (through participation) and of milieu relationships (through modification) are functions of intervention.

The five intervention components are the action arenas of ISB. Their effects become manifest in the responses to these actions within the interpersonal and/or milieu components. Therefore, to alter any interpersonal or milieu component, the supervisor must act through one or more of the intervention components.

The particular combination of cirmumstances obviously influences the type, degree, and timing of an intervention. Nevertheless, the various components of the matrix do generate a number of general hypotheses that merit field testing.

Intervention on Interpersonal Components. Different patterns of action or intervention behavior are dictated by the nature of each of the interpersonal components in which the supervisor seeks to achieve change. The action patterns suggested are different if he seeks changes in the respective interpersonal components. Establishment of the reference of the supervisor as a member of a group of teachers, for example, is most appropriately initiated through participation. Once the supervisor has been accepted by the group, he can assist the teachers with planning and then move on to strategizing. Support subsequently is provided to increase the probability of success. The accomplishment of a change serves to alter the internal relationships of the group. If the supervisor has intervened effectively, the focus of leadership will be shifted to him.

To provide the supervisor with esteem requires quite a different sequence of intervention components. Rather than reserving support until last, it is appropriate for him to demonstrate immediately that he can bring resources to bear upon projects in which teachers engage. Having demonstrated this ability, the supervisor can become involved in planning and later in participation. The strategizing component will occur last because it is only through his own competencies that the supervisor can best earn esteem.

Status is likewise substantiated and enhanced through the intervention component of strategizing. However, as defined earlier, status is a relationship based upon position in an organization. It exists in two forms. Official status is conferred upon supervisors by the authority for intervention (through the components of planning and strategizing) vested in their positions. Both of these components are highly significant to effectiveness. However, if within the formal organization the supervisor cannot command support or does not participate actively with the teachers, the planning and strategizing components may not permit him to intervene successfully. In fact, principals who can utilize the support system (by providing resource materials, additional personnel, or released time) establish status positions within the formal organization. The ability to utilize these same components (by political pressure, professional pressure, or personal charm) enables teachers to wield tremendous influence within the informal organization. It is not an uncommon occurrence for this unofficial status in the informal organization to be so exerted that the official status of the supervisor within the formal organization is completely thwarted. To eliminate this phenomenon may be both impossible and undesirable. However, the supervisor must be invested officially with the authority to intervene through all four components if his probability of success in changing the status component is to be enhanced.

It is important to reemphasize that the modification component is not applicable in terms of the interpersonal dimensions of ISB.

Intervention on Milieu Components. The action patterns suggested by the matrix are quite similar if the supervisor seeks to achieve changes in the respective milieu components. Regarding expectation, perception, and suitability, the four intervention components are applied in the same order. When dealing with the milieu dimension, modification emerges as the most significant among the intervention components. It serves to alter the status quo, to suggest new alternatives, and to broaden horizons. Once the established norm has been at least questioned and perhaps condemned, planning is pursued in a new key. Strategizing follows, to determine implementation procedures for revising the relationships between the teachers and the school environment. Support is applied only after the changes are underway. It is vital to withhold support until the new direction has been charted. Bringing support to bear too early may only serve to further entrench the existing expectations, perceptions, and/or suitability.

Note also that the participation component is applicable only to the interpersonal dimension, and is not considered in terms of intervening on the milieu dimension of ISB.

The Critical Components Matrix thus gives substance to relationships between cause and effect. However, it is not possible to translate the intervention components directly into the actions that affect interpersonal and milieu dimensions. The supervisor gives meaning to intervention through the intelligent selection and application of technical skills. Such skills and their relationships to the intervention components are described in Chapter 10.

INTERVENTION EFFECTIVENESS PROFILE

This section attempts to examine the interrelationships of Instructional Supervisory Behavior, the school organization, and the larger sociocultural system. It also suggests a procedure by which the supervisor can review his performance through an ISB Intervention Effectiveness Profile.

Understanding of the interrelationships requires attention to a number of dimensions, as illustrated in Figure 9-2. The sociocultural system dimension represents the broad characteristics of the society or social setting within which social institutions develop and out of which organizations are formed. Organizations operating within a particular society

FIGURE 9-2

ISB EFFECTIVENESS PROFILE

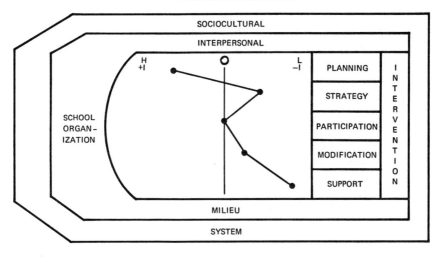

reflect in their structural elements those values to which that society has made a commitment. The relationship between the larger society and the organization is significant in that the larger society's occurrences, problems, conflicts, developments, and struggles toward priorities affect and shape the work of the organization.

This relationship is particularly pronounced in the case of service organizations such as schools. It has been a principle of long standing that schools should be concerned with the communities they serve; this concern should be made evident as faculty and supervisors work to shape a school program and the perspectives that will be used to guide instruction and learning. The interrelationship between school and community is particularly acute today. In many instances, vigorous reactions have been provoked when the public perceives that a school's instructional program is unmindful of, insensitive, or irrelevant to the needs of its constituency, proceeding instead with "business as usual." A school that operates in this way is usually more concerned with the maintenance of tradition than with the design of curricula and instructional processes responsive to contemporary demands. Those schools which *have* flourished, have done so by creating organizational and instructional arrangements and by developing a skilled staff dedicated to the primary goal of making the school organization serve the community. It is clear that organizations, particularly schools, have a basic and continuing responsibility to be a part of the communities they serve, instead of merely existing or being "located" within a particular area of the city and state.

The school as an organization, then, is the second dimension of this diagram. As described, it operates within the social environment and must respond to the constraints of the setting as well as employ environmental strengths in shaping an effective educational program. There is no one formula or best design. In each instance, the development of a positive interface between school and community will only be achieved through strong mutual effort. While there is ample evidence to suggest that the results of such efforts are of consequence and mutually enhancing, the coordination of action requires adroit leadership.

Although the supervisor primarily improves instruction and affects teacher behavior by acting within the formal organization of the school, he can also serve as a link to the larger community. This, too, is an important role. Obviously, he cannot proceed simply as an individual in providing such linkage; he must be aware of his total organizational responsibilities. However, to work solely within the organization on the improvement of instruction, in utter disregard of the school's presence within and relationship to the larger social system, may cause his efforts to be of little consequence or to be rejected and dismissed. The knowledge and application of the critical components of ISB will enable a supervisor to work effectively on improving the instructional program through influencing teacher behavior. Such performance will reflect knowledge of the critical interaction of the school organization with the social system.

In this diagram, attention is called to the fact that ISB is actually that behavior expressed when the individual supervisor *intervenes* within the organization of the school to affect teacher behavior. This suggests that effective ISB (intervention) is the result of interpersonal properties and the supervisor's knowledge of the organization's internal and external milieu conditions. Stated differently, ISB can be thought of as the action taken by the supervisor within the school setting. This action is logically a behavioral extension of existing knowledge and experience, and is drawn and designed from the interaction of the supervisor's understanding of the interpersonal and milieu components. From the interaction and analysis of these elements, the supervisor can determine a course of action, thereby applying his conceptual and technical expertise through the intervention components. Given a particular instructional problem, for example, the supervisor will elect to act (intervene). The effectiveness of ISB in influencing teacher behavior will depend upon the supervisor's capacity to create an approach to a problem vis-à-vis his knowledge of the organizational environment and the interpersonal conditions that characterize it.

The diagram also provides the supervisor with a way of viewing his performance of ISB in terms of the qualitative effectiveness of each phase of the intervention process. Planning could be analyzed separately, as could any of the other intervention components, and judgments could be made concerning the relative effectiveness of the supervisor's action through each element of the intervention components. In some cases, the supervisor's behavior might be such that his intervention could be classified as neutral, productive, or deleterious to the successful resolution of the situation under study. A scale could be created for each of the intervention components and a range established, from +1 (high degree of effectiveness), to 0 (neutral in effect), to −1 (negative in effect). As the intervention components were studied, an ISB profile could be charted based on the effectiveness of the information accumulated. It could be hypothesized that where the profile of the supervisor's efforts on the intervention components ran toward the +1 level, the more likely it would be that ISB was appropriate to the efficient and effective resolution of the instructional problem under study.

This diagram obviously requires further development. There is a need for more precise definitions of all components, but particularly the intervention elements. More exact definitions would provide a better base for securing descriptive information on ISB. It is suggested, however, that this model may provide a basis for more careful and analytical interpretations of supervisory efforts.

FUTURE STUDY

The identification of the eleven components, which it is postulated will help explain effective or ineffective instructional supervisory behavior, leads toward the development of a theory of ISB by defining certain questions for further investigators. Any number of questions might be posed; the following are suggested for future study: First, is effective ISB really a function of the eleven components? This has to be verified through experience. Second, are there additional components, and if so, what are they? For example, there has been some research evidence to indicate the possibility of competition as a critical element within the interpersonal components, although it was not strong enough to warrant inclusion at this time. Third, given the components of effective supervision, how can they be predicted and controlled? For example, if esteem is verified through experience as one predictor of effective ISB, then it becomes most important to find out by which factor esteem can be increased—by knowledge, ability, or self-concept. Perhaps what is needed is a theory of each of the components. It is hoped that a start has been made in an appropriate direction. Much work still needs to be done, but this work holds significant promise for education.

PART IV

Technical Skills of Instructional Supervisory Behavior

For supervisors to translate aspirations into practice requires the application of various skills. In previous literature, considerable emphasis has been placed upon the interpersonal dimension, through the use of human skills, and the milieu dimension, through the use of managerial skills. Many of the skills in these two areas are shared in common with counseling, administrative, and other leadership positions. Scant attention has been devoted to the technical skills that distinguish supervision as an educational specialty.

The principle is advanced here that the intervention components, which are the action areas of instructional supervisory behavior, are manifest through technical skills, and that the latter must be selected by the supervisor to fulfill particular purposes through an appropriate skill-mix.

The single chapter of Part IV describes nine technical skills that illustrate significant practices for supervision in education.

Chapter 10

Technical Skill-Mix
for Intervention

The intervention dimension of the ISB matrix corresponds to the technical skills needed by supervisors.* The technical area in the skill-mix concept is broadly conceived. It surpasses the notion of machine or engineering skills, including in its meaning the ability to use knowledge, methods, techniques, and equipment needed in order to perform the activities and tasks of supervision.

The technical skills, identified and interpreted briefly, present a more concrete and operational expression of the intervention components of the ISB matrix. The components of planning, strategizing, participation, modification, and support must be achieved through action and performance, if the supervisor is to contribute responsibly to change and growth of the organization. Systematic and objective approaches to such steps as planning, decision-making, instructional design, analysis of teaching and learning, and evaluation of teaching enable the supervisor to impact upon the school and the instructional system. Technical skills are the action states of intervention.

The ISB matrix portrays the intervention components as expressed by the application of technical skill areas in a functional relationship to the interpersonal or human components and the milieu or managerial components. Intervention itself is not expressed, nor does it exist, in isolation.

Human relations are expressed through the interpersonal dimension of the ISB matrix. They provide a connection between the intervention or technical aspects and the interpersonal or human dimension, by establishing a strong human character for the supervisory process.

Skills characterized as managerial or administrative are expressed through the milieu dimension. They provide a connection between the intervention and technical aspects and the organizational conditions that

* See Chapter 1.

affect or, in fact, determine the nature of supervisory behavior, establishing a strong environmental character for the supervisory process. The statements that follow are intended to identify and interpret some of the technical skills that the skill-mix concept and the intervention components of the critical components matrix require if ISB is to be concerned with the improvement of instruction. This definition of technical skills is not complete, nor is the treatment of the technical skills comprehensive. These summaries and ideas are intended to be a start at developing the technical skill area.

A fully developed set of technical skills would include techniques and procedures drawn from the social sciences, particularly political science, sociology, and economics. Applied skills from social work that have been created in the crucible of community interaction offer great promise in this regard. Certainly preparation programs for supervisors should be examined in terms of their outcomes, particularly as related to the technical competence of graduates.

PLANNING

The most encompassing of all technical skills in supervisory practice is the process of planning. Planning includes the range of organizational needs as expressed in the intervention components of ISB defined in the critical components matrix previously presented (planning, strategizing, participation, modification, and support). There can be little argument about the necessity for reflection and constructive analysis in determining the best course of action for an individual or group effort within an organization. In spite of the obvious need for planning, there is a tendency to set it aside in preference for a more immediate reaction to the perceived problem or situation. The frequent oversight of the planning process is related to the lack of any definition or design to follow in demonstrating its application. As organizations, including schools, become increasingly complex, the significance of the planning process increases. This condition is related to the human and technological sophistication of organizations as centers of service and productivity.

Considering those factors that contribute to the ability of the modern organization for innovation and vitality, Ewing states:

. . . Planning is one of the newer concepts of management—new, at least as compared to approaches like control, organization, policy, and financial management. . . . Planning is far more important to the modern corporation than it was to corporate ancestors of the early twentieth century and nineteenth century. This is because new technologies, proliferation of public needs, product diversification, accelerating social change, and other trends put an enormous premium on the ability of management to select skillfully from among many possible goals to make its selection at an opportune time, and to channel the organization's efforts swiftly in the desired direction. Indeed, to understand planning is to understand a process which, as much as or more than any other resource or capability, gives the modern corporation its unique ability to prosper in a world of continuing change.[1]

Ewing also outlined the contribution of effective planning to the work of complex organizations. He specified that such planning would accomplish at least seven things. They were:

1. It would lead to a better position or standing for the organization.
2. It would help the organization progress in ways that its management considers most suitable.
3. It would help every manager think, decide, and act more effectively for progress in the desired direction.
4. It would help keep the organization flexible.
5. It would stimulate a cooperative, integrated, enthusiastic approach to organizational problems.
6. It would indicate to management how to evaluate and check on progress toward the planned objectives.
7. It would lead to socially and economically useful results.[2]

In exploring the strategies of planning, Ewing interprets the rationale, potentials, and potholes associated with the *outside-in* and *inside-out* approach to planning.

Outside-in thinking always emphasizes fitting the organization to the market or the public need, adapting to anticipated opportunity, responding to external change. Its trademark is the primacy of the forecast. It centers the attention of management on opportunities that events are creating—events in the marketplace, in economic development or in national and international affairs.[3]

Continuing, Ewing described the inside-out approach to planning as focusing within the organization. He wrote:

The cornerstone of the inside-out approach is the key abilities, strengths, and apitudes of an organization. In some cases, as already indicated, these may prove to be in the marketing, engineering, or financial departments. In other cases, the key might be an unusual forecasting talent or a unique manufacturing capability. Then again, it might be simply location as when a company, store, or college finds it has the most advantageous spot in the area from which to serve many people.[4]

In effect, Ewing's emphasis on the critical role of the practice of planning conveys the position of this process—as bedrock in support of effective leadership and its consequence, successful organizations. Goal definition, the selection of appropriate strategies, and the use of human talents to the application of a plan are basic requirements of moving from the planning to the actualization stage. Reverse the sequence, as is often done under the pressure of program and system needs, and witness the dysfunctional change and development. In addition, the educational organization as both a production system and service institution is compelled to use the combination of what Ewing calls the *outside-in* and *inside-out* perspectives or organizational planning. The examination of internal strengths and milieu conditions, including the goal structure of the school, needs to be studied in relation to the environment being served. Only through the balanced view (inside and outside) can the school leadership, including supervisory personnel, project a plan that is likely to meet organizational goals and social needs.

DECISION-MAKING

Berman refers to responsible action in a variety of situations as a major quality of the educational leader. She asserts that responsible action requires expertise in decision-making. Berman describes the purpose of decisions within an organization as follows:

> Decisions serve different purposes within an organization. Some decisions make for increased coherence. They help provide the stabilizing influences, the traditions, the good feelings that come from knowing what the score is—from understanding. For example, the decision to have a mid-year seminar for staff, if it has been done in the past and if it is sanctioned by the staff, is a decision which helps provide coherence. Decisions for coherence help establish the boundaries of the school or organization.
>   On the other hand, some decisions establish new precedents or create the setting for innovation. These are "cuts"—a turning from what has been to something new. . . . A school or organization needs to study decisions made to maintain coherence and those made to initiate innovation. The balance between decisions for coherence and those for innovation can mean the difference between satisfied, productive individuals and organizations, and discontented individuals or institutions.[5]

These preceding ideas on decision-making remain as theoretical considerations that will not in isolation promote clear prescriptions as to a procedural framework to be followed by the supervisor in formulating strategies for their implementation. Feyereisen, Fiorino, and Nowak[6] have come closer to the definition of a decision-making model that holds promise, in terms of practical and applied planning needs of the supervisor. Their work provides a precise set of guidelines for the decision-making process. They were constructed in accord with systems concepts and procedures in mind. This model is presented as a guide rather than a formula. In addition, the assumption of this decision-making model is that the school system has a statement of objectives. Feyereisen *et al.* point out that stated objectives are crucial in a systems context, particularly with respect to the design and use of a decision-making model. This model is specifically designed for supervisors working on problems related to the instructional system. The model, together with its full interpretation, is a significant portrayal of a competence area for educational supervisors. The decision-making steps as outlined by Feyereisen *et al.* are the following:

1. *Identification of the Problem.* Within an organizational setting there are many problems, some relevant and some irrelevant to the attainment of organizational goals. Therefore, before we proceed we must define what is meant by a problem, and in this way provide guidance to the problem-solver's functioning within the school system.

2. *Diagnosis of the Problem.* The problem-solver must attempt to determine the causes of the problem so that appropriate action can be taken. It may be that the solution of the problem can be found in a curriculum guide, manual, or some other source. Easily solved problems in the curriculum and instruction system fall into this category. A more thorough investigation might begin by communicating with the problem-raiser to obtain as much information as possible. Observation of the instructional process may provide clues to the cause of the problem. Following the investigation and diagnosis, it will be necessary to define the problem clearly, listing probable causes before the next step—search for alternative solutions—can be taken.

3. *Search for Alternative Solutions.* Of all the steps in the decision-making process, this is probably the best structured because all the possible alternatives are not known. The creativity of the people involved in the decision-making process will certainly affect the alternatives that come to light.

4. *Selection of the Best Alternatives.* The selection of the best alternative might be considered the fulcrum upon which the problem-solving process rests.

Understandably, then, much deliberation and thought should precede the choice of the best alternative. Among the considerations to be weighed in making the final selection are payoff, risk, resources, and feasibility. Two obvious problems come to light when this concept is applied in the selection of alternatives in education. First, while the cost can be readily determined, the output or improvement generated by a solution may be rather nebulous, if known at all. Second, on occasion, a given community may desire a particular alternative of cost, if it will produce the greatest output. When this is the case, the educator has an obligation to provide the best education possible at a price the community can afford and is willing to pay. Should the implementation of a particular solution mean curtailment of other important activities, the public should be alerted to the possible consequences before a final decision is reached. . . . If the technology, personnel, equipment, or other resources are not available or cannot be acquired by the school system, the solution should be discarded as a possible alternative. In addition, systems analysis requires that the impact of the selected solution on the total solution be taken into account.

5. *Ratification of the Solution.* Following the selection of the solution, the subsystems of the total system determine the affect of the plan or decision upon their operation. This review points to flaws or weaknesses that had escaped notice and need to be corrected before the solution is implemented. This review also promotes coordination of effort between each of the subsystems.

6. *Authorization of the Solution.* The authorization may be routine or very troublesome. The delegation and definition of authority is very important in this step. Every effort should be made to define the conditions under which a particular individual is authorized to approve a particular action.

In delegating authority, the laws governing education must be considered, but beyond laws, the board of education, with the guidance of the administrative staff, would have the final authority. Whether to centralize or decentralize authority to authorize solutions is a decision to be made by each school system.

7. *Solution Used on a Trial Basis.* The authorization to use a solution on a trial basis might well be called the testing of solutions because the trial step in the decision-making process requires the application of all the techniques associated with testing and research.

8. *Preparation for Adoption.* This step is important enough to be considered as a separate one. It calls for thorough and appropriate preparation by a competent staff. This step includes such factors as supplies, building alterations and installations, adjustment of schedules, and employment of needed staff. Many potentially valuable solutions such as team teaching, modern math, nongraded organization, and so forth, have failed because the staff has not received adequate preparation.

9, 10, 11. *Adoption, Guidance, Evaluation.* The final steps in the decision-making process are adoption of the solution, guidance of the process, and evaluation. Since solutions are typically being applied in complex human organization, unforeseen problems may arise that require solutions. Despite efforts expended in preparing the staff, confusion, misinterpretations, misunderstandings, and mistakes will occur. This is particularly true when new procedures are adopted. At this point, the appropriate personnel, usually a supervisor, should be available to the staff to provide the needed guidance.

In sum, the Feyereisen, Fiorino, Nowak decision-making model is a systems type definition. It sets forth a series of steps that, if followed, will support the educational supervisor's efforts in the analysis of compound instructional problems. A design or definition such as this increases in importance as schools and the variety of instructional systems expressed within them continue to multiply.

APPLYING PROGRAM EVALUATION REVIEW TECHNIQUE (*PERT*)

There have been relatively recent technical developments in the planning and decision-making skills areas. One of these developments is Program Evaluation Review Technique (PERT). Sometimes this technique is referred to as critical path management (CPM).* L. Linton Deck, Jr. wrote the following interpretation of PERT: "PERT is an integrated system to bring about improved control and more efficient planning. Although imperfect in many respects, it has prime importance and usefulness in the logical thinking procedure that must be undertaken prior to the actual analysis of a project." [7] The technique forces the consideration of a total plan rather than a segmented approach. Feedback of the input information allows control to be exerted quickly on critical activities of a project. The construction and verification of the PERT network provide the basis for better communication and coordination between the individuals responsible for the achievement of the objectives of the project.

School administrators are beginning to extend the applications of PERT to large research projects supported by federal or foundation funds, and a growing number of local administrators are applying PERT to small but essential planning functions. The evidence now available indicates that the future will bring increasing applications of PERT for more efficient, more precise, and better administration at all levels of the educational enterprise.

Work Breakdown Structure. Application of the PERT technique must begin with the identification of objectives of the project to be planned. The prime objectives of the program must be carefully determined, and the supporting objectives necessary to the attainment of each of the prime objectives must also be carefully defined. Objectives, properly developed and applied, indicate the directions in which a project must move for successful completion. They provide guidance for the activities of the

---

* *Note:* See the statement on PERT and CPM presented in *Educational Decision-Making Through Operations Research* by Ralph A. Van Dusseldrop, Duane E. Richardson, and Walter J. Foley (Boston: 1971), Allyn and Bacon, Inc., pp. 114–133.

project and thus increase the effectiveness and efficiency of the under-taking. Once identified, the objectives must be organized and interrelated to enable attainment of the overall program goals. The organization of objectives, in the PERT system, is accomplished by the construction of a work breakdown structure. The process consists of subdividing the total project into smaller and more easily managed program elements.

Network Development.   The foundation of the PERT system is a network that is a logic diagram or flow chart derived from the work breakdown. The network shows the work plan established to reach the objectives of the project, the interdependencies and interrelationships of the work ele-ments in the plan, and the priorities of the elements of the program plan.

A network is composed of events and activities. An event does not consume time or resources but represents the start or completion of acti-vities. It is a specific, definable occurrence that is recognizable as a par-ticular instant in time.

An example of a simple PERT network is shown in Figure 10-1. In the figure, events are represented by circles. An arrow represents an acti-vity that connects two events, with the head of the arrow indicating the direction of time flow and touching the later event. One dummy activity is shown in the network, and is represented by the dotted arrow.

Precise and thorough descriptions of events and activities make it possible to keep networks simple, and networks should include only those

FIGURE 10-1.   Simple PERT Network

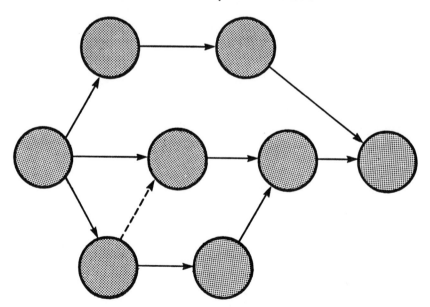

activities and events that are necessary to depict the work plan adequately. The process of combining networks for segments of a project into one network for the total project is called *network integration*. The element used to integrate network drawings MUST be an event, and not an activity. Events are used to preclude misunderstandings about the responsibility for accomplishing the activities that lead to and from integrating events.

ANALYZING LEARNING STYLES

Supervisors work to promote learning. They do so in all kinds of complex settings. Irrespective of locale and the peculiar requirements of a particular place, supervisory decisions in support of learning should be made out of knowledge about the learning process and the conditions required for the promotion of learning.

The supervisor's work should reflect a concept(s) of learning including the use of such conceptualization in the analysis of curricula and instructional processes. This proposal may be obvious to a fault. Unnecessary petitions will not be made, but conscious recognition of the legitimacy of this area is important.

Schools, as formal centers of learning, testify to the general acceptance of the notion that learning is not a mystical process. Also, learning promoted in the formal setting is not restricted to performance in prescribed areas of the curriculum. It has long been known that the school serves as an instrument of socialization. The school as a center of learning is expected, systematically and effectively, to provide instruction in traditional areas of knowledge; the school is also expected to promote learning in an environment and under conditions that nurture the self, the potential of all students, not in the form of toleration but in the belief that the traditions of our culture and their projected refinement into the future is best accomplished by a vital concern with the invigoration of people in the cognitive, affective, and totally humane sense. While responding to this expectation and cultural requirement is awesome enough, it is the essence of what schools are all about.

The supervisor needs the conceptual tools related to learning styles if he is going to make intelligent decisions about changing teacher behavior. He must be able to assist the teacher to analyze learning style in order that appropriate prescriptions of methodology and content can be made.

Schools, and the instructional processes they reflect, provide the observer with an eclectic view of learning. The supervisor must face the reality that differences are likely to be as dramatic within a school as between schools. There may be open space arrangements where teaching teams are working to determine an individual learner's profile of need and the implications of such diagnostic review. In a diagnostic approach to instructional decisions, it is not unusual to find the use of a range of programmed and autotutorial materials. These materials may be used as a method of reinforcement or as an initial learning mode in accord with a carefully constructed plan for an individual or group of students. In a reverse pattern, school curricula and instructional processes that emphasize patterned practice methods in accord with a use of stimulus-response psychology are likely to provide more "holistic" experiences in relation to the systematic and step approach to learning. Some teachers may concentrate their instructional decisions on an in-depth commitment to what is grossly labeled an S-R approach to learning, while others may concentrate their efforts through humanistic or field theory perspectives.

It is likely that in any given school or department the supervisor will find a combination of these perspectives on learning. The reality and need become clear. As the supervisor works with teachers, as individuals or in groups, there will be present a range of views on learning, what it is, and how the teachers' work is geared to promote learning through the curricula and the instructional decisions made. If assistance is to be provided by the supervisor, it must be drawn from a depth of understanding of the nature of learning, its various theoretical positions, and their implications for guiding the development of instructional arrangements and processes.

A vast body of literature and research makes up the discipline of human learning. This field must be explored in depth by the supervisor who proposes to make any kind of a difference in terms of teaching effectiveness as expressed in student learning performance and in total personal development. However, only a broad, illustrative review is provided here.

In terms of the nature of ISB as presented in this book, it is appropriate to refer to the work of psychologist Robert M. Gagne.[8] The great significance of Gagne's work rests in the fact that he proposes a view of learning based upon varieties of learning (*learning types*), whereby variations in learning (*changed behavior*) move on a continuum from signals and stimulus-response learning to the learning of principles and problem-solving. Gagne established a clear and critical relationship between less complex learning types and the more complex conceptual learning, and the combinations of concepts in principle learning and beyond to problem-solving and the creative leaps possible from the application of human rationality through problem situations. Gagne's learning types enable supervisors and teachers to study a complex learning performance. Its less complex components and subordinate learning can then be arranged in a logical and systematic fashion so that instruction and learning can proceed sequentially toward the expression of the more complex learning or performance. A learning sequence so constructed is called a *learning hierarchy*. One of the teacher's tasks in this approach to learning is to assess the student's entry performance against the learning or performance definitions contained in the hierarchy. In addition, each part of the learning hierarchy needs to be designed in relationship to the best possible instructional mode. There is ample room for instructional creativity and accomodation of the needs and dispositions of the student.

Here is a brief identification of Gagne's varieties of learning: [9]

Type 1: Signal Learning. The individual learns to make a general, diffuse response to a signal. This is the classical conditioned response of Pavlov (1927).

Type 2: Stimulus-Response Learning. The learner acquires a precise response to a discriminated stimulus. What is learned is a connection (Thorndike, 1898) or a discriminated operant (Skinner, 1938), sometimes called an instrumental response (Kimble, 1961).

Type 3: Chaining. What is acquired is a chain of two or more stimulus-response connections. The conditions for such learning have been described by Skinner (1938) and others, notably Gilbert (1962).

Type 4: Verbal Association. Verbal association is the learning of chains that are verbal. Basically, the conditions resemble those for other (motor) chains. However, the presence of language in the human being makes this a special type because internal links may be selected from the individual's previously learned repertoire of language. (*cf.* Underwood, 1964.)

Type 5: Multiple Discrimination. The individual learns to make n identifying responses to as many different stimuli, which may resemble each other in physical appearance to a greater or lesser degree. Although the learning of each stimulus-response connection is a simple type 2 occurrence, the connections tend to interfere with each other's retention. (*cf.* Postman. 1961.)

Type 6: Concept Learning. The learning acquires a capability of making a common response to a class of stimuli that may differ from each other widely in physical appearance. He is able to make a response that identifies an entire class of objects or events (*cf.* Kendler, 1964.)

Type 7: Principle Learning. In simplest terms, a principle is a chain of two or more concepts. It functions to control behavior in the manner suggested by a verbalized rule of the form "If A, then B," where A and B are concepts. However, it must be carefully distinguished from the mere verbal sequence "If A, then B," which, of course, may also be learned as type 4.

Type 8: Problem-Solving. Problem-solving is a kind of learning that requires the internal events usually called thinking. Two or more previously acquired principles are somehow combined to produce a new capability that can be shown to depend on a "higher-order" principle.

As a learning or performance system is designed, it is possible to view the system in terms of the types of learning or varieties of learning that comprise it. It is then possible to design and develop instructional strategies for the different clusters of learning or performance called for in the hierarchy or total instructional system. These strategies in turn can be defined and used in accord with the conditions outlined by Gagne as being necessary for the promotion of the learning types called for in the hierarchy.

This systematic view of an instructional or learning system may evoke cries of mechanism, human engineering, and anti-intellectualism. Granted the intensity of the reaction, supervisors nevertheless do need to know learning and the designs that promote it, as well as practical techniques for the analysis and cooperative construction of learning systems with teachers. General and vague knowledge about the nature of curriculum, what it is, how learning can be planned—and most critical today, how it can be evaluated—will not suffice. Supervisors must have analysis skills that are based in a substantive sense on the nature of learning and organizing techniques for its promotion.

ANALYZING TEACHING STYLES

The main data bank for the supervisory process is the teaching act. This interaction of teacher, student, and content (cognitive, affective) within a particular environment is the reality of the instructional system. The refinement of instruction requires that the supervisor know and apply structured approaches to the observation and analysis of teaching. This scientific approach even has been defined as a way of viewing supervision.[10] Analysis of teaching emphasizes description of overt behavior. This description is facilitated by predetermined frameworks as tools that ensure exactness and precision. The scientific analysis of teaching style is a significant technical skill in the supervisory process. The strengths of this approach have been interpreted as follows:

> The use of carefully designed frameworks to describe teaching behavior adds a new kind of precision to teaching and to supervision. With the collection of data that can be analyzed and quantified within predetermined categories, the supervisory observation and conference moves from the realm of "I think" to "This is what happened." The teacher has objective baseline data from which to make desired changes in his own behavior, even if the data do not account for all the variables within the classroom.[11]

Work by Biddle and Ellena;[12] Berman and Usery;[13] and Simon and Boyer,[14] offers assistance in attaining competence in the analysis of teaching. Training and practice in the application of selected observation systems will enable the supervisor to develop the required skills.

Biddle provides a multivariate model for teacher effectiveness and presents careful summaries of educational research on teacher effectiveness in the hope of stimulating thought and research related to teaching competence and effectiveness. For the supervisor, the Biddle model suggests areas of needed definition, in-depth study, and possible intervention. It is a point of departure, more an attempt at the total view needed if knowledge and the range of human and technical skills are to be applied by the supervisor in a rational way.

Biddle introduces his model in this way:

> It has been said that the central problem in understanding teacher effectiveness is establishing relationships between teacher behaviors and teacher effects. The statement suggests that two classes of variables are minimally necessary in the study of effectiveness: *teacher behaviors* (an independent variable) and *teacher effects* (a dependent variable). The problem becomes complex because teacher-pupil interaction is embedded in historical, social, and physical contexts that constrain and interact with it.[15]

In interpreting his model, Biddle wrote:

> These variables are represented visually [in Figure 10-2] in terms of a system of postulated, cause-and-effect relationships. More explicitly, five of the above variables are postulated to form a cause-and-effect sequence.
> 1. Formative experiences, teacher properties, teacher behaviors, immediate effects, and long-term consequences form a sequence such that

FIGURE 10-2.   A Seven-Variable-Class Model for Teacher Effectiveness (Note: *Variables listed in each class are examples*) (*From Bruce J. Biddle and William J. Ellena, eds.*, Contemporary Research on Teacher Effectiveness, *New York: Holt, Rinehart and Winston, Inc., 1964*)

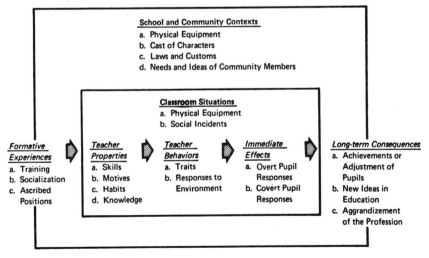

each variable class in the sequence causes effects in the next variable class listed.

The other two variables are postulated to be contexts for portions of the main sequence.

2. The classroom situation embeds (and interacts) with teacher properties, teacher behaviors, and immediate effects.

3. School and community contexts embed (and interact) with formative experiences, teacher properties, teacher behaviors, immediate effects, and long-term consequences.[16]

Given an instructional situation that requires supervisory attention, the use of a model such as this would substantially help in focusing attention on the possible points of intervention by the supervisor.

The variables of "teacher behavior" and "immediate effects" form the core of supervision in the Biddle model. The analysis of their interaction requires structured frameworks. Berman and Usery have provided supervisory personnel with a direct and clear statement of analysis of teaching employing such structured frameworks. More importantly, they have illustrated how the Flanders[17] and Hughes[18] systems apply to the supervisory process.

Other structured systems for the analysis of teaching have been developed, tested, and reported. Many of these interaction systems are reported by Simon and Boyer.[19]

It must be emphasized that as important as the structured approach to the analysis of teaching is, it is but one skill of intervention. It must be balanced and used in accord with supportive expressions in the areas of management and human relations.

DESIGNING INSTRUCTIONAL SYSTEMS

In addition to command of particular skills that can be applied separately, the supervisor must be able to synthesize several skills in concert. This blending and combined focus results in a more complex skill area of a higher order. The combination of skills can be illustrated in the designing of instructional systems.

The initial skill in this area is that of identifying the needs of the students for whom the system is intended. The second is that of determining the outcomes anticipated for learning. Task analysis skills can then be applied to systematize the approach. Skill in analysis of learning styles is necessary in order to enable the supervisor to develop a conceptual hierarchy of learning.

Translation into performance criteria or behavioral objectives for students is another skill on the continuum of designing instructional systems. The formulation of instructional objectives is one of the four elements of a classroom instructional system.

The given conditions to be met in the instructional objectives must subsequently be assessed. The skill of evaluating student learning must be applied to measure the same type of performance called for in the instructional objectives. Such evaluation may be summative, in that it comes at the end of a sequence of tasks, or criterion measures may be developed for tasks at each level of a performance hierarchy.

Similarly, the appropriate method or strategy must be selected by the teacher. The supervisor must assist him in choosing an instructional process that also has "performance agreement" with the instructional objectives and with the evaluation procedures. In other words, an instructional process must be determined that will enable the students(s) to acquire (at least) the competencies specified in the instructional objectives as well as the type of competencies in which he will be tested.

It is important that the supervisor possess the skill of distinguishing clearly between instructional objectives and process objectives.*

The effectiveness of teaching is measured by the degree to which the students learn that which the teacher intends. That is, a measure of teacher effectiveness moves beyond the description of the teaching decisions and strategies used during the instructional process to an appraisal of the *outcome* of that teaching—an appraisal of the learning by students of those instructional objectives initially selected by the teacher. The instructional process is certainly of value in itself, but its reason for existence lies in facilitating the achievement of the *instructional objectives* by the students. Differentiating among the components of the instructional system enables a teacher to plan properly for the achievement of each student in his class. The teacher who sees his role as facilitator—that is, one who is a *diagnostician*, a *prescriber*, and an *enabler* for each student's educational growth—finds that decision-making becomes more rational and more humanly responsible when it is done within the perspective of a classroom instructional system characterized by performance agreement between its components. Being accountable as teachers includes being accountable to oneself and to the child for increasing his competence level in respect to specific instructional objectives. The emphasis should not be merely upon accountability, however. It should be more upon student achievement. To assure such achievement, it is proper that teachers be accountable at the point of each component of the in-

---

* *Note:* Many of the ideas presented in the following material on design were developed by J. Marvin Cook, Associate Professor of Education, University of Maryland Baltimore County, in a paper prepared for the Ohio State Department of Education.

structional system. In like manner, failure by the teacher at the point of assuring performance agreement between each component of our instructional system means that the students cannot be expected to reflect the level of achievement desired.

Concern for a student is a necessary but not sufficient condition for helping him or her to achieve. Systematically planning for the student's achievement is one effective way to express such concern.

The fourth element in the instructional system design is classroom management. The supervisor must be able to determine the materials and equipment required for the instructional process and arrange for their availability at a particular time and place. This element also includes the arrangements for appropriate conditions to test outcomes and to secure logistical support.

These four elements of a classroom instructional system are illus-

FIGURE 10-3. Model of a Classroom Instructional System

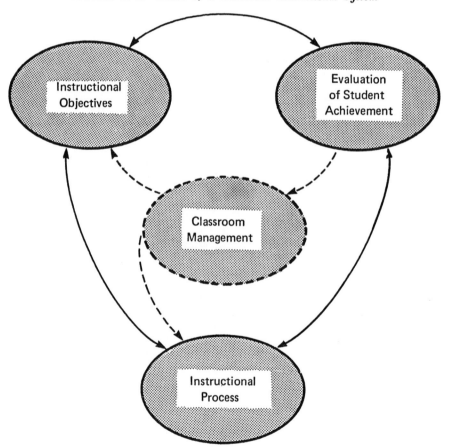

trated in Figure 10-3. The arrows indicate that congruence must exist among all four elements.

Instructional Objectives: Statements of what the students will be able to do as a result of teaching. A usefully stated instructional objective is one that helps teacher and students to see where they are heading and tells them how to know when they have arrived. Ideally, it will identify what a student would be doing when demonstrating his achievement of the instructional objective, suggest conditions under which the desired performance is to be exhibited, and suggest the minimal level of performance that the teacher will accept as evidence the learner has reached the objective.

Instructional Process: The teaching strategy (both planned and implemented) that is designed by the teacher to enable his students to attain the instructional objectives.

Process Objectives: Statements of what the teacher or the student will be doing DURING the instructional process. A *teacher process objective* is one that states what the teacher intends to do personally during the instructional process. A *student process objective* is one that states what the student will be doing during the process.

Classroom Management Objectives: Those objectives of a management nature that facilitate the accomplishment of the other three components of the classroom instructional system.

Related skills involve the determination of the worth and appropriateness of instructional objectives. Although some objectives may be well stated in behavioral terms, the supervisor must be able to assist the teacher in determining whether time and energy should be expended to enable students to attain them. Possibly some objectives will not be appropriate for a particular group of students.

Supervisors would be providing a much needed service if they would take the next step and work with teachers to sequence the objectives of curriculum units into performance hierarchies. Beginning with a terminal objective of an instructional unit stated in terms of the performance the students are expected to be able to exhibit at the completion of the unit, a performance hierarchy is developed by analyzing this final capability into subordinate skills in an order such that lower-level skills enable the higher level ones to be learned. The completed set of ordered skills forms a hierarchy.

In addition to *diagnosing* the curriculum, the supervisor *diagnoses* the teacher to determine competencies available as compared to those needed to facilitate the students in attaining the instructional objectives.

Having obtained data about the teacher and in like manner about the curriculum, the supervisor then assumes the role of a *prescriber* both for the curriculum and for the teacher.

The supervisor may prescribe the steps necessary to assure that the instructional objectives are quality objectives. Decisions may be made about the sequencing of curriculum objectives into performance hierarchies. Summer workshops may be required to construct such hierarchies for the various parts of the curriculum. Perhaps the supervisors will identify and prescribe new materials that may be secured, based on performance hierarchies.

For the teacher, the supervisor may prescribe specific training sessions. If the diagnosis shows that the teacher has competencies required to enable the students to achieve, but not the necessary equipment, then the supervisor might prescribe such equipment. In all cases, for both the curricula and the teachers, the prescription is based upon diagnosis.

As an *enabler,* the supervisor enables the prescribed changes in the curriculum to occur. Workshops can be conducted for the construction of curriculum using performance hierarchies, or the purchase of new curriculum can be expedited based upon the supervisor's prescriptions. Similarly, the supervisor provides for the multifaceted, multisensory instruction (in-service workshops, etc.) that enables the teachers to attain those new teaching competencies identified by the diagnosis and named in the prescription as necessary for the students to achieve the instructional objectives of the school.

The supervisor facilitates the students' attainment of the instructional objectives by:

Diagnosing the curriculum (in particular, the behavioral objectives) and the teachers;

Prescribing steps to remedy areas of concern with respect to the curriculum and the teachers; and

Enabling changes in the curriculum to occur while at the same time enabling the teachers to acquire those new competencies they need in order for the students to succeed.

The importance attributed to performance objectives in behavioral terms might suggest that the supervisor possess this skill for independent utilization. This is considered appropriate for other elements of the instructional system design, particularly analysis of learning and evaluation of learning. However, to isolate the preparation of behavioral objectives from the other elements of an instructional system is to increase the possibility of inappropriate or inconsistent objectives. It is precisely the excessive concern for such performance criteria in the abstract that has delayed the careful development of total instructional systems design.

EVALUATING STUDENT LEARNING

The definition of instructional supervision used in this book states that the supervisor directly affects teacher behavior in such a way as to "facilitate pupil learning." The supervisor helps achieve this end not by working with students, but by working *through* the teacher. Nevertheless, implicit in the definition is the need for him to be concerned and knowledgeable about the evaluation of learning.

The evaluation of student learning outcomes is an important vehicle through which a supervisor can gain leverage in working with teachers. Most teachers are genuinely concerned about the success of their students; through the analysis of these outcomes, the supervisor can move a teacher toward analysis of teaching and a consideration of instructional objectives and other key elements in improving the instructional process. Through such evaluation, a supervisor can work within the modification component of the matrix. Through data on student learning, he can modify a teacher's expectations concerning his own behavior and achievement. Such a successful joint effort on a problem of critical personal and professional concern can also alter their interpersonal relationships.

Supervisors must facilitate the analysis of the results of instruction, while cooperating with teachers and other colleagues in the definition of comprehensive evaluative processes, including the transfer of evaluative skills and techniques. They must also contribute to the professional analysis of student needs and performance levels as the basis for promoting the most reasonable and valid plan of study. Inherent in this statement is the principle of individual differences: students differ, and only infrequently are large groups of students in need of and interested in the same concepts or operations. This suggests the breadth of evaluation. There is need to apply evaluative procedures throughout the phase of instruction—from the start, at the point of defining entry behavior, through subsequent stages of teaching and instruction, to the summative analysis of student performance at the conclusion.

The concept of evaluation in education entails mixed images and meanings. Evaluation, for many individuals, connotes judgmental processes and the subsequent attachment of labels such as "good" or "bad," "pass" or "fail." In a real sense, this is a major component of the concept of evaluation, but by no means are the judgmental processes and "labeling" the full measure of evaluation in education. The labeling or categorizing that takes place in evaluation is often based upon information and analysis sadly lacking in detail. Frequently there is little emphasis on performance except of the paper-and-pencil variety, and there is typically no attention paid to the direction or rate of progress. Most disturbing is the avoidance of any action, in terms of instructional needs and prescriptions, as a result of thoughtful and specific analysis of the total performance of students. Indeed, in only severe cases of psychological malfunctioning are the behavior of the student and the underlying psychological state of the individual considered in their relationship to total functioning and performance in the school setting. Evaluation must reach beyond the combining of discrete scores that in turn are reinterpreted into another form—until such interpretative processes end in the unfortunate labeling or detailing of "what he is" based upon limited and possibly inaccurate measures of what the student has done.

Benjamin Bloom, J. Thomas Hastings, and George Madaus, in their *Handbook on Formative and Summative Evaluation of Student Learning*,[20] comprehensively examine the "state of the art" of evaluating student learning. The major sections of this volume concentrate on education and evaluation, the use of evaluation for instructional decisions, techniques for evaluating cognitive and affective objectives, and evaluation systems. The knowledge, insights, and techniques identified and interpreted in this handbook represent a compendium of perspectives on evaluation of student learning that a supervisor needs in order to apply and to help others apply evaluative processes and procedures to the design and improvement of instruction. The breadth of evaluation in education has been stated in these terms.[21]

1. Evaluation as a method of acquiring and processing the evidence needed to improve the student's learning and the teaching.
2. Evaluation as including a great variety of evidence beyond the usual final paper and pencil examination .
3. Evaluation as an aid in clarifying the significant goals and objectives of education and as a process for determining the extent to which students are developing in these desired ways.
4. Evaluation as a system of quality control in which it may be determined at each step in the teaching-learning process whether the process is effective or not, and if not, what changes must be made to ensure its effectiveness before it is too late.
5. Finally, evaluation as a tool in education practice for ascertaining whether alternative procedures are equally effective or not in achieving a set of educational ends.

The need for evaluation of learning suggests several areas in which the supervisor must be able to provide help for teachers. Examples are: establishing consistent and realistic criterion measures for student performance; validation, the process of determining whether or not the evaluation system is providing the data needed; test result interpretation, assisting teachers in determining the meaning and applicability of test results from standardized tests and from data obtained from such surveys as the National Assessment Project; knowledge of appropriate evaluation instruments; the ability to aid in the construction of local or teacher-designed tests; basic statistical competence necessary for the analysis of data obtained through evaluation processes, and skill in converting such data into useful information for teachers.

The views on evaluation set forth above, as well as the view of student learning and its evaluation defined in "Mastery Learning," are consistent with and supportive of previous ideas developed in this chapter on the technical skills of instructional supervision. Clearly, planning, decision-making, learning, instructional design, and the analysis of teaching—including the proposals and models reported here—are consonant with this interpretation of evaluation of learning. In each of these technical skill areas, there is a rich array of concepts over a range of knowledge levels in addition to models, techniques, and structures. These elements provide a knowledge base and the operational introduction to technical skill areas. In evaluation, as among the other areas of technical skills, the supervisor is required to perform in accord with the knowledge and techniques of the area.

CONDUCTING THE SUPERVISORY CONFERENCE

Probably no single supervisory performance is more critical to changing (if not advancing) the instructional process than the supervisory conference. The supervisory conference is a direct and practical testing ground for all of the human and interpersonal skills possessed by the supervisor. In order to use this important skill area effectively, there must also be the support of many of the other technical skill areas of supervision. Certainly knowledge and competence in the areas of learning, instructional design, and the analysis of teaching will be generously evidenced whenever a supervisor becomes engaged in supervisory planning, observation, and follow-up with a teacher or teaching team.

In accord with positive human relations factors, the preplanning for any observation and the supervisory conference that follows should be thoughtfully and sensitively arranged with the teacher(s) concerned. Here are some guidelines for the supervisory conference, including the pre-observation visit and the follow-up conference.*

Young indicates that the following items make up the functional parts or related purposes of the supervisory conference:

1. Plan teaching strategies
2. Provide encouragement to teachers

---

* The ideas presented on the supervisory conference are based upon a paper entitled "Using a Systems Approach to Develop and Research Supervisory Conference Strategies," presented by Dr. David B. Young, University of Maryland Baltimore County (New York: AERA symposium, 1971).

3. Provide training for the acquisition of specific teaching behavior
4. Provide for the improvement of the teacher's self-concept
5. Provide teachers with feedback on performance—to improve their accuracy of perception about their behavior
6. Develop a teacher's ability to analyze his own performance without the aid of a supervisor
7. Modify teacher behavior
8. Evaluate teacher performance

It is not enough, of course, merely to enter purposefully into a conference. Along with purposes the supervisor needs specific conferencing techniques in order to employ this method successfully. The following is a list of skills to be employed sequentially in conducting a supervisory conference.

Establishing Communication

For the supervisor this phase of the supervisory conference is a crucial one. He should attempt to reduce the teacher's anxieties through expressions of support, confidence, and interest. Teacher and supervisor alike must adjust their communication patterns to accommodate each other's "style."

Reflecting on Classroom Performance

The supervisor asks the teacher to reflect on his teachings, to recall those aspects of his teaching that went according to his plans and those that did not. During the course of this discussion, the teacher will probably identify one or two problems he thinks he encountered. As the teacher reflects on his performance, he should be guided toward relating his course of action to the learning objectives and to their effect on pupils.

Clarifying Learning Objectives

The supervisor asks the teacher to review the learning objectives for the instructional period. Using probing questions such as "Could you be more specific?," "What, specifically, are the pupils able to do at the end of the period?," or, "Can you put the objective into terms of pupil behavior?," the teacher is guided to a delineation of his specific objectives.

During these three phases of the supervisory conference, a "Rogerian counseling" model is suggested as a basis (screen) for determining essential supervisory behavior/strategy. The following counseling behaviors are illustrative of some skills that the supervisor needs to be able to employ during the conference:

Response Behaviors

Accepting
Reflecting
Clarifying
Summary Clarification
Probing
Silence

Initiating Behaviors

Assurance
Approval
Questions (thought level)
Perceiving
Patterning
Redefining
Predicting
Analyzing

The foregoing list should serve to illustrate the process. The following skills are described in general terms without an accompanying list of specific supervisory behaviors.

Feedback

The supervisor provides objective feedback to the teacher. This feedback may be in the form of a graphic summary of selected aspects of teacher-pupil behavior and/or patterns of teaching.

Analysis of Data

Given the data recorded during the observation, the supervisor engages the teacher in an analysis of his performance in terms of the stated learning objectives.

The conference should be an opportunity for describing, exchanging feelings, interpreting, and providing the feedback that is so critical if modifications or refinements are to be forthcoming. This exchange, particularly as it relates to feelings and the effect of behavior on one another, is part of feedback. In providing this information or feedback, Johnson [22] recommends that it be nonthreatening and be characterized as follows:

1. Focus feedback on behavior rather than the person.
2. Focus feedback on observation rather than inference.
3. Focus feedback on description rather than judgment.
4. Focus feedback on descriptions of behavior in terms of "more or less" rather than "either or."
5. Focus feedback on behavior related to a specific situation, preferably to the "here and now," rather than on behavior in the abstract, or "there and then."
6. Focus feedback on the sharing of ideas and information rather than on giving advice.

7. Focus feedback on exploration of alternatives rather than answers or solutions.
8. Focus feedback on the value it may have to the receiver, not on the value of "release" that it provides the person giving it.
9. Focus feedback on the amount of information that the person receiving it can use, rather than on the total amount that you might have available.
10. Focus feedback on time and place so that personal data can be shared at appropriate times.
11. Focus feedback on what is said rather than why it is said.

The supervisory conference is a crucial interpersonal interaction. The circumstance is compounded if the teacher or teaching team considers the pre-observation visit, the observation, and post-observation conference to be primarily inspectional and evaluative in the sense of assigning some value to the instructional episode observed and discussed. It is realistic to recognize that supervisory observation and conference do become (in part) the source of information for the evaluation of teaching. In the main, however, supervisory visits and conferences should be rich exchanges between teacher(s) and supervisors in unit level production systems. These interactions should be clear and productive, while evolving out of a positive human and interpersonal framework.

EVALUATION OF TEACHING

The systematic design of the school curriculum, in the form of instructional systems and the scientific or structural framework analysis of the teaching act, quite naturally leads to the attachment of some value judgments about teaching effectiveness. Where judgments on effectiveness impinge upon the position, job security, and professional role of the teacher, it is the responsibility of the supervisor to complete evaluation decisions with humaneness. Perhaps this is best done through a rational and carefully constructed approach to teacher evaluation. In the following statements, the *indirect* and *direct* approaches to teacher evaluation are interpreted. The procedures for implementing such measures, as well as the definition of instrumentation to be used in the evaluation process, have to be determined by teachers and supervisory personnel together. The evaluative processes cannot be imposed nor administratively constructed if increased effectiveness is the desired outcome. These ideas about teacher effectiveness, then, were constructed out of an instructional systems framework.[23] The basic premise of this statement is that measures of teaching effectiveness must be devised and used in formulating value judgments or evaluations of teaching efforts. This area is most complex.

The extent of the complexity results from the combined psychological and professional nature of teaching as well as from the lack of precise (if not measurable) instructional goals.

The supervisor will find this statement on the evaluation of teaching consistent with and related to the other technical skills developed in this chapter. Skills in learning, analysis of teaching, and instructional design and evaluation all merge as the supervisor observes, collects data, and makes judgments about the effectiveness of teaching. In the past, the phrase "teacher effectiveness" has too often been used as a synonym for: traits of teachers; classroom skills exhibited by teachers; student ratings received by teachers; classroom interaction or participation produced by teachers; classroom climate established by teachers; as well as student achievement effectuated by teachers. The same factors have been called "competence," "criteria for competence," "ability to teach," "value of a teacher," and other things. In this statement, a distinction is made between teaching traits and skills, "effectiveness," "rating," and "evaluation." The following definitions incorporate these discriminations:

Teaching functions refer to the categories of the role of the teacher as a facilitator of learning. These categories are established on the basis of the different ways a teacher relates to the student's learning process. For example, there might be three teaching functions that the teacher fulfills as a facilitator of learning: diagnostician, prescriber, and enabler.

Measurement of teaching traits and skills (including methodology and academic competence) is the act of determining what and how different traits and skills (methodology) are used by a teacher for the different teaching functions.

Teaching effectiveness is the ability of a teacher to facilitate the acquisition by his students of those ways of thinking, feeling, and acting that have been previously defined as his instructional objectives.

Measurement of teaching effectiveness is the act of measuring the extent to which students have learned what the teacher is trying to teach.

Inference refers to the process intervening between the objective data seen or heard by an observer and the coding of those data on a classroom observational instrument.

Rating a teacher is a procedure by which the rater observes the teacher's performance in a classroom and then infers from his perception of a series of such performances whether or not the teacher is "enthusiastic," "communicates clearly," "has rapport with students," etc. Such ratings yield general impressions that lack specificity.

Delineating a set of values involves the act of identifying the set of justifiable values that is to be superimposed upon a set of collected data.

Evaluating a teacher is the act of weighting the measured data obtained about a teacher by superimposing a set of values onto the data.

These definitions, by distinguishing between the various acts in the teacher evaluation process, should remove a primary roadblock to solving

FIGURE 10-4.   *The Relationship of the Different Components in the Act of Evaluating Professors in the Teaching Role at a University*

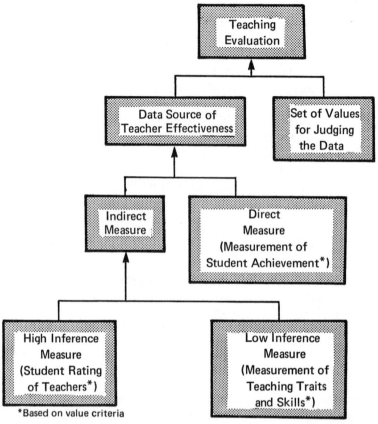

*Based on value criteria

the problem of teacher evaluation. Figure 10-4 displays these definitions hierarchically to clarify their functional interrelationships. Referring to the illustration, teacher evaluation can be seen as consisting of two major components: a data source of teacher effectiveness, and the set of values used to judge the data. When the measurement data have been obtained on a teacher's effectiveness, and a set of values has been decided upon by a promotion or tenure committee, the process of evaluation consists of weighting the measured data by superimposing a set of values predetermined by the committee onto the data known about a teacher.

For example, suppose the data collected showed that a teacher's students learned what he intended them to learn; and suppose what he intended them to learn were listed as instructional objectives A, B, C, and D. If the set of values of the supervisor or review committee were such that objectives A, B, and C were not acceptable instructional objectives, then the superimposition of these values onto the data collected about the teacher would give the teacher credit only for having taught objective D. Of course, the outcome in this example could have been prevented by making clear to the teacher what instructional objectives were to be included in the evaluation.

As shown in Figure 10-4, the data source of teacher effectiveness can be divided into two distinct types of measurements: direct and indirect. A *direct measurement* quantifies the effects of teaching and can be defined as the extent to which students have learned what the teacher is trying to teach as determined by the teacher, his department, and other qualified judges. An *indirect measurement* is a measure of what the teacher does to facilitate learning; for example, the teacher selects instructional objectives, selects course materials, establishes a learning environment, prepares himself academically, organizes and presents materials, diagnoses students, and interacts with students.

Indirect Measurement. Based on Figure 10-4, such information as student ratings of teachers and the measurement of teaching traits and skills are seen as indirect measures of teacher effectiveness. To use such data, a correlation must be established between what a teacher does to facilitate learning and what students do as a result of a teacher's activities. Correlating the activities of a teacher as a facilitator of student achievement is no easy task, but it must be done if indirect measures are to be used to assess teaching effectiveness.

Direct Measurement. The complexity of the task of evaluating teachers can be substantially simplified when a direct measure of teacher effectiveness is used. While many factors impinge on the behavior of the student, the teacher does have an extended opportunity to effect a change in the students' competence levels, and this change in competence becomes a relatively accurate barometer of a teacher's effectiveness. If a value is placed upon students achieving the instructional goals, then the task of evaluating a teacher, as noted by Tyler,[24] is that of determining "the extent to which the purposes of the [teaching] activity are actually realized."

Hite [25] noted that the object of teaching is to bring about learning, and stated:

> . . . when [teachers] teach pupils, the pupils should demonstrate learning. . . . But I don't think all that's learned is taught. Inasmuch as we teach, we have purpose, and I think that without purpose behind it, you don't have teaching. The object, then, is for the teachers to define the evidence that they'll accept as proof that this learning has taken place, and then to arrange matters so that the individual learner does demonstrate this evidence.

Pierrel[26] supports this attitude and expands upon it by suggesting that underlying any measure of effective teaching must be specification of the desired end behaviors, both in the classroom and, hopefully, well beyond the college years. These end behaviors should be defined in testable terms, and requires observation of the students as well as the teacher. Ideally, Pierrel would require follow-up studies of alumni to determine long-term retention of learned behaviors. Her position is encapsulated by this remark: "Not only is what the student *hears* more important than what the professor says, but it is what the student *does* about it and continues to do about it that demonstrates his professor's effectiveness." [27]

Biddle [28] concurs with Hite and Pierrel: "Teacher effectiveness [is] the ability of a teacher to produce agreed-upon educational effects in a given situation or context." These educational effects are those desired by the teacher and may be exhibited by the students during the teaching process as well as at the end. This direct approach to measuring teacher effectiveness is well expressed by Tyler: [29]

What is involved in evaluating teaching? In essence, the task is similar to that of evaluating any other purposeful activity. It is one of finding out the extent to which the purposes of the activity are actually realized. This seems simple enough[,] but as we examine the purposes of teaching, we find certain complications. The purposes of teaching are to facilitate various kinds of desirable learning on the part of the students. Hence, *the evaluation of teaching involves appraising the learning of students.* But learning is the acquisition by the student of ways of behaving, that is, ways of thinking, feeling, and acting, which he has not previously followed. Thus a college student may develop an understanding of the physical structure of the atom, an understanding which he did not possess before, or he may acquire the ability to analyze a problem in plant ecology which he could not do before, or he may develop greater skill in reading literary works than he had before, or he may acquire intellectual or aesthetic interests which he did not have previously. These are a few random illustrations of kinds of learning which college teachers may seek to bring about in their students.

Of course, not all things students learn in college are desirable, so that the evaluation of college teaching is not simply finding out whether students have learned, but *whether they have learned the things which the instructors were trying to teach.* Students may learn bad habits as well as good ones, they may acquire misinformation as well as sound understanding, they may acquire a distaste as well as an interest in various intellectual and aesthetic fields, and these, too, are cases of learning, but not cases of the learning which college teachers are trying to bring about. Furthermore, since the college years are relatively short—far too short to learn all that we wish could be learned—teachers must make a fairly rigorous selection of those kinds of behavior, that is, of those ways of thinking, feeling, and acting, that they consider most important for students to acquire. This, then, makes the evaluation of teaching a matter of finding out how far the students are acquiring the important ways of thinking, feeling, and acting on which the teachers are focusing their attention.

Supervisory efforts in teacher evaluation must be designed as an extension of a rationally conceived instructional system. The intentions of the teacher evaluation process, as well as the procedure to be followed must be constructed with teachers if the process is to be understood and accepted. Although the substance and the procedures involved in teacher evaluation require the most thoughtful and often arduous deliberations, there can be no denial of its necessity.

The contemporary scene is replete with power struggles between school administrators, school boards, informal community groups, and teachers' representatives. Not infrequently these struggles reflect the notion that teachers must be inspected, labeled, and categorized through processes that are ill-defined, and applied by individuals who are perceived, by teachers, to be incompetent to approach the evaluation process. If teacher evaluation is to advance student learning through increased teacher effectiveness, the process must be conceptualized, examined, and revised mutually by administrative, supervisory, and teaching personnel; and communicated, and then implemented, by competent professionals. However delicate the proposition, the definition of ISB and the nature of supervision as presented in this text mandate that the evaluation be a part of supervisory behavior.

RELATIONSHIPS OF TECHNICAL SKILLS TO THE MATRIX

The technical skills identified and interpreted in this chapter are not all-inclusive. Rather, they represent an important sample of the critical mass of techniques—the "skill-mix"—that the supervisor should be able to employ as he makes operational the intervention components of ISB.

A reexamination of the Critical Components Matrix makes it evident that only the intervention components are action areas. Intervention is expressed through the technical skills, while the results of their application are made manifest in the interpersonal and the milieu dimensions.

In some instances, the translation of theory into practice is clear and direct; in others, the relationship is indistinct and oblique. Perfect correlation of technical skills with respective components is unlikely. Some skills serve several components; most components may be served by a variety of skills. Also, the skills selected for inclusion in this description were created under other stimuli. They are fully developed in their own right. While it is possible to indicate their applicability to the intervention components, to alter the conditions drastically is to demean the basic integrity of the skill itself.

The technical skill of planning is one instance in which the intervention component can be readily translated into action. Decision-making is an element of the component of strategizing; or, put another way, strategizing invariably demands that certain decisions be made. The other technical skills have broader potential and should be considered as appropriate in degree rather than kind.

The application of Program Evaluation and Review Techniques (PERT) is most likely to be in the modification component. However, it is possible to use such techniques for planning and/or strategizing, particularly in affecting the milieu dimension.

Analysis of learning styles is a technical skill more closely associated with the milieu than the interpersonal dimension, while the reverse is true of analysis of teaching styles. Yet, both types of skills lend themselves to the planning and strategizing components. Much the same comparison can be made for evaluation of teaching—which implements planning or strategizing in the interpersonal dimension, and for evaluation of learning—which makes the same intervention components operational in the milieu dimension.

The technical skills of conducting the supervisory conference are applied in the interpersonal dimension through the intervention components of strategizing as well as support. The skills involved in the design of instructional systems have the potential for affecting the milieu dimension and are also implemented through the components of strategy and support. However, the former skill also has applications to the participation, and the latter to the modification component.

These skills are only exemplary arrows for the quiver of instructional supervisory behavior. The supervisor must master his intervention archery in programs of professional preparation and improve his marksmanship through practice with problem targets in the field.

The impression may be given that technical skills will replace both the human and managerial skills of the supervisor. This is not so. The emphasis placed upon the technical skills stems from two rationales, one philosophical and the other pragmatic. It is believed that human skills and, to a lesser extent, managerial skills have been overly stressed in previous treatments of supervision. Some have viewed supervision as a specialized application of counseling, while others have viewed it as a specialized application of administration. Both views ignore the third element of the skill-mix, technical ability. Moreover, both leave the supervisor with different philosophical stances but deny him the skills to practice his beliefs.

The second rationale is that of consistency with the original definition of ISB. To behave is to act. Therefore, the supervisor must be equipped to implement the intervention components that constitute the action areas of the ISB matrix. He takes action through the application of various technical skills. It is through participation that the interpersonal (or human) dimensions are involved. It is through modification that the milieu (or managerial) dimensions are involved. No priority of function or appraisal of value is implied or intended. The ISB matrix simply works through the intervention components, not through either interpersonal or milieu components.

It does not follow that the supervisor can intervene by using the technical skills without regard to human or managerial skills. He must give conscious and careful attention to all three.

There can be little doubt regarding the centrality of the human or interpersonal dimensions of an organization in its success or productivity. The research studies reported in Part II substantiate the reality of this assertion. It is documented by empirical findings in the areas of leadership theory, communication theory, organization theory, and change theory.

Moreover, a broad knowledge base of and demonstrated competence in the technical skills are insufficient for success as a supervisor. The behavior must be accompanied by human skills and directed toward improved interpersonal relationships. When the supervisor is not in tune with the reference norms of the teachers, when he is not esteemed as a colleague, and when his status is not officially confirmed by authority delegated to the position he occupies, no level of technical competence will be sufficient.

Much the same validation can be mustered for managerial skills. It is not by coincidence that preparation programs for supervisors and curriculum workers are frequently offered as adjuncts to programs for administrators. Nor is it accidental that in some states both supervisors and administrators earn the same certificate jointly. These are indices of the accepted fact that supervisors must apply managerial skills in the performance of their responsibilities.

The research findings document the pervasive influence of the social system, hierarchy, and environment in which individuals function. Leadership theory, communication theory, organization theory, and change theory all offer empirical data on the need for possession of managerial skills by the supervisor.

When the supervisor has expectations quite different from the teachers, when his perceptions of the situation vary markedly from those of others, and when he finds suitability in circumstances that are unacceptable to his professional colleagues, no level of technical competence will suffice.

Just as guidance personnel may adopt some manifestations of ISB, so the supervisor must utilize portions of skills from the counseling behavior system. And just as administrative personnel may adopt some of those manifestations, so the supervisor must utilize portions of managerial skills.

The attention of this chapter is focused almost exclusively on the technical skills of the supervisor because it is these that make his behavior unique. They give action to the intervention components. It is through the intervention components that ISB affects the interpersonal and/or milieu components.

ENDNOTES

1. David W. Ewing, *The Practice of Planning* (New York: Harper & Row, 1968), pp. 6–7.
2. *Ibid.*, pp. 9–14.
3. *Ibid.*, p. 42.
4. *Ibid.*, p. 60.
5. Louise M. Berman, *Supervision, Staff Development and Leadership* (Columbus, Ohio: Charles M. Merrill, 1971), pp. 55–56.
6. Kathryn V. Feyereisen, A. John Fiorino, and Arlene T. Nowak, *Supervision and Curriculum Renewal: A Systems Approach* (New York: Appleton-Century-Crofts, 1970), pp. 60–85.
7. L. Linton Deck, Jr., "Program Evaluation Review Technique." Unpublished manuscript, 1969.
8. Robert M. Gagne, *The Conditions of Learning* (New York: Holt, Rinehart and Winston, Inc., 1965).
9. *Ibid.*, pp. 58–59.
10. Louise M. Berman and Mary Lou Usery, *Personalized Supervision: Sources and Insights* (Washington, D.C.: Association for Supervision and Curriculum Development, NEA, 1966), pp. 36–37.
11. *Ibid.*, p. 39.
12. Bruce J. Biddle and William J. Ellena, eds., *Contemporary Research on Teacher Effectiveness* (New York: Holt, Rinehart and Winston, Inc., 1964).
13. Berman and Usery, *op. cit.*
14. Anita Simon and E. Gil Boyer, "Mirrors for Behavior," in *Classroom Interaction Newsletter* (Philadelphia: Research for Better Schools, 1970).
15. Biddle and Ellena, *op. cit.*, p. 5.
16. *Ibid.*
17. Ned A. Flanders, "Analyzing Teacher Behavior," *Educational Leadership* (December 1961), pp. 173–180.
18. Marie M. Hughes, "Teaching Is Interaction," *Elementary School Journal* 58, no. 8 (May 1958).
19. Simon and Boyer, *op. cit.*
20. Benjamin S. Bloom, J. Thomas Hastings, and George F. Madaus, *Handbook on Formative and Summative Evaluation of Student Learning* (New York: McGraw-Hill, 1971).
21. *Ibid.*, p. 7.
22. David W. Johnson, *Reaching Out* (Englewood Cliffs, N. J.: Prentice-Hall, Inc., 1972), pp. 16–17.
23. Marvin J. Cook and Richard F. Neville, "The Faculty as Teachers: A Perspective on Evaluation," Report 13, ERIC Clearing House on Higher Education (Washington, D. C.: George Washington University, 1971).
24. Ralph W. Tyler, "The Evaluation of Teaching," in *Preparing College Teachers*, ed. A. D. Albright and John E. Barrows (University of Kentucky, 1960), pp. 109–119.

25. Herbert Hite, "A Model for Performance Certification," in *The Assessment Revolution: New Viewpoints for Teacher Evaluation,* ed. Robert C. Burkhart (State University College at Buffalo, New York, 1968).

26. Rosemary Pierrel, "The Evaluation of College Teaching: The View of an Administrator-Psychologist." Ph.D. diss. (Providence, R.I.: Brown University, 1966).

27. *Ibid.*

28. Bruce J. Biddle, "The Integration of Teacher Effectiveness Research," in Biddle and Ellena, *op. cit.*

29. Tyler, *op. cit.,* p. 110.

PART V

Organizational Considerations of Instructional Supervisory Behavior

Supervision is typically neglected in the organization of the school enterprise. Allocated positions are pawns adjusted at will to conform to situations based upon administrative preference or teacher needs. The result is inconsistency in function, inefficiency in service, and inadequacy in staffing.

The principle is advanced here that those engaged in instructional supervisory behavior deserve an appropriate environment in which to operate. Supervisors must gain experience in various structures. Moreover, they must undergo professional preparation through programs at approved institutions and be able to meet increased and realistic standards for certification.

The three chapters of Part V explain the interplay of organizational dynamics and supervision in education.

Chapter 11

The Impact of School Environment

Instructional supervisory behavior is manifest only in specific situations. ISB is a complex of performances played out within a particular school context. The phenomenon of ISB and its components may be isolated, but only for the convenience of analysis. The implementation of ISB requires the dynamic of an educational environment. The dynamic quality of the educational environment results from the interplay of three major dimensions: the administrative structure, the faculty characteristics, and the learning setting. These dimensions provide a useful way of analyzing the impact of the school environment on instructional supervisory behavior. The intent of this statement needs to be made more exact. Throughout this book, the responsibility of the educational supervisor for the improvement of instruction has been the primary theme. And supervisory roles have been defined in terms of intervention. Supervisors act or perform by applying a wide range of conceptual and technical skills to the analysis and refinement of the instructional efforts of the school. In shaping his efforts, the supervisor needs to sense and respond to the impact of constraints present in the school environment.

Earlier, in Chapter 3 (Figure 3-1), ISB was conceptualized as one behavior system existing within the larger behavior system, or the environment of the school. Supervisory behavior does not exist in isolation, nor does it gain focus independent of the social system of which it is a part. The nature of the parent social system—the school environment—must be understood, and the design and implementation of any system of supervisory behavior must be in harmony with the expectations and possibilities of the school environment.

The behavior subsystems in Figure 3-1 are circumscribed by broken lines, indicating that these are not closed but open systems and that they are not independent but interdependent systems. The supervisor behavior system is in constant interplay with the other behavior systems of the school environment. This conceptualization of ISB suggests that effective performance requires congruence between the nature of the subsystem behavior and the nature of the environment in which it is exercised.

Consequently, in considering the context of the school environment and its implications for ISB, three dimensions must be considered. These are: administrative structure, differences in the characteristics of the faculty, and the nature of the teaching-learning process as well as its setting, which may be the classroom, the school, or the community.

ADMINISTRATIVE STRUCTURE

The authority base as defined by the school district and the prevailing leadership style, in combination with the organizational levels at which supervisory activity occurs, are the significant administrative structures that work to direct the expression of ISB. Figure 3-1 portrayed management behavior as one subsystem existing with and impacting on supervisory behavior.

Administrative structures of schools may be simple or complex. The most significant aspects of structure relate to the loci of authority and style of leadership. In some school districts, authority is concentrated in the central office. In such instances, plans and decision-making are handled by the board of education and superintendent. Only relatively minor decisions are shared with school principals and, in turn, with teachers. In other districts, considerable autonomy is delegated to the individual school, while in still others, particular teachers are invested with authority to operate specific programs.

The basic concern in regard to providing supervision within different authority bases is the issue of position. If authority is concentrated in the central office, individuals assigned and housed there become recipients of reflected authority. It matters little whether the supervisor is considered in a line (directing) or a staff (advising) capacity on the organizational chart. To those in the schools, principals as well as teachers, representatives of the central office are automatically cloaked with influence, treated with respect, and their directives usually followed. On the other hand, if authority is delegated to principals, with the result that schools operate as semi-autonomous units, a supervisor assigned to the central office frequently is faced with quite a different reaction. Viewed as an outsider seeking to inspect, monitor, and perhaps impede operations, the supervisor may be regarded as unfriendly to their interests —if not as an actual enemy. Even if genuine hospitality is displayed, teachers tend to defer to the authority of the principal and to their colleagues. The recommendations of the supervisor, rather than being accepted as legitimate requests or orders, may be substantially modified and even completely ignored. A supervisor within the school family, however, such as a resource teacher, department head, or team leader, is invested with authority by virtue of proximity of setting and appointment by the principal.

The funding of particular projects through grants from the federal government and philanthropic foundations has more recently created autonomous units under the direction of teachers. As these entities are outside the typical administrative channels and are supported without local tax funds, their personnel are frequently permitted considerable authority. On the assumption that the staff is responsible to the funding agency, such projects are often allowed to move outside the mainstream of the regular school program and receive little more than general surveillance by administrators. It is difficult for supervisors to mount the type of assistance needed in such independent and specialized operations, and the tendency to remain aloof is encouraged by both those engaged in ISB and the project staff.

In fact, if supervisory personnel are involved early enough in the conceptualization and design of the special project, they can see it as an innovative effort in contrast to a competitive one, and not as a threat to their supervisory role. Out of this development process, the supervisor may be seen as a contributor to change, innovation, and shared authority.

Authority can be expressed in the light of different leadership styles. This aspect of the school environment may be viewed by analyzing three general types of administrative styles—autocratic, democratic, and laissez-faire. In an autocratic administrative style, orders are passed from top to bottom with little consideration of the desires, interests, and aspirations of those at lower echelons. There is virtually no provision for input and decision-making except from other status leaders of the hierarchy. The intent of supervision in this situation is to fit the behavior of teachers into a pattern already determined by those in authority. The scope of a supervisor's efforts usually is limited to the monitoring and improving of classroom presentations. Like the administrator, the supervisor is assumed to be superior to the teacher. It is therefore justifiable for him to impose his opinions on the teachers and to insist that they comply with his prescriptions for adopting "correct" procedures.

In a democratic administrative style, it is assumed that leadership will be shared and cooperative relationships will be developed. The premise is held that the supervisor and teachers will work together to improve instruction. In this situation, there is a strong effort made to capitalize on the variety and collective strengths of the faculty. Also, formal leadership must be confirmed by the informal system. That is, the legal or traditional authority of the administrator or supervisor must be validated by performances, by demonstrated ability to contribute to the refinement of the school setting through work with people.

The laissez-faire administrative style, in education as in economics, abrogates formal authority and leadership responsibility while extending (generally by default) decision-making prerogatives to individuals at all levels. The result is close to anarchy. There will be confusion over goals. Consequently, ordering the internal resources of the school to the support of teachers will become an exercise in confusion. There will be so many voices that the organic concept of organization will be thwarted. This will quickly lead to competitiveness, which will be divisive. The supervisor in such a setting cannot be seen as an instructional leader in any positive sense. More likely, as he attempts to bring balance to the setting he will find out that he cannot rely on formal authority. As a result, he may find it impossible to intervene directly, and an absence of instructional leadership may occur. In such a situation, the supervisor must rely on the authority of competence, and much of what he does will be engineered on the basis of interpersonal relationships. This laissez-faire setting has the potential for destroying programs and, in some cases, the very institutions themselves.

ISB, in addition to being affected by authority and leadership style, is also affected by the level at which supervisory activities are performed. If all supervisory activity occurs, by definition of the school district, at the total school level, then ISB activities are likely to be gross attempts at coordination and the issuance of directives that require compliance in instructional concerns across the total school district. In other instances, the authority structure and leadership style of the school district may focus the expression of ISB at the local school level. Supervisory activities promoted at this level are likely to be related to local school needs and conditions, and teachers are more likely to perceive supervision as being concerned with the ongoing needs of the individual school, the students, and the defined professional concerns of the teachers. In this situation, the supervisory process will tend to be viewed as colleagual and professionally supportive. The organizational level at which a supervisor operates will make a substantial difference with respect to his supervisory activities and the potential for effectively impacting upon instruction.

The supervisor may understand this message more clearly by considering the issue of level of activity in relation to the teachers' role. The compatibility of a teacher's style is judged in terms of a particular set of circumstances. It assumes a certain place in which the students will function under predesignated conditions or within established boundaries. The discussion of whether the setting is the classroom, the entire school, or the community at large is not the most significant point, but rather, the recognition that a teacher's contributions to student learning will be enhanced or reduced by the setting in which they interact. Simply stated, a teacher may be more successful under some conditions than under others. It is assumed that the setting chosen for a particular activity will call for teachers to conduct themselves in different modes. Therefore, the major principle involves compatibility of supervisory style and situation.

FACULTY CHARACTERISTICS

The context of ISB may also be viewed in terms of the characteristics and the perceptions of the people who comprise the instructional staff— their characteristics in terms of preparation, experience, and competence. A survey of these factors is vital to the performance of ISB, in that their description provides strong leads into the analysis of the teacher behavior system—which, as presented earlier, is one of the major subsystems in the educational organization.

The provision of supervisory services for teachers is linked to the preparation, experience, and competence of the faculty. In some states and districts, teachers are not employed unless they have earned a master's degree; in others, college graduates who have had no professional preparation for teaching are granted so-called "emergency certificates." The latter are required to take the required courses for licensure, but study may proceed at a relatively slow pace. Every school staff includes members with a wide range of educational preparation. Experience is often equated with preparation or competence. However, experience is the result of actual participation in teaching. Because the employment of teachers may be interrupted for one or more extended periods, age alone is not an accurate index of experience. Also, some individuals spend an entire career in a single situation, while others, often considerably younger chronologically, are able to obtain greater experience by teaching in a variety of different schools under vastly different circumstances. Although preparation and experience obviously contribute to the development of competence, this factor is never assured by additional education or extended service. Moreover, some individuals, through greater potential, intuitive judgment, and enthusiastic dedication, either possess a high level of competence initially or attain it soon after entering the teaching field. The varied combination of education, experience, and competence ensures that the faculty characteristics will substantially influence ISB.

It is often assumed that supervisory service is most needed and offers the greatest potential rewards if applied to beginning teachers. Many suggestions and recommendations for the improvement of instruction are consciously or unconsciously developed with this target group in mind, in the belief that supervisory efforts directed to teachers during their first year or two on the job are likely to produce highly skilled practitioners by the time that tenure consideration is reached. While there can be little doubt that neophytes deserve and are especially responsive to appropriate assistance in establishing themselves as full-fledged members of the faculty, an ISB program geared predominately or exclusively to these teachers fails to include the largest portion of the teaching staff. Beginning teachers are more receptive to advice from colleagues, but they may be less skillful in identifying and isolating their problems.

Supervisory service is also needed by the veteran faculty, but it obviously must be of a different type. Many experienced teachers face changes in their assignments due to shifting school populations, developments in their subject fields, and improvements in methodology, as well as continuous refinement of their own professional skills. A substantial number of teachers have sufficient experience to be extremely successful in one situation but are unable to cope with the problems confronting them in another. While veteran teachers may have developed greater insight into their needs, they are reluctant to approach colleagues for assistance. Reputations are at stake, which may require a subtle or diplomatic approach. This is particularly true when teachers have achieved tenure and carefully protect themselves and the assignment of their time from involvement in supervisory and staff development activities. Maintaining openness and involvement of veteran faculty in supervisory processes tests the interpersonal skill of the supervisor. It is clear, however, that interpersonal skill is not enough; the reward system of the organization must support the supervisor's efforts. Much of this problem will be reduced if the group eventually accepts the idea that ISB is needed by all faculty at different times, in varying degrees, and for different reasons.

Another teaching group often ignored in discussions of ISB are those teachers who can only be described as professionally incompetent. They are far more numerous than most are willing to admit. Even if this were not true, however, such individuals cause difficulties far in excess of their number. It is possible to rationalize that many incompetents were employed under the stress of need and that th..e who remain among the present faculty are the price of meeting that emergency. While this may be partially true, politics, nepotism, and intimidation too frequently have overridden professional judgment and personal conscience. Because the employment of such persons was an administrative decision, the other teachers typically abrogate professional responsibility for the incompetent, leaving it to the administrators to recognize the problem and to take steps to rectify it. All too frequently, an administrator will substantiate his original decision by recommending tenure. Education continues to remain a bastion of the Pollyanna belief that even poor judgment may result in good outcomes. While there can be little quarrel with the claim in many supervisory texts that most teachers desire to improve, at issue are the degree of effort such teachers are willing to devote to the pursuit of greater skill and the amount of time, maximum effort, and supervisory skill needed to raise them above the minimum acceptable level.

It is necessary to differentiate between personnel who are basically incompetent and those who have become less effective after long and adequate service. In the first group are those individuals who have never possessed adequate skills and who have failed to acquire them even though they have held their teaching positions for several years. The second group is composed of teachers who at one point in their careers were acknowledged as adequate and even successful practitioners. As some individuals age, they may face special physical, emotional, and personality adjustments that impair their effectiveness with students.

It would appear essential that ISB be utilized in the decision-making related to the denial of tenure status to an incompetent. Although this may appear to be a hard-line position, it is only proper that those who are close to the instructional program share in the determination of competence and tenure. This is a reasonable expectation. Given the wide-ranging responsibilities of administrators, their time allocation to the analysis of programs and instruction is minimal. Therefore, for administrators alone to make such decisions borders on the absurd. The rationale supporting the position that the supervisor should contribute to the evaluation of teaching competence and tenure is inherent in the definition of ISB presented in Part I of this book: *Supervision is behavior officially designated by the organization that directly affects teacher behavior in such a way as to facilitate pupil learning and achieve the goals of the organization.* In activating this definition, it is the supervisor who establishes the most complete understanding of teacher performance. The exception to this would be a situation in which the teacher's peers interact with him as colleagues in a department or on a teaching team. Where the organizational context for teaching provides for this kind of peer interaction, it should also provide for the contribution of peer reviews as part of the information base in evaluating and deciding on tenure.

THE LEARNING SETTING

The third dimension of any environment is the physical locale in which learning activities are conducted. The school accomplishes its basic purposes through the provision of appropriate learning settings for students. It is most common to consider the classroom as the "unit," whether it be self-contained, combined with others in clusters or pods, or an "open classroom." The school itself is frequently conceived as a conglomerate of classroom units housed within a single structure or located on the same campus, although open-space facilities are not so readily categorized. The external classification of schools is more difficult when the schools are combined to form subdistricts or pyramids that may include a senior high, one or more junior highs or middle schools, and several elementary schools.

Another factor in the learning setting is the educational community involved. The population of a setting is usually seen as the number of students, generally in a limited age range, who actually are in attendance or on the rolls of the respective schools. Another viable concept is the nature of different cultural areas to be served rather than those based on demography. Thus, the inner-city areas inhabited by minority groups may require programs that differ from those in other subdivisions of the system. Still a third possibility is for the educational unit to embrace the entire city, metropolitan area, or county, with facilities utilized to serve the program needs of different groups on a flexible basis. Students might be transported from any part of the district to a particular school where a program is offered, or various schools might be sufficiently responsive to changes so that ad hoc programs would be phased in and out as circumstances demand. Because different learning settings call for varied teaching arrangements, the physical classrooms and schools, as well as the geographic, demographic, and cultural characteristics of the community, will operate to shape the expression of ISB.

The typical framework in which the supervisor functions is with a single teacher with a particular group of students in a specific classroom. The self-contained classroom still remains as the basic instructional unit in the elementary grades and as the unit for specialized education at all levels. In such a classroom, the individual teacher is responsible for the development of activities within a prescribed space. Such activities may include several curricular areas simultaneously or separately. The teacher seldom ventures from this base except for infrequent field trips to other parts of the school campus or into the community, although the students may move to other locations within the school for instruction in art, music, and physical education as well as to the cafeteria and library. In any event, both teacher and students usually regard the classroom as the "homeroom." It is both the hub of activity and a sanctuary from the outside world. The supervisor is considered an emissary from beyond the classroom who is assisting the teacher over the full range of instructional concerns.

As has been amply demonstrated of late, however, the entire school can become the potential and actual setting for learning. The trend toward open-space facilities, with team and diagnostic instruction supported by staff specialists, induces the concept of the entire school as a learning setting without the contrived limitations of human interaction, time, and space. Where this happens, teaching teams may be organized around a grade level, a subject field, student needs, or faculty competencies. Several teachers may draw upon the resources of the school to the extent that the students regard campus facilities as their learning setting. Small groups may participate in seminars, and individual students may pursue independent study in a coordinated program that views the school as the rightful province of all students. While some designation is applied for administrative purposes, groups of various size are developed within a large block of time as activities are changed. The supervisor himself may be a member of the teaching team. The master-teacher concept often associated with teaching teams carries with it many of the responsibilities previously considered exclusively those of the supervisor. In such cases, the officially designated responsibility for supervision is distributed horizontally throughout the organization.

A third learning setting is extremely difficult to define. It can be seen only as a shadow and "through a glass darkly." Institutions outside of the traditional educational pattern—such as the home, social agencies, government, business firms, industrial corporations, community organizations, and the media—must be helped to play a positive role in the development of the human being. Obviously, all of these do play a role but it is too often a negative one. Perhaps it was such a measure of the universal nature of the education task and of the provincial extent of efforts to date that led Frances Keppel to admonish that education is too important to be left to educators. Another former U.S. Commissioner of Education, the late James E. Allen, Jr., emphasized the need to help various "non-education" resources in the communities become aware of their responsibilities and to develop proper roles for offering educational opportunities to people of all ages. "Although the school would continue to accept heavy responsibility for formal instruction, the need is pointed up for a wide variety of agencies, including the vast private enterprise system of the United States, for accepting responsibility and defining its role as an education agent in society." This broadened concept of education in terms of the entire environment in which people live, is without regard to the limitations of space, time, resources, and traditions imposed by the existing formal structures for schooling.

As the professional staff sees its role as working with and coordinating agencies throughout a total community in a large-scale education enterprise that involves students presently out of school as well as adults, the concept of the instructional supervisor will be exceedingly different from the traditional one. It is quite possible, for example, that an instructional supervisor will be working with a team of individuals representing many kinds of professions and occupations. While he will be looked upon for expertise in educational matters, he will be required to possess a broad range of information regarding potential ventures within the community in which programs could be developed beyond the walls of the school. This may be the threshhold of a new horizon in education. The "school without walls" and "open-space schools" are hints of what may come. The instructional supervisor will then serve not as a member of the organizational hierarchy and not as the leader of a professional group, but as a coordinator of a total community effort in education.

There can be little doubt that the activities, priorities, and accomplishments of the instructional supervisor will be influenced to a significant degree by the environmental context in which he operates. It is not uncommon for the supervisor to select his behavior in light of factors present in or absent from a particular situation. It is not unusual for the environment to shape the supervisor in more subtle ways also, so that his behavior is actually a function of his surroundings rather than a conscious selection on his part. The impact of the school environment upon ISB is, therefore, both conscious and subconscious, both direct and oblique, both momentary and lasting.

INTERPLAY OF ENVIRONMENT AND SUPERVISION

The mere location of a supervisor has its effect on the various components of ISB. A supervisor assigned to a particular school is likely to be closely identified with members of the faculty; one assigned to the central office is likely to adopt the administrative personnel as his reference group. A supervisor who is immediately available has a greater opportunity to gain esteem from teachers than one who is remote and requires time to contact. Status, however, is less frequently associated with a field assignment than with a central office one, particularly when accompanied by a title, office space, and secretarial assistance virtually unknown to most teachers, department heads, and instructional team leaders. The converse is also applicable to the interpersonal dimension: it is more difficult for a supervisor from the central office to gain acceptance by teachers in the reference group of his concern or to obtain esteem from them, although he may be accorded status more readily.

A similar interplay can be seen in regard to the milieu dimension. Teachers have different expectations for a supervisor assigned to "their" school than for one who visits from the central office. They perceive his behavior in a different light and judge its suitability against different criteria. It is a manifestation of the cultural phenomenon that allows a subgroup to accept many criticisms from its own members that would be considered intolerable if stated by strangers. In reverse fashion, the supervisor from the central office has different expectations for teachers in particular schools than does one who operates almost continuously as a faculty member. Moreover, he perceives the actions of teachers in a different light and judges their suitability by different standards.

Such examples merely serve to illustrate that the choice of intervention components, the sequence of implementation, the nature of managerial, human, and technical skills, and the results obtained will be strongly influenced by the environment. Variations in administrative structures, faculty characteristics, and learning settings will often exert profound influences upon ISB.

Types of School Environments

Some concept of the magnitude of the influence of school environments may be obtained through consideration of certain of their gross characteristics. These contexts exist in operation. Respective descriptions of traditional, contemporary, and emerging school situations serve as a means of illustrating the impact of the situation on the behavior and activities of the supervisor. It should be emphasized, however, that the three illustrations are not descriptions of particular schools but represent composites on a continuum; many schools fall somewhere between these categories. The descriptions of the schools and the implications for ISB are illustrative only; they are not full-blown descriptions, nor are the implications fully developed. They are only brief examples of the analysis of school environment that is necessary before engaging in ISB.

Traditional. The supervisor in the traditional school operates within certain organizational constraints. The administrative structure tends to be autocratic. The purpose of instruction is to impart to students knowledge that they do not possess and that is considered essential to their subsequent development. Decisions are made by the teacher to adapt the curriculum from the standard textbook to the norms of the largest group and, as well as possible, to those few students who deviate furthest from the central range. Performance is rewarded by promotion to the next level of achievement and, at the end of the year, to the next grade. Faculty are assigned in the elementary school on the basis of the grade level that each prefers or has interest in teaching. At the secondary level, assignments are a function of the subject(s) the individual is prepared to teach. The student typically plays a passive role, with the teacher being largely responsible for determination of appropriate learning objectives and activities.

The learning setting is the classroom unit. Grouping in the elementary school usually is directly related to the age at which students are permitted or required to enter first grade. This pattern may be modified by the existence of multiple sections of a grade, although schools that prefer heterogeneous grouping deliberately maintain similarity of students in all sections. The election of particular courses or the pursuit of particular programs at the secondary level achieves homogeneous grouping of sorts. The students are expected to follow directions, to indicate need for further clarification, and to devote the necessary effort to make up existing deficiencies.

Given such a situation, the instructional supervisor must consider the type and sequence of intervention components he will utilize to alter the interpersonal and/or milieu dimensions. Planning and strategizing with and through the principal and influential teachers may be the most advantageous approach to making the power structure work *with* the supervisor rather than thwart his efforts. Moreover, the results of instructional supervision will be judged in terms of altering teacher behavior within the limits of manpower and environment. The selection of managerial skills may be crucial.

Contemporary. The organizational parameters facing the supervisor in the contemporary school differ from those in the traditional school in several respects. The administrative structure tends to be democratic. The purpose of instruction is to provide opportunities for students to learn citizenship responsibilities within a controlled environment while developing their own unique styles of learning. Decision-making in regard to the curriculum and learning activities is gradually transferred from teacher to student, with the hope that the latter will be able to function as an adult prior to leaving the confines of the school environment. Those who excel are allowed greater freedom within which to operate; those who are unable to profit from freedom are provided a structure within which they can function comfortably until they attain the next level of accomplishment.

Present attempts at corporate staffing in contemporary school environments are inclined toward teaching teams that offer a composite capability amounting to more than the sum of its constituent members. Such teams may contain individuals who are versed in different aspects of a subject (e.g., reading, speech, composition, and literature in English), who represent each of the subject fields for a particular grade at the elementary, junior high, or middle school levels, who are able to deal with certain learning disabilities or unusual abilities, or who are effective as lecturers, discussion leaders, or tutors. Learning is conceived as the right and responsibility of every student, with teachers charged with the fashioning of opportunities suited to the various students comprising a particular group.

The learning setting is less restricted and may encompass the school as a whole rather than a single classroom or a designated set of rooms. The classification of students determines the nature of the team assignment and even the composition of the team membership. Students are encouraged to experiment with new approaches, while the teachers monitor their continuing improvement.

In this type of situation, participation is a high priority in supervisory behavior. Planning, strategizing, and support of team activities offer appropriate additional areas for intervention. It is important to his effectiveness that the supervisor be able to alter the interpersonal dimensions. Therefore, reference and esteem take on greater significance than status. The selection of human skills may be crucial.

Emerging. The organization of the emerging school will provide still another challenge to the supervisor. The administrative structure tends to be eclectic, even approaching laissez-faire. The purpose of instruction is to allow students to test themselves and evaluate their qualifications through actual participation in loosely structured activities. Decisions on alternative experiences are made by students in consultation with members of the school faculty and representatives of community agencies. Some indication of the satisfactory completion of a venture or the attainment of a specific level of behavior provides indices of performance. Rather than augmenting the regular teaching faculty with resource personnel, instructors for the emerging school will be secured from any and all agencies embraced by a community. It is the obligation of the faculty to assist students in ascertaining their interests and aptitudes so that appropriate learning experiences may be arranged within the school or in the community at large. The qualifications of an instructor are his capacities to assist students in fulfilling a particular learning objective.

Students group themselves, with the aid of counseling, for activities conducted at various locations within and beyond the usual school facilities. Under this learning setting, there would not be a sharp break between the school and the community at a specific point in time (as now occurs at graduation). Instead, there would be a gradual shifting of emphasis as the student demonstrates his ability to cope with a variety of situations. Hopefully, the student will never completely sever his relationship with the school; instead he will return now and then for educational experiences (full- or part-time) long after the usual graduation date.

In this type of context, intervention must be initiated through modification. Planning, strategizing, and support also provide possibilities. It is important for the supervisor to be able to alter the milieu dimensions. Therefore, expectation, perception, and suitability must be given emphasis. The selection of technical skills may be crucial.

These three descriptions offer a kind of quasi-operational statement of school philosophy—that is, they provide a sense of the vitality of the instructional program, as well as a basis for making inferences about administrative structure and the educational setting. Little can be gleaned about the characteristics of the faculty in these schools. If, in fact, schools in operation reflect the above characteristics, they will be maintained by a combination of an administrative structure, faculty, and setting. It is the particular interaction of these environmental factors that constrains ISB. The factors must be understood discretely as separate elements in an organizational complex. They must also be understood— through rational attempts at identification, description, and interpretation —as primary knowledge in the implementation of an approach to ISB.

UNRESOLVED ISSUES

There are a number of issues that remain to be resolved by the supervisor through analysis of the environment in which he operates. Some indication of the importance of this determination can be provided by an illustration of a major issue in regard to administrative structure, faculty characteristics, and learning setting, respectively.

The administrative structure poses the problem of *operational prerogatives*. In an authoritarian context, the instructional supervisor must be aware of the positional status occupied by himself and others. This is particularly important in regard to the principal who has proprietary attitudes about his school and its faculty. Such an environment also requires that the supervisor be accorded appropriate status within the organizational structure, and an organizational leverage of his own. Otherwise, no countervailing force will be available, and the supervisor must settle merely for making recommendations as a staff officer. A more democratic environment, however, will encourage contributions from all team members to collective and collaborative action. The instructional supervisor will have greater opportunities for input. However, he—like the principal—must recognize that the acceptance of proposals will be based on their merit rather than on the position of a powerful advocate. In a community of equals, operational prerogatives are *earned* by those involved, not conferred by the organization. This phenomenon is complicated further in an eclectic situation such as the laissez-faire and community-wide operation suggested in emerging schools. Teachers, considered virtually autonomous in the classroom, principals in their schools, and superintendents and boards of education in the district must realistically share operational and decision-making prerogatives with representatives of power groups within the community. While school leadership stands to gain significantly from such an arrangement, it nevertheless raises many questions in regard to operational prerogatives that are currently given no more than cursory attention in many schools.

Faculty characteristics pose the problem of *involvement*. Any faculty presents a wide range of preparation, experience, competence, attitudes, and various other qualities. It is traditional for supervisors to concentrate their activities on beginning teachers and those who have not yet received tenure; the primary concern is to assist an individual to perform at the minimal acceptable level. Those teachers who have the most problems consequently receive the most assistance. Experienced teachers and those who are able to cope with the environment in which they function receive virtually no attention, because the remedial nature of the typical supervisory program has little to offer them. It is precisely this group of individuals, however, who must be groomed for future leadership roles in contemporary situations. They must have the assistance of supervisors if they are to provide instructional leadership to teams, provide for variable student grouping in flexible time blocks, and make curriculum decisions previously made by others.

The involvement of resource personnel outside of the professional staff, such as that advocated for the emerging school, presents other types of problems. While the supervisor is now able to utilize the services of many competent individuals not previously available to the school, he is faced with the responsibility of harnessing the efforts of many individuals who have none of the knowledge, attitudes, or skills embraced by any random group of professionally prepared teachers. The supervisor must minister to a much broader span of needs and orchestrate a greater range of competencies.

The nature of the learning setting poses the problem of *accessibility*. It is extremely difficult for an instructional supervisor to be available when needed if teachers are widely separated in classroom units. Secondary teachers, who conduct several different classes with only a single preparation period per day, find it difficult to utilize supervisory services.

Similarly, teacher-supervisor conference time disrupts classes in the self-contained elementary grades unless the conference is held while a class is engaged in instruction in a special subject such as art, music, or physical education. The sporadic visitations of supervisors, with lengthy intervals between, is a severe handicap to continuous faculty development. Instructional teams, which have become increasingly common, open the contemporary school more fully to the efforts of the supervisor. He is able to deal with teachers as groups, thereby increasing the frequency of contacts while decreasing the intervals between contacts. Since the team usually has a larger block of time at its disposal, and since time is built in for planning, there is more flexibility in arranging activities by supervisors than is possible in a classroom-by-classroom operation.

The utilization of the entire community as the learning environment may simultaneously provide the greatest advantage and the greatest disadvantage to supervisors. Supervisors, who in traditional or contemporary schools could either control certain facets of the school directly or through the administrators, will be required to respond and react to situations that are far more freewheeling. Moreover, they will have to arrange instructional supervisory activities in light of circumstances that most schools have tended to ignore completely or treat cavalierly, such as the beginning hour of the business day, vacation schedules of managers and representatives of other professions, and the personal proclivities, interests, and preferences of persons who receive no monetary compensation from the school budget.

The ISB Matrix (Figure 9-1) portrays the dynamic interrelationships of intervention, milieu, and interpersonal components. It is the effective use or altering of the milieu and interpersonal components of the school environment that makes ISB possible. The milieu components are especially helpful in understanding the impact of school environment on supervision. It is important to note that while the school environment—the milieu—is a major determinant of appropriate behavior, an analysis of the ISB Theoretical Model suggests that, through use of the intervention components, the milieu may sometimes have to be altered before teacher behavior can be influenced.

Chapter 12

The Structure of
Supervisory Services

Supervisory services are a part of the formal organization of the school system. In order to apply the concepts of ISB in the vitalization of supervision, some attention must be directed toward the understanding of existing patterns of supervisory services.

In many school systems, supervisors operate as individual agents. As an organizational structure, the school is similar to governmental bureaucracies. In many respects, it takes on the characteristics of complex organizations. There is a single line of command that descends from the board of education and its executive officer, the superintendent, down through the principals, to the teachers. Like complex organizations, the school system pattern includes both line and staff officers. Line officers are in command positions; they have authority delegated to them and are clearly responsible for certain functions and to certain other people in the organizational hierarchy. Staff positions, as in a military staff organization, are advisory and have only the authority of competence. There is a long-standing division of opinion within the educational ranks concerning whether instructional supervisors, particularly at the elementary level, should be assigned staff positions, where their responsibility to teachers would be a function of their capacities. The argument has been less strongly advocated at the secondary level, where the powerful position of the principalship often overshadows that of the supervisor assigned by the central office. It is not uncommon to have line positions within the school, that is to say department chairmen, team leaders, or assistants of one kind or another operating as an extension of the principal's office. Therefore, a supervisor at the secondary level who operates as a staff officer has serious limitations imposed on the scope of his work and the magnitude of his influence. It is strongly recommended that the conferral of line authority in this sort of circumstance receive careful consideration.

The need for line authority is supported by the analysis of research in the fields studied during the construction of the critical components of ISB. It was found, for example, that communication is affected by the respective positions occupied by the sender and receiver. In fact, communication effectiveness of an individual is at least partially a result of the authority of the sender. Similarly, it was found that leadership is more likely to be accepted if the leader has power and status in the organization. What is being emphasized here is not the isolated value of organizational status and authority, but rather, the fact that supervisors need the support (as a complement to competence) of the authority mechanisms of the formal system.

In the sections that follow, three examples of patterns or structures of supervisory services in education will be reviewed. The intent of describing some of the characteristics of these patterns is to aid in conceptualizing staffing structures and to prompt more thoughtful consideration of ISB in terms of prevailing and, in one case, an anticipated organizational context. These patterns are: the individual agent as supervisor, the professional supervisory team, and what is referred to in this book as the total delivery system structure for ISB.

THE INDIVIDUAL AGENT

The structure of supervisory services in terms of an individual agent is largely one of position. This can be clarified by examining such an assignment under three patterns—central office, specific schools, and what might be called neutral locations.

The titles conferred upon those engaged in ISB are legion. However, such positions usually may be categorized as four types: general all-level supervisor, general specific-level supervisor, special all-level supervisor, and special specific-level supervisor. In smaller systems, such supervisors operate out of the central office. One supervisor may be directly responsible to the superintendent for instructional improvement in all schools. An intermediate district is likely to have at least one supervisor in the elementary schools and may also provide some assistance for the supervisory responsibilities of the high school principal. It is not until a district is of substantial size that multiple supervisors are found.

The organization of supervision in small districts may be either vertical or horizontal. In the vertical structure, supervisors exercise responsibilities in all grades, K–12. This sometimes suggests the lessening of authority or role of the principals. This is not the intended interpretation, for the principal also needs to turn his attention to the management system of the school. As the one responsible for the effectiveness of the total effort of the school, the principal needs the direct support of leadership personnel in the instructional areas. In the small district, however, where the supervisor functions as the general supervisor across all grade levels, articulation of programs may be achieved at the expense of coordination.

In the small district, the general supervisor is also inclined to perform more heavily in the management aspects of the position, such as in overall systems planning and contributing to the definition of long-range instructional goals of the district. This makes it extremely difficult for the general small-district supervisor to demonstrate the level of intervention or technical skills needed for effective supervisory programs.

The most prevalent form of intraschool supervision is the teacher-principal pattern, and it is found in both large and small schools. The lack of planning and training are the most serious limitations. Variations of the teacher-principal form can be discerned: a supervisory, helping, or resource teacher may be freed from some instructional duties to assist other teachers through visitation, demonstration, and similar methods; a faculty committee or study group may be appointed to develop curriculum materials, adopt textbooks, and investigate techniques or strategies; departments may be organized under chairmen elected by the teachers for the study of common problems. In such departmental arrangements, the chairmen may be poorly chosen, and as a consequence, a rotation system may be followed. This pattern militates against both action and continuity.

Another pattern for organizing supervisory services is by objectives. In this pattern, supervisors are appointed to handle each cluster of objectives, with those who have authority over all teachers contributing to the attainment of these objectives. The objectives being pursued may be singular in nature or compound, in the sense that their attainment will require considerable time, coordinated effort, and resources. This format of supervision by objectives emphasizes focus of effort on the part of supervisors and participating teachers. There is usually a strong action orientation to the work undertaken, with design, implementation, and evaluation of efforts thoughtfully conceived. The supervision-by-objectives approach, although infrequently used at present, offers a productive framework for the efficient use of the school's resources in the challenge of constantly moving the program and its effectiveness forward.

In the cabinet type of school organization, various high school officials are delegated administrative and supervisory authority over certain school activities, under the general direction of the principal. A guidance counselor, for example, may also serve as supervisor of social studies. The principal coordinates the activities of the various units, but unfortunately, supervisory duties are often relegated to second rank because of the urgency of administrative duties. In addition, the selection of cabinet officers is not always based on their ability to supervise.

Another example of the individual-agent pattern of supervisory services is the special supervisor or director of instruction within the school. At one time the special supervisor or assistant principal for instruction was a rare phenomenon, but in recent years these positions have increased in number. In such a pattern, department heads usually are responsible to the special supervisor or assistant principal. The strength of such a structure is that it provides for the appointment of a qualified supervisor who coordinates all supervisory and instructional development activities.

The potential problems created by the appointment of a school-wide director of instruction are noteworthy. There is the surface impression, for example, that the principal is losing status as a result of assigning an assistant to what is most often proclaimed to be the focus of all school leadership; it must be made clear that this kind of assignment is in recognition of the importance and time requirements of the supervisory role. Additionally, the principal remains as the overall statesman for the school, drawing upon the views and recommendations of his supervisory or instructional assistant as decisions are made. Whenever the requirements for effective leadership demand delegation, it should be done—as an indication of responsive leadership—and not avoided because of concern about sharing authority.

No matter what particular definition of the individual-agent structure is used, there is strong evidence to support the generalization that the individual supervisory agent remains predominantly a staff person within the total organization. The implications are clear. The individual supervisor can study problems, and can help teachers, students, and administrators, but the system stops the supervisor short of pushing initiatives beyond the limits of his prescribed "helping" role. There is a high level of frustration possible in such a role. Priorities for action will likely exist elsewhere, and the individual supervisor may sense that he is moving from one definition and description of a problem to another without any sense of closure for himself and for those with whom he has been working.

It is clear that the supervisor operating as an individual agent is often faced with a scope of responsibility that simply defies reason in terms of the promotion of effective ISB. There may be too many schools to know, to visit, and to make any impact upon; there may be too many departments and special needs in the departmental structure; there may be too great a range of problems calling for a wide array of supervisory competencies. In sum, the individual supervisory agent suffers, first, from the accent of staff concept of his position, and secondly, from the sheer magnitude of people, schools, departments, and problems that impact upon his mind and energy.

On the other hand, when controls or some more precise definition can be employed to lessen both the constraints and the demands of his role, the individual-agent concept does have positive features. The predictability of supervisory efforts and intentions is one such feature. When a supervisor combines the human, technical, and managerial competence required to be esteemed by teachers, the individual-agent arrangement can become a significant factor in advancing the instructional process. Such an individual supervisor can provide the most productive human and communications base for the supervisory program. In any supervisory effort, the human and communications base is critical, but for the individual agent, it is mandatory. By knowing and having esteem for the supervisor, by being able to grasp the supervisor's style and predict his intention, the teachers will have a potentially active resource in the intervention sense, and can respond beneficially to his support and talents.

Another advantage of the concept of the individual agent as supervisor is that of stability. While it is true that too much stability can lull people into lethargy, a certain amount of stability is essential to smooth functioning. In this case, however, stability is not characterized by inactivity, incompetence, or lack of direction, but by confirmation of the supervisor's performance through instructional improvement and by recognition that supervisory efforts are directed at supporting the primacy of the role of the teacher in the learning process. Furthermore, the individual-agent approach to supervision can provide the supervisor with a continuous and total view of the instructional program, a view that promotes coordination and articulation throughout the range of supervisory services.

THE PROFESSIONAL SUPERVISORY TEAM

A second structure for instructional supervision is that of a professional team established on the principle of service. This type of colleagual relationship is represented by attorneys banded together in a firm, and perhaps epitomized by physicians serving in a hospital. While there is a hospital administrator, many of the professional responsibilities are handled through the chief of staff. This official is elected by the physicians, and eventually he returns to the role of physician and a successor takes his place. In the team approach, there will likely be varied competencies and professional interests. The important aspect is the concerted team approach to the resolution of instructional problems.

The structure of supervisory services in terms of instructional teams, rather than depending on location as in the individual-agent concept, is one that is dependent on the selection and organization of people. The composition of the teams can be viewed by contrasting those which have official sanction, those which operate parallel to the formal supervisory pattern for a temporary period, and those which are intended ultimately to displace the existing formal pattern.

The creation of a supervisory team structure officially approved by the formal organization appears as a logical complement to teaching teams. Position descriptions of complementary types could be developed, with individuals selected from among the existing personnel or from candidates outside the system. A particularly important consideration in formulating instructional supervisory teams is to match the professional competence and program commitments of individuals to appropriate team assignments.

Another manifestation of this concept would involve a temporary parallel authority structure to serve with the existing structure. Such a structure would provide an umbrella to guarantee organizational protection and support over a short time span. In such a situation, the label "supervision" could be avoided and replaced with "cadre," "nucleus team," "educational development task force," or some similar term to communicate the temporary nature of the unit.

The existence of teaching teams in schools also appears to mandate a new type of supervisory organization. The leader of the teaching team provides coordination for planning, instruction, and evaluation. As coordination clearly implies, the team leader is not responsible for the effectiveness but, in this arrangement, he operates primarily as a colleague with coordinating rather than supervisory responsibilities. The leadership of the team, in terms of overall evaluation or individual efforts, remains the responsibility of the principal, his assistant in charge of instruction, or the other appropriate supervisory or administrative personnel in the school system.

The supervisory team gives the school system a responsive, hard-hitting mechanism for acting on instructional problems identified by the more traditionally assigned supervisory or administrative personnel. When problems or program development issues emerge, the capacity of broad-based expertise is critical, and is clearly a significant intervention technique. Although it is a complicated system to manage, due to the overlap of responsibilities and roles, the supervisory team can bring to a school or department the help needed to provide for ongoing responsibilities while also further defining, planning, and strategizing on the particular problem at hand. In this type of operation, there is the obvious need for some flexibility in budget if the broad competence base of the school system is going to be incorporated in the team. Membership of the team must encompass the range of available competence. Members must not be excluded on the basis of official title, task, or organizational status.

Put another way, the potential of the instructional supervisory team is greater than the sum of its participants. The basic principle of this concept is the knowledge-and-skill-diversification of membership. This diversification should be determined primarily by the nature of the instructional problem being investigated and the competence or skill requirements that it poses. One significant dimension is the direct and massive impact made upon that part of the school system where the team directs its energies.

The membership of the team need not be made up entirely of full-time supervisory personnel. That is, teachers belonging to it might serve for only a portion of their time. Supervisory personnel from different sectors of the total system could, in like manner, be assigned to temporary team membership; the team is, in essence, task-organized. The problem or issue under consideration may occasionally point to the need for individuals who are outside of the formal school system. Community resources, when determined appropriate, should be tapped. There may be parents, agents of various community organizations, business leaders, and specialists from various academic and service agencies.

Clearly, then, instructional supervisory teams are dynamic units. As noted earlier, they are not easy to manage, as their deliberations subtly suggest the inadequacy of formal supervisory structure. Formal role occupants can become defensive and, through their behavior, interfere with the work of the team. The instructional supervisory team is not intended to be a replacement for the supervisory structure; rather, it can assure openness and extension of the formal structure, and can magnify the status of supervisory personnel. In terms of the theoretical matrix of ISB presented in this book, the perception and support of formal supervisory personnel are likely to be strongly related to the esteem and status in which they are held.

To carry out the organization and operation of the team concept in supervision strongly suggests the need for an organized effort within the school system to inventory the special training, expertise, and accomplishments of the entire staff, as well as those special resources and strengths available in the larger community. This will establish a profile of ability, interests, and skills that should be available if supervisory efforts—team concept or not—are to be kept at a vitalized level. In addition to knowing what is available, the school system needs to provide ongoing leadership preparation for individuals who are interested and who possess the potential skills to help in the area of instructional leadership. Therefore, an outgrowth of the supervisory team concept is the requirement that potential participants be identified and be given opportunities for professional enrichment and training in the technical, management, and human skill areas of ISB. This concern will communicate to all observers that the system is flexible, responsive, and conscious of its long-range planning requirements. It will also demonstrate a personalized approach to leadership development, an area that has too frequently been a void in many school systems. It is recommended that the identification and preparation of instructional supervisory personnel—particularly those who will participate in a team approach—be undertaken jointly by school systems and institutions of higher education. It is critical that strong working relationships between schools and colleges be established as a way of enriching and promoting the operational effectiveness of both organizations. The instructional supervisory team approach is a real challenge for leadership and management, but well worth the efforts required to bring it into existence.

THE TOTAL DELIVERY SYSTEM

Thus far, discussion has dealt with two structures or patterns of supervisory services. In the individual-agent pattern, the supervisor(s) may be organizationally stationed in the central office of the school system, in a specific school, or in a neutral location. Although formally vested with supervisory responsibilities, the supervisor as an individual agent typically operates as a staff person reporting to an administrative officer. The second pattern is that of the professional instructional supervisory team. This pattern calls for the combining of diversified talents and efforts as a means of impacting directly upon the school or unit with whom the team is working. The character, location, and stage of evolution of the school system will play an important part in determining which structure or combination of structures will be used in shaping an approach to instructional supervision.

A third pattern of supervisory services is that of instructional supervision as a total delivery system. This approach builds on the team concept. Examples of actual implementation of instructional supervision as a total delivery system are few in number. Obviously, this pattern is rooted in a set of perspectives that views education as a community-wide enterprise, and not solely as one of educators. The educators retain certain responsibilities for coordination, but all agencies of the community are involved in the total educational operation. This means that the resources for ISB may encompass a wide range, even beyond that of the team approach.

The schools have always been perceived as close to the people. Whether true or not, this is a generally accepted precept. The school-community interaction concept holds that the future success of youngsters in society is directly affected by the success and failure of the school. This implies the direct and continuing involvement of lay people and community agencies in the definition and interpretation of the work to be accomplished by the school. In most instances, the operations of the school in implementing these decisions become the responsibility of the educators. In the school-community concept, however, involvement of the community in determining the goal structure of the school is not a "hit-

and-run" affair. There is an intense continuity and dedication in all efforts. There is the conviction that educators alone cannot do all the work that has to be done, and there is frequently expressed community exasperation with the way it is done. There is the frequent criticism that the school system is more concerned with keeping itself together than with providing the programs and commitments needed to change the potential productivity of its students—and, in the more immediate sense, enriching the quality of life of the entire community. The result of these circumstances is an extensively shared responsibility for decision-making on educational programs, personnel, materials, activities, and policies—the gamut of concerns related to running a school and its programs. The supervisor in this community-school structure is an active participant in the process of goal definition. Resources for the improvement of instruction are numerous, extending beyond the school into the total community.

It is clear that the total delivery approach wrenches many educational prerogatives from the existing formal structure and makes them available to a varied group, many of whom have no official authority. In this sense, the community coordinating council may emerge as a threat and contender for power and authority. If there are serious communication problems between community and school officials, the result can be disastrous to the work of the schools and to the community's purposes. If the total delivery concept is to work, some basis for trust must be cultivated so that the rich combination of community and school can be used productively. Threat and acrimonious competition are inimical to the shaping of mutually productive efforts.

This general concept of a total delivery system is not easily achieved. It is, however, a surging effort to open up the formal system, to ask and ascertain the assumptions upon which the school and its programs are based. When this happens, a greater degree of vulnerability will result. Unknown and uncharted areas will be opened for consideration; questions will be posed about acceptable alternatives to present approaches. Justification will be difficult, and often defensive. This position will be uncomfortable and frustrating for those in the formal organization who believe they know what needs to be done, and who see involvement by outsiders as merely wheel-spinning and public relations. It may well be that a narrow and negative response by instructional leaders to such community-based efforts will promote and hasten alternative educational programs outside the formal educational system.

In the total-delivery-system concept, ISB is one resource in the search for the best fit between community, students, and the educational system. Supervisory behavior must be characterized by performance and technical skills that include the functional-structural analysis of organizations, value clarification, and a strong commitment to intense interpersonal relationships. In addition, ISB must assist all participants in this social experiment to define educational goals while assisting in the design of programs to meet these goals, including substantial work on the means for examining the results of programs. Accountability is to be shared by all, and ISB in the total delivery pattern is a bridge of communication among disparate groups who have one common bond: the students and the community to be served.

It is contended that ISB must be based upon some theoretical rationale and guidelines for action. The research and theoretical perspectives reported in this work, including the propositions as guidelines to action, are impinged upon by the context and structure of supervisory services. The ISB matrix, with its milieu, interpersonal, and intervention dimensions, calls for rational instructional leadership. That leadership must be knowledgeable about and sensitive to people, time, place, and alternative options for action, for no ISB equations as yet contain any proofs or checks.

Chapter 13

The Preparation and Selection of Supervisory Personnel

It is obvious that the performance of effective, intelligent instructional supervisory behavior cannot be left to chance, and those individuals officially designated to demonstrate it must be prepared and selected with extreme care. While the training of all personnel who periodically engage in ISB within the school enterprise is neither possible nor practical, those with major responsibility for supervision must possess particular qualifications, and preparation and selection processes must ensure that they do.

The concept of instructional supervision as participation in the interpersonal components and modification of the milieu components through intervention is complex, and the translation of the intervention components into appropriate technical skills is unlikely to occur naturally in most situations. Moreover, the precision necessary to function as an individual agent, as a member of an instructional service team, and/or as a school representative for a total delivery system must be developed over time and in an organized fashion.

This view of the professional supervisor is quite at variance with current preparation practice. It may be that the concept of instructional supervision as a distinct behavior system, coupled with the theoretical propositions distilled from research findings, can provide the impetus for designing improved programs of preparation, programs that focus on the nature of supervisory behavior and on the acquisition of the necessary skills.

Gordon Mackenzie asserts that the underdeveloped state of theory in the fields of supervision and curriculum has contributed to the low levels of preparation for those engaged in such fields:

Certainly if there were well developed descriptive theories as to the nature of curriculum and of supervision, as areas of knowledge, there would be more clarity and understanding as to the functions which the workers in these areas could perform to maximize the output of the educational program. However, the present absence of this knowledge does not excuse the tendency on the part of many to oversimplify the nature of supervisory and curricular work and to assume that any good teacher or any good administrator with sound professional intentions can perform the implied functions effectively.[1]

It is significant to note that supervision has lagged far behind other educational specialties in altering the historical practice of appointment to leadership positions. It was once quite common for administrators, counselors, and supervisors to be appointed directly from the teaching ranks without regard to formal preparation or the possession of qualifications deemed appropriate by the education profession. In more recent times, largely through the pressure of professional organizations such as the American Association of School Administrators (AASA), the National Association of Secondary School Principals (NASSP), and the National Association of Elementary School Principals (NAESP), states have enacted legislation requiring that the individual named to such a position possess a valid administrative certificate as a condition of appointment. While this is becoming increasingly true for counselors, supported by the American Personnel and Guidance Association, many persons still are assigned to guidance services and given a specified (and often flexible) period of time during which to complete licensure requirements.

Despite efforts by such organizations as the Department of Supervisors and Curriculum Directors, the Society for Curriculum Study, and the Association for Supervision and Curriculum Development—resulting from their merger in 1943—there has been no similar coalescence of influence regarding the preparation and licensure of instructional supervisors. Consequently, personnel are still too frequently named to supervisory positions on the basis of locally-oriented criteria and are not required to obtain more than nominal preparation to become certified.

It would seem appropriate to move supervision toward professional specialization by defining the essential competencies, including knowledge, attitudes, and skills, by establishing preparation programs geared to the development of such competencies in preservice, inservice, and retraining phases, and by developing clear selection processes with regard to identification, certification, and appointment. It is only through such processes that educational roles become professionalized.

ESSENTIAL COMPETENCIES

The absence of a theoretical base for supervision and the lack of systematic research on supervisory behavior are largely responsible for the unavailability of evidence of the competencies that are really essential for effective supervision. While much has been written on supervision, a substantial portion of such writing deals with "role" and is often little more than an endorsement of the need for supervision and an emotional treatise that implores supervisors to "go out and make a difference"; but these people have too often been denied the training and the tools that would permit them to do so.

Supervision is too frequently filled with good intentions, but lacking in the essential competencies needed to translate good intentions into behavior that can move a teacher and the school organization toward the attainment of important objectives. Supervision has been subjected to very little research; much of its operational base is little more than folklore. Among other reasons, supervision has been less effective than it ought to be because preparation programs have either been virtually nonexistent or, when they did exist, have dealt too much with discussions *of* supervision and too little with the development of necessary skills.

As a start toward the identification of essential competencies, Chapter 3 established a concept of ISB while Chapters 4 through 7 presented some theoretical propositions. The critical components—interpersonal, milieu, intervention—and the ISB matrix represent a step toward the identification and isolation of competencies for supervision.

It is important to note, however, that essential competencies include not only what are typically thought of as skills, but also three essential elements or areas in which supervisors must be competent. These elements are: 1) *a knowledge base*—the possession of a theoretical and conceptual base in the area of supervision and in related social and behavioral sciences; 2) *a supervisory skill base*—the possession of "the tools of the trade," the mix of technical, managerial, and human skills that are essential; and 3) *an affective base*—the possession of healthy personal characteristics, a functional value system, and a belief in others.

It is important that each of these elements be adequately represented in any preparation program. While this text has placed a strong emphasis on the acquisition of skills, the supervisor must of necessity have a deep theoretical, conceptual, and research base to undergird his efforts and to enable him to employ his supervisory tools intelligently. Nothing could be so fraught with potential disaster as to employ the skills of intervention without understanding the base of knowledge on which supervisory behavior rests. This essential competency area will draw heavily from the social and behavioral sciences and from such areas of research as those utilized in Part II of this text. It is these areas, plus research and writing directly within the field of supervision, that can provide the base of knowledge needed.

The need for a supervisory skill base has been treated extensively in this text and it has been suggested earlier that there is an important "skill-mix" needed by supervisors, a mix that includes technical, managerial, and human skills. Chapter 10 identifies some of the technical skills related to ISB. All of these should become a focus of attention in preparation programs, and preparing institutions should be asked to provide evidence of the possession of such competencies. It is through the application of skills that theory is translated into practice, and it is through the intervention components that technical skills are applied. While not all-inclusive, those skills identified in Chapter 10 suggest specific competencies that should be present in preparation programs. These programs should differ from the traditional ones, by emphasizing skill development, field experience, simulation, and competence assessment.

The third area of competency is that of an affective base or a personal competency. What a supervisor knows and what he can do, while important, are not enough. What he believes—his value-system, his own self-concept, and his view of others—are essential components of an affective competence base. This area has traditionally been emphasized in writing about supervision, often to the virtual exclusion of skills.

While affective competencies are more elusive and perhaps more difficult to identify and develop, they are nevertheless extremely important, especially for a professional role that entails directly influencing the behavior of others. While selection processes should seek to identify psychologically healthy, warm, empathetic individuals, preparation programs, through formal study and through real and simulated experiences, can assist a prospective supervisor to understand himself and the world around him.

These three essential competency bases should be represented in the programs of every supervisor. They do not exist in isolation. Their interrelationship can be illustrated as follows: a supervisor should be a student of change processes; he should have a deep understanding of the dynamics of change, and be familiar with the research and theory in this field—a *knowledge* base; he must also possess those skills necessary to the planning, strategizing, and carrying out of change efforts—a *skill* base; he must also be concerned about the human consequences, the welfare, and psychological well-being of those involved in and affected by his change efforts—an *affective* base.

PROFESSIONAL PREPARATION

There can be little doubt that preparation programs for supervisors currently are less than professional in terms of specialized offerings, selection and evaluation of students, the identification and commitment of faculty, the relationship of such programs to certification, national standards, and continued professional growth.

Maurice Eash describes the lack of consensus regarding the professional education of supervisors and curriculum workers:

At the present stage of development in preparatory programs for supervisors and curriculum workers, the programs can best be defined as combinations of idiosyncratic projections of staff and compromises generated by the exigencies of academic politics. The wide variation in programs bears out the lack of systematic foundations. Some curriculum and supervisory programs parallel almost exclusively the programs for school administrators; others do not define any specific program; some mandate specific courses, others define broad experiences, or attempt to predicate programs on desired behavioral outcomes. In short, systematic approaches to investigating and defining suitable programs have been lacking and the landscape of preparatory programs viewed as a whole reflects the resultant chaos.[2]

The absence of specifications regarding the knowledge, skills, and attitudes necessary to perform as an effective supervisor is reflected in the fact that there is little or no selective admission to programs of preparation. Robert Thurman states that

As a result, it appears that currently there are only two kinds of selection procedures being carried on in most of the preparing institutions. One is self-selection. The decision is left to the individual to decide whether or not he has the background, talent, or commitment to become a supervisor or curriculum worker. If he decides he does have such qualities, the second step of the screening procedure is employed. He needs only to meet the general requirements for admission to graduate study, which are basically the same for English, supervision, or any other field.[3]

Criteria should be established for the selection of students based upon promise to successful completion of such a program. Follow-up studies geared to successful performance on the job could provide important data for continuously improving the preparatory program.

Eash also points out that

An attendant problem in present programs of preparation organized around a course or two in supervision and/or curriculum is that few staff members are involved full time in the concerns of the area. Pursuing a divided responsibility is not conducive to development of the specialty or identification of the graduate professor with the area.[4]

It is quite common for the faculty member responsible for the supervision program to have primary allegiance to educational administration, curriculum development, or both. Seldom does a professor choose supervision per se as his field of scholarship or expertise, seldom does he devote himself almost exclusively to the teaching of supervision, and few university professors systematically pursue advanced study and research in this area.

The identification and subsequent acceptance of a conceptualization of ISB, a supporting theory based upon research, and the identification of the technical skills to implement the intervention components through both the interpersonal and milieu dimensions could alter this picture markedly. It is possible to establish programs of professional preparation with essential competencies defined in knowledge, skills, and attitudes.

It is axiomatic that the performance of supervisory candidates should be geared to the types of educational contexts in which they are to serve. This seems to mandate a change from programs defined solely as "supervision courses" to one that includes practicum experiences in selected field situations. The prospective supervisor should be required to function under various types of administrative organizations, with faculty representing a broad array of characteristics, and should be given expanding responsibility from classroom, through school, to community settings. A given supervisor may be required to function during his career in traditional, contemporary, and emerging settings, so he should be exposed as much as possible during his education to each type.

Moreover, the internships, clinical experiences, and/or practica must anticipate the multiple structures for supervisory services. The same individual may at one time operate as an individual agent, at another as a member of an instructional service team, and at still another as school representative to the total delivery system. A series of supervised assignments should determine the strengths and weaknesses of each candidate as he functions in varied structures.

It is not the purpose here to design a specific program for the preparation of supervisors or to describe in any detail what it should be composed of. Rather, the purpose is to identify major elements that ought to be represented in a professional program of preparation. Eash and Thurman have pointed out the casual, unstructured, and unfocused nature of most preparation programs. An analysis shows that they differ little from the preparation programs for general school administration, with the possible exception of an additional course in supervision and in curriculum. Few, if any, have focused on the development of skills, a knowledge base, and the attitudes essential to effective supervision.

Preparation programs must focus on the nature of ISB, and they must be so conceived, maintained, and evaluated that they do in fact produce supervisors possessed with the skills and understandings necessary to function effectively in changing teacher behavior. While teacher education programs have come under severe criticism in recent years, it is probably true that the profession knows even less about the ability of a supervisor upon graduation than it does about the competencies of teacher education graduates. There is far more focus, skill development, and evaluation of the competencies of a teacher prior to certification than there is for the supervisor who is expected to be responsible for and to influence the behavior of the teacher. While an undergraduate in teacher education is placed in a controlled situation for a field experience and is evaluated both by a practitioner and by his college supervisor, virtually no such experience is provided for supervisors. More recent requirements in a number of states for a "planned field experience" prior to certification are beginning to change such professionally irresponsible practices, but in many cases field experiences are still random and unspecific.

Just as preparation programs should avoid the random selection of course experiences and programs completed on a cafeteria-style basis, so should the development of experiences for supervisors avoid a random, unstructured, and unsupervised activity in the field. Field experiences or internships for supervisors should be carefully selected, and the supervisor matched with the setting. Practice should be designed to give the prospective supervisor the chance to demonstrate the skills he has, to refine them, and to test himself in real situations under the direction of skilled professionals. It is an opportunity to try out in a real setting what he has been developing in a "hothouse" environment.

The field experience should not be left entirely until the end of a program. Rather, an early field-based experience would enable the prospective supervisor to "test out" his conceptual and theoretical development in the light of reality. Working as an adjunct or an aide to a supervisor would help provide him with a needed perspective. Experiences such as this are not only "reality checks" but give the student the chance to exercise early some of the understandings and minimal skills he may have acquired. Field experiences are necessary components of a sequential and developmental preparation program that culminates in the certification of a supervisor who possesses knowledge, skills, and attitudes.

Local school systems have a necessary and important role to play in the design and conduct of field-based experiences. Such experiences provide real opportunities for schools and universities to become partners in the preparation of supervisors. The role of school systems should be an active one, not merely that of the passive acceptor of university program decisions, nor that of the uninvolved medium through which practical experience is gained.

School supervisory and administrative staffs need to be systematically involved not only in the design of such experiences but in their supervision and evaluation. Just as other professions apart from education assume responsibility for the intelligent, controlled introduction of trainees into a professional role through internship, so should practicing supervisors be willing to shoulder responsibility of field experiences for those who will eventually join their ranks. Such responsibility is continuous, beginning with the design of early field experiences and culminating in internship. School system personnel, along with university faculty, should be responsible for the supervision of field experiences, for the provision of significant activities, and for the assessment and evaluation of the intern's strengths and weaknesses.

Those involved in preparation programs need to guard against any single model of supervisory staffing, lest programs become geared exclusively to a particular kind of school organization or staffing pattern. Most supervision programs, if they have any form or substance at all, are oriented to a rural or suburban model in almost complete disregard of the different patterns and needs within an inner-city, an urban, or a large school system. Insofar as possible, preparation programs should enable supervisors to understand and to function effectively in different kinds of situations. While this factor should be recognized in formal course work, students should also have field experience in more than one kind of setting.

The professional development of the supervisor cannot, however, terminate with preservice programs, as is too typically the case. While the supervisor himself has the responsibility for his continued education and professional development, he cannot take advantage of opportunities that do not exist. Chapter 15 emphasizes the need for preparing institutions and for professional associations to respond to the needs of supervisors for their continuing education. It is a paradox that supervisors who have as a major responsibility the inservice education of teachers have had so little opportunity to engage in such systematic programs themselves. Nationally, supervisors have had to rely largely on the work of the Association for Supervision and Curriculum Development. While the Association has made many contributions to the advancement of supervision, its many other interests have made it less effective as a force for the continuing education of supervisors than would be so if it could focus directly on that role. A similar situation exists at the state level.

An example of an exception to this situation is an extensive inservice program that has been conducted by the University of Georgia for a number of years. Reba Burnham[5] describes the program, which begins with an internship, includes seminars conducted in various locations of the state, seminars on the university campus, summer institutes, regular graduate courses, and less formal types of experiences such as district meetings, experimental projects, participation in state and national professional associations, and professional reading and study.

It is virtually impossible for supervisors now in service and for those being prepared in traditional programs to assume the responsibilities as defined by the concept of ISB presented in this text. Extensive retraining programs are essential to provide them with the technical skills to utilize fully the intervention components and to operate from a research base. Other retraining will be required, for example, to enable individual supervisory agents to become members of instructional service teams and for the latter to join the cadre of total delivery systems. Both dimensions emphasize the need for institutions of higher learning to maintain pre-service and retraining programs in addition to assisting inservice develop-ment of supervisors. The medical model, in which a doctor returns periodically to a medical school or a teaching hospital in order to acquire a newly-developed technique, is an example of the kind of continuous at-tention to his professional expertise that must characterize a supervisor's educational development.

CERTIFICATION AND SELECTION PROCESSES

Even the most appropriate preparation programs will be ineffective unless they are the logical and exclusive means by which supervisors find their way into service. The concomitants of identification, certification, and appointment are extensions of the professional development of instruc-tional supervisors. Often, however, individuals are "tapped" by adminis-trators in a particular district to occupy supervisory positions. Those who seek formal preparation subsequent to such identification or those who aspire for supervisory assignments do so on the basis of personal prefer-ence. Active recruitment of supervisors is not standard procedure, as it is for administrators and more recently for counselors.

Not the least among the various problems related to the design of preparation programs and certification is the absence of clarity in defini-tion and the lack of agreement on functions associated with the super-visor. The role of the supervisor and curriculum worker has become increasingly ambiguous as a result of the various titles assigned to them and of the multitude of functions they perform. Gordon Mackenzie em-phasizes this condition:

> There is a wide range in both the titles used and in the assignment of responsibilities to supervisors and curriculum workers. The diverse origins in the positions, some being in administration and others being in teach-ing, curriculum, and the improvement of instruction, cause initial diffi-culty. A strong supervisory or administrative lineage is apt to result in a stress on such functions as quality control, the provisions of needed infor-mation for administrators, and the management and coordination of var-ious kinds of organizational activities. The teaching, curricular, and instructional improvement lineage suggests a possible emphasis on direct assistance to teachers, curricular planning, and in-service education. The local variations in skills and interests of holders of various positions, and the differing patterns of organization further cloud the picture as to what any specific individuals do and how the supervisory and curriculum improvement functions are performed. In fact, to diagnose the manner in which supervisory and curriculum improvement functions are per-

formed, it may be necessary in specific school systems to analyze the functioning of such diverse but related performers as the chief school administrator for instruction, directors, coordinators, general and special subject supervisors, principals, building curriculum coordinators, and department heads.[6]

The lack of agreement on the professional role of the supervisor reflected in preparatory programs is mirrored in certification. Maurice Eash describes the varied provisions for licensure:

Certification for supervisors alone ranges from fourteen states which have no certification to four states with four separate certificates. If added to these figures are certifications for curriculum workers, the number of certificates is further multiplied. The chaos is further compounded when the bases for certificate preparation programs are examined in further detail. In some cases the supervisory certificate is an ancillary licensure to the administrative certificate, requiring little or no preparation; in others it is an extension of the classroom teacher's certificate.[7]

. . . Most commonly when a special certificate is awarded for supervision or curriculum it represents the taking of some courses, usually limited in numbers, and as an additive to some other program. At this time the preparation does not appear to be either specific to a function or specialized in program. Consequently the licensure of supervisors and curriculum workers, being vague and supplementary to other licenses and goals, frequently results in a serious imbalance of number of preparing institutions, and of number of licenses issued in relation to market demand. As examples underscoring this imbalance, one state has issued over 7,000 licenses and counts only a little over 260 positions; another state has twenty-eight institutions offering preparatory programs for supervisors, when in all likelihood one would produce a sufficient number. Even these normative figures do not disclose what is believed to be the most serious resultant, the quality of preparatory programs.[8]

Irene Hallberg also comments on the certification dilemma:

A study of the certification requirements for supervisors and/or curriculum workers completed in 1964 revealed wide discrepancies in these standards among the 50 states. There was a total of 71 certificates for supervision and/or curriculum workers available in 36 of the 50 states. Some certificates were for supervision of special subject matter areas and two entitled the holder to supervise both general and special subject areas.[9]

As a result of such lack of clarity about function and the multitude of titles and certificates, the title of supervisor is virtually without meaning. Two alternatives exist regarding appropriate designations for individuals engaged primarily in ISB. The first is to replace the title of "supervisor" with one that is less burdened with historical precedent and inspectorial connotations. Such practice would allow a more accurate description of the duties actually performed. The second alternative is to retain the title of "supervisor" and demand more restricted use of it. This practice would define the position by generic category rather than by local option.

The latter possibility follows the pattern established for administrators, both superintendents and principals, and for counselors. It would allow greater specificity of requirements in preparation programs and protection against cavalier utilization through state certification. The elimination of a time-honored term appears to serve no useful purpose, while the introduction of new designations seemingly would further complicate an already confused situation. The title of supervisor should be used more sparingly and much more accurately. The use of such a title should imply the possession of skills, the execution of them, and the particular responsibilities that go with the practice of a profession.

It is essential to restrict preparatory programs to those institutions willing and able to provide sufficient resources. One aid to this would be to raise the standards for certification. Higher requirements are necessary, but these should be expressed qualitatively in terms of performance, rather than quantitatively in terms of courses.

Increasingly, state certification for teachers is reflecting a move toward competency-based teacher education, or, at least, toward the recognition that universities must be held accountable for ensuring that their graduates possess some basic competencies. Such a move in supervision is long overdue. At present, there is very little assurance through certification of the possession of any essential or identifiable set of competencies. It is recognized that certification requirements in themselves do not guarantee competencies, and that too typically merely *more* requirements rather than more rational and precise ones have been seen as the means to professional upgrading.

Universities, schools, and certification agencies need to work together in establishing certification requirements that lead to the attainment of essential competencies. Rather than being expressed in terms of credit hours, however, the emphasis should be on the attainment of professional competence; rather than a single model of preparation in a state, the possibility should exist for multiple models among universities or within a university. This calls for an approved program approach to the accreditation of university programs. In turn, this approach requires that universities assess their graduates' performance so as to be able to provide evidence that they do possess essential competencies. One of the significant weaknesses, not only in supervisory certification but in professional education in general, is licensing based too exclusively on completion of courses rather than on demonstrated ability.

The certificate for supervisors should be separate and distinct from those for administrators and curriculum workers. Supervisors should be expected to demonstrate competencies unique to ISB. Such licensure procedures would limit the use of the designation "supervisor" to those who are fully qualified, and companion regulations would be necessary to curtail the use of other titles coined at local convenience for persons who actually are engaged in ISB.

Appointment of supervisors could then be made from among those already qualified, as is standard procedure for administrators and counselors. It would also preclude the assignment to individuals designated as supervisors of numerous tasks completely unrelated to the instruction. Perhaps supervisors should be selected, at least in part, by the teachers with whom they are to serve.

While it would be unrealistic to expect certificates to be endorsed in such a way as to indicate effectiveness either as an individual agent, as a team member, or as a member of a total delivery system, it should at least be the responsibility of those in charge of preparation programs to possess this knowledge about candidates and to be prepared to make recommendations. They should assess the capabilities of supervisors and indicate the kind of structure in which they are likely to be most effective.

Universities must be held responsible for reducing the distance between themselves and the realities of the public schools. Moreover, the lack of congruence between universities and school systems on what a supervisor is and what he ought to do is a serious detriment to the development of effective, skill-based preparation programs. All too often, the approach taken to supervision in a university denies the reality of school organization, staffing, the disarray of the supervisory profession, the differences among school organizations, and the related social and cultural factors.

Preparation programs must cease to prepare supervisors for a world that doesn't exist. Such programs must be designed in full recognition of the reality of the world of the public school and with the commitment to the development of supervisors who can help create the kind of educational world that should exist.

RECRUITMENT OF CANDIDATES

Important as the clarification of essential competencies, the development of professional preparation, and the improvement of selection processes are, they will not in and of themselves ensure the availability of supervisory personnel. Thurman emphasizes the problem of finding individuals within the leadership pool who possess the personal attributes, intellectual abilities, and professional commitment to fulfill the roles of supervisors and curriculum workers:

The profession can no longer afford the luxury of hoping that enough persons with promise will decide to prepare to be supervisors or curriculum workers but must take decisive steps to identify persons with the potential talent and to encourage them to consider the opportunities in the field of supervision and curriculum.[10]

Any person contemplating a career or entering a program of professional training gives careful consideration to such factors as the nature of preparation programs, opportunities for employment, job security, and the prestige or status of the occupation. In addition, one also makes some assessment of the risks involved in pursuing a particular career. While there are certainly elements of doubt and risk involved in the selection of any preparation program and career, one must weigh these against the known, positive elements. The risks involved in becoming a racing car driver, for example, are clear. First of all, one may never make it to the "big time" where the real financial rewards are. Secondly, the risk of serious injury or death is an ever-present one. In the medical profession, the greatest element of risk is in committing oneself to the career only to fail to gain entry to medical school. Once entry is achieved, there is substantial assurance of unusually high income, prestige, and long-term job security. Usually the more clearly defined the role, the greater the prestige, and the more sophisticated the programs of preparation, the lower the risks that are involved.

A fundamental difficulty in attracting educators to supervisory careers lies in what they perceive as the number and degree of risks involved in preparation, employment, and career opportunities. The absence of specifications for supervisors in terms of knowledge, attitudes, and skills results in professional dependence on generalized concepts that are just as applicable to other leadership roles, including administration and curriculum work, and to some teaching assignments as well. It has been difficult to differentiate between those competencies which are equally appropriate for many leadership positions and those peculiar to supervision. As a result, an individual runs considerably greater professional or career risk in attempting to acquire competencies as a supervisor than in acquiring competencies for leadership generally—competencies that would be transferable.

The nature of most existing preparation programs likewise contributes to the elements of risk and doubt perceived by the person contemplating a career in supervision. Because there is seldom a clearly defined program for preparing supervisors, and seldom anyone clearly in charge of a program that does exist, it is logical to question the worth of the program and the status and importance of the professional role. It is seen as less professionally risky, therefore, to pursue identifiable programs that exist for teachers, administrators, counselors, and occasionally even curriculum workers. The absence of many inservice and retraining opportunities also contributes to the conclusion on the part of many prospective supervisors that other leadership roles contain fewer risks and more rewards. The combined effect of competition from more stable leadership possibilities and obscure criteria for supervision as a professional career seriously restricts its attractiveness to prospective candidates.

The element of individual risk is increased by the fuzziness and overlapping of supervisory roles and by the haphazard processes of selection. Fluid role definitions allow persons with similar supervisory titles to have quite different functions; conversely, persons with different titles often perform the same functions. Consequently, it is extremely difficult for a person to visualize a supervisory position clearly; he knows, or thinks he knows, what a principal does, but he does not know what a supervisor does. Added to this is the ambiguous nature of certification for supervisors, in which licensure is not a well-defined professional category but more nearly an adjunct to other leadership positions. It is not surprising, then, that an individual may prefer to minimize professional or placement risks by earning certification primarily as an administrator and subsequently (or concurrently) extending it into supervision via endorsement or by obtaining separate licensure.

The way in which appointments to supervisory positions are often made by administrators and school boards further serves to increase perceived and actual risk; such positions too frequently tend to be idiosyncratic, assuming the conformation of a particular situation. Supervisory positions historically have been created to meet particular problems, often ones of limited duration. Further, qualifying for a specific position as a supervisor has been more a function of chance and timing than a result of professional preparation and survival of a rigorous selection procedure. The entire process, from identification through preparation and certification to appointment, provides little assurance that an individual can obtain a supervisory position, even though he may possess the appropriate qualifications.

An organizational corollary to individual or employment risk factors is found in the nature of the organizational opportunities and restrictions offered to the supervisor in the situation in which he works. While much the same battery of technical skills is needed by supervisors in all structures, their form, application, and the opportunity to exercise them will be influenced by the particular system in which they function.

The choice of intervention components to be used is limited in the more traditional staffing configuration, in which the supervisor is assigned a staff position and placed in the central office. In such a position, he must operate through the building principal, not in a direct relationship to teachers—and, in some larger districts, through department heads or team leaders as well. As a result, the supervisor has less opportunity for influence and he runs fewer individual leadership risks. Performance expectations may be low; he may make recommendations to teachers or others, but they may be considered and then disregarded. This may occur by administrative inaction, contradiction, or through rejection by teachers.

While individual leadership risks are few, guarantees of security in the traditional structure may be correspondingly low. For example, a strong desire for an addition to or revision in a program may bring about the establishment of a particular supervisory position. When a position is created for such a specific purpose, however, the greater the effectiveness and efficiency of the supervisor, the less likely the retention of that position. In some cases, the need for certain supervisory responsibilities is only of limited duration; as teachers and administrative personnel become schooled in new programs and techniques, the need for external leadership decreases and the supervisory position may be eliminated. Many supervisory positions tied to specific needs came into being following the Elementary and Secondary Education Act of 1965, usually supported by federal funds, and were abandoned later as change became solidified or as federal funding expired.

In the contemporary staffing configuration, individual leadership risks increase to a moderate level for supervisors but they entail in turn a stronger degree of guarantee within the organization. Membership on an instructional service team enables the supervisor to expand the range of opportunities for applying intervention components. This structure enables all personnel to play multiple roles on the same team and/or to serve more specific needs on different teams as circumstances warrant. The numerous combinations possible utilizing the same manpower reduce the probability of obsolescense, while the accompanying flexibility permits access to and assignment of the individuals considered most suitable for executing a particular mission.

Situational guarantees are similarly enhanced, because the pool of resource personnel can be maintained in a fluid form while providing opportunities to explore other needs and staffing services. Consequently, the team concept is less affected by alterations of assignments and temporality of specific needs.

The emerging staff configuration brings high leadership risks to supervisors, matched by substantial guarantees. The broad frame of reference of a total delivery system places new multiple and complex responsibilities upon those involved in ISB. They must contact and work with external agencies and they are projected into positions of substantially greater school and community visibility. The sanctions they receive derive from the community at large rather than from professional colleagues. Therefore, their accomplishments and deficiencies will be more widely known.

The potential for redeployment of such cadre personnel into many situations enhances the probability of matching skills with needs and of giving the most appropriate individual a particular assignment. Moreover, the resources of an entire community are available to be focused upon a specific problem. Consequently, no one person becomes the fulcrum for the lever of too large and varied a load of supervisory tasks.

The significance of the above considerations for those engaged in ISB cannot be minimized. The initial step in staffing is the identification of the essential competencies for those who will function in supervisory roles. Agreement is needed on appropriate designations for such personnel. Utilizing established and accepted criteria, professional accreditation of preparatory institutions will then be possible, and the title of "supervisor" will merit the same protection under certification standards as is now accorded other professional roles in education.

Because the particular competencies essential for supervision have not been previously defined, the role has been particularly vulnerable. Acceptance of the ISB concept means that it is no longer possible to assume that such knowledge, skills, and attitudes as may be required for instructional improvement can be found readily or automatically among those serving in other leadership positions, notably administrators and curriculum workers, or even experienced teachers. Consequently, district staffing categories can be established for supervisors, who can be retained during periods of austerity budgets and protected against the encroachment of other responsibilities. The distinctive characteristics and competencies of supervisors are likely to keep them from being recycled to various other assignments; in this way, they will be like teachers, administrators, or counselors. This will reduce the tendency of supervisors to obtain administrative certification merely as an added protection.

Certification, which presently does little to provide an anchor to the chameleon-like character of supervision, can operate to make supervisors independent of administrators, curriculum workers, and teachers. It should project a separate identity by establishing supervisors as organizationally legal entities in their own right.

The selection process can restore professional stature to supervisory staffing and assignment, rather than matching supervisors with needs as perceived at a particular time and place. It will no longer be possible suddenly to convert a supervisor into the director of a project upon receipt of funds from a federal agency or philanthropic foundation. The same recognition of stature and job qualifications would be needed to justify the assignment of a supervisor as is required for an administrator, curriculum worker, or teacher.

Institutions of higher education will be required to establish bona fide programs for preparing supervisors, as well as including appropriate aspects of supervisory training in the preparation programs of administrators and curriculum workers.

ENDNOTES

1. Gordon N. Mackenzie, "Roles of Supervisors and Curriculum Workers." Statement prepared for discussion purposes by Dr. Mackenzie as a former member of the Committee on Professionalization of Supervisors and Curriculum Workers of the Association for Supervision and Curriculum Development (no date, ca. 1964).
2. Maurice J. Eash, "Preparatory Programs for Supervisors," *Educational Leadership* 23, no. 5 (February 1966), pp. 358–362.
3. Robert S. Thurman, "Identifying Potential Leaders for Supervision and Curriculum Work," *Educational Leadership* 23, no. 7 (April 1966), pp. 587–593.
4. Eash, *op. cit.*
5. Reba M. Burnham, "In-Service Education of Supervisors," *Educational Leadership* 19, no. 2 (November 1961), pp. 103–106.
6. Mackenzie, *op. cit.*
7. Eash, *op. cit.*
8. *Ibid.*
9. H. Irene Hallberg, "Certification Requirements for General Supervisors and/or Curriculum Workers Today-Tomorrow," *Educational Leadership* 23, no. 8 (May 1966), pp. 623–625.
10. Thurman, *op. cit.*

PART VI

Accountability in Supervision

Much has been advocated recently in regard to holding various school personnel accountable for their level of achievement or degree of progress. While the major concerns have thus far involved administrators and teachers, it is presumed that supervisors also will be evaluated in terms of performance criteria. Their contributions to the success —or failure—in the improvement of teaching are amenable to assessment.

The principle is advanced here that there are appropriate indices of ISB that should be utilized as standards for accountability. The supervisor should be accountable to himself, to the school, and to the profession for technical competence. Conversely, the organization should be accountable for structures and support essential to supervisory effectiveness.

The three chapters of Part VI analyze the respective features that fix accountability for supervision in education.

Chapter 14

Indices of Effective
Instructional Supervisory
Behavior

At a time when educational systems in general are asked to be accountable for the outcomes of instructional effort, it would also seem appropriate for all professional subunits and all personnel in school systems to be held accountable within their own area of assignment and expertise. Accountability is an enormously complex concept, and one cannot discuss it seriously without considering an entire system and its interrelatedness and interdependence. No total system should be held accountable for the learning of children unless all contributing parts of the system are also to be held accountable for their own discrete effectiveness. While not attempting to minimize the importance or responsibility of any other phase of the school operation or its own significant linkage in the whole chain of accountability, the effectiveness of ISB in a system-wide concern for accountability is of critical importance.

Many functions of the school contribute to its overall objective—the learning and development of children—but instructional supervision is directly, consciously, and systematically brought to bear on achieving that goal. In the first chapter of this book, ISB was defined as "behavior officially designated by the organization that directly affects teacher behavior in such a way as to achieve the goals of the organization and to facilitate student learning." This definition has, among others, three useful functions:

1. It enables a supervisor to sort out which of those behaviors in his daily activity are supervision and which are not. It provides some way of knowing whether one is really engaging in supervisory activity or whether he is simply engaging in a host of activities that, while important to the existence and functioning of the organization, are *not* supervisory.

2. Such a clear definition makes it impossible for a supervisor to delude himself into believing that his day was well spent simply because it was filled with activity. It forces him to examine his activity in the light of educational objectives and by the yardstick of whether or not teacher behavior has been affected or improved in any way. Such a definition also forces a supervisor to be selective in his activity, to organize his time, and to design some systematic way of proceeding in his responsibilities. Moreover, this definition forces him to establish some priorities. Clearly, not everything is equally important, although many supervisors have behaved as though all tasks were equally important, and priority has not always been given to those which most directly affect instruction. This definition—given the multitude of tasks too often heaped on supervisors—is helpful in establishing priorities of time and effort.

3. The definition is of primary value in a supervisor's own system of personal/professional accountability or in any system-wide effort of accountability. Without such definition, without some focusing of activity and influences, no serious discussion of accountability can take place. The first step in any system of accountability is to know what it is one wants to accomplish. Too often this is not spelled out even in the most general terms, and the "catchall" nature of supervision in this country makes accountability for instructional supervisors a particularly elusive goal.

It should come as no surprise that a heavy emphasis on accountability in supervision is advocated, for the whole thrust of this text is that supervision should "make a difference." There is, in fact, very little evidence around that supervision has truly made much of a difference in what takes place in schools or, ultimately, in the learning of children. This is not to say that it has not had a positive effect; perhaps it has, but the evidence is simply not available. Just as the educational system in general has not truly been held accountable for learning outcomes, supervisors have not been held accountable for the effectiveness of their own work and for improving the effectiveness of teachers. If school systems are seriously concerned about holding teachers accountable for the outcomes of their instruction, then they should also be concerned about holding supervisors accountable for intelligently, directly, and effectively influencing the behavior of teachers.

SOME INDICES OF EFFECTIVENESS

How do supervisors know when they are effective? How do they know when their time is well-spent, and how do they know when their activity is contributing directly to the goals of the organization? How does the system know when the money spent for supervision is reaping positive benefits? Answering such questions is no more difficult than attempting to assess teacher effectiveness; in many ways, in fact, supervisory effectiveness might be easier to assess though more difficult to measure.

Although the definition of ISB provides a useful framework within which to develop an accountability process, it contains certain assumptions basic not only to assessing effectiveness but also to determining whether ISB can function at all in a system. For example, unless the goals of the larger organization are clear, understood, and accepted, it is unlikely that effective ISB can exist. If such goals do not exist, what is the organizational yardstick along which a supervisor's behavior is evaluated? And if such organizational objectives are not known and accepted by a supervisor, how can he hold himself personally accountable in any way except to those objectives that he identifies and drives toward on his own, on a day-to-day or month-to-month basis?

Presuming the existence of clear, attainable organizational objectives, school leaders would have to identify and describe those contributing objectives that a supervisor would attempt to achieve, while he himself would be responsible for organizing the strategy and engaging in the behavior that would bring about the realization of those subobjectives. Accountability for supervisors simply means *that they are going to be held responsible for the achievement of those tasks and behavioral changes that will contribute to the larger, all-embracing objectives of a school system.*

Figure 14-1 suggests seven essential elements in an "Accountability/Effectiveness" sequence or feedback loop that could enable supervisors and organizations to establish clear objectives and to assess the effectiveness of supervisory behavior: Definition of Organizational Objectives, Derived or Contributing Objectives, Planning, Strategizing, Evaluation, Evidence of Achievement, and Analysis by Superior. These seven elements provide for specificity of objectives, joint planning and evaluation, development of specific strategies and evidence of achievement, and responsibility for finally judging achievement and redefining organizational objectives at the next higher level. This loop provides a sequence of movement, allows for accountability and assessment in any of the seven elements, and also makes possible the development of a time frame for each of the elements as well as for the entire sequence.

Briefly, these elements might be described as follows:

1) *Organizational Objectives.* The objectives of the larger organization ought to provide the genesis of supervisory behavior, yet it is not uncommon for supervisory personnel to determine almost entirely on their own what the objectives of their activity will be. Such decision-making often takes place almost in an organizational vacuum, without reference to the objectives of the larger organization and without consultation with the superiors to whom the supervisors are responsible. In fairness to supervisors, the larger organization often has no clearly stated objectives, or those which exist are so all-encompassing as to be of no help to super-

FIGURE 14-1. *Supervisory Accountability/Effectiveness Feedback Loop*

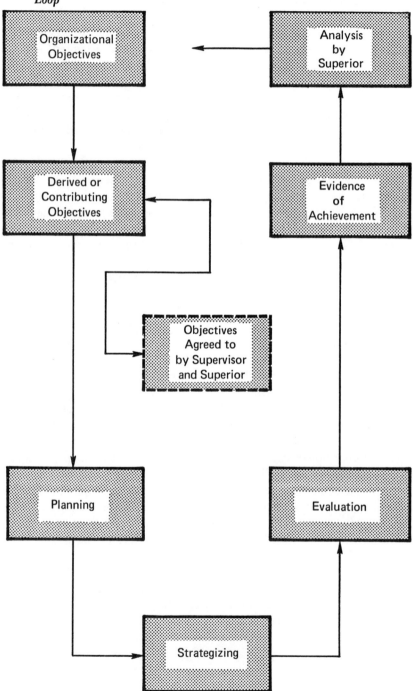

visors and other staff personnel. These people must not be left solely to their own devices in determining organizational objectives or in deciding on what activities they are going to spend their time and energy. No effective profit-making organization allows supervisory personnel to decide on their own what the focus of their responsibility is going to be. On the contrary, their activity, their time, and their continuing education are all organized in such a way as to achieve the goals of the organization. It is in that context precisely that they are held accountable; they are not granted the privilege of gaining personal and professional comfort out of achieving tasks that, while worthwhile in themselves or satisfying personally, do not contribute directly to the objectives of the organization. A system of accountability for supervisors must start with clearly defined, understood, and accepted organizational objectives.

Yet, supervisors too often work on a problem at a time with a teacher at a time, on issues that are brought to them, rather than on specifically identified and targeted problems whose solution contributes to the long-range objectives of the organization. The realization of immediate gains and the disposition of short-range problems, while needing attention, are not vital links in the chain of organizational achievement and accountability.

2) *Derived or Contributing Objectives.* It is usually unlikely that a supervisor will work directly on the general objectives of the organization. Instead, he, with his superior, needs to identify those objectives appropriate for him, objectives that are derived directly from the larger organizational objectives and that clearly contribute to their solution. No system of accountability can be effective unless the supervisor and the person to whom he is accountable have mutually agreed on what is to be accomplished. It is essential that *both* people be involved in extracting and specifying these objectives and the time frame in which they are to be accomplished.

3) *Planning.* A general assessment of time, resources, the skill of the supervisor, the organizational milieu, and agreement between the supervisor and the superior on the general conditions of priority, urgency, and operating procedures lays the groundwork for more specific elements to follow. The planning element involves situational data collection and analysis, a kind of organizational and situational reconnaissance following the identification of an objective and serving as a necessary prelude to development of a comprehensive strategy.

4) *Strategizing.* Supervisors, if they are to be responsible for changing teacher behavior, must be held accountable for designing well-thought-out, logical strategies. Such strategies must be consistent with their own abilities and institutional capabilities, must focus clearly on end results, provide for direction of activity, and conform to the value system of the organization. In this element, as in each of the others, ac-

countability for achievement should be required. Unless a supervisor is able to do more than verbalize—unless he is able to identify and define, in written form, the essential ingredients of his scheme of action—it is unlikely that sustained and effective strategies will result. Moreover, one cannot be held accountable for that which is not known or agreed to. Accountability for developing a workable strategy is, therefore, an essential element in the feedback loop.

5) *Evaluation.* The process of evaluation of ISB ought to be continuous. The strategy ought to provide for self-correcting mechanisms, an ongoing process that evaluates not only the operational activity, but the results being obtained. Any strategy ought to provide for evaluative checkpoints. Such evaluation might—depending on the nature of the objective—be either informal or highly specialized, with a thorough collection and analysis of data. In any case, supervisors ought to be held accountable for continuous and systematic evaluation of their behavior and outcomes.

6) *Evidence of Achievement.* In any system of accountability, "achievement" is a key concept. Neither good works nor faith is sufficient. In Figure 14-1, the evidence of achievement is whether or not, and to what degree, the derived objectives agreed to by the supervisor have been reached. Using the earlier definition of ISB, which specifies that it "directly influences teacher behavior," evidence should exist that the teacher's behavior has in fact been altered, and altered in such a way that it contributes to the general objectives. Since the focus of ISB is on "behavior," it follows that the derived objectives will be behaviorally stated and that there will, therefore, be evidence that teachers either are or are not behaving differently.

Evidence of supervisory effectiveness has not been generally noticeable. The reasons for this dismaying lack of data are multiple, but it is probably caused most by failure to identify and specify clearly what was to be accomplished. With clear objectives, however, the positive results of ISB can be observed, described, or made available in some form that can be analyzed and evaluated against the intended outcomes. A supervisor should be held accountable for performing the kind of evaluation of his achievement that is necessary for his own feedback as well as for the provision of data for his immediate superiors. Accountability within a profession suggests that its members hold themselves personally accountable for achievement in addition to any evaluations, analyses, and sanctions that may be performed by superiors. A personal commitment to accountability, and to achievement, is the essence of professionalism.

7) *Analysis by Superior.* In addition to a supervisor's own and professional accountability, the officially designated person in the organization to whom he is responsible must ask for and scrutinize the evidence of supervisory achievement. Accountability exists and is continuous at all

levels, but it is a spiral of responsibility that makes each designated leader accountable for the achievement of those within his unit. It is the task of such a person to analyze, evaluate, and discuss with the supervisor the evidence of achievement that has been presented, drawing directly on the objectives that he and the supervisor have jointly identified. Such an analysis means the supervisor's work will be analyzed on the basis of "hitting the target," on changing teacher behavior, rather than on the basis of a host of extraneous activities and achievements, or inappropriate responsibilities suddenly imposed on him. Such a focus of analysis and evaluation protects both the supervisor and the organization. It requires that *both* be held accountable—the supervisor for achieving specific objectives, and the organization for evaluating him.

The final value of such an accountability/effectiveness feedback loop is that the analysis of the supervisor's achievement is fed directly into the larger organizational objectives, providing evidence of contributing to them, making data available for alteration or refinement, and leading to the identification of new objectives, either primary or derived. Such a process makes possible supervisory planning and behavior that is sequential, reinforcing, and priority-based.

EFFECTIVE SUPERVISORY ACTIVITY

The above discussion of accountability deals with evidence of achievement; it suggests that a supervisor has the skills and can marshall his time and talents in ways that will bring about the desired results. Yet, there exists a need to ensure that supervisors be held accountable not *only* for the end result but also for the planning and conduct of their total ISB endeavor. There is an accountability of means as well as of ends.

A vital ingredient in any system of supervisory accountability is a requirement that holds a supervisor accountable for planned, coordinated, systematic, sustained, and focused activity. He must be held accountable not only for the nature and focus of his daily activity, but also for the effect it has on other people and on the organization. One must guard against a blind commitment to accountability that considers only the end in sight and fails to recognize the responsibility of accountability to oneself, to others, and to the organization. Supervisors, especially, since they work directly on teacher behavior, must be particularly conscious of those human values and needs that exist in every organization. Attainment of objectives and respect for human values are not in conflict; a supervisor must be responsible for both.

Studies of supervisory role and activity have shown an alarming array of behaviors and assignments. Supervision has too often become a dumping ground for a countless number of unrelated tasks that need to be performed by "someone" in the system. Without a definite focus of activity, without a delineation of responsibility, a professional role cannot exist. The need for such a focus for supervisors and the need for a clear concept of ISB is the central concern of this book. The random nature of supervisory behavior has been a serious deterrent to the objective of improved teaching and learning and is, in fact, antithetical to the concept of accountability. Precision, logic, focus, organization, and achievement are all key ingredients of accountability. There is no room for the kind of haphazard and frenetic behavior that has too long characterized instructional supervision.

In Figure 14-2, a sequence of suggested activity is portrayed that could be useful to supervisors and others interested in assessing supervisory effectiveness and, more specifically, in applying the concept of accountability to supervisory activity within specific time frames, whether a day, a week, or a year. First of all, the use of such an "ISB Activity/ Accountability Sequence" helps a supervisor to stay "on target," to plan his time and activities, to assess his expenditure of effort in the light of stated objectives, and to refocus his activity when other institutional stimuli divert him from his priority effort. As a professional, a supervisor ought to feel accountable first of all to himself for organizing and conducting his professional affairs and for engaging in the behavior for which he was hired.

Figure 14-2 suggests comprehensive and detailed analysis and planning. The concept or framework of this sequence is consistent with the definition of ISB given in Chapter 3 of this work, and with the constructs developed in Chapters 8 through 12. It might be useful to study this sequence in relation to the Critical Components of ISB and the ISB Matrix (Chapters 8 and 9). In addition, the direct relationship between this sequence and the "accountability/effectiveness feedback loop" is readily apparent. This figure does not pretend that there is a single sequence of activity or that all major elements are included in it. It is merely an example of the kind of organization that a supervisor needs to bring to his efforts, and it provides one means of assessing accountability. This model picks up Figure 14-1 at the point of agreement on "derived objectives," and portrays a sequence of activities involved in achieving the specific objectives(s).

Neither is it suggested that there can be only one activity/ accountability sequence underway at any one time. The number of sequences can vary, depending not only on the ability of the supervisor, but more directly on the nature and complexity of the change effort. One sequence might be all-consuming, while in other cases, there might be several sequences underway at once. Charting supervisory efforts in such a way would make multiple efforts considerably more manageable and would tend to ensure adequate attention to all essential elements. In this way,

FIGURE 14-2.   ISB Activity/Accountability Sequence

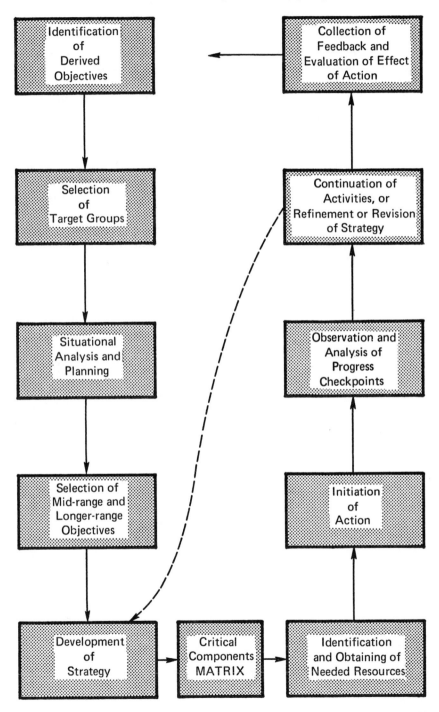

a supervisor would hold himself more accountable; this is a type of "personal accountability system," while the model shown in Figure 14-1 is an organizational accountability sequence for supervision.

The element described as "selection of mid-range and longer-range objectives" provides for what might be called "a self-correcting accountability mechanism." Such objectives serve as "progress checkpoints" for observation, analysis, and interim evaluation of effectiveness. These checkpoints thereby enable revisions or refinements in strategy and provide for corrections and recycling prior to the completion of the action sequence. Such progress checkpoints are consistent with the position taken earlier in this chapter that evaluation and accountability should be continuous and should occur at all levels.

In Figure 14-2, attention is also called to the suggested close relationship between the development of a strategy, the usefulness of the ISB Critical Components Matrix, and the identification and obtaining of needed resources. The Matrix is injected into this sequence as a highly useful analytical tool, juxtaposed between "strategy" and the "identification of needed resources"—the kinds of human, material, and technical resources and competencies that must be brought to bear, given the nature of the situation and the strategy devised.

Chapter 15

Technical Competence

School organizations are filled with well-intentioned supervisors. Their motives are good, and most of them have a reasonably well-thought-out philosophical position as well as a sense of direction. Most of them do have some understanding of the needs of the system in which they work. If there is a startling gap between the ideal and the actual behavior of supervisors, however, it is because they have all too infrequently been in possession of the technical competencies necessary to carry out their assigned responsibilities and to act on their professional commitment. Change has come slowly in schools and teacher behavior has been remarkably similar over the years because those persons with the responsibility for instructional leadership, while brimming with good intentions, have been virtually devoid of the technical knowledge and skills necessary to bring about dramatic changes in educational systems.

This book places a high value on knowledge, skills, objectives, precise planning, research, and evaluation. Chapter 2, which traced the history of educational supervision, criticizes the recent supervisory writing and practice that place an emphasis on "human relations" almost to the exclusion of intellectual and technical competence. While it is essential that a supportive environment be established and that employees feel good about themselves and each other, this work challenges the naive and almost implicit assumption that if such conditions exist, "everything else will turn out all right." Clearly, it hasn't.

The purpose of this chapter is not to identify and describe the array and the nature of technical competencies needed by supervisors, but to discuss the acquisition, demonstration, and refinement of skills as a vital aspect of supervisory accountability. The preceding chapter discussed accountability for *results*, for achievement in accordance with specific objectives. Such a process presumes the existence of technical skills, for without these a change-focused supervisory effort will be a shallow one, predestined to fail.

Accountability is multidimensional and interrelated. While a supervisor has the clear responsibility for his own competence, the development and assurance of technical competencies are not exclusively his concern. This chapter will analyze accountability for technical competence in three categories: supervisor accountability, organizational accountability, and the accountability of the larger profession. Such a three-pronged concept of accountability for technical competence holds that the supervisor, his organization, and the profession all have arenas in which they must be held accountable if a high degree of technical competence is to be assured.

SUPERVISOR ACCOUNTABILITY

A supervisor is accountable to himself, to the organization, and to the profession for the possession of technical competence. The concept of "profession" means that its members do, in fact, possess a body of information, understanding, and skills acquired through training and experience, and that these technical competencies are not to be found among the general public. Professional preparation programs and the literature on supervision, however, have a disappointing record of coming to grips with supervisory skills.

Much of the focus of this book is on technical competencies; Chapter 10 identifies a range of competencies needed by supervisors and discusses them in depth. It is important to note that these skills are derived from the research- and theory-based ISB model, from empirical data and not through speculation. For an understanding of what is meant by "technical competencies," references should be made to Parts III and IV of this book; it is recognized that these competencies are identified and described as clusters of skills of professional expertise, rather than as specific, narrowly-defined skills, such as "the ability to write behavioral objectives." There is an essential body of skills appropriate for all supervisors, given the definition and the model of ISB developed earlier. Beyond this there are needs related to a given change, an institution, or the nature of the situation that require the application of a specific skill. No list of competencies can be all-inclusive. Surely one aspect of technical competency is the ability to recognize—and the willingness and the capacity to acquire —those additional specific skills which are needed. Further, the distinction is made between those general, essential, technical competencies generic to the nature of ISB, and those skills of a different order that are primarily situational in origin and function.

Supervisory accountability for technical competence means that a supervisor can demonstrate that he possesses the basic technical competencies of ISB, and that he can identify and acquire such other situational skills as may become necessary. If "profession" implies a body of knowledge and competence, then "professional" implies accountability for their possession. Accountability also suggests personal responsibility for such technical competence. If one desires to become a supervisor, he must also be willing to be held accountable for technical expertise, and he should not expect to be employed or rewarded if he cannot engage effectively in such behaviors. Accountability entails ethical as well as organizational connotations; as a professional, a supervisor has the *ethical* responsibility for competence.

A supervisor is, therefore, responsible for his own competence and for his continued learning. Any supervisor seriously concerned about his effectiveness and committed to the concept of accountability must conscientiously pursue his own learning and should plan and engage in a systematic program of professional development. Such a program should have multiple purpose: enhancing those competencies considered generic to the field of supervision, and also including opportunity to acquire essential short-range or situational competencies. A professional should not expect someone else to provide him with such opportunities, nor should he wait to be asked to engage in professional development. The responsibility is, first of all, his own.

Technical competence implies growth, continued learning, and professional self-renewal. Even the most extraordinarily skilled artists, craftsmen, and professionals the world has known have always felt accountable for refining their skills and for learning new techniques. Regardless of the quality and the range of competencies a supervisor possesses, he is not eternally competent. Simply maintaining one's skills at the level of initial acquisition is to fail to be accountable professionally. A professional university program of preparation tuned to the conditions of the 1960s or 1970s may prove all too inadequate for the 1980s.

Figure 15-1 portrays four essential elements in a system of supervisory accountability for technical competence. Within the large construct of "supervisory behavior," the possession of identifiable technical competencies is placed at the center. The three key ingredients in the acquisition and maintenance of these competencies are identified as: 1) a well-conceived formal program of professional preparation; 2) a focused program within the organization itself of inservice development and competency testing and refinement, and 3) a long-term, continuous, and carefully planned career program of professional activity and development. The highest level of accountability—and in the long run, the one that is probably the most satisfying as well as the most effective—is one in which a supervisor holds himself personally accountable for possession and use of technical competence.

FIGURE 15-1. *Supervisory Accountability for Technical Competence*

SUPERVISORY BEHAVIOR

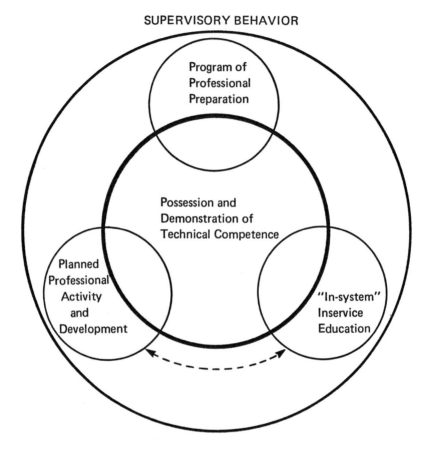

ORGANIZATIONAL ACCOUNTABILITY

The preceding section dealt with the supervisor's personal responsibility; this section describes the significant role played by the larger organization in ensuring the possession and application of technical competence.

Individual employees must not be left on their own to determine the requirements of a position or to specify the kinds of competencies they are to hold. Yet, too few school systems provide any more than a very general description of the role to be performed by a supervisor, and fewer still have considered the tougher professional question of the technical competencies they expect a new supervisor to possess. There has been a dismaying absence of organizational insistence on adequate qualifications and on the monitoring and evaluating of supervisory skills. It is not unusual for a supervisor to be hired virtually without a job description and with little or no evidence that he possesses any kit of professional tools.

In general, supervisory preparation programs have failed to equip supervisors with the "tools of the trade." Every true profession should be genuinely concerned about providing its new members with the basic elements of professional expertise.

School systems need to be held accountable for ensuring the existence and use of the technical competencies necessary to the performance of ISB. Just as a supervisor is held personally accountable, the school system bears an organizational responsibility. The frequent assumption that an outstanding teacher will make a good supervisor ignores the fact that the skills of teaching are not the same as the skills of supervision and that outstanding success in a classroom is no assurance whatsoever that a person possesses the competencies related to the management and leadership functions of supervision. School systems have been indifferent at best in the specification and insistence on demonstration of technical competence by supervisory personnel.

There are several ways in which school systems can ensure higher technical competence, and they should be held accountable for a sequence of decisions and processes that aim at creating and maintaining a technically competent staff of instructional supervisors. The following five items are key phases of this sequence:

Job Description.   The specifications for the role and responsibilities of a supervisory position need to be carefully determined and clearly spelled out. A clear statement of the nature of the position and the qualifications expected in a supervisor should give some indication of the essential technical competencies required. Such a job description should not be abstract, generalized, or even idealistic. Rather, it should be derived from the nature and needs of the particular organization, it should represent its beliefs about instructional supervision, it should indicate how much a position fits into the staffing pattern, and it should include those competencies which are not only generic to ISB but those which are needed to "fill out" the broader spectrum of competencies that an organization desires in its staff.

Not only the concept of accountability but basic organizational ethics mandate that supervisory skills be made known at the time of employment. If, for example, a supervisor is expected to work frequently in small-group situations as a group leader and facilitator, certain skills should be required. These are skills peculiar to the group process; if such a process is seen as a vital ingredient in instructional improvement efforts, then these skills need to be spelled out in the job description.

Hiring.   The concept of "staffing for supervisory services" discussed at length in Chapter 12 deals with the need to design a range and a pattern of supervisory services and skills in order to provide "total service" to the organization. Hiring officials are accountable for seeking out and verifying that an applicant does in fact possess technical competence, both generally in the area of supervision and specifically as might be needed to complete the staffing model.

Admittedly, it is difficult for an organization to be certain that a new supervisor is technically competent. Few preparation programs are sufficiently competency-based so as to guarantee the possession of even a minimum set of skills. Nor, as pointed out earlier, are present state certification requirements of much help. When programs have been competency-based and when students have undergone skill exercise—either real or simulated—some evidence is available. The ability to use a given skill can be at least partially verified by checking with former instructors and employers. Too often such checking is of a very general nature, not delving into the specific kinds of competencies desired.

Partially, at least, the burden of proof should be on the applicant himself. What sources of evidence can he provide that he possesses the competencies called for in the job description? Elaborate job descriptions, carefully structured staffing patterns, and organizational commitment to instructional supervision will be hollow exercises, unless hiring processes ensure that new supervisors are technically competent. While some judgments must continue to be subjective, increasingly more objective evaluations and observational data will become available, especially as preparation programs emphasize competencies and require planned field experiences for aspirants.

Monitoring and Evaluating Supervisory Performance.   It is not uncommon for employees in many fields to find that the competencies they were asked to possess go virtually unused, or if used, go virtually unevaluated. An organization is interested in end results, but it must also be concerned about how the results were achieved. This book has been critical of the failure to emphasize sufficiently the need for supervisors to achieve objectives, to change teacher behavior, to "make a difference." This should not be interpreted as disregard for the *process* of supervision. On the contrary, the bulk of this work deals with developing a theory of ISB and then extracting from it those critical components that will enable a supervisor to design and move systematically through an effective process of goal attainment.

Because behavior is critical, and because the process and what happens to people and the organization as a result are also important, the organization should be held accountable for the monitoring and evaluating of supervisory performance. Analysis and evaluation for the purpose of assessing technical competencies and improving them is quite different in form and intent from evaluation based on the achievement of objectives.

Objectives may be reached by utilizing different competencies, with varying strategies, and in considerably different lengths of time. Moreover, the positive or negative side effects of ongoing supervisory activity must also be assessed. A technical competency efficiently employed and resulting in a desired change, yet having deleterious effects on other aspects of the organization, can hardly be described as an example of competence in action.

The evaluation of supervisory behavior attempts to assess the degree of technical competence demonstrated throughout the range and duration of ISB. In Chapter 14, Figures 14-1 and 14-2, respectively, describe indications of effective supervision and an accountability system for supervisory activity. In both of these figures, there are elements that suggest technical competence and provide checkpoints for monitoring it. To cite only one example, both figures refer to the use of "derived or contributing objectives." One kind of technical competence a supervisor must demonstrate is the ability to analyze the objectives of the organization, relate the functions of supervision to these objectives, extract concerns appropriate to his responsibility, and identify and state an appropriate derived objective.

Figure 14-2 is of particular help in visualizing how an organization might analyze competence, because it deals more precisely with supervisory activity and lends itself to the assessment of technical competencies. When an organization hires an employee, it "contracts" for technical competencies. It should then determine whether those competencies are being made available with the frequency and at the quality level contracted for; it should insist on this and it should provide for the refinement of competencies as well as the development of new ones.

Inservice and Professional Development.   No system of organizational accountability for technical competence would be complete without a supporting and regenerative system of inservice education and professional development. No professional can remain at his entry competence level and continue to be a productive team member. First, his technical competence, although at the same level descriptively, will be less in proportion to the changed nature and needs of the organization; second, professional growth ought to be an expectation of continued employment; and third, new techniques and competencies will continue to become identified and available to the profession. It is important to judge supervisory behavior not simply in terms of what was done, but also in comparison to the options available.

A school system should be held accountable for insisting on the professional growth of its supervisory personnel, and for providing not only the impetus but the implementation of it through opportunities both within and without the organization. Such implementation should be planned, focused, identifiable, understood, and financially supported. The size of a school system and its supervisory staff will dictate the nature and extent of "in-system" professional development, but every system, regardless of its size, ought to allocate some portion of its budget to its own internal renewal and, specifically, to the enhancement of professional competence.

Similarly, money should be made available for advanced professional development through activities external to the system. A distinction needs to be made between those activities deemed professionally worthwhile in a general sense and those more specifically focused on the development of technical competencies. It is possible, for example, for one to spend much time and effort in attending conferences, with little noticeable change in skills and behavior. No criticism is intended of the host of general professional activities available; however, the school organization needs to insist on professional development activities that contribute demonstrably to overall technical competencies. Increasingly, skill-oriented training sessions are being made available to supervisors. With the advent of more research-based approaches to supervision and the analysis of effective supervisory behavior, more opportunities for advanced, professional, competency development will become available. It is ironic that supervisors, traditionally given the responsibility for inservice programs for teachers, have had very little opportunity themselves to partake of a planned and supported program of professional development.

The Reward System.   The last of the five phases suggested as critical in organizational accountability for technical competence is the existence of a reward system that recognizes such competence and that "pays off." Employees become quickly disenchanted with an organization if it fails to reward competence and punish incompetence. Behavior that is valued and rewarded is repeated. Supervisors who engage in high-level professional behavior and who demonstrate exceptional technical competence deserve to have such activity rewarded. The organization, in turn, needs to reward such behavior, not only because it is the human thing to do, but also because rewarding such behaviors reinforces it in the *behaver,* and serves as clear notice to others of the kind of competence that is expected and valued.

A school system is accountable for distinguishing among levels of performance in supervision and for giving tangible recognition to the most competent people on its staff. Uniform recognition of unequal competence does not generate increasingly higher levels of competence. Rather, it destroys initiative, provides no incentive for quality performance and continued development, and is destructive of morale. Organizational rewards should follow performance; an organization fails in its responsibilities if it continues to reward and reinforce behavior that is not consistent with its expectations, and if it tolerates the absence of the technical competence specified and contracted for at the time of employment.

The reward system is seen as a final and necessary element of organizational accountability for technical competence. It presumes the existence and effectiveness of the other four components.

Finally, then, organizations are to be held accountable for technical competence. The stance taken by their major spokesmen in regard to the technical competence of their members creates either a climate in which technical competence is recognized as of critical importance, or one in which imprecise, uncoordinated, and ineffective professional activity is accepted. The more professionally responsible the organizational climate and the clearer the expectations for its members, the greater is the likelihood of technical competence from its instructional supervisors.

THE ACCOUNTABILITY OF THE PROFESSION

By profession, in the context of this discussion, is meant the total combination of people and organizations involved in the preparation of supervisors, their certification, maintenance of standards, and the organizational and professional activities of development, publication, and research. It includes all those bound together by the common concern of providing, through their own unique contributions, more effective instructional supervision.

The existence of technical competencies at the local level can also be powerfully affected by attitudes and actions to that setting. Frymier, discussing the "profession" of supervision, notes that among other characteristics of a profession "those groups which are truly professional use the power of the professional organization to impose a discipline upon their membership. . . ."[1] He then criticizes the profession, claiming that it fails to impose a discipline on itself which would guarantee that every member would function in "the most effective, the most ethical, the most professional manner known."[2]

Supervision is, in many respects, the "unorganized profession." Even the Association for Supervision and Curriculum Development, which purports to speak for supervisors, has made only spasmodic efforts to develop a research-based approach to supervision, and has given little emphasis to the technical competencies related to supervision. Allen, writing for ASCD's *Educational Leadership*, stated,

> Professionalism implies the possession of a certain and particular knowledge which can be brought to bear on problems. It implies concerted action to raise the level of practice within the profession and to maintain a mutually acceptable level of performance through policies enforced by the professional group. It also implies selective admissions, specialized training in duly accredited institutions, and certification procedures approximating licensing.[3]

By the standards suggested by Allen, supervision lacks many of the attributes necessary for the emergence of a profession and for the guarantee of the existence and delivery of an identifiable set of technical competencies.

While a "profession" consists of multiple contributing components, only three will be discussed here: the universities—or training component; the state certification—or licensure component; and the professional organizations—or development and standards component. Each of these has a special contribution to make to the development of technical competence, and each should be held accountable for its own contribution.

Accountability of Universities.   While other sections of this book deal specifically with the nature of preparation programs for supervisors, it is appropriate to note here that it is empty and meaningless pontificating to discuss the technical competencies of supervision if preparation programs themselves do not focus on the identification, development, and verification of technical skills. Such programs must be held accountable for graduating students who do in fact possess the "tools of the trade," who know what their competencies are, and who have tested and verified them in real or simulated situations. In short, university programs must be held accountable for producing professionals, in the full range of the meaning of that concept.

Little attention has been given to supervisory competencies in most institutions, as well as in most of the literature. Writings by such people as Goldhammer,[4] as well as Sergiovanni and Starratt,[5] are indicative of more recent scholarly interest in supervisory behavior and competence.

Clearly, universities are a key link in establishing accountability for technical competence. The roots of a supervisor's skills lie in the philosophical and actual experience he receives during his preparation. Universities can, and should, be held accountable for ensuring a competence level. Just as competency-based programs are being developed for prospective teachers, so should graduate programs include guarantees of the attainment of a set of basic technical competencies at some minimally acceptable level. Such an expectation is a normal one for any "professional" program.

To be truly accountable in this area, university programs should:

1. Identify the competencies needed by supervisors,
2. Develop a program that provides for the acquisition of those competencies, and
3. Evaluate prospective supervisors in such a way that they can ascertain the presence and the degree of technical competence on completion of a program.

A survey of university programs, however, discloses an almost total absence of emphasis on technical competencies. While there are exceptions, this area remains one of major weakness.

Accountability of State Certification.   Obviously, the relationship between university programs and state licensure is a close one. One follows the other. While poor programs can exist despite certification standards, a licensure system for supervisors based on demonstrated competency rather than on mere acquisition of courses would be a powerful influence on preparation programs. Moreover, state departments of education would then be behaving with professional responsibility, for they would be holding themselves accountable for ensuring that the schools were getting supervisors trained and able to provide specific identifiable skills.

Most certification standards prescribe areas of study or knowledge, rather than enumerating competencies. There is probably more available evidence of the competencies of teacher education graduates than there is about the vast majority of newly licensed supervisors—an incredible situation! State certification agencies bear a special kind of accountability burden, for theirs is the *legal* accountability for the guarantee of performance competence.

Accountability of Professional Organizations.   State and national organizations must be held accountable for the status of the entire profession and for taking a professional stance that requires technical competence in order to be admitted and to remain a member in good standing. Theirs is a unique role: an insistent one with their own membership, a persuasive one within the larger educational profession. They should be held accountable for the development and enforcement of standards of technical competence; they should also be held accountable for providing national and regional leadership in the improvement of preparation programs and in the setting of standards of certification. They should insist on competence.

Professional organizations should be held accountable by their members for assisting them in their professional development. The vital, continuing importance of the work by the organizations of the profession in improving knowledge, skills, and attitudes for the development of new technical competencies cannot be overestimated. Such functioning is essential if the first two elements of this tripartite accountability are to be fully possible—the accountability of the supervisor himself for technical competence, including the acquisition of new competencies and professional development; and the accountability of the organization for technical competence, including provision for continued competency development, both within and without the organization.

The acquisition, guarantee, provision, maintenance, refinement, reward, and continued development of technical competencies require accountability on a broad professional front, with first and major accountability resting—as it should with any professional—on the supervisor himself.

ENDNOTES

1. Jack Frymier, "The Supervisor and His Professional Identity," in *The Supervisor: New Demands—New Dimensions*, ed. William Lucio (Washington, D. C.: Association for Supervision and Curriculum Development, 1969), p. 93.
2. *Ibid.*, p. 95.
3. Rowanetta S. Allen, "Role and Function of Supervisors and Curriculum Workers," *Educational Leadership* 23 (January 1966), p. 333.
4. Robert Goldhammer, *Clinical Supervision* (New York: Holt, Rinehart and Winston, Inc., 1969).
5. Thomas G. Sergiovanni and Robert J. Starratt, *Emerging Patterns of Supervision: Human Perspectives* (New York: McGraw-Hill, 1971).

Chapter 16

Organizational Viability

A complex social system cannot be depicted by a table of organization. The dynamics, thrust, and vitality of organizations are represented in the interaction of human beings, not in descriptions of staffing and purposes. An organization is a communications network as well as a production system. In a myriad of ways it establishes and communicates a system of punishments, approvals, and rewards. Certain behaviors are seen as appropriate; others, as ones to be avoided. In most efficient, mature organizations expectations are clear, and even when not written down, a hierarchy of behaviors and functions is evident. Not all functions of an organization have equal status; by virtue of size, financial commitment, visibility, or other less tangible factors, every organization establishes a value graph. By the amount, quality, and consistency of its support for an endeavor, the organization indicates its centrality and its value.

The organization of the public school, if it is seriously concerned about improving teaching and learning, must be held accountable for establishing a support system that ensures the existence of conditions which favor ISB and make it possible. In short, does the organization value instructional supervision, and does it provide support for such functions? School systems must be held accountable for more than organizational platitudes concerning the improvement of instruction; they should be held accountable for designing and maintaining a strong system of support—philosophically, structurally, materially, and financially.

By "organizational viability," then, is meant a school system that is: 1) a living, dynamic organization which places a high priority on change and instructional improvement; 2) oriented toward teaching and learning rather than maintenance and control; 3) realistic but insistent on quality teaching performance; 4) clear in its objectives and expectations; 5) fully supportive of a system of instructional supervision that will ensure the achievement of objectives considered essential by the organization and the community it serves.

In the two preceding chapters, organizational accountability was discussed briefly in relation to evaluation of supervisory effectiveness and also as a vital ingredient in guaranteeing technical competence. This chapter discusses organizational accountability from a more general, but basic standpoint—the requirement of "organizational viability" if instructional supervision is to be an effective instrumentality for improving instruction and, as a result, to facilitate student learning.

Leadership is needed at the top. The administration of a system creates a climate that can either support instructional supervision or render it a pathetic and ineffective endeavor. School boards, superintendents, and other key central office and building administrators are accountable for the organizational factors that support a strong program of supervision. No organization has the right to hold supervisors accountable unless it is willing itself to be held accountable for providing the support system necessary for effective ISB. A viable organization should be held accountable for providing in three broad areas: accountability for philosophical support and interpretation; accountability for structural recognition, and accountability for adequate staffing and services.

Organizational components, or operating units, do not exist independently of each other. They are creations of the larger organization and depend on it for organizational life and subsistence. A subunit either has such support, or it atrophies; it ceases to make an effective, sustained effort, even though it may technically continue to exist. It is not uncommon for organizations to withdraw from a group or a subunit as a means of bringing about change or establishing organizational priorities. Frequently used techniques are: reduction in personnel; alteration in chain of command, resulting in a lower reporting level; redesignation of titles, or withdrawal of support through reduced budget allocations. There are also other techniques. It is important to note the consequences of such lack of support, especially if the actions are not deliberate attempts to alter the organizational hierarchy of values. If the actions are not strategically taken but, rather, random and uncoordinated, the result may be communications and consequences that were not intended.

ACCOUNTABILITY FOR PHILOSOPHICAL SUPPORT

Belief in the purposes of instructional supervision is essential. The philosophical position of the leadership of a school system must represent a commitment to change, a belief in the necessity and possibility of improving teaching, and a value position that the system has the responsibility to expect and help bring about the highest level of professional performance possible. Such a position is rooted in the belief that a school system is a human organization, goal-oriented, responsible to the society, and that it has a mandate to achieve objectives held to be important by its constituency. Such a belief supports the existence and behavior of persons employed to assist in achieving these objectives; it supports the role of instructional supervisors as essential elements in structuring, guiding, and affecting such changes as will help the organization reach its objectives.

In subtle but philosophically powerful ways, a superintendent communicates to an organization whether or not he "believes" in the functions of supervision. For one thing, does he himself speak to the importance of organizational concepts? Does he have confidence in the ability of supervisors to influence the behaviors of teachers? Is an effective charge given to supervisors, and does the teaching faculty comprehend the strong support of the superintendent for "intervention behavior" by supervisors? The values communicated by a superintendent do more than simply support supervisors; they give their activity and influence-attempts organizational validity. They answer the questions of teachers as to whether or not supervisors have the "right" to influence the teaching process directly. Such philosophical support confers organizational status; it gives supervisors the credentials needed to gain acceptance. By so doing, supervisors become official spokesmen for organizational objectives, rather than individuals making personal requests of teachers.

Such organizational support cannot give supervisors esteem; it cannot endow them with skills; it cannot automatically make them effective; but it can create in them a confidence that their work is highly valued, and this is a vital precondition of establishing effective instructional behavior in the organization.

Finally, the perception of the leadership of a school system concerning the purposes of instructional supervision is extremely important. It is not unusual for some superintendents to view supervision as an arm of administration, organized to carry out a variety of activities designated by the central office, and existing largely for purposes of efficient management of the educational processes. Such a view absolutely destroys effective instructional supervision. Administration must philosophically support the definition of supervision that focuses it on directly affecting teacher behavior, on being an active, deliberate agent for improving teaching. Philosophical support in the organization means that supervision can and should be accountable for changing teacher behavior; it means that effective activity is asked for, recognized, and rewarded. The organization must create a philosophical climate in which instructional supervision is legitimatized and valued so that it will flourish.

ACCOUNTABILITY FOR STRUCTURAL RECOGNITION

Organizational support can be communicated in tangible ways as well as in philosophical terms. In fact, apparent philosophical support can quickly turn to meaningless platitudes unless visible evidence of commitment manifests itself. The supervisory position in the table of organization, reporting routes, access to the major decision-makers, job titles, and the typical organizational symbols of status and power are all examples of the way in which the placement and treatment of instructional supervision can be given institutional support. The *position* of people and units in the structure of an organization lends credibility to them; it accords them status; it gives them a "leverage" that those without it do not possess. One's position in the structure conveys a degree of authority.

In all too many cases, supervisors have spoken with little authority. Unsure of their own esteem and organizational status, they have too often spoken timidly and behaved conservatively. They have been reactors, consultants, and instructional counselors almost exclusively, rather than intervention agents seeking to influence teachers directly. They have responded, rather than initiated. The structure has often placed them in a "power limbo"—neither line nor staff, neither administration nor faculty, but somewhere in between, with uncertain and greatly varying degrees of power and authority. Such status-and-legitimacy confusion breeds weak and ineffective supervision.

If an organization is going to hold supervisors accountable for influencing teacher behavior and improving instruction, it must itself be held accountable for supporting them through according supervisors appropriate status and reward within the structure. The two must go hand-in-hand. An organization grants power to its members; placement, rewards, titles, and other tangible symbols communicate that power.

A viable organization must also give attention to the system of financial reward. Compensation for supervisors must be in keeping with their degree of authority. One test of another's legitimacy to make demands within an organization is, "What right does he have to ask me to do this? I make more money than he does." Salary verifies authority. Instructional supervisors must be placed at a level within the salary structure that is consistent with their responsibilities and that gives them significant "financial advantage" over those whom they are expected to influence.

It is important to note that the above discussion on authority treats only the responsibility of the organization to confer *formal authority* on supervisors. The necessity for authority and power gained through competence, experience, and the exercising of leadership is clear. Sergiovanni and Starratt summarize the literature on authority and apply it to the unique roles of supervisors, observing that bureaucratic authority is being challenged increasingly by the authority of competence and functional authority.[1]

Clearly, supervisors cannot draw their base of power exclusively from the formal organization, and caution is urged lest one be misled into such an overreliance. The above discussion is limited *solely* to the responsibility of the organization to ensure that legitimate and appropriate formal authority is conferred. It is expected that accountability for technical competency (as described in Chapter 15) will bring about the authority of competence; in tandem with formal authority, the ability of the supervisor to act as a change agent is vastly increased.

ACCOUNTABILITY FOR STAFFING AND SERVICES

In addition to philosophical support and formal status support, organizational viability also means being accountable for providing the number and quality of personnel and adequate logistical support for them. By "adequate" is meant sufficient support to meet the expectations of the organization, in keeping with its mission and nature. No one should be held accountable for achieving an objective that is hopeless, for which he is not equipped and not supported. Before supervisors can be held accountable for achieving objectives, the organization must meet its responsibility to provide adequate human, financial, and material tools. Seldom have school systems invested heavily enough in supervisory personnel. The number of teachers and the number of buildings for which the typical supervisor has responsibility renders truly effective supervision almost impossible. The financial and material support given to their work is correspondingly inadequate.

Appropriate Staffing Patterns.   Chapter 12 of this book discusses patterns of supervisory services in considerable detail; it suggests three basic forms of services: the individual agent, the instructional service team, and the total delivery system. Supervisory staffing can range all the way from a single supervisor, working across the board and at all levels, to a complex supervisory staff representing many specialties and with carefully delineated responsibilities. Reference should be made to Chapter 12 for a description of the many kinds of patterns for the delivery of supervisory services and for an analysis of the positive and negative aspects found in almost every one of them.

School organizations must design a pattern of supervisory services consistent with the philosophy of the system and one that provides for adequate delivery of instructional services, be the system a large one or a very small one. A pattern cannot just grow, with tasks added haphazardly and additional supervisors hired randomly as finances permit. Much has been said in this book about objectives. The staffing structure should begin with a clear perception of the objectives of supervision—within the context of that system; it should move through a careful analysis of the number and nature of the population to be served; it should assess the existing supervisory capability; and, finally, it should culminate in a design for supervision that is situational and uniquely appropriate. Chapter 11 deals with the "context of school environment" and how it affects the nature of instructional supervision.

In a small system, articulation is not a significant problem, but the issue of providing a range of skills, covering all grade levels and all subject areas, becomes a critical one. In a large system, provision for coverage is much easier, but problems of coordination and articulation become acute. In a large system, a combination of skills can be developed; in a smaller system, a few people are expected to possess a vast array of technical competencies and human characteristics.

Regardless of size, every school system must give time and in-depth analysis to its needs if it is going to provide instructional services of the kind needed, in the amount needed, and at the time needed. Supervision should not be held accountable for effectiveness in a structure that is poorly designed, uncoordinated, inadequately staffed, and lacking in the clear support of the parent organization. People can be held accountable only when they are working within a structure that *provides* the conditions for effective professional behavior.

Human Resources.   It is essential not only to have numbers of persons, but also to provide the skills and qualities needed to "round out" a staff. Chapter 15 discusses accountability for technical competence. A viable organization selects its employees not only on the basis of the most objective evidence it can find of competence, but also on the basis of the *particular* skills needed to complement the existing staff. In other words, the design or pattern devised for delivering supervisory services determines what skills are sought and who gets hired. Anything less perceptive is a random staffing process based not on the needs of the system but on any other criteria that happen to be operative at the moment.

To be held accountable in this area, an organization must continually be involved in self-study and need-analysis. On the other hand, it must seek for evidence of training and competence in the personnel it hires. Concerns about staffing are not merely structural and quantitative. There are major qualitative concerns as well. Organizations support instructional supervision not only through devising a pattern but by employing people of the highest professional quality possible. Supervisory services will not be effective simply because of structure; while appropriate staffing is vitally important, the professional and personal qualities of the staff will make the difference in the effectiveness of the services rendered. Employment of outstanding persons also communicates within the system the leadership's commitment to the importance of instructional supervision.

Financial and Material Resources. No one would think of asking an engineer to build a bridge without providing him the necessary money, manpower, and material. Yet, supervisors are very often charged with making substantial change in school programs with few supporting material resources other than their own energy and personal technical competence. This is no simple matter, and educational organizations are naive to think that change can be achieved with virtually no investment of financial and material resources.

Budgets for improving instruction are typically modest. Supervisors have little access to funds other than those which can be coaxed out of the central administration. They have little or no "seed" money; lacking a program budget, their plans for the year must often preclude the use of any sizable expenses for staff development and for other activities to improve instruction. How much of their total budgets, for instance, have most systems invested in instructional resource centers? While there are some exemplary centers, most of them are visible denials of the verbal support given to the importance of improving teaching and learning. The organization must provide the necessary tools if supervisors are to be effective. Supervisors are expected to possess technical competence; by the same token, the organization should be expected to provide the setting, the finances, and the resources that will enable this competence to be exercised. Philosophical commitments must be backed up by resources if goals are to be realized.

Accountability is cyclical. Either everyone connected with an enterprise is accountable, or no one is. The effectiveness of one part may be absolutely dependent on the effectiveness of another. Instructional supervision cannot be effective without organizational viability, structure, and supportive activity.

Early in this book, ISB was defined as "behavior officially designated by the organization that directly influences teacher behavior in such a way as to facilitate student learning and achieve the goals of the organization." This definition charges supervision with being focused, identifiable, goal-oriented, and change- and achievement-oriented. It also implies organizational endorsement—behavior officially asked for and approved by the organization. Along with the organizational request for such behavior exists the corresponding organizational obligation to ensure that the necessary conditions exist in support of effective ISB. Supervision cannot create such conditions by itself; the organization must provide a strong, viable, organizational support system.

ENDNOTE

1. Thomas G. Sergiovanni and Robert J. Starratt, *Emerging Patterns of Supervision: Human Perspectives* (New York: McGraw-Hill, 1971), pp. 37–50.

PART VII

Future Directions for Instructional Supervisory Behavior

There can be no "final" chapter in a book that attempts to redirect thought regarding supervision in schools. The previous parts have served to define concepts and describe their application. Acceptance requires that the theoretical construct be tested to determine whether it adequately describes the phenomenon of ISB. The processes suggested by the theory remain to be documented through actual practice resulting in teacher improvement.

The principle is advanced here that ISB must be subjected to careful study in field situations that are controlled as much as is feasible. Individuals must be prepared to utilize technical skills for the implementation of the intervention components. Only if the ISB matrix is tested can its possibilities be realized.

The single chapter of Part VII points the way toward application of this model for supervision in education.

Chapter **17**

Toward a Theory of Instructional Supervisory Behavior

Supervision as a field of professional study has been long neglected. It has lagged far behind administration, counseling, and teaching in the quest for conceptualization and analysis. With the possible exception of curriculum development, with which it shares a number of common elements, supervision remains a virtually uncharted territory. The time is long past due to replace folklore with fact, to substitute data for opinion, and to utilize experimentation rather than observation.

While initial steps can be taken by rational thought, borrowed information, suggested implications, and fabricated models, these merely open the door to a new direction. Movement across the threshold and into the future demands the translation of such steps into action. The improvement of supervision in general, and of instructional supervision in particular, necessitates the investigation of various possibilities.

A RATIONALE FOR SUPERVISORY BEHAVIOR

If the concept of instructional supervision as a distinct behavior system is viable, it follows that other behavior systems in education—administering, counseling, teaching and the like—exist as well. The analysis of research studies to determine their implications for these behavior systems will allow comparison and contrast, and will be more profitable than the isolated study of supervisory behavior.

The procedure followed to isolate the concept of ISB might also be used to clarify differences among behaviors demonstrated by various individuals within the same school and by the same person responding to varied stimuli. The subtleties and nuances of ISB must be understood if it is to be explained and preparation for it obtained through recognized programs. The quest for distinguishing among behaviors is particularly appropriate in efforts to isolate curriculum development behavior from ISB. The tendency persists to assume a high degree of similarity and to expect both behaviors to be manifested by one individual.

A RESEARCH BASE FOR ISB

Only four areas of research, selected through arbitrary criteria, served as the research base of this text. Numerous sources other than leadership theory, communication theory, organization theory, and change theory might have been tapped. It is quite possible that sociological theory or psychological theory would lead to the generation of additional, or even more appropriate, propositions.

However, these are pure, vicarious, and secondary sources; they will suffice only until research studies can be conducted under similar controls in different organizational settings. Assuming the imperative character of supervision, it seems appropriate to investigate supervision as the primary source. Moreover, supervision is a real and an applied field. The possibility exists that application of supervision theory will have direct implications for instructional supervision much as sociological theory contains direct implications for social work.

CRITICAL COMPONENTS OF ISB

To assume that the eleven components cited are the only possible combinations of research propositions is to defy astronomical odds. Since the evolution of the matrix stems entirely from the critical components, identification of others must be a task of high priority. The painstaking sorting by hand should be replaced by a computerized process that could provide printouts under various categories for more careful analysis. Propositions from other research fields may, when added to the data bank, suggest different clusters and require a redefinition and redesignation of the categories.

Another possibility is that there are other ways of arranging the components themselves, and the emergence of more than three dimensions—intervention, interpersonal, and milieu. Therefore, the matrix must be assumed to be as incomplete in regard to supervision as Mendeleev's periodic chart of the elements in regard to chemistry. Use of the matrix may help to uncover other components, just as the periodic chart led from 96 elements to the discovery of 106. The ISB matrix may be as rudimentary as the four elements of earth, air, fire, and water. The issue will remain merely speculative until some attempt has been made to experiment with the present components. Substantiation in practice will provide clues to further refinement, while refutation will suggest alternative possibilities for investigation.

TECHNICAL SKILLS OF ISB

The technical skills utilized were selected for illustrative purposes from among various possibilities that appeared in the educational literature. They are not all-inclusive; most of them have a distinct integrity and were developed to fulfill other needs, not as a direct response to the quest for developing the skills of supervision.

Attention needs to be directed to technical skills that are consistent with and evolve from application of the intervention components to actual situations. Many of the technical skills may continue to serve ISB in their present form. Some of them may be altered in some way to conform appropriately to the matrix. However, other technical skills still need to be developed in order to expand the range of possible intervention behaviors and to improve ISB.

A similar emphasis should be considered in regard to both managerial skills and human skills, but the differences between those skills utilized in ISB and those associated with administrative and counseling behavior are more of degree than of kind. It is the technical skills, however, that distinguish instructional supervision from other forms of educational leadership behavior. Consequently, the technical skills require analysis, development, and incorporation into preparation programs.

ORGANIZATIONAL CONSIDERATIONS

The existence of ISB in actual practice can only be partially achieved by supervisors themselves. The possibility of its realizing its full potential and the form it takes are powerfully affected by the context of school environment. Administrative structure, faculty characteristics, and the learning setting are major determinants of the form ISB takes, and one or more of these elements may have to be altered before ISB can be utilized most effectively. In typical situations, supervision is rooted in an autocratic administrative structure and is directed primarily at novice or beginning teachers scattered widely throughout the school district. Perhaps a less autocratic form, one that includes continual attention to the needs of experienced teachers, and one that serves and utilizes the community at large, is more desirable and is more conducive to effective ISB.

Issues such as these are highly significant to the establishment of graduate programs for the preparation of supervisors. The investigation and resolution of these questions could be a major step toward refinement and precision in preparation. The acceptance of the conceptualization of instructional supervision as a distinct behavior system would be sufficient in itself to alter the form of many existing programs. In addition, a commitment within the profession and on the part of university professors to supervision as a professional field would also be a major help in revising the courses and programs offered; both knowledge and attitudes need to be affected. While the widespread distribution of supervisory programs throughout many colleges and universities in the nation must be questioned, the issue of concentrating professional preparation at a fewer number of major institutions demands further study and evidence. Preparation programs themselves should be subjected to research and study, and projects need to be undertaken for the creation of model programs, for the experimental design of clinical experiences and internships, and for follow-up studies in real-life field situations.

Such elaborate ventures will require the cooperative and collaborative efforts of public school leaders, university faculties, and state education department staffs—particularly those engaged in certification and regional accreditation. The advent of visible programs with substantial resources and under combined auspices would in itself offer inducements for qualified candidates.

A clear designation of supervisory trainees at the program level, combined with reinforcement through licensure, may serve to curb the tendency for the creation and description of supervisory positions according to local and temporary deployment needs.

ACCOUNTABILITY IN SUPERVISION

The problems of supervisory accountability, while vital, are complex and vexing. The action orientation of the ISB concept places major emphasis on influence, on the effective application of the intervention components. These components are translated into action through the use of technical skills. Such a process provides an entry point for the assessment of performance accountability. It is possible to observe and evaluate the application of technical skills in specific situations. These skills, which distinguish the supervisor from other educational leaders, are a major focus of accountability, especially as directed at preparation programs. The measure of the appropriateness of such skills will be the degree to which they accurately represent ISB. The ability to employ technical skills is one indication of the success of a university program in preparing the supervisor for his responsibilities, and it is for the teaching of technical skills that preparing institutions should be held accountable.

The successful employment of technical skills in schools—the translation of intervention components into action—is a performance for which the supervisor himself must be held accountable. Major indices of effectiveness of technical skill are the extent of change wrought in the interpersonal components—as affected by the application of technical skills through the participation component, and/or the extent of change in the milieu components—as affected by the application of technical skills through the modification component. Ultimately, of course, accountability depends upon change and improvement in teacher performance as a result of such efforts.

It should be noted that the concept of ISB has been formulated and a matrix developed on the basis of propositions drawn from selected research in four areas. It is almost certain that further development will refine and perhaps considerably alter these eleven components. Since the present analysis of technical skills is based on an incomplete behavior system, accountability must also be incomplete. As supervisory behavior systems become further researched and more carefully delineated, and as technical skills become more distinctive and precise, the assessment of accountability for their possession will become increasingly accurate. Many of these same concerns apply to managerial and human skills, as they pertain to the total skill-mix.

The accountability of the organization for supervision is measured by the extent to which support is provided for the functions of supervision and for the technical skills considered essential. An organization gets what it supports, and the introduction of or request for a new skill may require a different kind or degree of organizational support. Congruence is needed between supervisory behavior and the skills that the organization supports.

In addition to the need for the school organization to be held accountable for supporting supervisory behavior, preparing institutions, state departments of education, and professional associations should also be held accountable. To use a medical analogy, accountability for sound hospital practice would be incomplete without parallel concern by the medical school, the certification board of physicians, and the American Medical Association. A similar situation exists in regard to supervisory accountability. School systems alone cannot be held responsible for sound practice; in addition, university graduate programs, state certification agencies, and the Association for Supervision and Curriculum Development are all part of the cycle of accountability.

FUTURE DIRECTIONS

The possibility of implementing instructional supervisory behavior depends upon organization and resources. Contractual relationships need to be established between major universities and school systems to develop model preparation programs and to experiment with various prototypes. Only after a number of highly trained personnel are available can the effectiveness of the implementation of the intervention components through the application of technical skills be truly studied and assessed.

Until a critical mass of resources and data can be assembled and utilized, the practice of supervision will remain among the superstitions of American education. An organizational imperative mandates a better fate.

Appendix

Critical Components:
Proposition Groupings

The following outline indicates the grouping of the propositions ocurring as a result of the interfacing process.

1. INTERPERSONAL COMPONENTS

Reference Component

A leader will be more effective if he recognizes that follower behavior is at least partly a function of leader behavior.

Leadership and its effectiveness is a function of the dynamic interrelationships of numerous conditions within an organization.

Communication will verify group norms, which in turn will determine the nature of internal communication and receptivity to external communication.

To be effective in modifying individual behavior, communication must achieve a comparable change in the norms of the group to which the individual belongs.

Effective organization is a function of the integration of formal and informal systems.

An organization will be more efficient when it seeks to reduce human submission and alienation of persons within it.

The success of change efforts will be affected by the cohesiveness and the longevity of the group to be influenced.

A change effort will be more effective when it recognizes and utilizes the strength of group norms.

The effectiveness and stability of a change will be enhanced when a cohesive group commits itself to it, thereby setting up a new force field.

A change effort will be more effective if recognition is given to the presence and influence of group norms.

Esteem Component

Esteem will contribute to the possibility of successful leadership, and successful leadership enhances the leader's esteem.

Communication will be more frequent and in greater amount with a peer whose expertise is accepted as superior.

Organizational effectiveness will be enhanced when leadership behavior is characterized by interpersonal strength, technical skills and management ability.

The effectiveness of a change effort will be increased when one sees the nature of the change as enhancing his own personal relationships and status in the organization.

Change efforts will be more effective if the change is not perceived as causing a loss of prestige or group esteem.

Change will be more effective when leadership and acceptance from within the group to be influenced come from an individual with group membership and esteem.

Change efforts will be more effective when the change agent, as perceived by other group members, has prestige and acceptance within the group.

The change agent will be more effective if he has prestige and acceptance in the eyes of those in the client system.

Status Component

Leadership is more likely to be accepted and effective when the leader has status and power in the organization.

Communication will be affected by the respective positions occupied by sender and receiver, particularly in regard to centrality.

Communication effectiveness of an individual occupying an official position is at least partially a function of the authority of that position.

Communication will be more effective if it is recognized that messages will differ in kind with a person perceived as having higher status than with one perceived as having lower status.

Communication will be less precise and accurate if it proceeds in an upward direction through the hierarchy, than if it proceeds in the downward direction.

Effective organizations will indicate the lines of responsibility and the authority upon which the responsibilities are based.

Change will be more effective if it does not appear to disturb the existing organizational structure of status, relationship, and recognition.

2. MILIEU COMPONENTS

Expectation Component

Leadership will be more effective when the style employed is consistent with the nature and expectations of the group to be led.

Leadership will emerge from within a group when a member fulfills the needs and expectations of the group or when the formal leader does not measure up to the group's expectations.

Communication will be more effective when the views of the sender and the receiver(s) are in harmony.

Communication will be more effective if the style and techniques selected by the sender are consistent with the expectations of the receivers.

Communication will be more effective if the sender considers the connotative value of language to the receiver.

Communication will be more effective if the sender organizes the content of his message to maximize receptiveness by the receivers.

An effective organization will continue to examine its stated goals in relation to its real goals as defined in the behavior of its membership.

The effectiveness of change efforts will be improved when those restraining factors which inhibit an individual's normal desire for change are recognized and dealt with deliberately.

Perception Component

A leader will be effective, as evaluated by a group, if he is perceived as performing needed group functions.

A leader will be more effective if he recognizes that his leadership will be evaluated and perceived differently by subordinates and by superiors.

Communication will always be inaccurate because sender and receiver can never share common perceptions.

Communication will be more effective if the message is perceived by the receiver as within acceptable limits of possibility, and/or the distance from his own opinion is not considered excessive.

Communication will be more effective if verbal messages and nonverbal cues from the sender reinforce each other.

Organizations will be more effective if the membership understands the organization's structure and uses this understanding as a basis for contributing to its work.

Organizations will be more effective when there exists a clearly understood definition of goals or purposes.

The morale of an organization will be enhanced when its goals are understood and perceived as important.

A change effort will be more effective if it is perceived as building on existing practice rather than threatening it.

Change will be more effective when it is recognized that change efforts will be perceived differently by different people as a result of the many forces at work within each individual.

Suitability Component

The traits that characterize effective leaders are at least partly related to the situation and the perceived needs of the group.

Leadership will be more effective if it considers the needs of human beings as well as providing for the initiation of structure.

Communication will be more effective if the sender and receiver are dealing with situations in which both have obtained previous experience.

Communication will be more effective if the message from the sender indicates compatibility and common basis of interest with problems confronting the receivers.

Communication will be more effective if the sender takes into account social and educational similarities and differences between himself and his receivers, as well as those among his receivers.

Communication will be more effective if the sender takes into account his own personality characteristics and those of the receivers.

If an organization is to operate effectively and make a significant contribution to social purpose, its services and/or products must be consistent with the values of the society.

The nature of a particular organization, along with its stage of historical and technical development, are factors that will determine the system's supervisory and management requirements.

An organization will be more effective when its structure and designed modifications are consonant with the cultural milieu within which it exists.

Change will be more effective within groups that do not see themselves in competition with each other.

Change will be more effective if it is not perceived as giving advantage to some other group or area within the organization.

Change will be more effective if it does not threaten the vested interests of powerful groups or individuals.

The effectiveness of a change effort will be increased when it is recognized that the characteristics of some changes make them easier to accept than others.

Change will be more readily accepted if it can be demonstrated to be practicable in the target system or in a close approximation of it.

Change will be more readily accepted if it is not perceived as requiring a shift in one's attitude or belief system.

3. INTERVENTION COMPONENTS

Planning Component

The possibility of successful leadership will be enhanced when a leader is aware of his dominant leadership motivation style and plans his activities in light of it.

Participatory leadership will be more effective when it is based and planned on intelligent assessment of the value system of the leader and the nature, ability, and perceptions of the group.

Leadership will be more effective when it is a consequence of careful analysis and planning in the light of the nature of the organization and the task to be achieved.

The nature of supervisory structure in organizations should be directly related to their production systems.

The assessment of an organization's effectiveness should include its analysis as a total complex structure and as a laboratory of human interaction.

An organization should construct and use mechanisms for the analysis of its efficiency and effectiveness.

Planning and initiating change will be more effective when the objectives and policies of the organization are clear, realistic, and understood.

Change efforts will be more effective when they are carefully planned, have goals, and incorporate some functional method of problem-solving to attain the desired ends.

Change will be more effective and more likely to occur when it is brought about not by chance, but deliberately, and is initiated and guided by some active person or group.

Strategy Component

A leader is likely to be more effective if he recognizes that democratic and autocratic leadership styles generate different and predictable responses and patterns of achievement among followers.

The effectiveness of language as a symbol system will be improved by two-way (verbal) rather than one-way (written) communication.

Communication will be more effective in promoting change if the sender utilizes many communication channels rather than a few.

Communication will be more effective if the sender utilizes the capabilities of mass media for appropriate message transmission to receivers.

In an effective organization, leadership behavior will be distributed between maintenance activity and more creative, goal-directed activity.

Change efforts will be more effective if they are supported by an appropriate systematic and comprehensive strategy.

Change will be more effective when the choice of a strategy is consistent with the focus of the change effort.

Change will be more effective when, at the appropriate point in the change process, the change agent's efforts shift from "selling" to "diffusion."

Change is more likely to occur if there is a recognized role-responsibility for initiating and directing change in the system.

Participation Component

Successful leadership is not a result of, and cannot be predicted on the basis of, any known single personality trait or pattern of traits.

The probability of successful leadership will be increased if the leader maintains some degree of psychological distance from his subordinates.

A leader is likely to be more effective if he sees and provides for the possibility of leadership coming from any member of a group.

Leadership will be more effective when it provides for the active participation in decision-making of those to be affected.

Communication will be affected by the nature of the network and the channels it provides for interaction between sender and receiver.

Communication will be more effective in influencing group behavior and attitudes when it utilizes discussion and decision-making.

Communication will be more effective if the sender considers the rates and kinds of interactions that his message promotes or discourages with the receivers.

Communication will be more effective if the sender takes account of factors that tend to apply pressures for increased interaction among receivers.

Communication will be more effective if the sender utilizes feedback from receivers to enhance the accuracy of the message.

Communication will be more effective if the sender employs factors that increase interaction rate and reduce hostility among receivers.

An organization will contribute effectively to the needs of people to the extent that it maintains an open and responsive posture.

The effectiveness of a change effort will be enhanced when the people who are to be affected are involved in the planning and decision-making about it.

A change effort will be more successful if recognition is given to the different roles that individuals within a system play in accepting change.

A change agent will be more effective if he remains free from intimate involvement with the client system.

Modification Component

Leadership attempts will be determined partly by favorable or unfavorable conditions that exist at the particular time.

The effectiveness of an organization will be increased when there is provision for continuity of interaction and structural integration.

Organizational effectiveness will be expressed in attempts to modify the existing structure as a response to changing conditions and circumstances.

Change will be more effective if it recognizes differences in acceptance of change according to the personality fluctuations that occur with age.

Change will be more effective when external contact and influence are components of the change process.

Change will be more effective if linkage occurs between external and internal agents of change.

Support Component

Leadership will be more effective if the organization provides conditions that support such behavior.

The potential for effective leadership will be increased through the provision of rewards and satisfaction of the needs of members.

Communication will cause change by providing both ample preparation and continuous reinforcement.

An organization will be more effective if there is a conscious effort to blend the resources needed for production and the psychological commitment of the membership.

When there are changes in the goal(s) of an organization, continued effectiveness will require accompanying changes in its internal structure and in the distribution of its resources.

Change efforts will be more effective and durable when they are buttressed by supportive forces.

A change effort will be more effective if it takes into account the demands of time, money, and energy that the nature of the change requires.

Changes that are primarily technological will be more effective if they are buttressed by direct experience and support in their implementation.

A change is more likely to be lasting if it receives continuous evaluation after initial adoption.

Change will be more effective when the conditions existing within the target system are those that encourage change processes.

Name Index

Subject Index